Lone Star Generals in Gray

RALPH A. WOOSTER

EAKIN PRESS ◈ Austin, Texas

FIRST EDITION

Published in the United States of America
By Eakin Press
A Division of Sunbelt Media, Inc.
P.O. Drawer 90159 ⬐ Austin, Texas 78709-0159
email: eakinpub@sig.net
🖳 website: www.eakinpress.com 🖳

1 2 3 4 5 6 7 8 9

1-57168-325-9

Library of Congress Catologing-in-Publication Data

Wooster, Ralph A., 1928-
    Lone Star generals in gray / Ralph A. Wooster.
      p.   cm.
    Includes bibliographical references and index.
    ISBN 1-57168-325-9
    1. Generals—Confederate States of America Biography. 2. Generals —Texas
Biography. 3. Confederate States of America. Army Biography. 4. Texas—History—
Civil War, 1861-1865 Biography. 5. United States—History—Civil War, 1861-1865
Biography. I. Title.
E467.W897   2000
973.7'464'0922
[B]--DC21   99-23919
                                                                                                    CIP

Cover illustration: Lee and Gregg at the Wilderness by Gary Zaboly
Maps by George Farrar

Contents

Preface

Several years ago when working on a study of the role played by Texans in the American Civil War, I determined to learn more about the thirty-seven Texans who as general officers commanded armies, divisions, and brigades in that great conflict. Several of these men, notably Albert Sidney Johnston, John Bell Hood, Ben McCulloch, Samuel Bell Maxey, and Tom Green, have been the subjects of full-scale biographies. Brief biographies of others are contained in William C. Davis' multi-volume *The Confederal General,* Ezra J. Warner's *Generals in Gray,* and in the *Handbook of Texas.* While these sources are informative I believed that a study incorporating recent research published in scholarly journals and monographs could provide additional insights into the careers of these men, both individually and collectively. Ed Eakin, publisher and long-time friend of Texas history and historians, agreed that such a work would have merit. Thus the present volume.

One of the most difficult tasks was determining who the Texas Confederate generals were. As those who have studied the Civil War will recognize, there is no complete agreement as to who held the rank of general officer. Various lists exist, but often they differ. I generally follow Marcus J. Wright, comp., *Texas in the War, 1861-1865,* ed. Harold B. Simpson (Hillsboro: Hill Junior College Press, 1965). In doing so I include five individuals assigned as brigadier general by Edmund Kirby Smith, commander of the Trans Mississippi Department, but never confirmed by President Davis and the Confederate Senate. This will trouble Civil War purists, but since these men were considered general officers by their peers and performed the duties as such I include them.

The question as to who among these generals should be considered a Texan is also troubling. I include John Bell Hood because he stated that Texas was his adopted home and took his Confederate commission as an officer from the Lone Star State. Tom Rosser, born in Virginia and commander of Virginia troops in the war, is considered a Texan because he and his family lived in Texas before the war and he was appointed to the U.S. Military Academy from Texas. Most of his classmates, including his good friend George A. Custer, considered him a Texan.

More difficult were the decisions to include John C. Moore as a Texan and to exclude James P. Major. It would have been easy to include them both or to exclude them both, but for reasons stated in the book Moore is in and Major is out. I suspect some readers will disagree with these decisions.

A word about the organization of the book. In Chapter One I present an overall view of the thirty-seven Texans who served as general officers, including such information as age, place of birth, education, prior experience, date of rank, service experience, and postwar careers. Chapter Two is devoted to the two Texans, Albert Sidney Johnston and John Bell Hood, who held the rank of full general commanding large armies in the field. Biographical sketches of the five Texans who served as major general make up the third chapter. Similar information for those Texans who served as brigadier general is provided in Chapters Five and Six. In the final chapter I evaluate the performance of these Lone Star generals in gray. Such an evaluation is highly subjective but will provide the reader with my views based upon considerable study of their performance as a general officers. Perhaps, too, it will stimulate some discussion and debate. An appendix furnishes some information about Texans such as James W. Throckmorton and John S. Ford, who are often mistakenly referred to as Confederate generals. A bibliographical essay describes the sources used in this study.

Many people contributed both directly and indirectly to the book. I wish to thank particularly those historians such as Alwyn Barr, Anne J. Bailey, Norman Brown, Tom Cutrer, Donald S. Frazier, T. Michael Parrish, and Jerry D. Thompson, whose works have prevented Texas and the Trans Mississippi Department from being overlooked by students of the Civil War. My thanks also go to religious historian Ron Ellison of Beaumont for sharing information pertaining to the Harrison brothers, two of the Texas generals included in this study. W. D. "Bill" Quick, authority on Sabine Pass and Texas-Louisiana coastal waters, once again was helpful in a variety of ways, not the least of which was being a good listener. Gary Zaboly, military artist from New York, provided the splendid painting of John Gregg and Robert E. Lee for the cover of the book. My good friend George Farrar designed the maps that illustrate some of the campaigns and battles in which Texas generals were involved. Peggy Fox, director of the Harold B. Simpson Confederate Research Center at Hill College, made available most of the photographs of the Texas generals included in the book. John Rager of Digital Photographic Imaging in Beaumont was most helpful in preparing photographs for reproduction. My son, Robert Wooster, professor of history at Texas A&M University–Corpus Christi and himself a recognized military historian, was helpful as always. Melissa Locke Roberts, editor at Eakin Press, did another outstanding job in editing the manuscript for publication.

The book is dedicated to my wife, Edna Jones Wooster, who for more than fifty years has listened to me talk about the events and personalities of the American Civil War. She has shared much of her life with the men and women of that great conflict. For her patience, understanding, and love I am most grateful.

RALPH A. WOOSTER
Beaumont, Texas

CHAPTER ONE

Confederate Generals
from Texas

ON FEBRUARY 23, 1861, the voters of Texas approved the ordinance passed by the state convention dissolving the ties that bound the state with the United States. This step, endorsed by three-fourths of those voting, followed the actions of six other slave-holding states of the lower South that seceded from the Union during December and January. A week before Texans voted to secede, Brig. Gen. David Twiggs, commanding U.S. forces in Texas, agreed to turn over all Federal property and withdraw all Federal troops from the state. Six weeks later Federal efforts to supply the garrison at Fort Sumter in the harbor of Charleston, South Carolina, led to the outbreak of the Civil War, in which more than 600,000 Americans lost their lives.

Although a frontier state, Texas played a significant role in the war. More than 70,000 Texans served in the military during the war, the majority in the Confederate army and others in state forces protecting the frontier. Slightly more than 2,000 Texans enlisted in the Union army during the conflict. Texans fought in every major battle of the war except First Manassas (Bull Run) and Chancellorsville. In several major engagements, notably Gaines Mill, Pea Ridge, Vicksburg, Sharpsburg, Gettysburg, Chickamauga, Atlanta, the Wilderness, and Franklin, units from the Lone Star State played particularly important roles.[1]

Texans fought in New Mexico Territory, Indian Territory,

1

Maryland, Pennsylvania, and every state of the Confederacy (including Kentucky and Missouri) except Florida.[2] They recaptured Galveston from the enemy in January 1863, and drove Union invaders away from Sabine Pass, Corpus Christi, and Laredo. Texans helped defeat Nathaniel P. Banks in the Red River campaign and turn back Frederick Steele in southern Arkansas. The last battle of the Civil War was fought at Palmito Ranch in South Texas a month after Lee surrendered at Appomattox Courthouse.

Thirty-seven Texans served as general officers in the Confederate army during the war. Thirty-one of those Texans were appointed to the rank by President Jefferson Davis and confirmed by the Confederate Senate. One other, Felix Robertson, was appointed brigadier general by President Davis but was never confirmed by the Senate.[3] Five Texans—Arthur P. Bagby, Xavier B. Debray, Wilburn H. King, Horace Randal, and A. W. Terrell—were recommended for general officer rank by Edmund Kirby Smith, the Confederate commander in the Trans Mississippi Department, but for various reasons were never appointed by the president and confirmed by the Senate. Yet these five and Felix Robertson acted as general officers in the field, wore the uniforms of generals as surviving photographs indicate, and were listed in various accounts as general officers. They are therefore included in this study of Lone Star generals in gray.[4]

The majority of Lone Star generals were natives of the slaveholding states. Twenty were born in states of the upper South, ten in Tennessee. Kentucky was the birthplace of six Texas generals, including the only two (Albert Sidney Johnston and John Bell Hood) to attain the rank of full general. Thirteen Texas generals were natives of states of the lower South. Only one of these, Felix Robertson, was born in Texas. Lawrence Sullivan Ross, Texas Ranger and future governor, was a native of Iowa, and William Steele, West Point graduate and career soldier, was a native of New York. Two Texas generals, Xavier Debray, born in France, and Walter P. Lane, born in Ireland, were natives of Europe.

Among the Texas generals were a father and son, Jerome B. and Felix Robertson, and two sets of brothers, James and Thomas Harrison and Ben and Henry McCulloch.

Two-thirds of the Confederate generals from Texas were in their thirties and forties in age; thirteen were aged thirty to thirty-nine; and twelve were forty to forty-nine when the war began. Only three Texans, Albert Sidney Johnston, fifty-eight years, Joseph L. Hogg, fifty-five years, and Ben McCulloch, fifty years, were fifty years or older in 1861. Nine future Texas generals were in their twenties when the war began. Youngest of the group were Wilburn H. King and Felix Robertson, each twenty-two, and Lawrence S. Ross and William H. Young, each twenty-three.

The Texas Confederate generals were fairly evenly distributed throughout the state in places of residence in 1861. Twelve future generals resided in towns or counties east of the Trinity River, twelve resided in the region between the Trinity and Colorado rivers, and ten lived in towns or counties south or west of the Colorado.[5] Waco was the home of more generals than any other Texas community. Hiram Granbury, Sul Ross, and the two Harrison brothers all resided in Waco at the outbreak of war. Three future generals, Louis T. Wigfall, Elkanah Greer, and Walter P. Lane, lived in Marshall. Three other generals, A. P. Bagby, Ben McCulloch, and Thomas N. Waul, were residents of Gonzales County.

Twenty-three of the Texas generals attended college before 1861. Nine matriculated at the United States Military Academy at West Point. Seven of these (Albert Sidney Johnston, John Bell Hood, A. P. Bagby, Samuel Bell Maxey, John C. Moore, Horace Randal, and William Steele) graduated from the academy. Felix Robertson and Thomas L. Rosser were both students at West Point when Texas seceded but resigned prior to graduation.[6] Three future Texas generals, Thomas N. Waul, John A. Wharton, and Louis T. Wigfall, had attended South Carolina College. Wigfall also attended the University of Virginia, as did William H. Young. Tom Green graduated from the University of Tennessee. William P. Hardeman also enrolled at that institution but apparently left before graduation to come to Texas. French-born Xavier Debray attended a French college or academy. Several sources state that Debray attended the prestigious St. Cyr military academy, but historian Bruce Allardice, author of *More Generals in Gray*, questions this. Allardice believes Debray attended a national college in Paris but not St. Cyr.[7]

Four of the future Texas generals, Albert Sidney Johnston, John Bell Hood, Horace Randal, and William Steele, were soldiers on active duty when the Civil War began. Thirteen of the future Texas generals were lawyers. Eight others were working for the state or federal government in some civilian capacity. Three were merchants, two were planters, and three were still students in early 1861. Richard Gano of Tarrant County and Jerome B. Robertson of Washington County were physicians, and John C. Moore was a professor at Shelby College in Kentucky. Adam R. Johnson was a surveyor and overland mail contractor prior to the war.

Twenty of the Lone Star generals were slaveholders in 1860. Most of these owned only a few slaves, but eight of the future generals held twenty or more slaves and thus would be classified as "planters," as the term is accepted by historians. John A. Wharton, wealthy young lawyer and a future major general in the cavalry, owned 133 slaves on his plantation in Brazoria County. Wharton, whose total property was valued at nearly $237,000, was one of the wealthiest individuals in Texas on the eve of the Civil War. Hamilton P. Bee, owner of sixty-seven slaves and $109,300 in total property, and Richard Waterhouse, owner of fifty-two slaves and $117,300 in total property, were two other future Confederate generals among the wealthiest Texans in 1860.[8]

TABLE 1
Confederate General Officers from Texas

Name	Place of Birth	Age in 1861	Education	Occupation
Bagby, Arthur P.*	Alabama	58	West Point	Lawyer
Bee, Hamilton P.	S. C.	39	———	Government
Debray, Xavier*	France	43	Academy	Publisher
Ector, Matthew D.	Georgia	39	Centre	Lawyer
Gano, Richard	Kentucky	31	U.Louisville	Physician
Granbury, Hiram	Miss.	30	Oakland C.	Lawyer
Green, Thomas	Virginia	47	U.Tennessee	Government
Greer, Elkanah	Tennessee	36	———	Planter
Gregg, John	Alabama	33	LaGrange C.	Lawyer
Hardeman, W. P.	Tennessee	45	U.Nashville	Planter
Harrison, J. E.	S. C.	46	———	Government
Harrison, Thomas	Alabama	38	———	Lawyer
Hogg, Joseph L.	Georgia	55	———	Lawyer

Hood, John Bell	Kentucky	30	West Point	Military
Johnson, Adam	Kentucky	27	———	Surveyor
Johnston, A. S.	Kentucky	58	West Point	Military
King, Wilburn*	Georgia	22	———	Merchant
Lane, W. P.	Ireland	44	———	Merchant
Maxey, Samuel B.	Kentucky	36	West Point	Lawyer
McCulloch, Ben	Tennessee	50	———	Government
McCulloch, Henry	Tennessee	45	———	Government
Moore, John C.	Tennessee	37	West Point	Educator
Nelson, Allison	Georgia	39	———	Lawyer
Randal, Horace*	Tennessee	28	West Point	Military
Robertson, Felix**	Texas	22	West Point	Student
Robertson, J. B.	Kentucky	46	Transylvania	Physician
Ross, Lawrence S.	Iowa	23	Wesleyan(Al)	Government
Rosser, Thomas	Virginia	25	West Point	Student
Scurry, William R.	Tennessee	40	———	Lawyer
Steele, William	New York	42	West Point	Military
Terrell, A. W.*	Virginia	33	———	Lawyer
Waterhouse, R.	Tennessee	29	———	Merchant
Waul, Thomas N.	S. C.	48	S.C.College	Lawyer
Wharton, John A.	Tennessee	33	S.C.College	Lawyer
Whitfield, John	Tennessee	43	———	Government
Wigfall, L. T.	S. C.	45	S.C.College	Lawyer
Young, William H.	Missouri	23	U.Virginia	Student

*Appointment never confirmed by president and Confederate Senate
**Nominated by president but not confirmed by Confederate Senate

Of the future generals twenty-two held some form of public office or political appointment before the war. Eleven of the group served in the Texas legislature during early statehood. Tom Green, Joseph Hogg, and William R. Scurry were members of the Congress of the Texas Republic. Matthew Ector and Allison Nelson served in the Georgia legislature before coming to Texas, and James Harrison was in the Mississippi state senate prior to his move to the Lone Star State. Hiram Granbury, John Gregg, and A. W. Terrell were county or district judges before the war. Louis T. Wigfall, who had served in the Texas legislature, was elected to the U.S. Senate in 1859. John Whitfield was territorial delegate to Congress from Kansas prior to moving to Texas on the eve of the

TABLE 2
Slaveholding of Texas Civil War Generals

General	*Slaves Held in 1860**
Bee, Hamilton P.	67
Ector, Matthew D.	20
Gano, Richard	21
Granbury, Hiram	1
Green, Thomas	10
Greer, Elkanah	12
Gregg, John	13
Hardeman, William	31
Harrison, Thomas	8
Hogg, Joseph	26
Lane, W. P.	6
Maxey, Samuel	1
McCulloch, Ben	6
McCulloch, Henry	1
Terrell, A. W.	6
Waterhouse, Richard	52
Waul, Thomas	45
Wharton, John A.	133
Whitfield, John	10
Wigfall, Louis	10

* This represents slaves held in county of residence and enumerated in the manuscript returns of Schedule No. 2, Slave Population, U.S. Census, 1860. Neither Thomas Rosser nor Lawrence S. Ross owned slaves, but in both instances their fathers did. Albert Sidney Johnston owned two slaves but sold them before moving to California in 1860.

Civil War. Seven of the future generals were members of the Texas secession convention. Three future Texas generals, John Gregg, Thomas N. Waul, and Louis T. Wigfall, were representatives to the Montgomery convention which drafted the Confederate constitution and elected Jefferson Davis president.[9]

Nearly two-thirds of the Texas generals had some type of military service prior to 1861. Sixteen of the group fought in the Mexican War. Some, like regular army officers Albert Sidney Johnston, Samuel Bell Maxey, and William Steele, were recognized for gallantry or bravery in Mexico. Others, like the McCulloch brothers, Tom Green, Hamilton Bee, Allison Nelson, and Walter P. Lane, were officers of volunteer or ranger companies. Elkanah Greer and Thomas Harrison served in the Mississippi Rifles under the command of Col. Jefferson Davis. Richard Waterhouse, only a lad of fourteen at the time, ran away from his home in Tennessee to take part in the Mexican War.

Future Confederate generals Tom Green, Walter P. Lane, and Ben McCulloch fought in the Battle of San Jacinto. William P. Hardeman accompanied a group heading to the Alamo, but the garrison fell to Santa Anna's army shortly before relief arrived. Hardeman missed the Battle of San Jacinto because of illness. Jerome Bonaparte Robertson, a lieutenant in a company of Kentucky volunteers, offered his services to the Texas army, but he and his company were delayed in New Orleans and arrived in Texas after Santa Anna's defeat. Hardeman, Robertson, Tom Green, and the McCulloch brothers were in the Somervell expedition, which was ordered to the Rio Grande after the Vasquez invasion in 1842. The McCulloch brothers accompanied the Texans who crossed the Rio Grande and headed for the Mexican town of Mier, but returned to Texas after warning Col. William S. Fisher that the Mexican army heavily outnumbered the Texans.[10]

At least sixteen of the future Confederate generals participated in Indian campaigns before the Civil War. Some, such as the McCulloch brothers, Tom Green, and Sul Ross, were noted for their prowess in fighting hostile Indians. Ross, the son of Texas Ranger and Indian agent Shapley P. Ross, established a reputation for boldness and courage in campaigns against the Comanches. His rescue of Cynthia Ann Parker from her Comanche captors in December 1860 gained recognition for him throughout the state.[11]

Two of the Texas Confederate generals, Allison Nelson and John Whitfield, fought in the disturbances in Kansas during the 1850s. Nelson also served as a brigadier general under Narcisco Lopez in the Cuban insurrectionary movement during the 1850s. After he moved to Texas in 1856, Nelson was an Indian agent as well as Indian fighter, serving under Sul Ross.[12]

Albert Sidney Johnston had the greatest prewar military reputation of any Texan. His standing as a military officer, based upon service in the Texas Republic, Mexican War, and Indian campaigns, was probably higher than that of any American, including Robert E. Lee, who served under Johnston in the elite Second Cavalry Regiment in Texas. When Texas seceded, Johnston was stationed in California as commander of the Department of the Pacific. He resigned his commission and headed back to the South when the conflict began. He was appointed full general in the Confederate army on August 31, 1861, to rank from May 30, 1861. Johnston was appointed commander of Department No. 2, the Western Theater, by his former West Point classmate, President Jefferson Davis.[13]

Although Johnston was the highest ranking field officer in the Confederacy, he was not the first Texan appointed as a general officer. That honor went to the veteran Ranger captain Ben McCulloch. His biographer, Tom Cutrer, points out "McCulloch was one of the most celebrated Texans, and his reputation as a scout and Indian fighter was known throughout the United States."[14] Even so, appointment by President Davis as one of the Confederacy's first general officers on May 11, 1861, surprised McCulloch and his friends. McCulloch had sought appointment as colonel of the U.S. Second Cavalry in 1854, only to see Davis, then secretary of war, appoint Albert Sidney Johnston. Once the Civil War began, McCulloch was convinced that Davis, whose preference for West Point professionals was well known, would not appoint him general. However, the Confederate president gave McCulloch not only the rank of brigadier general but also command of the Army of the West charged with defense of Texas and Indian Territory.

Louis T. Wigfall, the stormy, passionate secessionist leader, was the only other Texan appointed to the rank of general in 1861. A native of South Carolina, Wigfall was an active proponent of southern rights during the 1850s. After service in the Texas legislature and the United States Senate he was elected to the Montgomery convention in 1861 and later as senator in the regular congress of the Confederacy. He was commissioned lieutenant colonel of the First Texas Battalion and later promoted to colonel of the First Texas Infantry Regiment. On October 21, 1861, he was appointed brigadier general of the Texas Brigade. He held this position only briefly, resigning his commission on February 20, 1862, to take his seat in the Confederate Senate.[15]

Fourteen Texans were named brigadier general during the year 1862. Joseph Hogg, father of the future Texas governor James

Stephen Hogg, was the first of this group to receive his appointment. Although he had only limited experience in the Mexican War, Hogg had strong political connections, leading to his commission as a brigadier general from Texas on February 14, 1862. His military service in the Confederate army was brief. He was stricken with dysentery and died at Corinth, Mississippi, on May 16, 1862.[16]

John Bell Hood, Samuel Bell Maxey, Hamilton P. Bee, and Henry E. McCulloch were appointed brigadier general in early March 1862. John C. Moore received his general's stars in May of that year. In late summer and early autumn nine other Texans were advanced to general office rank. One of these was Dr. Jerome Bonaparte Robertson, colonel of the Fifth Texas Infantry, who was given command of the Texas Brigade when John Bell Hood, who had succeeded Wigfall in that position, was advanced to division command with the rank of major general in October 1862.

Five Texans were appointed brigadier general in 1863. Later that year Hood, wounded at both Gettysburg and Chickamauga, was made a corps commander and advanced to the rank of lieutenant general. John A. Wharton, last of the Texans appointed brigadier general in 1862, was promoted to major general in November 1863. Thirty-three years of age when the war began and with no military experience, Wharton showed considerable ability, first as a company commander and then as regimental commander of Terry's Texas Rangers. Wounded at Shiloh, Wharton recovered and distinguished himself at Murfreesboro and Chickamauga. His rise in rank and stature was the most rapid of all of Texas' citizen soldiers in the Civil War.[17]

Hiram Granbury, who proved to be one of the state's most capable brigade commanders, was the first Texan to receive his stars as a general officer in 1864. Promoted brigadier general in February, Granbury led his Texas Brigade throughout the campaign in northern Georgia and at Atlanta. At the Battle of Franklin, Tennessee, in late November 1864, Granbury was one of six Confederate generals killed or mortally wounded.

Nine other Texans, including four (King, Randal, Debray, and Bagby) promoted by Kirby Smith but never confirmed by President Davis or the Confederate Senate, were made brigadiers in 1864. Samuel Bell Maxey and Tom Green were also recommended by their superiors for promotion as major general that same year. John

Bell Hood was appointed commander of the Army of Tennessee with the temporary rank of full general in the summer of 1864, but after the disastrous Tennessee campaign reverted to his regular rank of lieutenant general.

Thomas Rosser, the young Texan who left West Point prior to graduation, was promoted to major general in November 1864. A native of Virginia, Rosser spent the war commanding troops from the Old Dominion. His advance in rank was steady as he performed well at Second Manassas, Chancellorsville, and Gettysburg.[18]

TABLE 3
Date of Rank, Texas Confederate Generals

1861

May 1	Ben McCulloch	Brigadier General
May 30	Albert S. Johnston	General
Oct. 21	Louis T. Wigfall	Brigadier General

1862

Feb. 14	Joseph Hogg	Brigadier General
Mar. 3	John Bell Hood	Brigadier General
Mar. 4	Hamilton P. Bee	Brigadier General
Mar. 4	Samuel Bell Maxey	Brigadier General
Mar. 14	Henry McCulloch	Brigadier General
May 26	John C. Moore	Brigadier General
Aug. 23	Matthew D. Ector	Brigadier General
Aug. 29	John Gregg	Brigadier General
Sept.12	Allison Nelson	Brigadier General
Sept.12	William R. Scurry	Brigadier General
Sept.12	William Steele	Brigadier General
Oct. 8	Elkanah Greer	Brigadier General
Oct. 10	John Bell Hood	Major General
Nov. 1	Jerome B. Robertson	Brigadier General
Nov. 18	John A. Wharton	Brigadier General

1863

May 9	John Whitfield	Brigadier General
May 20	Tom Green	Brigadier General
Sept. 18	Thomas N. Waul	Brigadier General
Sept. 20	John Bell Hood	Lieutenant General

Sept. 28	Thomas L. Rosser	Brigadier General
Nov. 10	John A. Wharton	Major General
Dec. 21	Lawrence S. Ross	Brigadier General
1864		
Feb. 14	Tom Green*	Duties as Major General
Feb. 29	Hiram Granbury	Brigadier General
Apr. 8	Wilburn King*	Brigadier General
Apr. 8	Horace Randal*	Brigadier General
Apr. 13	Arthur P. Bagby*	Brigadier General
Apr. 13	Xavier Debray*	Brigadier General
Apr. 18	Samuel Bell Maxey*	Duties as Major General
June 1	Adam R. Johnson	Brigadier General
July 18	John Bell Hood	General (temporary)
July 26	Felix Robertson**	Brigadier General
Aug. 15	William H. Young	Brigadier General
Nov. 1	Thomas L. Rosser	Major General
Dec. 22	James Harrison	Brigadier General
1865		
Jan. 14	Thomas Harrison	Brigadier General
Mar. 17	Richard Gano	Brigadier General
Mar. 17	William Hardeman	Brigadier General
Mar. 17	Walter P. Lane	Brigadier General
Mar. 17	Richard Waterhouse	Brigadier General
May 10	Arthur P. Bagby*	Duties as Major General
May 16	A. W. Terrell*	Brigadier General

    * Appointed by Edmund Kirby Smith; never confirmed by President Davis or Confederate Senate

    ** Appointed by President Davis; never confirmed by Confederate Senate

The Harrison brothers were among the last Texans to be appointed brigadier general. James, serving in Polignac's Division in Louisiana, was the last Texan promoted to the rank of general officer in 1864, and Tom, who succeeded John A. Wharton as commander of Terry's Texas Rangers, was the first Texan elevated to brigadier general in 1865. He was wounded just prior to his appointment and never actually exercised brigade command before the war ended.[19]

Four Texas Confederates, Richard Gano, William P. Hardeman, Walter P. Lane, and Richard Waterhouse, were appointed brigadier general by President Davis on March 17, 1865, and confirmed by the Senate on March 18, the final day the Confederate Congress met. A. W. Terrell, serving in East Texas, was the last Texan to be named a general officer, receiving his appointment from Edmund Kirby Smith on May 16, 1865.[20] On that same day Smith assigned Texan Arthur P. Bagby to duty as major general (to rank from May 10), but this rank, like his earlier appointment as brigadier general, was never approved by higher officials.

Fourteen of the thirty-seven Texans who served as general officer spent their entire Civil War careers west of the Mississippi River. Two of these, Ben McCulloch, mortally wounded at Pea Ridge on March 7, 1862, and Allison Nelson, who succumbed to disease in Arkansas on October 7, 1862, died early in the war. McCulloch fought in two of the biggest battles in the Trans Mississippi, commanding Texas, Louisiana, and Arkansas troops both at Wilson's Creek and Pea Ridge. Allison, on the other hand, took part only in a minor engagement at DeVall's Bluff on the White River before dying from typhoid fever.[21]

Ben McCulloch's younger brother, Henry, spent the early and latter parts of the war defending the Texas frontier from Indian raids and dealing with deserters, draft dodgers, and bushwhackers. In the autumn of 1862 he joined thousands of Texans defending Arkansas from Federal invaders. He served as a brigade commander in John G. Walker's division in the unsuccessful attack on Union defenders at Milliken's Bend in June 1863. In late summer of that year he returned to Texas as commander of the northern subdistrict of the state, a position he held until the war's end.[22]

Twelve of the fourteen Texas general officers who spent the entire war west of the Mississippi River took part in the Red River campaign. Ten of these were in the Battle of Mansfield on April 8, 1864. William R. Scurry and Horace Randal commanded brigades in Walker's Texas Division in this battle. Richard Waterhouse led a regiment in Scurry's brigade and Wilburn King led a regiment in Thomas Waul's brigade. Tom Green commanded the army's cavalry at Mansfield. Hamilton P. Bee commanded one of the four cavalry brigades under Green. Colonels A. W. Terrell and Xavier Debray led cavalry regiments under Bee. The Second Cavalry brigade was commanded by Missourian James P. Major, who was married to

Tom Green's sister-in-law. Major's regiments were led by future brigadiers A. P. Bagby, William P. Hardeman, and W. P. Lane.[23]

James Harrison, another future Confederate general from Texas, normally would have commanded one of the infantry regiments in Polignac's Brigade, but was afoot in Texas at the time.[24] Harrison rejoined the army shortly after the Battle of Mansfield, however, and took part in the pursuit of of Banks' retreating army. Brigadier William Steele also missed the Battle of Mansfield. The veteran Steele, who had earlier commanded troops in New Mexico and Indian Territory, was on assignment in Texas when the Red River campaign began. Like Harrison, he arrived after Mansfield but played a role in pursuing the retreating Federal army.[25]

Ten Texas Confederate generals commanded troops both in the Trans Mississippi and in the vast area between the Mississippi and the Carolinas that historian Thomas Connelly has described as the "Confederate Heartland." As noted earlier, one of these, Joseph Hogg, died after only brief service. A second officer, John Whitfield, led Texas cavalry at Pea Ridge, Iuka, and the early phases of the Vicksburg campaign, but left the army in the autumn of 1863 due to failing health. Walter P. Lane, who commanded a regiment in the battle at Mansfield, spent most of his Civil War service west of the Mississippi, but was in the fighting around Corinth, Mississippi.[26]

Sam Maxey, Richard Gano, and Elkanah Greer held commands in the Heartland and the Trans Mississippi. Maxey, a West Point classmate of Stonewall Jackson, was one of the first Texans appointed brigadier general. After serving with Albert Sidney Johnston in Kentucky, he commanded a brigade in the 1863 fighting in Mississippi. He was transferred to the Trans Mississippi in August 1863, and in December assumed command in Indian Territory, a position he held until February 21, 1865. Richard Gano, a physician and former state legislator, commanded a cavalry brigade in Indian Territory under Maxey. Earlier in the war Gano was with John Hunt Morgan in his first Kentucky raid. Elkanah Greer, who commanded the Third Texas Cavalry in 1861-1862, spent most of his career in the Trans Mississippi but served briefly in the siege of Corinth in May 1862, before becoming commandant of the Conscription Bureau of the Trans Mississippi Department.[27]

John A. Wharton, Thomas N. Waul, Matthew D. Ector, and

Lawrence "Sul" Ross were among the successful Texas generals who fought in both the Trans Mississippi and the Heartland. Although Waul was fifteen years Wharton's senior, the two men had several common characteristics. Neither had prior combat experience, both attended South Carolina College, both were lawyers as well as owners of sizable plantations, and both were staunch secessionists. Wharton was a delegate to the Texas secession convention and Waul represented Texas in the Montgomery convention that created the Confederate States of America. Waul returned to Texas to form Waul's Legion, which served in the Vicksburg and Red River campaigns. Wharton became commander of the Eighth Texas Cavalry, or Terry's Texas Rangers, after the deaths of Benjamin Terry and Tom Lubbock. After service at Shiloh and in Bragg's Kentucky invasion, Wharton was promoted to brigadier general. Differences with his superior, Joe Wheeler, led to Wharton's transfer to the Trans Mississippi Department. After the death of Tom Green, Wharton was promoted to command Richard Taylor's cavalry as the Confederates pursued the retreating Union army in the Red River campaign.[28]

Matthew D. Ector and Lawrence "Sul" Ross also served in both the Trans Mississippi and the Heartland. Ector enlisted as a private in the Third Texas Cavalry when the war began but was quickly promoted to captain. After taking part in the battles of Wilson's Creek and Pea Ridge he served in the Kentucky and Tennessee campaigns of 1862. By the end of the year he was commanding an infantry brigade. "Sul" Ross gained recognition as one of the South's most capable cavalry officers. As commander of the Sixth Texas Cavalry Ross led troops in battles at Corinth (October 1862) and Thompson's Station (March 1863) and in Wheeler's Tennessee raid in October 1863. Promoted to brigade command in December 1863, Ross led his Texas cavalry in the Georgia and Tennessee campaigns of 1864.[29]

Six Lone Star Confederate generals, one (Albert Sidney Johnston) an army commander and five brigade commanders, led Confederate troops only in the Heartland. Waco lawyer and judge Hiram Granbury was the most talented of the brigadier generals in the group. Granbury proved his ability at Fort Donelson, Raymond, and Chickamauga before his promotion to brigadier. Under his leadership the brigade distinguished itself in the north Georgia-

Atlanta campaign in late spring and summer of 1864. Granbury was killed in November 1864 while leading his brigade in the attack at Franklin, Tennessee. West Point graduate John C. Moore commanded the Second Texas Infantry at Shiloh prior to his appointment as brigadier general. As brigade commander he led his troops with skill at Corinth, Yazoo Pass, Vicksburg, and Missionary Ridge. Tom Harrison, like Granbury, served in the north Georgia campaigns of 1864. His promotion to brigadier general came late in the war as he commanded Confederate cavalry in the Carolinas campaign.[30]

Except for brief recruiting duty in Texas, Kentucky-born Adam R. Johnson spent his Civil War career in the Tennessee-Kentucky region, serving under John Hunt Morgan and Nathan Bedford Forrest. An injury to his eyes in August 1864 forced Johnson to return to his home in Texas.[31]

William Hugh Young was the sixth Texas general officer whose Civil War service was in the Confederate Heartland. Young commanded Texas troops at Shiloh, Perryville, Murfreesboro, Chickamauga, and Atlanta. Often wounded in combat, Young was captured late in the war and confined to prison at Johnson's Island until the war ended.[32]

Four Texas general officers, John Bell Hood, John Gregg, and the father and son Jerome and Felix Robertson, fought in both the Heartland and Virginia. Hood was highly successful as a brigade and division commander in the Army of Northern Virginia. After being wounded at Gettysburg he recovered sufficiently well that he could lead his division in the Battle of Chickamauga. Wounded again, he later commanded a corps and the Army of Tennessee. John Gregg, former district judge in Freestone County, served in Mississippi, Tennessee, and Virginia, eventually commanding Hood's old brigade in Virginia. At the time of his death in October 1864, Gregg was regarded as one of Lee's most capable brigadiers. Felix Robertson, the only native Texan to become a general officer, commanded troops in the Heartland and Virginia. Unlike Gregg, however, Robertson was a highly controversial officer criticized by contemporaries and historians for his treatment of captured prisoners.[33] Felix Robertson's father, Dr. Jerome Bonaparte Robertson, who served in Virginia and Tennessee, also became involved in controversy, leading to his removal as commander of Hood's Texas

Brigade. Robertson never held an active command in the Confederate army again. He was ordered to report to John B. Magruder, commanding the District of Texas, and soon thereafter took command of the reserve forces of the state.[34]

Tom Rosser, West Point classmate of George A. Custer, and Louis T. Wigfall, who briefly commanded the Texas Brigade in Virginia, were the only Texas general officers whose Civil War careers were spent entirely in the East. Wigfall resigned his commission in early 1862 to take a seat in the Confederate Senate. Rosser was with the Army of Northern Virginia from Manassas through Appomattox. He refused to surrender at Appomattox and planned to carry on the struggle with Joe Johnston's army but was captured in May 1865.[35]

Ten of the thirty-seven Texas Confederate generals died before the end of the Civil War. Seven were killed or mortally wounded in combat—Hiram Granbury at Franklin, Tennessee, Tom Green at Blair's Landing, Louisiana, John Gregg near Richmond, Albert Sidney Johnston at Shiloh, Ben McCulloch at Pea Ridge, and Horace Randal and William R. Scurry at Jenkins' Ferry, Arkansas. John A. Wharton was killed at Gen. John B. Magruder's headquarters in Houston by Col. George W. Baylor after an altercation in April 1865. Joseph L. Hogg died from dysentery in May 1862, and Allison Nelson died from typhoid fever in September 1862.[36]

In addition to those dying during the war, seventeen other Texas generals were wounded. Some of the wounds were not serious; others such as the wounds to Generals Ector and Hood resulted in the loss of a leg through amputation. Adam Johnson was blinded after he was accidentially shot in the head by his own men at Grubbs Crossroads, Kentucky.[37]

Several Texas generals were wounded more than once. Tom Rosser and William Hugh Young had the distinction of being the Texas general officers wounded most often. Rosser was wounded six times while leading cavalry in Virginia; Young was wounded five times while serving with the Army of Tennessee. Young was one of six Texas Confederate generals to be captured during the war. He was captured by Federal cavalry while being taken to the rear in an ambulance after his wound at Allatoona on October 5, 1864. After an operation in December 1864, he spent four months in Union hospitals prior to his transfer to Johnson's Island, where he remained a prisoner until July 1865.[38]

TABLE 4
Texas Confederate Generals
Injured, Wounded, or Killed in the Civil War*

General	Nature of Injury	Date	Place
Bagby, A. P.	Wound in arm	4-13-64	Bisland, La.
Bee, Hamilton P.	Facial wound	4- 9-63	Pleasant Hill
Ector, Matthew D.	Hit four times	9-19-63	Chickamauga
	Slight wound	6- 2-64	New Hope Ch.
	Left leg, amputated	7-27-64	Atlanta
Gano, Richard	Left arm broken	9-19-64	Cabin Creek
Granbury, Hiram	Wounded	9-19-63	Chickamauga
	Killed	11-30-64	Franklin
Green, Tom	Killed	4-12-64	Blair's Land.
Greer, Elkanah	Slight wound	3- 7-62	Pea Ridge
Gregg, John	Neck wound	9-19-63	Chickamauga
	Killed	10- 7-64	Charles Road, Vir.
Hardeman, W. P.	Slight wound	2-21-62	Valverde
Harrison, Thomas	Hip wound	1- 1-63	Murfreesboro
	Leg wound	3-10-65	Fayetteville
Hood, John Bell	Left arm shattered	7- 2-63	Gettysburg
	Right leg, amputated	9-20-63	Chickamauga
Johnson, Adam R.	Blinded	8-21-64	Grubbs Cross-roads, Ky.
Johnston, Albert S.	Killed	4- 6-62	Shiloh
King, Wilburn	Wounded	8-10-61	Wilson's Cr.
	Severely wounded	4- 8-64	Mansfield
Lane, Walter P.	Cut on head	6- ?-63	Donaldsonville, La.
	Thigh wound	4 -8-64	Mansfield
McCulloch, Ben	Killed	3- 7-62	Pea Ridge
Robertson, Felix	Elbow wound	11-28-64	Buck Head,Ga.
Robertson, Jerome	Shoulder wound	6-27-62	Gaines Mill
	Groin wound	8-20-62	2nd Manassas
	Right knee	7- 2-63	Gettysburg
Randal, Horace	Killed	4-30-64	Jenkins' Ferry
Rosser, Thomas	Arm wound	5-23-62	Mechanicsvil.
	Foot wound	3-17-63	Kelly's Ford
	Slight wound	10-12-63	Fleetwood,Va.
	Leg wound	6-11-64	Trevilian St.
	Arm wound	3-31-65	Five Forks

	Arm wound	4- 6-65	High Bridge
Scurry, William R.	Cheek wound	3-28-62	Glorieta
	Grazed	4- 9-64	Pleasant Hill
	Killed	4-30-64	Jenkins' Ferry
Waul, Thomas N.	Arm broken	4-30-64	Jenkins' Ferry
Wharton, John A.	Right leg wound	4- 6-62	Shiloh
	Wounded in arm	7-13-62	Murfreesboro
	Grazed in chest	2- 3-63	Ft. Donelson
	Killed	4- 6-65	Houston
Whitfield, John	Shoulder wound	9-19-62	Iuka
Young, William	Shoulder wound	12-31-62	Murfreesboro
	Thigh wound	7-13-63	Jackson
	Chest wound	9-20-63	Chickamauga
	Neck/jaw wound	6-19-63	Kennesaw Mt.
	Left leg wound	10- 5-64	Atlanta

* Sources: Jack D. Welsh, *Medical Histories of Confederate Generals* (Kent: Kent State University Press, 1995), the main source, is supplemented by Ezra Warner, *Generals in Gray* (Baton Rouge: Louisiana State University Press, 1959), Bruce S. Allardice, *More Generals in Gray* (Baton Rouge: Louisiana State University Press, 1995), Ron Tyler, et. al., eds., *The New Handbook of Texas* (Austin: Texas State Historical Association, 1996), 6 vols., and William C. Davis, ed.. *The Confederate General* (Harrisburg, PA: National Historical Society, 1991), 6 vols.

John Gregg and Hiram Granbury became prisoners when the Confederate garrison at Fort Donelson surrendered. Both were exchanged in the late summer of 1862 and rejoined the army in Mississippi. As noted earlier, they served with distinction at Chickamauga and were later killed while leading their brigades against the enemy. John C. Moore and Thomas N. Waul became prisoners when Vicksburg surrendered. Like Gregg and Granbury they were later exchanged and returned to their commands. Adam Johnson was also at Fort Donelson but escaped with Forrest's cavalry. He was later captured in August 1864 and transported to prison at Fort Warren in Boston harbor. He was exchanged in February 1865.[39]

Most of the Texas Confederate generals who survived the war had active postwar careers in government or business. Samuel Bell Maxey resumed law practice and in 1875 was elected to the United States Senate, where he served two terms. Sul Ross, popular cavalry commander, was a member of the 1875 constitutional convention, a state senator, governor of Texas, and president of Texas Agricultural and Mechanical College in the postwar years. Former generals Thomas N. Waul and John Whitfield were delegates to the state constitutional convention of 1866. Waul also practiced law in the postbellum period as did Felix Robertson, William H. Young, and Arthur P. Bagby. Matthew Ector and Thomas Harrison served as judges after the war. A. W. Terrell, the last Texan to be appointed a general officer in the Confederate army, served four terms in the Texas Senate and three terms in the Texas House in the post Reconstruction years. He was author of several important pieces of legislation including the Terrell Election Law.[40]

William P. Hardeman, Henry McCulloch, William Steele, and Wilburn H. King all held leadership positions in state government in the postwar years. Richard Gano, the physician-general who commanded a brigade in Indian Territory, became a minister of the Christian Church, a position he held for forty-four years. John C. Moore, who led the Second Texas Infantry at Shiloh and commanded a brigade at Chickamauga, became a schoolteacher and writer. Jerome B. Robertson resumed his medical practice. John Bell Hood, Walter P. Lane, and Richard Waterhouse were businessmen after the war. Tom Rosser, the tall cavalryman and close friend of George A. Custer, went to work for a railroad in the Reconstruction period and eventually became chief engineer for the Northern Pacific. Rosser was one of a handful of ex-Confederate general officers called into United States service in the Spanish-American War. Commissioned brigadier general by President William McKinley, Rosser donned the old uniform he had taken off thirty-seven years earlier when he resigned as a West Point cadet to take Confederate service. Adam Johnson returned to Central Texas after the war to pursue an active career in spite of the injuries to his eyes sustained during the war. During the next fifty-seven years Johnson founded the town of Marble Falls, developed water power of the Colorado River, and established the Texas Mining Improvement Company.[41]

Louis T. Wigfall, former commander of the Texas Brigade in the Army of Northern Virginia and Confederate senator throughout the war, was one of few Confederate generals from Texas who did not have a successful career after the war. Fearing arrest by Federal authorities, Wigfall fled to London, where he lived in

TABLE 5
Death of Texas Confederate Generals

General	Date of Death	Place of Death	Burial
McCulloch, Ben	3- 7-62	Pea Ridge	Austin*
Johnston, Albert S.	4- 6-62	Shiloh	Austin*
Hogg, Joseph	5-16-62	Corinth	Corinth
Nelson, Allison	10- 7-62	Austin, Ark.	Little Rock
Green, Tom	4-12-64	Blair's Landing	Austin
Scurry, William	4-30-64	Jenkins' Ferry	Austin*
Randal, Horace	5- 2-64	Jenkins' Ferry	Marshall
Gregg, John	10- 7-64	Charles R.Va.	Aberdeen, Miss.
Granbury, Hiram	11-30-64	Franklin	Granbury
Wharton, John	4- 6-65	Houston	Austin*
Wigfall, Louis T.	2-18-74	Galveston	Galveston
Harrison, James	2-23-75	Waco	Waco
Waterhouse, Rich.	3-20-76	Waco	Jefferson
Greer, Elkanah	3-25-77	DeVall's Bluff	Memphis
Hood, John Bell	8-20-79	New Orleans	New Orleans
Whitfield, John	10-27-79	Hallettsville	Hallettsville
Ector, Matthew	10-29-79	Tyler	Marshall
Steele, William	1-12-85	San Antonio	Austin
Robertson, Jerome	1- 7-91	Waco	Waco
Harrison, Thomas	7-14-91	Waco	Waco
Lane, Walter P.	1-28-92	Marshall	Marshall
Debray, Xavier	1- 6-95	Austin	Austin*
McCulloch, Henry	3-12-95	Rockport	Seguin
Maxey, Samuel Bell	8-18-95	Eureka Springs	Paris
Bee, Hamilton P.	10- 3-97	San Antonio	San Antonio
Ross, Lawrence S.	1- 3-98	College Sta.	Waco
Hardeman, William	4- 8-98	Waco	Waco
Young, William H.	11-28-01	San Antonio	San Antonio
Waul, Thomas N.	7-28-03	Greenville	Fort Worth
Rosser, Thomas	3-29-10	Charlottesville	Charlottesville
King, Wilburn	12-12-10	Sulphur Springs	Corsicana
Moore, John C.	12-31-10	Osage	Osage
Terrell, A. W.	9- 9-12	Mineral Wells	Austin*
Gano, Richard	3-27-13	Dallas	Dallas
Bagby, Arthur P.	2-21-21	Hallettsville	Hallettsville
Johnson, Adam R.	12-10-22	Austin	Austin*
Robertson, Felix	4-29-28	Waco	Waco

*Buried in Texas State Cemetery

humble circumstances for several years. He returned to the United States in 1872 and lived for two years in Baltimore. He planned to resume his law practice in Marshall but died in Galveston on February 18, 1874, at the age of fifty-seven, the first of the Texas generals to die after the war.[42]

Six other Texas Confederate generals—James Harrison, Richard Waterhouse, Elkanah Greer, John Bell Hood, John Whitfield, and Matthew Ector—died in the 1870s. William Steele was the only Lone Star Confederate general to die in the 1880s. In the next three decades, 1890-1920, sixteen Texas generals passed away. A. P. Bagby (1921), Adam Johnson (1922), and Felix Robertson (1928) were the last Texas generals in gray to die. The controversial and often criticized Robertson, whose promotion was never confirmed by the Confederate Senate, was the last Confederate general to die. He was eighty-nine at the time of his death.

CHAPTER TWO

The Army Generals:
Albert Sidney Johnston and
John Bell Hood

TWO TEXANS, BOTH KENTUCKY natives, held the rank of (full) general commanding major armies during the Civil War. Senior of the two, Albert Sidney Johnston, was the highest ranking field officer in the Confederate army at the time of his death at Shiloh on April 6, 1862. Johnston came to Texas in the closing days of the struggle for independence from Mexico and made the new Republic his permanent home. John Bell Hood, on the other hand, was first stationed in Texas with the Second Cavalry, commanded by Johnston, following his graduation from the U.S. Military Academy at West Point in 1853. When his native state Kentucky failed to secede in the spring of 1861, Hood adopted Texas as his second home. He was appointed commander of the Fourth Texas Infantry with the rank of colonel in September 1861. A born fighter, Hood rose rapidly in the Confederate army. He was promoted to brigadier general in March 1862, in command of what came to be called "Hood's Texas Brigade." He was elevated to division command with the rank of major general in October 1862, corps commander with the rank of lieutenant general effective September 1863, and army commander with the rank of general (temporary) in July 1864.

Although Johnston and Hood served together in Texas during the 1850s (Hood in a very junior capacity), the two men had no direct contact during the Civil War. Johnston, appointed commander of the Western Department in September 1861, spent his brief Civil War career in Kentucky and Tennessee, while Hood was serving in Virginia under Joseph E. Johnston and Robert E. Lee. A year and a half after Albert Sidney Johnston's death, Hood commanded a division in the Battle of Chickamauga and eventually became commander of the Confederate army Johnston was leading when killed at Shiloh. Two years after the war, Hood was a pallbearer when Johnston's body was moved from its original burial site in New Orleans to the Texas State Cemetery in Austin.[1]

ALBERT SIDNEY JOHNSTON (1803-1862)

Albert Sidney Johnston graduated from the United States Military Academy five years before the birth of John Bell Hood. Born in Washington, Kentucky, on February 2, 1803, Johnston initially hoped for a naval career, but opposition from his parents turned him elsewhere. For a brief period he pursued the medical profession like his father, but in the midst of his studies at Transylvania University his thoughts turned back to the military, this time the army. Nominated for the U.S. Military Academy by his older brother, Josiah Stoddard Johnston, then a congressman from Louisiana, Albert Sidney Johnston entered West Point in June 1822.

The young Kentuckian was a cadet during the academy's golden age. Under the leadership of Col. Sylvanus Thayer, who became superintendent in 1817, West Point developed into a first-rate school for the training of young officers. While emphasis was upon engineering and tactics, the institution on the Hudson provided solid instruction in the fundamentals of soldiering.[2]

By all accounts Johnston was a fine cadet. Impressive in stature and bearing, Johnston had the appearance of a leader. Highly regarded by instructors and fellow students, he was appointed sergeant major of the Corps of Cadets in his junior year. In his senior year he was made adjutant of the Corps, a highly coveted honor. He ranked eighth in the class of forty-one cadets who graduated in June 1826. He would have ranked even higher except for a poor performance in a senior mathematics final examination.[3]

Upon graduation Johnston was assigned to infantry duty at Sackets Harbor on Lake Ontario. Shortly later he was transferred to the Sixth Infantry stationed at Jefferson Barracks near St. Louis.

Albert Sidney Johnston
—Courtesy of Harold B. Simpson Research
Center, Hillsboro, Texas

In January 1829 he married Henrietta Preston, the daughter of a prominent citizen of Louisville. Their first child, William Preston Johnston, was born in January 1832. Three months later Johnston was appointed adjutant to Gen. Henry Atkinson in the campaign to subdue Black Hawk and the Sauk and Fox Indians. What seemed to be a promising career and happy personal life was soon cut short by tragedy. Within three years Johnston lost his father, oldest brother, infant daughter, and wife through death.[4]

At his ailing wife's insistence Johnston resigned from the army a year before her death. Now distraught with grief he considered moving west to establish a colony in Sioux territory. These plans were put aside, however, when Johnston, visiting friends and relatives in Louisville, heard the appeal by Stephen F. Austin for support of the Texans fighting for independence from Mexico. The Texas cause appealed to Johnston's democratic spirit and his desire for adventure on a new frontier. Two decades earlier two of his brothers had participated in the Gutierrez-Magee expedition to liberate Texas from Spain. Now Johnston had an opportunity to help free Texas from Mexican rule. Saying a temporary goodbye to his small son and daughter, whom he left with relatives, Johnston headed for Texas in the summer of 1836.[5]

When Johnston arrived in Texas he found conditions unstable. Independence had been won but threats of Mexican invasion, unrest in the Texas army, and financial difficulties caused concern for the survival of the new Republic. After meeting the Republic's president, Sam Houston, in Nacogdoches, Johnston joined the Texas army. Brief service as an enlisted man was followed by an officer's commission. Johnston's training and organizational skills soon brought him appointment first as adjutant general and then senior brigadier general of the army. A duel with an unhappy rival, Gen. Felix Huston, resulted in a serious injury to Johnston's right hip and left him incapacitated for several months.

As senior, and commanding, general of the Texas army, Johnston became unhappy with what he considered to be the vacillating policies of President Houston regarding Mexican incursions and Indian disturbances. To his delight a more aggressive Texan, Mirabeau B. Lamar, was elected to succeed Houston as president in 1838. When Lamar asked him to accept the position of secretary of war in his cabinet, Johnston readily accepted. During his tenure as secretary, Johnston fully supported Lamar's policies, particularly those dealing with the Indians. Johnston assembled an army of 900 men under Gen. Kesley Douglass and ordered the expulsion of the Cherokees from Texas. Johnston also endorsed firm action against the Comanches in Central Texas, gaining him the reputation as the "scourge of the red man."[6]

Distaste for administrative routine, coupled with a desire to improve his financial situation, caused Johnston to resign as Texas secretary of war in March 1840. In the next few years Johnston alternated between Texas and Kentucky. During this period he acquired both property and a new wife, Eliza Griffin of Louisville, cousin of his first wife. The outbreak of war with Mexico in 1846 brought Johnston back into the U.S. Army. Enlisting for six months' service, Johnston was chosen colonel of the First Texas Infantry Regiment in Zachary Taylor's army. As the army moved southward Johnston was appointed inspector general on the staff of Maj. Gen. William O. Butler, commander of a division of volunteers. In the battle for Monterrey in September 1846, Johnston distinguished himself by rallying green American troops who were fleeing from an attack by Mexican lancers. Both Generals Taylor and Butler praised Johnston for his skill and courage under fire.[7] Johnston fully expected to be offered a field command after the capture of Monterrey. None was forthcoming, however, and since his six-month enlistment as a volunteer expired he returned to his family in Galveston.[8]

Johnston and his family now moved to a sprawling piece of land called China Grove plantation, which Johnston had purchased several years earlier. Located on Oyster Creek in Brazoria County, China Grove consisted of 5,856 acres of rich alluvial soil, most of which was unimproved prairie and forest land. For the next three years Johnston struggled unsuccessfully to make the plantation profitable. In the autumn of 1849 creditors brought suit against him, and two years later the plantation was sold, with Johnston still in debt.[9]

Johnston was already back in the army when China Grove was sold. At the urging of Johnston's friends and relatives, President Zachary Taylor appointed Johnston paymaster of Texas with the rank of major in October 1849. Although this was not the field command he longed for, Johnston gladly accepted the position. For the next five years he traveled from military post to military post in Texas while carrying out his duties.

In March 1855, the drudgery of paymaster duty came to an end when Johnston was appointed commanding officer of the newly created U.S. Second Cavalry Regiment with the rank of colonel. The Second Cavalry was one of two new mounted units created by Congress to augment military forces in the American Southwest. Secretary of War Jefferson Davis took particular pride in the Second Cavalry, so much so that some referred to the regiment as "Jeff Davis' Own." The Second was staffed primarily with officers born in the southern states. In many ways Johnston was the logical choice as commander of the regiment, which would be stationed in Texas. He had the required experience, both in the American and Texas armies, and was endorsed for the post by the Texas legislature and governor. Johnston's wife, friends, and relatives had waged a campaign in his behalf. Secretary Davis and Johnston had known each other since their cadet days at West Point, where Johnston, two classes ahead of the Mississippian, befriended the younger cadet. Later they had been stationed at Jefferson Barracks as young infantry officers, had fought in the Black Hawk War, and had been two of the officers who negotiated the surrender terms for the city of Monterrey during the Mexican War. Davis had come to idolize Johnston. Davis' biographer, William C. Davis, pointed out that "even in his last years Davis spoke of Johnston's early friendship with pride [that] betrays the reverential admiration and love he felt for the older cadet who befriended him."[10]

Joining Johnston in the Second Cavalry were some of the most promising officers in the army. Robert E. Lee of Virginia was appointed executive officer with the rank of lieutenant colonel. A graduate of the West Point class of 1829 (three years after Johnston), Lee had a brilliant record during the Mexican War as one of the engineering officers on the staff of Gen. Winfield Scott, and had just completed a tour of duty as superintendent at West Point. William J. Hardee of Georgia and George H. Thomas of Virginia were the two majors of the new regiment. Among the company commanders were Earl Van Dorn (Mississippi), Edmund Kirby Smith (Florida), and George Stoneman (New York). Lieutenants included John Bell Hood (Kentucky), Nathan G. Evans (South Carolina), and Charles W. Field (Kentucky). Twenty-four of the thirty-four officers first assigned to the regiment were Southerners. Fourteen of the assigned officers became generals in the Civil War —nine Confederate and five Union.[11]

Under Johnston's direction, the new regiment completed its recruiting, organizing, and training at Jefferson Barracks, Missouri, in late summer 1855 and marched to its assigned duty stations in Texas that autumn. The primary task of the regiment was to protect the frontier from Comanches who had been raiding farms, ranches, and outlying settlements in West and Central Texas. This was an assignment for which Johnston was well suited as a result of his previous experiences as Texas secretary of war. The state of Texas had contributed land for a reservation for the Comanches on the Clear Fork of the Brazos, but the Indians stayed on the reservation only during the winter months. Johnston believed the Indians would remain on the reservation only after they had been severely chastised. Consequently, he ordered a series of operations against the Comanches in 1856 which resulted in temporary peace along the Texas frontier.[12]

In late July 1857, Johnston received orders to report to the secretary of war for a new assignment. He departed from Texas at once, leaving Robert E. Lee in command of the Second Cavalry. In Washington, Johnston received orders to take command of U.S. troops already on the march to Utah, where the Mormons were challenging Federal authority. President James Buchanan had appointed a non-Mormon, Alfred Cumming of Georgia, as governor of Utah, along with three new Federal judges. It was believed that the Mormon population would resist these appointments, so U.S. troops were to accompany the governor and the judges. When Brigham Young and church leaders learned that U.S. troops were coming, they prepared for war, declaring martial law, mobilizing the Mormon militia, and fortifying mountain passes leading into the Salt Lake basin.

Johnston had a difficult assignment. U.S. troops already on the march were badly scattered and ill prepared for the winter. When early snows made the advance impossible, Johnston ordered various units to concentrate at Fort Bridger on the Oregon Trail, only to discover the Mormons had burned the fort. Under extremely difficult conditions, Johnston's small army spent the winter in a temporary camp near the remains of Fort Bridger.[13]

Johnston's handling of the problems facing the Utah expedition during the bitter winter of 1857-1858 impressed his superiors in Washington, resulting in his promotion to brevet brigadier general in April 1858. Angry at the Mormons for the destruction of Fort Bridger and the Mountain Meadows Massacre in which more than one hundred emigrants to California were slain, Johnston prepared for a summer campaign. This became unnecessary when peace commissioners appointed by President Buchanan resolved differences between the Mormons and the Federal government.[14]

In late June 1858, Johnston's army entered Salt Lake City without opposition. After a march through the city Johnston moved his army southwest of Salt Lake City to a campsite in Cedar Valley. For the next eighteen months Johnston and his troops remained in the area as occupation forces to be available if needed by Federal officials. During this period the army helped maintain order, opened new roads through the mountains and desert, and provided protection for emigrant trains against the Indians.[15]

In February 1860, Johnston was relieved of his Utah command and granted an extended leave before reporting for a new assignment. Many of his friends believed that Johnston would be appointed to command the Department of Texas, but Johnston hoped otherwise. Normally he would welcome the return to Texas; however, sensing that the sectional controversy over slavery was nearing a climax, he wished to avoid choosing between the Federal government and Texas. He was pleased therefore when the secretary of war appointed him to command the Department of the Pacific with headquarters in San Francisco. In December 1860, one month after the election of Abraham Lincoln as president, Johnston and his family left New York City on a steamer heading for his new assignment.[16]

Johnston arrived in San Francisco on January 14 and took command of his new department immediately. He had barely arrived, however, when he heard rumors that several slaveholding states were seceding from the Union. On April 9 he learned that the people of Texas had endorsed the secession ordinance passed by the state convention meeting in Austin. He now faced a difficult choice. He was a staunch nationalist who had fought two wars to preserve national honor and had been prepared to fight a third against the Mormons to uphold Federal authority. But he was also a Southerner who supported the institution of slavery. Also, he had developed a strong commitment to Texas. He had hoped that somehow a conflict could be avoided, but that was no longer possible. Johnston made his decision immediately. He resigned his commission that day and asked to be relieved as soon as possible.[17]

Historian and biographer Charles P. Roland believes that Johnston left Federal service "resolved to join neither the Union nor the Confederacy in the impending conflict." Johnston told friends that he hoped to remain in California as a rancher. A week after he was relieved of his command, Johnston and his family left San Francisco to go to the Los Angeles home of Dr. John Griffin, Mrs. Johnston's brother and a prosperous physician. The news of Fort Sumter and President Davis' call for troops convinced Johnston that he must offer his services to the Confederacy. At first he planned that he and his family would sail to New York City, then travel to Virginia, but he learned that the secretary of war had ordered his arrest. He left the family behind and joined a small party of California Southerners riding overland to the Confederacy.[18]

The trip back to Texas was long and hazardous. Crossing 800 miles of desert and mountains, the party avoided hostile Apaches and Federal patrols. In late July they encountered Texas troops commanded by Lt. Col. John R. Baylor near Mesilla, New Mexico. At Baylor's insistence Johnston delayed his journey for a week to take temporary command of the Texas troops who were attempting to intercept a Federal detachment marching through the region. When it became apparent that the Federals could not be captured, Johnston continued his journey to Texas. From El Paso he traveled by stage to San Antonio, then on to Houston and New Orleans. From there he traveled by rail to Richmond, which he reached in early September.[19]

Johnston's safe arrival was greeted with enthusiasm throughout the Confederacy. When Johnston called at the Executive Mansion the president was ill, but when he heard the bell followed by footsteps, Davis sat up and exclaimed "that is Sidney Johnston's footstep. Bring him up." According to Johnston's son, William Preston Johnston, Davis said many times afterward: "I hoped and expected that I had others who would prove generals, but I knew I had *one*, and that was Sidney Johnston."[20]

Davis was delighted that Johnston was available for military duty. Davis' biographer, William C. Davis, stated that the Confederate president "worshipped Sidney Johnston as he did no other man in his life." He regarded Johnston as the finest soldier in America, an opinion shared by many others, in both the North and the South. Davis had already nominated Johnston to the rank of full general, second in rank only to Adj. Gen. Samuel Cooper. Since Cooper held a staff appointment, Johnston was the highest ranking field general in the Confederate army. Davis considered Johnston for various positions, but because of chaotic conditions prevailing in the western Confederacy he appointed him to command Confederate Department No. 2, a vast area stretching from the Appalachian Mountains on the east through Indian Territory on the west. The department included Kentucky, Tennessee, Missouri, and Arkansas and the northern portion of Alabama, Mississippi, and Louisiana.[21]

Johnston was faced with a difficult task. In his long experience in the military he had never commanded more than 3,000 troops. Now he commanded 40,000 soldiers defending a 500-mile front stretching from the Appalachians of Kentucky and Tennessee to the Ozarks of western Arkansas and Missouri. Felix Zollicoffer with 4,000 men defended the right flank of Johnston's Confederates at Cumberland Ford in eastern Kentucky, Simon B. Buckner with 4,000 men held the center at Bowling Green, Kentucky, and his old West Point classmate and Episcopal bishop of Louisiana, Leonidas Polk, occupied Columbus, Kentucky, on the Mississippi. Small garrisons defended Fort Henry on the Tennessee and Fort Donelson on the Cumberland, Sterling Price and 10,000 Missourians were in southwestern Missouri, and Ben McCulloch and 7,000 Texans, Arkansans, and Confederate Indians were in northwest Arkansas. Three or four thousand troops commanded by William J. Hardee were in northeastern Arkansas.[22]

On paper Johnston's army looked formidable, but many of his men were ill equipped, poorly armed, and inadequately trained. The Union forces they faced outnumbered them by 20,000 men and were supported by gunboats and transport vessels. There were no natural barriers to aid in the defense of the western Confederacy. The major rivers, the Mississippi, Cumberland, and Tennessee, were arteries offering pathways for invasion.

To offset enemy numerical superiority Johnston attempted to

create the illusion of great strength with stories in newspapers doubling the size of his army and hinting of a winter offensive toward the Ohio River. At the same time he worked diligently, but with limited success, to increase his own forces. His appeals to Maj. Gen. Braxton Bragg at Pensacola, Governor A. B. Moore of Alabama, and Governor Joseph E. Brown of Georgia for men and arms were rejected as each replied that there were no men to spare. Tennessee Governor Isham G. Harris did agree to send additional troops, and some Kentucky volunteers, including former Vice President John C. Breckinridge, joined Johnston's ranks. At the same time Generals Don Carlos Buell and Henry W. Halleck, commanding Union troops opposed to Johnston, received more reinforcements so that the disparity in numbers continued to mount. A personal appeal by Johnston to his friend President Davis proved unsuccessful as the chief executive responded that he had no reinforcements to send.[23]

Johnston received Davis' reply at the same time he learned that his right wing under Felix Zollicoffer and George Crittenden had been defeated at Mill Springs, Kentucky, by Federal troops commanded by Johnston's former subordinate in the Second Cavalry, George Thomas. In a confusing battle fought in a rainstorm, Zollicoffer was killed and Crittenden was forced to fall back across the Cumberland, abandoning artillery and valuable supplies to the enemy. The defeat at Mill Springs was a blow to Johnston; his right flank was now exposed and the center of his line at Bowling Green was in danger.[24]

Outnumbered two to one and with Bowling Green and Nashville in danger, Johnston once again requested that Richmond send additional troops. This time President Davis responded by sending two brigades from West Virginia and another general, P. G. T. Beauregard. The hero of Fort Sumter and First Manassas, Beauregard was one of five full generals in the Confederacy. He had shown some strategic ability but had disagreed with the Confederate president concerning the conduct of the war. For several months Davis had considered ways of removing Beauregard from the Virginia scene. This seemed an ideal opportunity; Johnston needed assistance and Beauregard was an experienced, capable officer. Beauregard showed some reluctance to accept a role in the West but agreed to go with the understanding that additional troops would be sent.[25]

Johnston received Beauregard warmly at his Bowling Green headquarters in early February. Beauregard, who had a creative if not always realistic mind, suggested a plan of operations. He proposed that Johnston mass his troops near Forts Henry and Donelson, attack and destroy Union troops in the vicinity commanded by one of Halleck's subordinates, Brig. Gen. U.S. Grant, and then turn upon Don Carlos Buell in central Kentucky. The plan had merit, but Johnston lacked sufficient troops to carry it out.[26]

Three days after Beauregard's arrival in Kentucky, Johnston received word that the small Confederate garrison at Fort Henry on the Tennessee River had surrendered after an attack by Union gunboats assigned to Brig. Gen. U. S. Grant. Grant was now moving his troops and gunboats for an attack on Fort Donelson, twenty miles to the east on the Cumberland River. After conferring with Beauregard and William J. Hardee, now commanding Confederate troops at Bowling Green, Johnston ordered his scattered commands to withdraw south of the Cumberland River, abandoning Columbus, Bowling Green, Fort Donelson, and, if necessary, Nashville. Such a move required courage as it would be widely criticized, but Johnston believed it was the only way to prevent his army from being outflanked.[27]

As the Confederates withdrew from central Kentucky, Johnston made what historian Charles P. Roland described as "the most grievous error in military judgment of his career."[28] Receiving additional information about the number of available forces in the area, and apparently troubled by the thought of surrendering the fort without a fight, Johnston decided to reinforce Donelson. Generals Gideon Pillow, Simon B. Buckner, and John B. Floyd were ordered to proceed to Donelson with troops under their command. As Roland pointed out, Johnston should have defended Donelson with all the troops in his command or stripped the garrison at Donelson of all but enough troops left to fight while he withdrew his forces from the Bowling Green line. He did neither.[29]

In his study of Confederate command in the West, Steven Woodworth contended that while Johnston made a mistake in reinforcing Donelson, it need not have been a disaster. The disaster, Woodworth declared, "was the work of the men he sent to reinforce the garrison."[30] John B. Floyd, the senior officer who now commanded at Donelson, and Gideon Pillow, second in command, were both inept political generals. Simon B. Buckner, their junior in rank, was a West Point graduate and professional soldier who was unhappy about serving under two amateurs. Together, the three completely mishandled affairs at Donelson. Grant surrounded the fort, and after several days of fighting the Confederates surrendered.[31]

The loss of Donelson and the surrender of more than 12,000 troops was a major blow to the Confederacy and a complete shock to Johnston. Earlier reports from Floyd had been optimistic; as a result Johnston had informed the War Department on February 16 that the Confederates had won a "brilliant victory." The next day he had to report that the fort had surrendered after a "most gallant defense."[32]

The loss of Donelson, coupled with Johnston's withdrawal from Nashville on February 17, sent shockwaves throughout the Confederacy. Newspaper editors, who five months earlier had lauded Johnston, now clamored for his removal. Tennesseans were particularly bitter over the loss of Nashville and the abandonment of western and middle Tennessee. The state's congressional delegation called upon President Davis, demanding Johnston's removal and stating their belief that Johnston was no general. But Davis publicly expressed confidence in his old West Point classmate, informing the delegation "if Johnston is not a general we had better give up the war, for we have no general."[33] Privately, Davis wrote to Johnston assuring him of his support but urging him to make a full report concerning recent events in Kentucky and Tennessee.[34]

On March 18, 1862, Johnston wrote to Davis explaining his reasons for the evacuation of Nashville. Johnston thanked the chief executive for his support and welcomed a possible presidential visit to the army. Johnston had no objections if Davis should himself choose to assume command of the army; "it would afford me the most unfeigned pleasure to help you to victory and the country to independence," he wrote the president.[35]

Johnston continued to have the support of many who served with him. John A. Wharton, colonel of the Eighth Texas Cavalry, better known as Terry's Texas Rangers, wrote Johnston that "I regard you as the best soldier in America, and . . . I desire to fight under no other leadership, and that such is the feeling of the Texas Rangers." Another Texan, Richardson Scurry, a veteran of San

Jacinto, approved Johnston's actions and urged him to ignore the critics; "pursue your course and follow the dictates of your own reason," he wrote.[36]

Aware of the various criticisms against him, Johnston was determined to bring his scattered forces together for a stand against the enemy. He ordered Hardee's Bowling Green garrison, Critten-den's eastern Kentucky troops, and the rear guard from Nashville to join him as he fell back toward Corinth, an important railroad junction in northern Mississippi. At the same time Beauregard pulled the western wing of the army away from Columbus and the Mississippi River toward Corinth. Four regiments from New Orleans commanded by Daniel Ruggles were ordered northward, and Braxton Bragg brought 10,000 well-disciplined troops from Florida to Corinth.[37]

As the Confederates gathered at Corinth, the Union army slowly moved southward. Johnston's movements confused Union leaders in late February as they thought he was heading toward Chattanooga, but they now believed he intended to make a defensive stand at Corinth because of its strategic importance. Grant moved his army south along the Tennessee River to Pittsburg Landing, about twenty-five miles north of Corinth. There the Federals awaited the arrival of Don Carlos Buell and his army from Nashville. Once Buell arrived, Grant planned to move against Corinth.[38]

By the last week of March, Johnston had 40,000 troops at Corinth. He was determined to attack Grant's army at Pittsburg Landing before Buell could join him. For some unexplained reason Johnston offered command to Beauregard, but the Creole general declined, preferring to serve as second in command to Johnston. Johnston then instructed Beauregard to draw up the operational plan for the advance and attack. Braxton Bragg was named chief of staff as well as commander of one of the corps. His task was to drill and discipline the green troops. Johnston himself obtained local guides to lead the army on the route to Pittsburg Landing. He attempted without success to convince area planters to assign their slaves to the army as cooks and teamsters, thus relieving soldiers for combat duty.[39]

On the evening of April 2 Johnston gave orders that the advance to Pittsburg Landing would begin the next day. He originally planned to attack Grant's army on April 4, but delays on the march made this impossible. Johnston still hoped to attack on the morning of April 5, but it was 4:00 P.M. before most of the Confederates reached the designated position for the assault. Beauregard, convinced that there was no longer any hope of surprising the enemy, urged that the offensive be canceled and the army return to Corinth. After some discussion with Beauregard and other officers, Johnston declared that "we shall attack at daylight tomorrow." As he closed the conference Johnston remarked to an aide, "I would fight them if they were a million."[40]

At 5:30 on the morning of April 6, Confederate troops in Hardee's Corps launched the attack against Grant's army. The assault took the enemy by surprise. Grant, who had not expected an attack, was at Savannah, nine miles downstream. His army had no entrenchments and was scattered in division encampments between a small Methodist church named Shiloh and the Tennessee River.

Although they gave ground, the Union troops fought stubbornly as they fell back. When Grant arrived on the scene at 9:00 A.M. there was great confusion as Union division commanders William T. Sherman, John McClernand, and Benjamin Prentiss attempted to stabilize their lines. The fighting went on throughout the morning with heavy casualties sustained by each side. Johnston left Beauregard in the rear to guide the battle while he himself rode along the front lines urging his men on. By early afternoon the Confederates under Hardee and Leonidas Polk had driven the enemy back on the Confederate left and in the center, but Union troops under Prentiss were making a desperate stand on the Confederate right near a spot called "the Hornet's Nest." Repeated assaults by Breckinridge's Corps failed to dislodge the enemy. At about 2:00 P.M. Johnston was on the extreme right, trying to rally an exhausted Tennessee regiment, when a musket ball ripped the heel of his boot on his right leg.[41]

At first Johnston did not believe he was injured, but he began to fall from his saddle. He was caught by Tennessee Governor Isham G. Harris and an aide, who laid him on the ground. Harris ripped open his shirt looking for a wound but failed to recognize the bleeding in his boot. Within thirty minutes Johnston bled to death from the bullet that had severed an artery on the back of his right leg near the knee.[42]

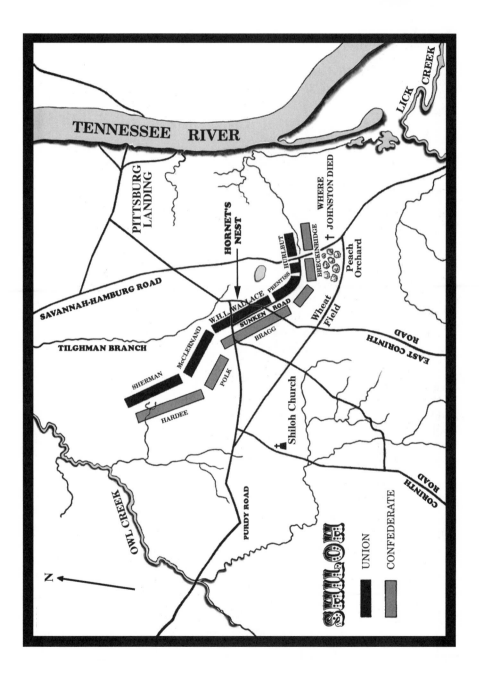

Johnston's death stunned members of his staff. His body was wrapped in a blanket and taken to Beauregard's headquarters. The battle continued with Beauregard now in command. Near dusk that evening Beauregard ordered Confederates to cease the attack. The offensive was resumed the next morning, but Grant had been reinforced by Don Carlos Buell. Momentum rapidly passed to the Federals as the Confederates were pushed back. On Monday evening, April 7, Beauregard ordered a withdrawal to Corinth.

Johnston's body was taken to Corinth and from there on to New Orleans, where it lay in state for two days. On the afternoon of April 11 Johnston was laid to rest in the St. Louis cemetery. After the war the body was removed from the cemetery with Generals Beauregard, Bragg, Hood, Richard Taylor, and James Longstreet among the pallbearers. The body was returned to Texas and buried in the State Cemetery on February 2, 1867.[43]

Many Southerners, including President Davis and Generals Bragg and Hardee, believed the Confederates would have won the Battle of Shiloh had Albert Sidney Johnston lived. They were convinced that in halting the attack at dusk Beauregard lost a golden opportunity to destroy Grant's army. Writing years later, Johnston's son, William Preston Johnston, declared that Beauregard had "complete victory in his grasp and he threw it away."[44]

Beauregard disagreed with this opinion. He argued that the decision to stop the Confederate attack when he did was correct. He contended that the Confederates were exhausted and dispirited after fighting all day. There was no possible way they could have broken the Federal lines that evening, Beauregard maintained.[45]

Contemporary historians are divided in their appraisal of Albert Sidney Johnston.[46] Johnston's biographer, Charles P. Roland, conceded that evaluation of Johnston as a general is difficult; "he died too early in the Civil War to demonstrate his full capabilities," wrote Roland.[47] Roland agreed that Johnston made errors, but pointed out that he had the capacity to grow. Roland noted that Robert E. Lee, U. S. Grant, and William T. Sherman all made mistakes in their early Civil War careers but went on to become outstanding field commanders. Had they died as early as Johnston their reputations would not be so high. More recently, Steven Woodworth in his thoughtful *Jefferson Davis and His Generals* (1990) argued that even had Johnston lost the Battle of Shiloh yet lived he "might still have changed the course of the war."[48]

JOHN BELL HOOD (1831-1879)

On the day (April 6, 1862) Albert Sidney Johnston was mortally wounded at Shiloh, John Bell Hood and his Texas Brigade began pulling out of the encampment near Fredericksburg, Virginia, and headed toward the York Peninsula. After two weeks' march the brigade went into camp near the site of the old Revolutionary battlefield. Assigned for the moment to John B. Magruder's command, the brigade readied itself to take part in efforts to block the advance by George B. McClellan's Union army.[49]

Hood had commanded the brigade consisting of the First, Fourth, and Fifth Texas and Eighteenth Georgia infantry regiments for more than a month. A native of Kentucky and a West Point graduate (1853), Hood served his junior apprenticeship under Albert Sidney Johnston and Robert E. Lee in the Second U.S. Cavalry on the Texas frontier. When the Civil War began, Hood resigned from the U.S. Army. As Kentucky had not seceded, Hood joined Confederate service from Texas, which he declared was his "adopted land." After brief service as a cavalry officer, he was appointed colonel of the Fourth Texas Infantry, which had recently arrived in Virginia. In October 1861 the regiment became part of a brigade consisting of three Texas and one Georgia regiment. Louis T. Wigfall, prominent Texas politician and commander of the First Texas, was given command of the brigade with the rank of brigadier general. When Wigfall was elected to the Confederate Senate he resigned his commission in the army. On March 6, 1862, Hood was promoted to brigadier general and named commander of the unit, which would soon become known as "Hood's Texas Brigade."[50]

The future commander of the Texas Brigade was born in Owingsville, Kentucky, on June 19, 1831. His parents wanted him to pursue a medical career like his father, but the young Hood preferred the adventure associated with a military life and convinced his parents to allow him to become a soldier. Appointment to West Point was relatively easy as his uncle, Richard French, was a member of Congress. The appointment was made on February 27, 1849, and Hood entered the academy in July.[51]

Hood's West Point years were difficult. His biographer Richard McMurry stated that "in no way did Hood distinguish himself, nor did West Point make any permanent change in his personal-

John Bell Hood

—Courtesy of Harold B. Simpson
Research Center, Hillsboro, Texas

ity."[52] His academic record was poor, and only through hard work did he survive. His conduct and disciplinary record was worse each year as he received demerits for "laughing in the ranks," "chewing tobacco," "smoking," "breaking ranks," and "trifling conduct." He was popular with his fellow cadets, however, and in September of his final year he was made lieutenant of the Corps of Cadets. But in December Hood was reprimanded and demoted to private by the new superintendent, Robert E. Lee, for being absent from quarters. In addition he received enough demerits to run his total to 196 for the year, only four short of expulsion from the academy. Hood was so depressed that he discussed leaving the academy with a fellow cadet and future Union general, John Schofield, who convinced Hood to stay.[53]

Hood managed to graduate in 1853, ranking forty-fourth in his class of fifty-five. Among his fellow graduates were future Union generals Schofield (ranked seventh), James B. McPherson (first), and Philip H. Sheridan (thirty-fourth).[54]

Upon graduation Hood was assigned as a brevet second lieutenant in the Fourth Infantry at Fort Jones in northern California. There he became a close friend of George Crook, an Ohioan who graduated a year ahead of Hood. To supplement their income Hood and Crook secured land and sowed a large crop of wheat. Just before the harvest, Hood was assigned to command a detachment of dragoons escorting a surveying expedition of the Topographical Engineers.[55]

In August 1855, Hood received orders transferring him to the newly created Second Cavalry being organized at Jefferson Barracks, Missouri. After being relieved by Lt. Philip Sheridan, Hood proceeded to San Francisco where he stopped to make financial arrangements for the trip through Panama. At the banking firm of Lucas, Turner & Company he met the bank manager, a West Point graduate and former army officer, William T. Sherman, whom Hood later recalled as possessing "a piercing eye and nervous temperament."[56]

Hood reached Jefferson Barracks in October 1855. Later that month the regiment, led by Col. Albert Sidney Johnston, began its march across Arkansas and Indian Territory to its duty station in Texas. The weather was bitterly cold as Hood first saw the state he came to love. The regiment reached Fort Belknap in Young County on December 27. There the regiment was divided with several companies moving to the Clear Fork of the Brazos and others, including Hood's company, continuing south to Fort Mason on the Llano River.[57]

For the next four years Hood was on duty with the Second Cavalry in Texas. During this time Hood and his fellow soldiers spent hours patrolling the frontier. There were occasional skirmishes, but often the troopers spent days in the saddle without seeing any hostile Indians. Hood's most serious encounter came in July 1857, while leading a detachment of twenty-four-men in the Devil's River country. After trailing what they believed to be a raiding party for two weeks, Hood's command was attacked by nearly 200 Comanches. In the fierce battle that followed, two cavalrymen were killed and five, including Hood, whose left arm was pierced by an arrow, were wounded. Nineteen Indians were killed and many wounded. Fortunately for Hood and his troopers, the Indians gathered up their dead and wounded as darkness approached and disappeared toward the Rio Grande. Hood and his men were later commended for gallantry by Gen. David Twiggs, commander of the Department of Texas, and Gen. Winfield Scott, commanding general of the army.[58]

Hood was promoted to first lieutenant in August 1858. He spent much of that year and 1859 either at Fort Mason or Camp Cooper on the Clear Fork of the Brazos. At Cooper he had the opportunity to renew his association with Robert E. Lee, who became commanding officer of the regiment when Albert Sidney Johnston was assigned to the Utah expedition. Hood frequently accompanied Lee when the Virginian rode over the country searching for a suitable location for a new fort. On one such occasion Lee advised Hood to "never marry unless you can do so in a family which will enable your children to feel proud of both sides of the house." Lee's kindness and fatherly advice deeply impressed the young Hood, who later wrote in his memoirs: "from those early relations first sprang my affection and veneration which grew in strength to the end of his [Lee's] eventful career."[59]

Like his commanding officer, Hood was concerned about the impending conflict between the Federal government and the slaveholding states. Hood decided to cast his lot with the slave states once his native state seceded. When it appeared that Kentucky would not take a decisive stand, Hood resigned from the U.S. Army and took a commission in the Confederate army as an officer from Texas. In his memoirs Hood later wrote that he was so impressed with Texas that he had determined to make it his home for life. "Therefore when Kentucky failed to act," he wrote, "I entered the Confederate service from the State of Texas, which henceforth became my adopted land."[60]

Hood was appointed first lieutenant in the Confederate army and ordered to report to his old commander, Robert E. Lee, in Richmond. Lee, then a major general in command of Virginia state forces, instructed Hood to proceed to the York Peninsula to assist Col. John B. Magruder. Magruder immediately put Hood in charge of all cavalry operations on the York River with the rank of major. In July, Hood's first Civil War action took place when he led eighty Confederate cavalrymen in a successful attack against Federal raiders. For his performance in this small engagement Hood was praised by Magruder, congratulated by Lee, and promoted to lieutenant colonel.[61]

In late September 1861, Hood was relieved of cavalry duties and appointed commanding officer of the Fourth Texas Infantry Regiment with the rank of colonel. The Texas companies that made up the regiment had recently arrived in Virginia. R. T. P. Allen, a West Point graduate and former superintendent of the Bastrop Military Institute, was the first commander of the regiment, but had been reassigned. Allen had earlier been a training officer in Texas, where he gained the reputation as a martinet which made him unacceptable to the Texas volunteers.[62]

Although there were some doubts expressed about the new commander, Hood, these soon disappeared. Rev. Nicholas Davis, chaplain and chronicler of the regiment, later wrote that "in a few days this feeling [of doubt] was gone, and every one seemed to be perfectly satisfied." Hood had a commanding presence—"about six feet two inches high, with a broad chest, light hair and beard, [and] blue eyes," and "gifted by nature with a voice that can be heard in the storm of battle," according to Chaplain Davis. His manly deportment, courteous manners, and decisive nature convinced the Texans that he was the man to lead them.[63]

On October 22, 1861, Hood's regiment was combined with the First Texas, Fifth Texas, and Eighteenth Georgia regiments to form a brigade, commanded by Louis Trezevant Wigfall, a stormy South Carolinian who had migrated to Texas in 1846. Although he had only limited previous military experience, Wigfall, recently a U.S. senator, had been instrumental in organizing and bringing the Texas companies to Virginia. The regiments, soon to be known as the Texas Brigade, were assigned to service with Joseph E. Johnston's army in northern Virginia. In early November, Hood and the Fourth Texas joined other units of the brigade at winter quarters near Dumfries, a small town north of Fredericksburg.[64]

The Texas Brigade spent the winter of 1861-1862 guarding the west bank of the Potomac against a possible Federal invasion. Except for patrol duty and work on fortifications there was little activity, but the cold, damp weather took its toll on the unacclimatized Texans. About twenty percent of the men in the three Texas regiments died or were discharged for disabilities that winter. Col. Hugh McLeod, commander of the First Texas, was among those who died from pneumonia. Hood spent several days recovering from the flux, but experienced no major illness that winter.[65]

In late February 1862, the brigade commander, Brigadier General Wigfall, resigned from military service to take his seat in the Confederate Senate. The senior regimental officer, Col. James J. Archer, a Marylander who commanded the Fifth Texas, temporarily assumed brigade command. In early March, however, Hood was appointed brigadier general and commander of the brigade that would henceforth be known as "Hood's Texas Brigade."[66]

Hood's Brigade was ordered to move southward in March as part of Johnston's efforts to meet the threat of a Federal invasion up the York Peninsula. In May the brigade saw its first major action. Assigned to W. H. C. Whiting's division to cover the Confederate withdrawal from Yorktown, the Texans engaged Union troops commanded by William B. Franklin near Eltham's Landing on the Pamunkey River. Franklin had moved his troops by water in an attempt to outflank the retreating Confederates. In fierce fighting Hood's Brigade drove the Federals back to the river, taking forty prisoners and capturing eighty-four wagons. The brigade losses, mainly in the Fourth Texas, were comparatively light.

Hood himself had a narrow escape at Eltham's Landing. A Union corporal drew down his musket to fire on Hood as the

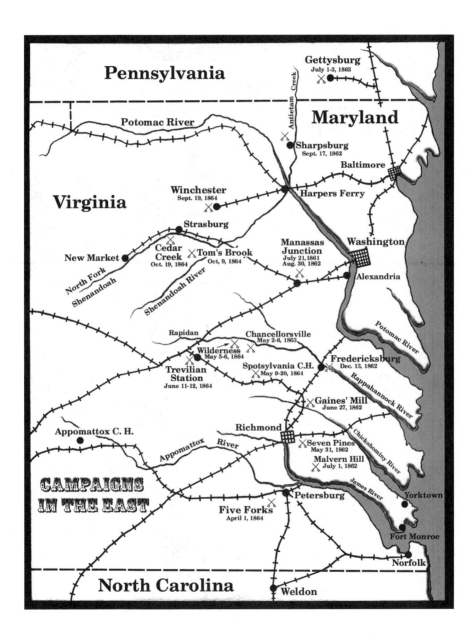

Pennsylvania

Gettysburg
July 1-3, 1863

Maryland

Potomac River

Antietam Creek

Sharpsburg
Sept. 17, 1862

Baltimore

Virginia

Winchester
Sept. 19, 1864

Harpers Ferry

Strasburg

Cedar
Creek
Oct. 19, 1864

Tom's Brook
Oct. 9, 1864

New Market

North Fork

Shenandoah

Shenandoah River

Manassas
Junction
July 21, 1861
Aug. 30, 1862

Washington

Alexandria

Potomac River

Rapidan

Chancellorsville
May 2-6, 1863

Wilderness
May 5-6, 1864

Trevilian
Station
June 11-12, 1864

Spotsylvania C.H.
May 9-20, 1864

Fredericksburg
Dec. 13, 1862

Rappahannock River

Gaines' Mill
June 27, 1862

Appomattox C. H.

Richmond

Appomattox River

Seven Pines
May 31, 1862

Malvern Hill
July 1, 1862

Chickahominy River

CAMPAIGNS
IN THE EAST

James River

Petersburg

Yorktown

Five Forks
April 1, 1864

Fort Monroe

Norfolk

North Carolina

Weldon

Texan led the attack. John Deal, a private in the Fourth Texas, fired and killed the Union soldier, who fell within a few feet of Hood.[67]

Hood and the Texas Brigade were commended by President Davis and Maj. Gen. Gustavus Smith, commanding the left wing of the Confederate army, for their role in defeating Franklin's forces at Eltham's Landing. The victory prevented the Union army from outflanking the Confederates as they withdrew toward the Richmond defense lines.[68]

As the Union army, commanded by George B. McClellan, neared Richmond in late May, Confederate general Joseph E. Johnston launched a major assault. In the fighting at Seven Pines and Fair Oaks, Hood's Texans saw only limited action as they formed part of the Confederate reserve. In the battle the Confederates halted the Union advance but in the fighting General Johnston was wounded. President Davis, who was on the scene, appointed his military advisor, Robert E. Lee, to succeed Johnston.[69]

Lee was a more aggressive general than Johnston. In late June he launched a series of assaults aimed at driving McClellan away from the Confederate capital. He planned to attack and destroy that part of the Union army north of the Chickahominy River and then deal with McClellan's larger forces south of the river. In this campaign, known as the Seven Days, the Texas Brigade, now reinforced by infantry from Hampton's South Carolina Legion, served as part of W. H. C. Whiting's Division assigned to Stonewall Jackson's command.

The opening battle of the Seven Days, fought near Mechanicsville, was indecisive. Jackson's troops arrived late and did little fighting. Lee resumed the assault the next day at Gaines' Mill, but the Union forces commanded by Fitz John Porter held a strong position along Boatswain's Swamp. Repeated assaults against the enemy lines failed with heavy Southern losses. Late that afternoon Hood led his brigade in a furious bayonet attack that broke the enemy's line. Hood's old regiment, the Fourth Texas, and the Eighteenth Georgia were in the forefront of the assault. The Union cavalry attempted to stem the Confederate advance but were driven back with heavy losses. Porter's Corps retreated south of Chickahominy as dusk ended the fighting.[70]

The Texas Brigade and its commander were praised for their role at Gaines' Mill. Generals Lee, Jackson, and Whiting all commended the brigade and Hood for their gallant efforts in breaking the Union line. The cost was high in terms of casualties: eighty-six members of the brigade killed, 481 wounded and four missing, or greater than twenty-five percent. Col. John Marshall, commander of the Fourth Texas, was shot in the neck and died instantly. Lt. Col. Bradfute Warwick, executive officer of the Fourth Texas, was mortally wounded, and Maj. J.C.G. Key, the other field grade officer of the Fourth, was wounded. Col. Alexis T. Rainey of the First Texas and Col. Jerome B. Robertson of the Fifth Texas were also wounded.[71]

The Confederates continued to attack McClellan as he fell back toward the James, but Hood's Brigade played little part in the fighting at Savage Station and White Oak Swamp. The brigade did suffer some casualties from enemy artillery fire at Malvern Hill but did not participate in the futile infantry attack against entrenched enemy positions. Although Lee did not destroy McClellan's army as he had hoped, he forced the enemy back to Harrison's Landing on the James River. In August President Lincoln ordered McClellan to return to the Washington area.

Historian Richard McMurry pointed out that Hood was one of few Confederate generals in the Seven Days to emerge with his reputation enhanced. Others, including Stonewall Jackson, John B. Magruder, Benjamin Huger, and Theophilus H. Holmes, performed poorly or indifferently. Hood handled his troops well and when ordered to attack at Gaines' Mill drove the enemy from the field.[72]

In late July, W.H.C. Whiting, who commanded the division consisting of Hood's Brigade and Col. Evander M. Law's brigade, left the army on medical furlough. As senior officer Hood assumed temporary command of the division. Since it was not clear at the time that Whiting would not return, Hood acted as both division and brigade commander during August and early September.[73]

In August the division moved to the area south of the old battlefield at Manassas as part of Maj. Gen. James Longstreet's command. A new Union army led by Maj. Gen. John Pope was advancing southward from the Potomac River. General Lee divided his forces with Jackson on the Union right flank and Longstreet to Pope's south. On August 29, Pope, not realizing that Longstreet was near, pounded away at Jackson's divisions. On the afternoon of

August 30, Longstreet launched a counterattack against Pope's exposed left flank. Hood's Division led the assault, smashing one New York infantry brigade and almost destroying another. Pope's army was driven from the field as the Confederates won a great victory at Second Manassas.[74]

Once again Hood performed well as a commander. As leader of the division he demonstrated his competency as a combat officer, carrying out his orders with precision and efficiency.

For his efforts at Second Manassas, Hood again received the praise of the army commander, Robert E. Lee.[75]

Following the defeat of Pope's army at Manassas, Lee moved his army northward into Maryland. Hood's Division crossed the Potomoc River near Leesburg and moved to Frederick, Maryland, where it camped for several days. Hood was not in command as the division crossed the Potomac. He had been placed under arrest following an incident that occurred at Manassas on the evening of August 30. Some of Hood's men had captured several much coveted new Federal ambulances. Brig. Gen. Nathan "Shanks" Evans, who was in command of operations in the sector, ordered the ambulances turned over to his own South Carolina brigade. Hood refused and Evans ordered his arrest. Longstreet ordered Hood to remain at Culpepper until the case was tried, but General Lee, not willing to leave one of his best combat officers behind while moving north, allowed Hood to accompany his men, but not in command and at the rear of the column.[76]

As the Army of Northern Virginia marched northward, Lee divided his forces. One wing of the army under Stonewall Jackson was ordered to capture Harpers Ferry. The other wing, under James Longstreet, and including Hood's Division, moved on north to Boonsboro and Hagerstown. When a lost copy of Lee's orders was retrieved by Federal troops, however, the Confederate commander moved quickly to bring his scattered forces together to avoid being crushed separately by the larger Union army again commanded by George B. McClellan.[77]

As Lee brought the two wings of the army together in western Maryland, Hood's Division participated in a delaying action fought at South Mountain. Just prior to the fighting the division passed by General Lee. As they approached Lee, men in the division began to shout for the return of Hood to command. "Give us Hood," they cried. Lee, caught up in the emotion, raised his hat and replied, "You shall have him, gentlemen." Lee then called Hood out of the column and offered to restore him to command if he would state that he regretted the affair over the ambulances. The proud Hood refused to do so, insisting that he could not admit to the justness of Evans' demand for the ambulances. Lee, who probably believed that the whole affair was ridiculous, brushed aside Hood's explanation but stated that the arrest was temporarily suspended. To the cheers of his men, Hood returned to the head of the column and resumed command of the division. The arrest was not mentioned again.[78]

Hood commanded the rear guard of Longstreet's wing as the Confederates pulled back toward the small village of Sharpsburg near the south bank of Antietam Creek. There, on September 17, one of the bloodiest battles of the Civil War was fought. McClellan, with vastly superior numbers, directed a major assault on Lee's army.

Early that morning the Union First Corps, commanded by Joe Hooker, opened the battle by delivering a powerful blow against one of Jackson's divisions commanded by Alexander R. Lawton. The outnumbered Confederates reeled from the attack. Lawton was wounded and half of his division were casualties as the Rebels gave ground. Hood's Division, which was immediately behind Lawton's forces, was ordered into the fray. Moving through the West Woods, across the Pike, and into Miller's corn field where the carnage was the greatest, Hood's Division, 2,300 men strong, drove the Federals back. Momentarily the Confederates controlled the field, but a second Union attack, this time by Joseph K. Mansfield's Twelfth Corps, forced Hood back toward the West Woods. With most of its ammunition gone and casualties high, the division was shattered, but held until relieved by Lafayette McLaws' Division.[79]

Hood's Division saw no major action after 10:00 A.M. that day. Unable to break through on the north, McClellan shifted his main assault first to the center and then to the south. The Confederates gave ground but held their lines. The battle, the bloodiest single day in the war, was tactically a draw but strategically a Union victory as Lee was forced to withdraw his army back into Virginia.

Sharpsburg, or Antietam as the Federals called it, was costly to both sides. McClellan's army suffered 12,401 casualties, or 25 percent of those engaged. Lee sustained 10,318 casualties, or 31 percent of those engaged. The casualty rate for Hood's old Texas Brigade was particularly high at 64 percent. The First Texas, led by Col. Philip A. Work, had 82.3 percent casualties, the highest of any regiment, North or South, for one day in the war. The Fourth Texas sustained 53.5 percent casualties; the Fifth Texas, 49.1 percent. The South Carolina Legion, a small unit of only 76 men, had 69.7 percent casualties, and the Eighteenth Georgia, 57.3 percent. Evander Law's Brigade, the other brigade in Hood's Division, had 23.2 percent casualties.[80]

Both armies were completely exhausted by the fighting. According to some sources that night at headquarters Lee inquired of various division commanders concerning their losses and strengths. When he asked Hood where his splendid division was, the Texan replied, "They are lying on the field where you sent them, sir. . . . My division has been almost wiped out."[81]

Hood's performance at Sharpsburg had been impressive. After the battle Stonewall Jackson, who directed Hood's operations in the West Woods and Miller's corn field, recommended Hood's promotion to major general, declaring that Hood's "duties were discharged with such ability and zeal, as to command my admiration. I regard him as one of the most promising officers of the army." General Lee agreed and in late October recommended Hood's promotion. The promotion was approved on November 6 with Hood's date of rank as major general set at October 10.[82]

As part of the army reorganization Hood's Division, assigned to Longstreet's Corps, was increased from two brigades to four. The Texas Brigade and Law's Brigade remained but with changes in regimental composition. The two new brigades were those now commanded by George T. Anderson and Henry L. Benning. Col. Jerome B. Robertson, who had commanded the Fifth Texas, was promoted to command of the Texas Brigade with the rank of brigadier general.[83]

Hood's enlarged division saw limited action in the Battle of Fredericksburg in early December 1862. Longstreet's Corps held Marye's Heights overlooking the town as Ambrose Burnside's Union troops attacked. Hood's Division was on the right flank of Longstreet's Corps and positioned next to Jackson's Corps. Although heavy fighting took place on both sides, the division itself was not heavily engaged. Only the Fifty-fourth and Fifty-seventh

North Carolina regiments of Law's Brigade suffered extensive casualties in the battle.[84]

After Burnside's defeat at Fredericksburg, Lee's Army of Northern Virginia went into winter quarters along the Rappahannock. Hood's Division spent the winter in the hills and pines just north of the Massaponax River, a tributary of the Rappahannock. The army saw little action during this time. An occasional scouting assignment, snowball fights, amateur minstrel shows, and foraging for firewood and food provided some activity during the long winter months. Hood's Texas Brigade acquired a reputation for foraging. On one occasion, while Hood was visiting Lee's headquarters, the subject of depredations against civilian property came up. General Lee complained to Hood that the army was guilty of burning rail fences, killing pigs, and committing other delinquencies. Hood spoke up in defense of his troops, declaring they were not guilty of these offenses. General Lee, who was walking up and down near the campfire, turned to Hood and laughingly said, "Ah, General Hood, when you Texans come about the chickens have to roost mighty high." With that the assembled officers all shared in the laughter.[85]

In early spring of 1863, Longstreet, along with Hood's and Pickett's divisions, was sent on detached duty to the Suffolk region of Virginia to counteract increased Federal strength in the area and to obtain meat and fish believed abundant in the vicinity. As a result Hood's Division was not involved in the Confederate victory over Joe Hooker's army at Chancellorsville in early May 1863.[86]

Hood was pleased when Lee recalled Longstreet and his two divisions from the Suffolk area. In Hood's opinion "nothing was achieved against the enemy" by the diversion to the south. He welcomed the opportunity to rejoin the main army which was preparing for another move across the Potomac River.[87]

Hood's Division rejoined Lee's army in time to participate in the invasion of Pennsylvania in June. Moving across the Blue Ridge and the Shenandoah River, the division crossed the Potomac near Williamsport, Maryland, on June 26 and camped near Chambersburg, Pennsylvania, on June 27. Lt. Col. Arthur Fremantle of the British Coldstream Guards was among those who watched as the division entered Pennsylvania. "This division," he wrote, "well known for its fighting qualities, is composed of Texans, Alabamians, and Arkansians, and they certainly are a queer lot to look at." He noted that they carried less baggage than other troops and that many had discarded their shoes in the mud. "All are ragged and dirty, but full of good humor and confidence in themselves and in their general, Hood," reported Fremantle.[88]

In the great battle that took place at Gettysburg in the first week of July, Hood's Division was deployed on the Confederate extreme right. After fighting around Culp's Hill on the Union right on July 1, General Lee ordered Longstreet to attack the Union left with two divisions the next day. On the afternoon of July 2 Longstreet ordered Hood and Lafayette McLaws to lead their divisions along the Emmitsburg Road against the Federal left flank on Cemetery Ridge and two hills, Round Top and Little Round Top. Just as the attack was ready, Hood's scouts reported the Round Tops were unoccupied by Federal troops. Hood, believing he could turn the Union flank by swinging around the Round Tops, asked Longstreet for permission to change the direction of the attack. Longstreet refused, stating that Lee had ordered the attack directly against the enemy positions. Hood repeated the request twice but was again refused. Accordingly, he directed his division to attack as ordered.[89]

In the attack Hood's Division encountered heavy enemy fire from Union artillery in the rocky formation known as the Devil's Den. The Confederates carried Devil's Den but were unable to exploit their gain. In the fighting Hood was severely wounded by a shell fragment that shattered his left arm. Brigadier Generals Jerome Robertson and George T. Anderson were wounded, and eleven of Hood's regimental commanders were killed or wounded. Determined efforts by the Texas and Alabama regiments in Hood's Division failed to wrest control of Little Round Top and the Rocky Ridge from the enemy. The division, under the temporary command of Evander Law following Hood's injury, broke off the battle at dusk.[90]

Hood's Division did little fighting on July 3 as Confederates led by George Pickett and James J. Pettigrew attempted unsuccessfully to break the center of the Union line. Casualties were heavy on both sides. There was no fighting on July 4 as the two armies watched each other like great wounded giants. That evening Lee began his withdrawal southward toward Virginia. Hood, suffering much pain from his wounded arm, rode along in an ambulance with a fellow wounded general, Wade Hampton of South Carolina.

Hood spent the month of August convalescing at Staunton, Virginia. In September he was in Richmond, where he visited various friends including Mary Boykin Chesnut, wife of one of Davis' aides, and Sally Buchanan Preston, a vivacious South Carolina belle whom Hood met earlier in the year. Hood had been quite taken by "Buck" Preston, as the young Carolinian was known, and their friendship was the talk of Richmond society. Buck was "capricious, coquettish, and moody," but Hood was determined to make her his wife. Before rejoining his division, Hood proposed. Although "Buck" refused to give him a direct answer, Hood believed they were engaged.[91]

In mid-September Hood, his shattered left arm still in a sling, rejoined his division on the eve of the Battle of Chickamauga. Braxton Bragg's Army of Tennessee had been forced out of Chattanooga into the northwestern corner of Georgia. The Confederate War Department sent Longstreet's Corps by rail to reinforce Bragg for a surprise attack against William Rosecrans' Union army along Chickamauga Creek, south of Chattanooga.

The Confederates were already skirmishing with the enemy when Hood rejoined his old division on the afternoon of September 18. After "a touching welcome" from his comrades, Hood led his division as it pushed the Federals back several miles before darkness halted the fighting. On the following morning Bragg ordered a major attack in an attempt to roll back the enemy's left flank, but a delay by Leonidas Polk, commanding the Confederate right wing, gave the Federals time to reinforce the sector and prevent a breakthrough. Heavy fighting raged throughout the day but with no change in positions.[92]

On September 20 Bragg resumed the attack. Longstreet, who arrived the previous evening, assigned five divisions to Hood for the assault. In the confusion of the fighting Rosecrans left a gap in his line in Hood's sector. Hood's troops poured through the opening, scattering the Federals and causing many, including General Rosecrans, to flee from the field. Only the firm stand by one of Rosecrans' corps commanders, George H. Thomas (who had been a field grade officer in the old Second Cavalry), saved the Union army from disaster.[93]

In the midst of the fighting that afternoon Hood was wounded once again. While conversing with the commander of the Texas Brigade, Jerome B. Robertson, Hood was hit by a minié ball in the upper part of his right thigh, shattering the bone. The surgeons who examined the wound concluded that amputation was required. The leg was taken off at the thigh by Dr. T. G. Richardson of New Orleans, the chief medical officer of the Army of Tennessee. After the operation Hood was taken to the residence of a friend, fifteen miles to the southwest, where he spent the next month recuperating.[94]

By late October Hood had recovered sufficiently that he was able to travel. After a brief visit to Atlanta he journeyed by train to Richmond, and there he spent the winter months being entertained by the social and political lions of the capital. His romance with Sally "Buck" Preston continued to be the talk of society. Friends, including Mary Boykin Chesnut, warned him that "Buck" was not serious but merely teasing him as she did other suitors, but Hood paid little heed. Hood was, as one biographer noted, "suffering from a disease as old as man himself—acute blindness due to passionate love."[95]

The courtship continued throughout the winter. In late December it appeared the affair was ending when Preston told Hood there was no hope, but Hood would not give up. He continued to pursue her and in February she reluctantly agreed to an engagement.

By this time Hood was able, with assistance, to mount a horse once again, although he had to be strapped into the saddle. Members of the Texas Brigade raised money to purchase a "cork leg" for Hood, but due to the nature of his amputation the fitting for the prosthesis was not altogether satisfactory and Hood needed crutches to walk. Hood himself seems to have borne no bitterness concerning his physical infirmities, but others noted his sad physical appearance. It is "bad for the head of any army to be so helpless," lamented the obiquitous Mrs. Chesnut.[96]

In January 1864 President Davis appointed Hood to the rank of lieutenant general. The Senate confirmed the promotion on February 11, with the date of rank September 20, 1863, the day of Hood's injury at Chickamauga. Hood was ordered to proceed to Dalton, Georgia, to join the Army of Tennessee as a corps commander.[97]

Hood arrived at Dalton on February 24 and assumed his new duties as corps commander on the 29th. The Army of Tennessee was now under the command of Joseph E. Johnston, who had been appointed to succeed Braxton Bragg after the defeats around Chattanooga in November 1863. Johnston greeted Hood warmly and the two officers appeared to work well together at first. Differences in military philosophy and temperament, however, were soon obvious. The older and more experienced Johnston was a cautious, stubborn, and suspicious individual who stressed defensive warfare and tried to avoid battle; Hood was a bold fighter who took risks and believed in the attack even if it meant heavy casualties. Hood was soon corresponding with President Davis, presidential military advisor Braxton Bragg, and Secretary of War James A. Seddon about Johnston's failure to take the offensive against the enemy.[98]

Even though their philosophies differed, Johnston and Hood had a close relationship in the early phases of the Georgia campaign. The two generals often dined together and regularly discussed military strategy and tactics. Johnston seemed to have more confidence in his junior corps commander than he had in his other corps commanders, Leonidas Polk and William J. Hardee. When Union general William T. Sherman began his drive toward Atlanta in May, Johnston entrusted Hood with the most critical points of the line. In the battles at Resaca, Pickett's Mill, Kolb's Farm, and Kennesaw Mountain, Hood's Corps played a key role in efforts to delay the enemy advance. Even so, the Confederates slowly gave ground in May and June as Sherman continued to push southward. On July 8 Union forces under Hood's old classmate, John M. Schofield, crossed the Chattahooche River, the last major natural barrier to Atlanta. To prevent being outflanked, Johnston withdrew his army south of the river only ten miles from Atlanta.[99]

For President Davis news of the retreat south of the Chattahooche was a serious blow. He was convinced now that Johnston did not intend to fight for Atlanta. Reports received from his military advisor, Braxton Bragg, who had been sent to confer with Johnston, confirmed his fears. On July 12 Davis telegraphed Robert E. Lee outlining his lack of confidence in Johnston and asking what Lee thought of Hood as his successor. Lee replied immediately, cautioning against a change in leadership at such a time and adding that while Hood was a bold fighter he might not have the other qualities necessary for army command. In a letter written to Davis that evening Lee noted that William J. Hardee, Johnston's senior corps commander, had more experience in directing an army than did Hood.[100]

Davis, who deeply respected Lee's judgment, gave serious thought to appointing Hardee, who was senior to Hood in both the old army and in Confederate service. Hood had directed a corps for only six months, whereas Hardee had been a corps commander for more than two years. However, Hardee had turned down the command earlier and was not an inspiring leader. Also, the president's military advisor, General Bragg, disliked Hardee, who led the cabal supporting Bragg's removal as army commander. Hood had ingratiated himself with Bragg in a letter in which the Texan claimed, not altogether truthfully, that he had consistently supported a vigorous, aggressive campaign against Sherman, but that Johnston, encouraged by Hardee, favored the retreat. Bragg, impressed (and perhaps deceived) by Hood, advised Davis that the appointment should go to Hood.[101]

Davis hesitated. On July 16 he telegraphed Johnston requesting a clear statement of his plans for defeating the Union army. Johnston replied that he was so badly outnumbered he could only react to the enemy's movements. He concluded by proposing to pull the Army of Tennessee out of Atlanta, leaving the defense of the city to the Georgia militia. The reply left Davis with little alternative. Convinced that Johnston meant to abandon Atlanta without a fight and that Hardee would only continue Johnston's tactics, Davis instructed Adj. Gen. Samuel Cooper to inform Johnston that he was removed from command and replaced by Hood, who was given the temporary rank of general.[102]

The removal of Johnston and his replacement by Hood was controversial. The other corps commanders, William J. Hardee and A. P. Stewart (who had replaced Leonidas Polk, killed at Pine Mountain), were surprised by the move, as apparently Johnston and Hood were also. Hardee, who was particularly bitter, requested and eventually received a transfer out of the Army of Tennessee. Many of the soldiers of the army were opposed to the change. Johnston, a mature, senior general, was popular with his troops, who appreciated his careful, deliberate style of campaigning which emphasized maneuver and defense rather than costly, aggressive attack. Hood, who was well liked and respected by members of his old brigade and division, was young, inexperienced in corps command, and new to the

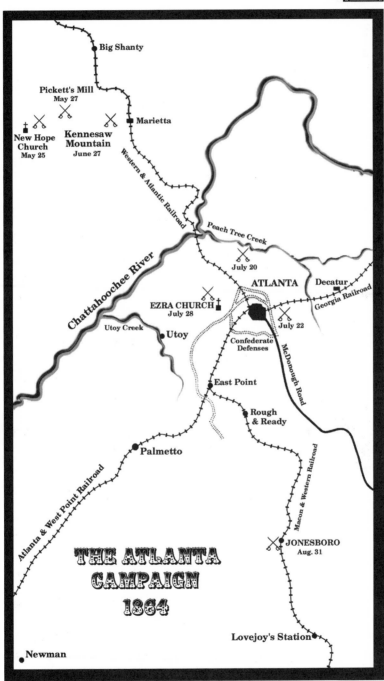

Army of Tennessee. Samuel T. Foster of Hiram Granbury's Texas Brigade summarized the feeling of many veterans when he wrote in his diary: "Gen. Johnson *[sic]* has so endeared himself to his soldiers that no man can take his place." Foster concluded that Johnston "has more military sense in one day than Hood ever did or ever well have." Another Texan, Capt. James P. Douglas, who commanded an artillery battery in Hood's Corps, believed the change in command was necessary. "One thing certain," Douglas wrote his wife, "Gen'l Hood will fight the enemy, and I believe he can whip them." One of Sherman's generals, John M. Schofield, agreed with Douglas. When asked by Sherman what sort of fellow his old West Point classmate was, Schofield replied: "I will tell you the sort of man he is. He'll hit you like h__l, now, before you know it."[103]

Douglas and Schofield were correct in their belief that Hood would fight. The day after he assumed command Hood determined to launch an attack upon the left wing of Sherman's army commanded by George H. Thomas as it attempted to cross Peachtree Creek about five miles north of Atlanta. On the morning of July 20 Hood directed two of his corps commanders, Hardee and Stewart, to attack Thomas before he could complete the crossing of Peachtree. Unfortunately the attack was delayed until late in the afternoon. Then it was a poorly coordinated affair, with the Confederates losing 2,500 men in an unsuccessful effort to stop the Union advance.[104]

Hood's first effort at army command was a failure. In analyzing the mistakes at Peachtree Creek historian Richard McMurry blamed both Hood and Hardee. Hood did not properly supervise the direction of the battle. This was due to his inexperience, his physical handicaps, and his attempt to imitate the methods of his mentor, Robert E. Lee. Lee's system of command in which he outlined his objectives and left execution to his subordinates worked well in Virginia; it did not work well elsewhere. It failed completely in reference to Hardee, who continued to sulk over Hood's appointment as army commander. Only one of Hardee's four divisions made full contact with the enemy in the battle, and his most experienced command, Patrick Cleburne's Division, was never sent into action.[105]

Hood was disappointed in the failure at Peachtree Creek but still determined to hit the enemy. He pulled his army back into the inter-defenses of Atlanta with Stewart's Corps on the west, Hardee on the north and in center, and Benjamin F. Cheatham's Corps (Hood's old corps) on the east of the city. On July 22 he sent Hardee's Corps to the south around Cheatham for a flank attack on the Union right wing commanded by Maj. Gen. James McPherson, a former classmate of Hood. For several hours Hardee, supported by Cheatham, pounded away at the Union lines.

In the fighting McPherson was killed and at times it appeared the Union lines would break. But once again the Confederate attacks were poorly coordinated and the Union lines held. The Confederates lost 5,500 men in the fighting.[106]

The Confederate assault on July 22 did cause Sherman to shift his army from the eastern side of Atlanta to the north and west in a sliding movement around the city. Hood moved quickly to use his army to check Sherman's advance on the west. He ordered Lt. Gen. Stephen D. Lee, who had just arrived to replace Cheatham as commander of Hood's old corps, to take and hold a road intersection near Ezra Church, three miles northwest of Atlanta. When Lee reached Ezra Church he discovered Union troops already controlling the road, whereupon Lee launched an immediate attack. Hearing the sound of battle, A. P. Stewart ordered two of his divisions into the fighting. Although the Confederates pushed the Federals back a short distance, they were unable to drive the enemy off. Once again lack of coordination prevented Hood's army from accomplishing its objective.[107]

The three major assaults by Hood's army against the enemy—Peachtree Creek, Atlanta, and Ezra Church—succeeded in keeping Sherman out of the city but at a heavy cost. In an effort to stop Sherman's slide around Atlanta, Hood now sent his cavalry under Joe Wheeler on a massive raid against Sherman's railroad supply lines in northern Georgia. The strategy was sound, but due to Wheeler's ineptness and Sherman's careful planning the raid accomplished little. Hood meanwhile was without his cavalry as Sherman swung his forces southward to cut the railroad lines leading into Atlanta. Hood dispatched Hardee and his corps to block Sherman; however, after heavy fighting at Jonesboro, Hardee was forced to withdraw. On September 1, Hood, fearing encirclement, ordered his two other corps to evacuate Atlanta. On the next day lead elements of Sherman's army occupied the city.[108]

Following the evacuation of Atlanta, Hood moved his army to the town of Palmetto, thirty miles to the southwest. During the next two weeks Hood reorganized units of the army, attempted to find additional supplies, and prepared for the next campaign. On September 25 he was visited by President Davis, who spent two days reviewing the troops and conferring with Hood and his generals. In the discussions Davis approved a proposal that the Army of Tennessee attack Sherman's supply line north of the Chattahooche. Davis and Hood both believed that such a maneuver would force Sherman to leave Atlanta to protect his communications. If Sherman, instead of following Hood, turned south, Hood agreed to move his army quickly to block the Federal advance.[109]

In late September, Hood crossed the Chattahooche and began attacking the Union supply line. At first the plan seemed to be working as Sherman moved part of his army out of Atlanta to deal with Hood. When it appeared, however, that the Army of Tennessee was not strong enough to engage Sherman's approaching troops, Hood decided to take his army into northern Alabama, pick up supplies and reinforcements, and advance northward against the major Union supply depot at Nashville. Such an operation clearly departed from the agreement with President Davis, but Hood believed this was the only practical course of action.[110]

In mid-October Hood's army moved into northern Alabama. His new departmental commander, P. G. T. Beauregard, questioned Hood on the details of his operation but gave tacit approval to the move. Beauregard, not fully understanding what Hood proposed, believed that the Texan intended to make a quick, direct thrust into middle Tennessee. Instead, Hood swung far to the west in Alabama, crossing the Tennessee River near Florence before heading into Tennessee. The move was slow as extremely bad weather, Hood's poor health, and inadequate staff delayed the operation.[111]

General Sherman, meanwhile, left Atlanta. Rather than moving north to follow Hood, Sherman headed south toward Savannah and the sea. Concerned that Hood might strike at Nashville, Sherman dispatched Maj. Gen. George H. Thomas to prepare the defense of that city. He also sent Maj. Gen. John Schofield with some 25,000 troops to reinforce the Nashville garrison under Thomas.

In November, while Sherman marched toward the sea, the two former classmates, Hood and Schofield, were marching their armies toward Nashville. As they approached the Tennessee capital they moved along the same pike. Hood hoped to intercept and defeat Schofield before he joined Thomas at Nashville. On the night of November 29 Schofield's troops slipped past the Confederates near Spring Hill, a small community thirty miles south of Nashville. The next morning Hood, furious that the enemy passed during the night, ordered his army to pursue the Federals. That afternoon, the Confederates overtook Schofield, who entrenched his troops in a strong defensive position on the outskirts of Franklin on the Harpeth River.[112]

Despite the opposition of his generals and without awaiting the arrival of his artillery and Stephen D. Lee's Corps, Hood ordered an immediate attack on the Union lines. The initial assault by Stewart's and Cheatham's Corps overran a Union division, but heavy enemy artillery and small-arms fire took a heavy toll on the advancing Confederates. Brig. Gen. Hiram Granbury, leading his Texas Brigade, was shot in the face and killed. At about the same time his division commander, Maj. Gen. Patrick Cleburne, fell with a bullet through the heart.

Throughout the late afternoon and evening the fighting raged but the Union lines held. In five hours the Confederates suffered nearly 7,000 casualties. In addition to Cleburne and Granbury four other Southern generals were killed and five wounded. Union losses totaled slightly more than 2,000.[113]

In spite of the heavy casualties, Hood planned to resume the attack the next morning. Further carnage at Franklin was spared, as Schofield withdrew his army during the night. Hood now had few options. His army was too small to challenge Sherman in Georgia, so he ordered his troops to follow Schofield. Hood's only chance was to take a strong position near Nashville, wait for reinforcements from the Trans Mississippi, and hope that Thomas would make a blunder.[114]

Hood's army, now less than 25,000 men, reached the Nashville environs on the afternoon of December 2. For two weeks the crippled army camped outside Nashville in the bitter cold. The Confederates held a thin line about five miles long that covered several of the major roads leading into Nashville from the south. Historian Thomas Connelly believed that "Hood could not have aligned his troops in a worse position." Hood's biographer Richard McMurry noted that "to make matters worse, Hood sent off a division of infantry and part of Forrest's cavalry to operate against Murfreesboro thirty miles to the southeast."[115]

There was little fighting during early December. Hood, who realized he was in no condition to attack the entrenched Federals, spent the time attempting to find more men and supplies. Thomas, a capable, deliberative officer, carefully strengthened his army and prepared for the attack.

Thomas struck on the morning of December 15. More than 50,000 well-equipped and ably led Union troops hit the outnumbered Confederates hard, first on the right flank held by Cheatham's Corps and then in the main attack on the left flank defended by Stewart's Corps. For nearly two days the Confederates held their thinly manned lines, but on the afternoon of December 16 Hood's lines collapsed. Cheatham's Corps gave way first and then Stewart's Corps retreated in wild disarray. Hood tried to rally his troops but in vain. Only Stephen D. Lee's Corps in the center maintained any order as the defeated Rebels fled southward.[116]

As the battered Army of Tennessee made its way south, Confederate cavalry and Lee's Corps fought a rear guard action against the pursuing Federals. On Christmas Day the Confederates reached the Tennessee River. As soon as a temporary bridge could be constructed the army began crossing the river. The march continued on to Tupelo in northern Mississippi. Less than 19,000 officers and men were present for duty on December 31, 1864.[117]

Hood's dreams of glory were shattered by the crushing defeat at Nashville. Although he continued to justify his actions, Hood requested to be relieved of command. General Beauregard, who was now at Tupelo, was authorized by Confederate authorities to replace Hood with Lt. Gen. Richard Taylor. On January 23, 1865, Hood turned over command to Taylor and left for Richmond. On his way to the Confederate capital he stopped in South Carolina to see "Buck" Preston. Hood still hoped to marry her, but opposition from her family and friends put a final end to the affair.[118]

Hood spent six weeks in Richmond, where he wrote a lengthy report of the Tennessee campaign in which he blamed Joe Johnston, William J. Hardee, and Benjamin Cheatham for many of the failures of the army. In the closing days of the Confederacy he left for Texas, arriving there in late June. After a brief visit he traveled to Washington, D.C., and then to Kentucky to see his mother. He decided to settle in New Orleans, where he became a commission merchant and insurance company executive. On April 13, 1868, he married Anna Marie Hennen, daughter of a prominent Louisiana Catholic family. During the next eleven years the couple had eleven children, including three sets of twins.

Hood was active in historical and veterans' affairs in the postwar years. He returned to Texas occasionally to attend meetings of the Hood's Texas Brigade Association. He spent much of his free time gathering material for his memoirs and answering criticisms, especially by Joe Johnston, concerning his military operations. His business interests prospered for a decade, but economic reverses in 1878 wiped out his property holdings. In August 1879, Hood, his wife, and oldest daughter died in a yellow fever epidemic. He was buried in Metairie Cemetery in New Orleans. His memoirs, titled *Advance and Retreat*, were published in 1880 for the Hood Orphan Memorial Fund by his former departmental chief, P.G.T. Beauregard.[119]

CHAPTER THREE

The Major Generals

DURING THE CIVIL WAR six Texans were appointed to the rank of major general in the Confederate army. Three of these Texans, John Bell Hood, John A. Wharton, and Thomas L. Rosser, were promoted upon the recommendation of President Jefferson Davis and confirmation by the Confederate Senate. Hood, whose date of rank as major general was October 10, 1862, was the first Texan so recognized. As noted in the previous chapter Hood was promoted to lieutenant general in September 1863, and general (temporary) in July 1864. John A. Wharton, with date of rank November 10, 1863, was the second Texan to become major general. Thomas L. Rosser, like Wharton a cavalry officer, was the third Texan nominated by President Davis and confirmed by the Confederate Senate as a major general.[1]

A fourth Texan, Samuel Bell Maxey, was assigned duties as a major general by Edmund Kirby Smith, commander of the Trans Mississippi Department, in April 1864, but there is some question whether he was ever confirmed by Richmond authorities. President Davis turned down Maxey's promotion in December 1864, but according to Maxey's biographer the promotion was later approved by the Confederate Senate. Maxey commanded a division, signed all official papers as a major general, and was so regarded by his fellow officers.[2]

Two other Texans, Tom Green and Arthur P. Bagby, were also

recommended for promotion to major general by Kirby Smith but neither appointment was approved by the president or the Senate. Green's nomination was made by Smith in February 1864, only two months before Green was killed at Blair's Landing, Louisiana. Neither the president nor Senate had acted upon the nomination. Bagby was appointed major general by Smith on May 16, 1865, a month after the collapse of the Richmond government and only two weeks before the surrender of the Trans Mississippi Department. Technically Green and Bagby were never major generals, but as both commanded divisions (an assignment normally performed by major generals), if only briefly, they will be considered major generals in this study.[3]

JOHN BELL HOOD

(See previous chapter for biographical information.)

JOHN AUSTIN WHARTON

John Austin Wharton, the second Texan appointed major general in the Confederate army, was born near Nashville, Tennessee, on July 3, 1828. His parents were members of a pioneer Texas family, but were in Tennessee at the time of Wharton's birth. Young Wharton was originally named Edwin Waller Wharton, after his father's friend Edwin Waller. His mother, Sarah Anne, was the daughter of Jared Groce, the largest slaveholder among Stephen F. Austin's Old Three Hundred. His father, William Harris Wharton, established Eagle Island Plantation on Oyster Creek in Brazoria County on land given to him and his wife by Jared Groce.[4]

As a lad the young Wharton, renamed John Austin in 1838 for his deceased uncle, was surrounded by individuals and events associated with the Texas movement for independence. His father, William, was a leader in the so-called War Party that favored independence from Mexico. He was president of the 1833 convention which prepared a list of grievances against the Mexican government. When the Texas Revolution began, William H. Wharton was one of the three commissioners sent to the United States to secure aid.

John Austin Wharton
—Courtesy of Harold B. Simpson Research Center, Hillsboro, Texas

When independence was won he was appointed the first minister of the new Republic of Texas to the United States. William's brother, John Austin Wharton (for whom the future general was re-named), was also an active participant in the Revolu-tion, serving on Sam Hous-ton's staff in the San Jacin-to campaign. John served as Texas secretary of war and later in the Texas Con-gress. He died in a fever epi-demic in 1838. Another uncle, Leonard W. Groce, was a delegate to the 1833 convention and an officer in the Texas army. He and his father, Jared Groce, helped provide supplies for Houston's army.[5]

When young John A. Wharton was eight years of age he was sent to Leonard Groce's home at Bernardo Plantation near Hemp-stead for instruction from a tutor from Boston hired by the family. Later Wharton attended a preparatory school at Galveston estab-lished by the tutor. From 1846 to 1850 Wharton attended South Carolina College (now the University of South Carolina), where he was chosen commandant of the cadet corps. While attending col-lege he met and married Penelope Johnson, daughter of South Carolina Governor David Johnson. When he returned to Texas, Wharton studied law with several prominent attorneys including future governor Elisha M. Pease. Wharton opened a law office in Brazoria County with Clint N. Terry, the younger brother of planter Benjamin F. Terry, the future commander of Terry's Texas Rangers.

Wharton was a prominent figure in antebellum Brazoria Coun-ty. In addition to his law practice he operated Eagle Island Plantation, which he inherited when his father was killed in an accident in 1839. In 1860 Wharton, enumerated in the federal census with $113,000 in real property and $123,950 in personal property (including 133 slaves), was one of the wealthiest men in the state and one of the largest slaveholders. Under his management the plantation produced 100 bales of cotton, 185 hogsheads of sugar, and 7,000 bushels of corn that year.[6]

Wharton opposed the efforts by Northerners to place restrictions upon the institution of slavery. He became increasingly active in politics in the late 1850s, serving as a presidential elector for John C. Breckinridge in the 1860 election. Following Breckinridge's defeat and Lincoln's election, Wharton favored resolute action to protect Southern interests. He was elected a delegate to the state convention called by secessionist leaders in early 1861 and was appointed a member of the Committee on Federal Relations. On the second day of the convention, he moved "that the state of Texas should separately secede from the Federal Union." The resolution passed by 152 to 6, indicating clearly the intent of the convention. Wharton voted with the majority three days later when the convention formally adopted an ordinance of secession by 166-8. In the festivities following adoption of the secession ordinance, women of Travis County presented a new Lone Star flag to the convention. On behalf of the delegates, Wharton thanked the women for their generosity.[7]

Once Texas voters ratified the secession ordinance, Wharton and other secessionist leaders prepared to defend their state in the coming conflict. After the firing upon Fort Sumter and the secession of the states of the upper South, Wharton accompanied Benjamin F. Terry, Thomas Lubbock, and Thomas J. Goree to Richmond, Virginia, to offer their services to the Confederate government. Terry, Lubbock, and Goree served as volunteer aides to James Longstreet at Manassas on July 21, 1861, but Wharton, who was ill, missed the battle. Goree stayed on with Longstreet for the remainder of the war, but Terry, Lubbock, and Wharton returned to Texas where they organized the Eighth Texas Cavalry Regiment. Terry was chosen colonel of the new regiment, soon to be known as Terry's Texas Rangers, and Lubbock was selected as lieutenant colonel. Wharton was elected captain of Company B, made up of men from Brazoria and Matagorda counties.[8]

The new regiment was originally intended for service in Virginia but was rerouted to Kentucky for duty under Albert Sidney Johnston, who had been appointed commander of the Western Department. The Rangers fought their first battle at Woodsonville, Kentucky, on December 17, 1861. Although the Texans drove back a Federal regiment in a fierce attack, Terry was killed in the assault.[9] Lieutenant Colonel Lubbock, then ill in a Bowling Green hospital, succeeded Terry as commander of the regiment, but died shortly thereafter. Wharton was elected colonel to succeed Lubbock. L. B. Giles, a member of the regiment, later recalled that Wharton was "a captivating public speaker," who was "enterprising and ambitious." These qualities and his close association with the previous commanders, Terry and Lubbock, undoubtedly played a part in his election.[10]

Under Wharton's command the Rangers carried out scouting, picketing, and patrolling duties in Kentucky during January and February 1862. When General Johnston ordered the withdrawal of the army southward after the fall of Forts Henry and Donelson, the Rangers served as a rear guard for the retreating Confederates. In late March the Rangers joined the main body of the Army of the Mississippi at Corinth, Mississippi, where Johnston finalized plans for an attack on Grant's army at Pittsburg Landing on the Tennessee River.[11]

On April 3 Johnston ordered the army to advance along the narrow roads leading from Corinth to the Tennessee River. Wharton's cavalry guarded the left wing of the army as it moved forward. A steady rain during the night drenched the Rangers. In the morning the men, fearing their weapons might fail them in battle, implored Wharton to allow them to fire them off. The inexperienced colonel consented. The firing "sounded like a brief skirmish," according to one of the participants. Wharton was immediately summoned to headquarters, where he was severely reprimanded for violation of security which might warn the enemy of the Confederate approach. On his return to the regiment Wharton informed the men of his serious blunder in allowing them to fire their weapons, and called upon them "to wipe out the stain by our gallant behavior in the coming engagement."[12]

The Rangers performed gallantly in the Battle of Shiloh as Wharton had hoped. Assigned to the Confederate left flank, the Rangers fought both as mounted and unmounted troops. When the enemy gave ground on the afternoon of April 6, Hardee ordered Wharton to pursue the retreating enemy. Unfortunately for the Texans, a large body of Federals was hiding in ambush and opened a heavy barrage against the hard-charging Rangers. Five of the Texans were killed and twenty-six wounded, including Wharton, who was shot in the leg. Although Wharton refused to leave the field, the regiment was forced to fall back. On the next day the Rangers were ordered by General Beauregard, who succeeded to command when Albert Sidney Johnston was killed, to ride around the Federal right flank. Once again the Texans met a massive fire and were forced to withdraw. They soon reformed, however, and fought as dismounted troops.[13]

Although Wharton's cavalry and other Confederate units fought stubbornly, the Southerners were pushed back by superior Union numbers on April 7. That evening Beauregard ordered a retreat back to Corinth. Once again the Rangers helped to cover the Confederate withdrawal.[14]

After a brief period spent at Corinth recovering from the effects of Shiloh, the Rangers were transferred to East Tennessee, where they were assigned scouting and patrol duties. A skirmish with Union troops near Bethel, Tennessee, in early May was followed by encounter with Federal infantry near Morrison's Depot in Warren County, Tennessee. In the summer the Texans were assigned to the cavalry brigade under Brig. Gen. Nathan Bedford Forrest. After a successful raid upon a Union garrison at Murfreesboro, Tennessee, in July, Wharton and the Rangers were praised by Forrest for their attack against the enemy. Once again while leading the charge, Wharton suffered a severe wound, this time in his arm.[15]

In the fall of 1862 the Rangers were part of Braxton Bragg's army in the unsuccessful attempt to liberate Kentucky. In this campaign Wharton commanded a brigade of cavalry consisting of the Rangers, the Fourth Tennessee, and the First Kentucky. Fighting occurred almost every day as Wharton's troopers covered the right wing of the army as it marched north. In the battle of Perryville, fought on October 8, Wharton's cavalry distinguished itself in helping drive the Union troops back. In their official reports of the battle both Bragg and Leonidas Polk praised Wharton. Of one attack Polk reported that "Wharton charged the enemy's extreme left with great fury, passing on over stone walls and ravines and driving back [the enemy] several hundred yards."[16]

Wharton's handling of the cavalry in the Kentucky campaign merited his promotion to brigadier general in November 1862. In keeping with his new rank Wharton was assigned additional troops so that his brigade now consisted of eight regiments and two battalions of cavalry, two cavalry escort companies, and an artillery battery.

The enlarged brigade saw its first major action in late December 1862, in the Battle of Murfreesboro, or Stone's River. In this engagement Bragg launched a major assault against the Union army commanded by William S. Rosecrans. In the attack on the morning of December 31, Wharton's cavalry slashed away at the Union right wing and rear, capturing 1,500 prisoners, a four-gun battery, and several hundred wagons. Wharton received the praise of both Bragg and William J. Hardee for his efforts. In his report Hardee wrote that "the conduct of Wharton and his brigade cannot be too highly commended." Once again, however, the Confederates failed to achieve their objectives, as the battle ended on an indecisive note after two days of fighting with heavy casualties on both sides.[17]

Wharton's brigade was in the cavalry division commanded by Maj. Gen. Joe Wheeler throughout most of 1863. In late January Wheeler led the brigades commanded by Wharton and Forrest in an ill-conceived attempt to recapture Fort Donelson on the Tennessee River. Neither Wharton nor Forrest believed the operation had much chance of success. The Federals were strongly entrenched, the weather was bitterly cold, and the Confederates were low on ammunition. Forrest vigorously protested the wisdom of the operation, but Wheeler was insistent. Although the Confederates carried the enemy's outworks, they were forced to abandon the campaign after they exhausted their limited supply of ammunition.[18]

After the failure at Donelson, Wharton's cavalry returned to its encampment at Sparta, Tennessee. The brigade took part in several skirmishes and raids during the spring and summer but was not involved in major action. In August Wharton's cavalry was divided into two brigades with Col. C. C. Crews commanding the First Brigade and Col. Tom Harrison, who succeeded Wharton as commander of Terry's Rangers, commanding the Second Brigade. Although Wharton was now a division commander, he was not promoted major general until November 10, 1863.[19]

During the spring and summer Wharton and the Rangers frequently had opportunities to relax. Wharton enjoyed horse racing and often participated in the sport. One member of the Rangers, Pvt. E. S. Dodd, noted in his journal on April 4 that Wharton and Colonel Harrison had a race, but did not reveal who won. Another Ranger, Dunbar Affleck, in a letter to his parents in early May, reported that Wharton was badly hurt a few days earlier when his horse ran into a tree. Wharton was knocked from his horse and injured his left leg and foot. He was in bed a week and then had to ride in a carriage and use crutches for several weeks. Apparently Wharton remained popular with his men, who contributed money to buy him a new horse which was given to him at a barbecue in early August.[20]

The lull in military action for Wharton and his cavalry ended in early autumn. During the summer the Union army under Rosecrans moved southward by outmaneuvering Bragg and the Confederates. In early September the Rebels evacuated Chattanooga and fell back into northern Georgia. The situation was so desperate the Richmond government rushed reinforcements from Virginia to Bragg, who hit Rosecrans' army at Chickamauga Creek, just south of Chattanooga, in the third week of September. Wharton's Division covered the left wing of the Confederate army in the battle. Since the heaviest fighting was in the center, the division escaped much of the carnage of the battle but did earn the thanks of the cavalry corps commander, General Wheeler, for its performance in the battle.[21]

The battle at Chickamauga was the last major engagement that Wharton fought under the command of Wheeler. In early October Wharton's cavalry rode with Wheeler in a highly successful cavalry raid against Rosecrans' supply line in middle Tennessee. Although Wheeler praised Wharton and his command for behaving "with their accustomed gallantry," relations between the two generals deteriorated.[22] Wharton and Nathan Bedford Forrest had been surprised when Bragg appointed Wheeler head of the army's cavalry. Both were convinced that Wheeler's appointment had not been merited but was based upon his West Point graduation and his ability to flatter Bragg. Some Confederate congressmen, particularly in the Texas delegation, believed that Wharton, not Wheeler, should command the cavalry in the Army of Tennessee. Wharton himself discussed Wheeler's shortcomings with Senator Louis Wigfall of Texas, a former Confederate brigadier and one of President Davis' most vocal critics. This led Wheeler to write to Joe Johnston, who succeeded Bragg as army commander, that Wharton had disobeyed orders and had tried to turn his troops against him. "General Wharton," charged Wheeler, "allowed his ambitions to completely turn his head, as his friend in Congress [Wigfall] has assured him that he should command the cavalry of this army, he being one of those politicians (not statesmen) who looked upon things we would consider dishonorable as legitimate tricks." According to Wheeler, Wharton "forgot that he was an officer instead of a frontier political trickster."[23]

The Wheeler-Wharton controversy was one of several problems that Joe Johnston inherited from his predecessor, Braxton Bragg. To improve the efficiency of his army Johnston made a number of changes in personnel in early 1864. When he learned that Wharton had applied for a transfer to the Trans Mississippi Department, he endorsed the application. In February 1864 an order was issued transferring Wharton to the Trans Mississippi.[24]

Wharton arrived in Texas in April. He was immediately ordered to Louisiana, where his services were needed. The Union army of Nathaniel P. Banks had been defeated at Mansfield and was now attempting to withdraw down the Red River. Confederate forces under Richard Taylor were trying to crush Banks' army before it reached the Misssissippi. Tom Green, who had commanded Confederate cavalry under Taylor, was killed at Blair's Landing on April 12. An experienced cavalry commander was needed to replace him. On April 21 Taylor appointed Wharton to command all the cavalry in his army. In announcing the appointment Taylor noted that Wharton came to the Trans Mississippi "with a reputation second to none in America."[25]

Wharton joined Taylor's army just before Union troops crossed the Cane River at Monett's Ferry. Taylor had hoped to delay the crossing by sending a cavalry division under Brig. Gen. Hamilton P. Bee to block Banks' army, but Bee abandoned his position, allowing the Federals to escape. The Confederate cavalry, now commanded by Wharton, continued to harass Banks' troops as they moved down the Red River but was unable to stop them. On May 18 Wharton led his cavalry and Polignac's infantry in two futile assaults against superior Union forces at Yellow Bayou. Confederate losses in the attacks were high, slightly over 600 men, but Banks' army made its withdrawal across the Atchafalaya. Effective pursuit was no longer possible.[26]

The failure at Yellow Bayou hurt Wharton's reputation. Most of his senior officers had opposed the attack. One, Col. William H. Parsons of the Twelfth Texas, had to be ordered twice before he led his men in the assault. Another, Col. Xavier Debray of the Twenty-sixth Texas, described Yellow Bayou as an "unfortunate and unnecessary affair." Lt. Buck Walton of the same regiment declared that he did not believe "the battle ought to have been fought." Henry Orr, an enlisted man in Parsons' cavalry, reported to his father that "Gen. Wharton is considerably censured for the manner in which he managed the fight."[27]

Wharton never admitted the assaults at Yellow Bayou were a mistake. Several days after the affair he praised his cavalry for its performance in the Red River campaign. In a congratulatory message he stated "the history of no other campaign will present the spectacle of a cavalry force capturing and killing more of the enemy than their own numbers. This you have done, and in so doing have immortalized yourselves, and added new luster to Texas."[28]

The Battle of Yellow Bayou was the last major engagement of the Civil War in Louisiana. During the summer of 1864, Wharton's cavalry saw little action. Some of the men, including Wharton, received short leaves of absence to visit family and friends in Texas. There were rumors of enemy movement, efforts to improve food and equipment, and patrols to be maintained, but little else. In early September Wharton and his cavalry were ordered into Arkansas to support a major raid into Missouri by Confederate general Sterling Price. Although there was much scouting and maneuvering by the cavalry, there was little contact with the enemy.[29]

In late November 1864, the commander of the Trans Mississippi Department, Kirby Smith, ordered Wharton to move his cavalry into East Texas, where winter forage for the horses might be found. For three months Wharton made his headquarters in Nacogdoches, but in February he was ordered to move to Hempstead. In the same order Kirby Smith instructed Wharton to reorganize his command by dismounting nine regiments. Such reorganization was never popular, but Wharton carried out Smith's orders. In the process of making these changes some officers and men were made unhappy. One officer, Col. George W. Baylor, a veteran of the New Mexico and Louisiana campaigns who earlier had difficulties with Wharton, was particularly displeased when he and his troops were placed under an officer (Col. David S. Terry) Baylor considered his inferior.[30]

Baylor's anger led to a confrontation with fatal consequences. On April 6, 1865, Wharton was visiting Gen. John B. Magruder's headquarters in Houston when he encountered Baylor on the street. A heated exchange occurred during which Wharton called Baylor a liar and Baylor took a swing at Wharton. Fellow officers separated the two, but the argument resumed inside the Fannin House Hotel, where Magruder was having breakfast. In this exchange a scuffle occurred, and Baylor pulled a pistol. Brig. Gen. James Harrison, who had accompanied the unarmed Wharton, attempted to grab Baylor's gun hand. The pistol fired. The ball went into Wharton's left side below the short rib. Wharton fell to the floor, dead.[31]

The death of the thirty-six-year-old Wharton was a shock to Texans everywhere. Baylor was arrested and taken to jail. Before he could be tried by court-martial the war ended. The case was later transferred to civil court, and Baylor was released on bond. The legal proceedings dragged on for three years. In May 1868 the jury was unable to decide the case, so a new trial was held. Six months later the second jury found Baylor not guilty.[32]

A military funeral with full honors was conducted for Wharton in Houston, with General Magruder leading the procession. Wharton was first buried at Hempstead but was later moved to the State Cemetery in Austin.[33]

THOMAS LAFAYETTE ROSSER

Thomas Lafayette Rosser, the third Texan to be appointed major general, was born in Campbell County, Virginia, on October 15, 1836. Since he was born in Virginia and commanded Virginia troops throughout most of the Civil War, Rosser is often thought of as a Virginian rather than a Texan. However, he spent his adolescent years living in Texas, was appointed to the United States Military Academy as a Texan, and was considered a Texan when he entered Confederate service. Most of his West Point classmates, including George Armstrong Custer, considered Rosser to be a Texan.[34]

Little is known of Tom Rosser's early years in Virginia. His fa-

Thomas L. Rosser
—Courtesy of Harold B. Simpson
Research Center, Hillsboro, Texas

ther, John Rosser, was of French Huguenot descent and his mother, Martha Melvina Johnson Rosser, was of English and Scandinavian ancestry. Martha was the third of four wives of John Rosser, and Tom was the second of five children born to the couple. The senior Rosser was a farmer in Virginia, but financial difficulties led him to move to Texas.[35]

Business reasons compelled the senior Rosser to stay temporarily behind in Virginia when the family moved to Panola County, Texas, in 1849. Young Tom Rosser, the oldest son, and his mother led the procession of wagons carrying family members and possessions to East Texas. With the help of Tom, three younger sons, and several slaves, John Rosser cleared timber land and developed a 640-acre farm in the Sabine River bottoms during the 1850s. Tom attended public school in Mount Enterprise for four years and gave some thought to becoming a teacher. However, his thoughts turned to becoming a soldier. In 1856 he secured an appointment to West Point from East Texas congressman Lemuel D. Evans.[36]

Rosser entered the U.S. Military Academy in the summer of 1856. Among his fellow cadets were a number of young men who would later distinguish themselves as cavalry officers in the Civil War: John S. Marmaduke was in his final year at the academy, Joe Wheeler was in his junior year, James H. Wilson and Wesley Merritt were in the class of 1860, and Judson Kilpatrick was in Rosser's class. George A. Custer entered the academy the year after Rosser.

Rosser was not an outstanding student. Although he excelled in horsemanship and, with his six-foot-two-inch muscular frame, black hair, and brown eyes, was impressive in physical appearance, Rosser was not strong academically. At the end of his plebe year he stood thirty-fourth in a class of fifty-nine. He did make friends easily, however, and was well liked by his fellow cadets. His roommate was a handsome blonde two years younger than Rosser, John Pelham of Alabama, who would later become an outstanding artilleryman in the Confederate army.

Rosser and Pelham soon became close friends with a young cadet from Ohio, George Armstrong Custer. The three shared many characteristics, especially their fondness for horses. They were regarded the best riders in the corps; most cadets agreed that if Rosser, Pelham, or Custer could not stay on a horse the animal could not be ridden.[37]

The growing tension between the North and the South over the issues of slavery and states' rights affected most West Point cadets. While remaining good friends throughout their lives, Rosser, Pelham, and Custer each remained committed to his section. Rosser, the oldest and perhaps the most impulsive of the three, was concerned about the prospects of a Republican victory in the 1860 presidential election. On November 5, 1860, he wrote Governor Sam Houston offering his services to the state if Texas seceded. Houston's response to Rosser was disappointing. The governor told the young Texan that he (Houston) could not for "a moment entertain the belief that any cause for secession or disunion" existed. Houston urged Rosser to stay in school and "give your whole time and attention to your studies."

Not satisfied with Governor Houston's response, Rosser wrote Senator Jefferson Davis, who had been secretary of war when Rosser entered West Point, expressing his determination to resign from the academy if Texas left the Union. On February 27, 1861, he sent a second letter to Davis, now president of the Confederate States, offering his services to the Confederacy.[38]

Several members of the Corps, including Price M. B. Young of Georgia, John H. Kelley of Alabama, and Felix H. Robertson of Texas, resigned from the academy during the winter months of 1860-1861. Rosser waited to see what his native state of Virginia would do. When the Virginia convention voted to secede on April

17, Rosser, Pelham, and James Dearing, a boyhood friend from Campbell County, Virginia, decided not to wait for graduation in May. They resigned immediately.[39]

Upon resigning from the academy Rosser and Pelham journeyed to Montgomery, Alabama, where they were commissioned lieutenants in the Confederate artillery. After brief service in Wilmington, North Carolina, Rosser was assigned to the famed Washington Artillery, a New Orleans elite organization created in 1840. The Washington Artillery was assigned to Gen. Pierre Beauregard's army defending Manassas Junction. On July 17 Rosser's battery of four howitzers was ordered to join Richard Ewell's brigade at Mills Union Ford, on the Confederate extreme right. As a result Rosser missed the action at First Manassas when McDowell's army crossed on the Confederate left on July 21.[40]

Rosser was promoted to captain in the Washington Artillery in September 1861. He and fellow roommate John Pelham served in the horse artillery under Brig. Gen. J. E. B. Stuart during the winter months and won Stuart's favor. In the Peninsula campaign Rosser was wounded in the arm during a skirmish at Mechanicsville on May 23, 1862, but returned to duty in two weeks. He was made lieutenant colonel of artillery on June 10, and on June 23 received word that he was transferred to Stuart's cavalry. The following day he learned that he had been promoted to full colonel in command of the Fifth Virginia Cavalry.[41]

Rosser was eager to show that his promotion and transfer were justified. In the Seven Days fighting around Richmond the young colonel handled his regiment with skill. On June 30, while scouting on the army's right flank, Rosser discovered the Union army moving hurriedly over Malvern Hill toward the James River. When his report was ignored by Generals Longstreet and Theophilus Holmes, Rosser sent the information directly to the army commander, Robert E. Lee. Lee came immediately to Rosser's outpost, where he observed the enemy movement and then ordered Holmes forward. Although Holmes moved too slowly to capitalize upon the information, Lee was impressed by Rosser's alertness.

The following week Rosser was praised by General Stuart for his conduct of defensive operations on the road below Westover. In his official report Stuart lauded the young colonel for inspiring his men and arranging them so that the enemy failed to achieve his objective. "From that day, in a service that boasted many daring and ambitious officers," noted Douglas Southall Freeman, "Rosser was a marked man."[42]

Rosser continued to impress Stuart in the campaigns of 1862. At Beverly's Ford, Catlett's Station, Second Manassas, and Crampton's Gap in August and September, Rosser's cavalry skillfully performed the tasks assigned by Stuart and brigade commander Fitzhugh Lee. In the Battle of Fredericksburg in early December, Rosser's cavalry helped defend the extreme right of the Confederate line. Here Rosser had an opportunity to display his artillery skills once again as he commanded several guns alongside his old West Point companion, the gallant John Pelham. Later that month Rosser and the Fifth Virginia took part in a major cavalry raid against the Union supply base at Dumfries, Virginia. Rosser's action in pursuing Federal cavalry across the Occoquan River gained him the praise of both Stuart and Fitzhugh Lee.[43]

In autumn 1862 Stuart wrote to Lee's chief of staff, R. H. Chilton, urging creation of a new brigade with Rosser as its commander, but no action had been forthcoming. In January 1863 Stuart renewed his efforts, recommending Rosser's promotion, but once again the recommendation was not acted upon. Rosser, who was extremely ambitious and sensitive about rank, was disappointed and bitter. He blamed Stuart for the delay in promotion, and became critical of Stuart's military ability. Stuart, never realizing the extent of Rosser's hostility, continued to work for Rosser's promotion to brigadier general, which was finally approved in October 1863.[44]

Before the promotion was approved Rosser won new laurels with the courage and bravery he displayed in the Battle of Kelly's Ford fought on March 16-17, 1863. He was severely wounded in the foot earlier in the fighting but remained with his regiment until victory was won, leading his brigade commander, Fitzhugh Lee, to praise him for "his habitual coolness and daring, charging at the head of his regiment." The Confederate victory was costly; in addition to Rosser, Stuart's cavalry suffered 132 casualties including the death of Rosser's West Point roommate, John Pelham of Alabama.[45]

Rosser did not rejoin his command until after the Battle of Chancellorsville in May 1863. Rosser and the Fifth Cavalry participated in the grand cavalry review Stuart held at Brandy Station on June 8, but were on picket duty at Warrenton the following day and missed the battle with Alfred Pleasonton's cavalry.

In the early phases of the Gettysburg campaign Stuart's cavalry was assigned the task of screening Lee's infantry as it moved northward along the Blue Ridge. When advanced elements of Fitzhugh Lee's cavalry brigade were attacked at Aldie by a much larger Federal force commanded by Brig. Gen. Judson Kilpatrick, Rosser and the Fifth Virginia countered with a saber charge that stopped the Union advance. Although the outnumbered Confederates were eventually forced to withdraw, they succeeded in shielding Lee's infantry as it moved north.[46]

Rosser and the Fifth Virginia were part of Fitz Lee's brigade when Stuart's cavalry swung to the east of the Confederate and Union armies as they moved northward in the Gettysburg campaign. Although Stuart and his troops captured 125 Federal wagons loaded with supplies, the swing eastward left Lee without most of his cavalry as his army moved across Maryland and into Pennsylvania. On July 3, the day that Pickett led the Confederate infantry against the center of the line on Cemetery Ridge, Confederate and Federal cavalry fought a fierce but indecisive battle near Rummel's farm east of Gettysburg. The next evening Stuart's cavalry was assigned the task of screening Lee's army as it withdrew toward the Potomac River.[47]

Rosser's promotion to brigadier general came three months after the Gettysburg campaign. A long-running feud between Stuart and William E. "Grumble" Jones, commander of a brigade in Wade Hampton's Division, led to Jones' reassignment elsewhere. On October 10 Rosser was appointed brigadier general in command of Jones' Brigade with the date of rank established as September 28. Soon thereafter, following a successful cavalry raid in the Shenandoah Valley, Rosser issued an order naming the unit "the Laurel Brigade," and directing each member to wear on his hat a laurel leaf, the foliage used by ancient Greeks to crown victors.[48]

In the autumn of 1863 Rosser and his new brigade were involved in several engagements with Federal cavalry as the Union Army of the Potomac, now under George Meade, attempted to push its way southward toward the Rapidan and Rappahannock rivers. Two days after assuming command of the Laurel Brigade, Rosser was wounded at Fleetwood, Virginia, but continued fighting until the enemy was defeated. Later, in repulsing the Union cavalry along Mine Run, Rosser again won the praise of General Stuart for his vigilance and daring.[49]

During the winter months of 1863-1864 Rosser's Brigade was assigned to support Jubal Early's operations in the Shenandoah Valley. The relationship between the exuberant Rosser and the dour, crusty Early got off to a rocky start. Rosser, who had married the previous spring, was deeply in love with his wife. When she came to Staunton, near the encampment of the Laurel Brigade, in December, Rosser visited her. Such visits by general officers with their wives was not all that uncommon, but Early, a bachelor, was displeased and complained of Rosser's actions in a letter to General Lee. Fortunately, the following month Rosser captured ninety-three loaded Federal wagons in a daring raid, a feat that delighted Early.[50]

In the Shenandoah campaigns that winter, Rosser formed an adverse opinion concerning the operations of Confederate irregulars. Such irregulars, Rosser wrote in a letter to General Lee, "are a nuisance and an evil to the service." Lacking any discipline, order, or organization, they constituted "a band of thieves, stealing, pillaging, plundering, and doing every manner of mischief and crime." Rosser concluded "they are a terror to the citizens and an injury to the cause. They never fight; can't be made to fight . . ."[51]

Rosser's message evidently had an effect. Lee, forwarding Rosser's comments to the War Department, recommended the law authorizing irregular or partisan forces be repealed. The Confederate Congress passed legislation doing away with Partisan Rangers, though allowing exceptions such as John S. Mosby's men.

The coming of spring meant increased military action as the massive Federal army, now under the direction of Ulysses S. Grant, pushed southward across the Rapidan and into the Wilderness. Robert E. Lee moved his army into the Wilderness in an effort to block the Federal advance. On May 5 Union cavalry commanded by one of Rosser's West Point classmates, James H. Wilson, moved west along the Catharpin Road in an effort to screen the advancing Federal infantry. Although outnumbered three to one, Rosser attacked and drove the Federals back. Fighting continued the following day with Rosser facing another West Point comrade, his old friend George Armstrong Custer. In some of the most fierce cavalry action of the war neither side gave ground, each later claiming they had the upper hand.[52]

Although the Confederates won the battle in the Wilderness,

fighting continued throughout the summer as Grant edged closer to Richmond. In the Spotsylvania campaign of early May, Rosser rescued approximately eighty wounded Confederates from a Union field hospital. In June Rosser's Brigade defeated Custer's cavalry at Trevilian Station. While leading his troops in the attack, however, Rosser was wounded in the leg. He did not return to the army until August 23.[53]

When Rosser returned to his brigade he found some changes. The campaign of maneuver around Richmond had been replaced by a war of attrition as the armies of Grant and Lee dug miles of trenches around Petersburg. Wade Hampton had been named to replace Jeb Stuart, who had been killed at Yellow Tavern. Matthew Calbraith Butler had been appointed to command Hampton's old division, a disappointment to Rosser, who hoped he would be chosen. Rosser had never liked Hampton; these appointments intensified his dislike. Even so, Rosser worked well under Hampton's command. In mid-September 1864, Rosser and the Laurel Brigade rode with Hampton on a major raid against Grant's supply base near Sycamore Church, just to the east of the Union lines at Petersburg. In this action, described by one writer as the "beefsteak raid," Rosser captured over 200 prisoners and brought in over 2,400 head of beef cattle. For several weeks Rosser and his men ate well.[54]

In late September Rosser and the Laurel Brigade were ordered back to the Shenandoah Valley to reinforce Fitz Lee's Division. Confederate fortunes there were at a low ebb. Jubal Early had been routed by the Federals at Winchester, Fitz Lee had been wounded, and Phil Sheridan's cavalry left a trail of devastation in the once rich valley. The morale of the army and the citizens was low; many had lost confidence in General Early. The arrival of the confident, self-assured Rosser and his brigade rekindled some hope in Valley residents who were soon calling the big Texan "the savior of the Valley."

Fitz Lee's interim successor as division commander, Carter W. Wicksham, resigned to take a seat in the Confederate Congress, so Rosser temporarily commanded Lee's Division as well as the Laurel Brigade. At Early's request Rosser was soon pursuing and harassing the Federal cavalry. Although his initial efforts were successful, Rosser and his cavalry were defeated by Union forces commanded by George A. Custer just south of Tom's Brook, a tributary of the

Shenandoah. In the fighting Rosser's troopers attempted to stem the Union attack; however, when the Confederate lines broke, a general stampede took place. Custer's cavalry chased the Southerners ten to twelve miles, capturing all but one of Rosser's twelve guns and virtually every weapon, ambulance, and caisson his cavalry had. And more humiliating, Custer captured a headquarters wagon containing a trunk with Rosser's dress coat and hat. The next day Custer appeared before his men wearing Rosser's coat, which was much too large for him. That night he sent Rosser a note thanking him for the coat, but asking if he would have his tailor make the coattails a little shorter the next time.[55] Historian Robert K. Krick has noted that Tom's Brook "was the most disastrous defeat of the war endured by any major cavalry component of the Army of Northern Virginia." Jubal Early, who always questioned the willingness of cavalry to fight, expressed to General Lee his belief that "it would be better . . . if they [Rosser's cavalry] could all be put into the infantry; but if that were tried I am afraid they would all run off." Even so, Early refrained from recrimination against Rosser. In a letter to Rosser, Early attempted to console the Texan, pointing to the Union advantage in numbers and equipment. Later that month Early endorsed Rosser's promotion to major general, which Lee approved on November 4.[56]

Rosser continued to lead Early's cavalry in the struggle against overwhelming numbers in the fall and winter of 1864. Ten days after the defeat at Tom's Brook, in a desperate attempt to reclaim control of the Valley, Early launched a surprise attack on the left flank of Sheridan's army at Cedar Creek. Rosser's horsemen kept the Union cavalry engaged on the Union right as Confederate infantry hit the Federal left. In the morning Early's troops pushed the Federals back and seemed on the verge of a great victory, but Sheridan rallied his men in the afternoon and sent the Confederates reeling. Rosser's cavalry covered the retreat of Early's crippled army as it withdrew southward. Among the Confederate dead was one of Rosser's West Point friends, Stephen Dodson Ramseur.[57]

After the autumn defeats, Early's army was in no condition to engage Union forces in major battle. Rosser, however, was able to stage several successful raids against Union supply depots. In November he attacked a large Federal supply base at New Creek near the Potomac River. In this raid he captured 700 Union troops and great amounts of clothing, equipment, food, horses, and mules. In January he surprised two Ohio regiments guarding the Union depot at Beverly in western Virginia. With the loss of only one man killed and one wounded, Rosser captured nearly 600 Federal troops, 100 horses, 600 weapons, and 10,000 rations.[58]

Raids such as these alleviated the serious supply problem facing the Valley army but could not offset the increasing Union numerical superiority. At Waynesboro on March 2, 1865, the war ended for Jubal Early and his Valley army. On that date Early made a futile attempt to prevent Sheridan from joining Grant near Petersburg. Early's smaller army was crushed. Most of his troops were captured. Early, his staff, and Rosser and the cavalry managed to escape. Four weeks later Early was relieved of his command. Rosser and the cavalry were ordered to join Lee's army in the defense of Richmond and Petersburg. They were assigned to support George Pickett, who held the right wing of the army near Five Forks.[59]

On his way to join Pickett, Rosser crossed the Nottoway River. Noting that the shad were running, Rosser borrowed a seine from a local farmer. With the assistance of his aides, he caught a number of fish, enough so that he invited Generals Fitzhugh Lee and George Pickett to share the bounty at a shad bake on April 1. What followed was the best known luncheon in the Civil War. While the three generals relaxed and enjoyed a leisurely meal, Sheridan launched a massive assault at Five Forks. By the time Pickett received news of the attack the Confederate line had broken. Sheridan took 5,000 prisoners and captured a road junction vital to Lee's defense line. While it is doubtful that Pickett's presence would have changed the outcome of the battle, the shad bake did not help the reputation of Pickett, Fitz Lee, or Rosser.[60]

Five Forks was the beginning of the end for Lee's army. The next day Lee informed President Davis that he must evacuate Petersburg and Richmond. For the next seven days Lee's army was on the move as the Confederates attempted to escape encirclement by Union forces. Rosser's cavalry carried on a desperate rear guard action during this week. On April 6 Rosser was wounded in his arm once again in fighting at High Bridge on the Southside Railroad. Rosser, whose bravery and courage had been demonstrated many times, ignored the wound while leading his troops in the last major cavalry victory of Lee's army. In a hand-to-hand encounter during the battle, Rosser killed the Union commander, Brig. Gen. Theodore Read.[61] The victory at High Bridge did little to change the outcome. Three days later Lee surrendered to General Grant at Appomattox Courthouse. Fitz Lee, Rosser, and most of their cavalry left Lee's army just before the surrender, hoping to join Joe Johnston's army in the Carolinas. They were able to get through Grant's lines but were captured before they could join Johnston.

When the war ended, Rosser was completely without funds. Twenty-eight years old, a husband and father, Rosser had no training or experience other than as a soldier. He decided not to return to Texas because he believed it was not safe "to go amongst the population that had flocked there since the war." He studied law briefly but decided this was not a career he wished to pursue. After several minor business ventures he determined to find a new career in the West. He went to St. Paul, Minnesota, where he found work as an axeman for the Lake Superior and Mississippi Railroad. He so impressed his employers with his hard work that he was soon promoted. In 1870 he became assistant engineer for construction for the Northern Pacific Railroad. Three years later he headed an engineering surveying party for the Northern Pacific in the Yellowstone country of Montana.[62]

On the Yellowstone expedition, Rosser resumed his friendship with his old West Point comrade and Civil War adversary, George A. Custer. Custer, then a lieutenant colonel in the Seventh Cavalry, was in command of the military escort for the engineering survey. For several weeks the two cavalrymen enjoyed each other's company retelling stories of their days on the Hudson and their battles in the Shenandoah. When Custer was killed on the Little Bighorn in 1876, Rosser was quick to defend his old comrade in the public press. "I knew Gen. Custer well," Rosser wrote in a letter to the Minneapolis *Pioneer Press and Tribune*, "have known him intimately from boyhood; and being on opposite sides during the late war we often met and measured strength on the fields of Virginia, and I can truly say now that I have never met a more enterprising, gallant or dangerous enemy during those four years of terrible war, or a more genial, wholesouled, chivalrous gentleman and friend in peace than Major General George A. Custer."[63]

Rosser believed that Custer would have been successful on the Little Bighorn had his subordinate officers carried out their assignments properly. Rosser was particularly critical of Maj. Marcus A. Reno for failure to support Custer. Although he later retreated from statements questioning the courage of Reno and other officers, Rosser never departed from his support for Custer.[64]

With money earned while working for Northern Pacific and later Canadian Pacific, Rosser purchased a 200-acre farm near Charlottesville, Virginia, in 1886. During the next decade he was active as a gentleman farmer and defender of his military record. He engaged in critical exchanges with a former brigade commander, Tom Munford, a former commander, Jubal Early, and a former opponent, Phil Sheridan. The exchange with Early was particularly heated as Early described Rosser as "a consummate ass" and a "falsifier," who might like "Judas Iscariot consider hanging himself."[65]

When the United States went to war with Spain in 1898, Rosser applied for and received a commission as brigadier general of volunteers in the U.S. Army. Poor health prevented him from going to Cuba during the war (although he did visit Cuba after the war), but the old Confederate cavalryman did report to the army assembly point at Chickamauga, where he helped train the Third Brigade of U.S. Volunteers commanded by another West Point classmate, Brig. Gen. James H. Wilson. After the war he returned to Charlottesville, where he served as postmaster from 1905 until his death. He died on March 29, 1910, from pneumonia and kidney failure, and is buried in the Riverview Cemetery in Charlottesville.[66]

SAMUEL BELL MAXEY

Future Confederate general and U.S. Senator Samuel Bell Maxey was born on March 30, 1825, at Tompkinsville, Kentucky. Sam Bell, as he was known throughout his life, was the third of four children of Rice and Lucetta Pope Bell Maxey. Sam's father, Rice, was a lawyer and county clerk. His mother, Lucetta, was a member of a prominent Virginia family that moved to Kentucky at the turn of the century. When Sam Bell was nine the family moved to Albany, Kentucky, where Sam and his older brother studied Latin and mathematics from a private tutor. Sam grew up in a comfortable upper-middle-class environment. The family knew and associated with the social and political leaders of Kentucky, including Henry Clay.[67]

Samuel Bell Maxey
—Courtesy of Harold B. Simpson
Research Center, Hillsboro, Texas

At the age of seventeen young Sam Bell wrote to Senator Bryan Y. Owsley of Kentucky requesting appointment to the U.S. Military Academy at West Point. Owsley was so impressed with the letter that he nominated Maxey for enrollment at the Academy. In the summer of 1842 the young Kentuckian became Cadet Maxey, class of 1846.

Like fellow Kentuckian John Bell Hood, who was a cadet several years later, Sam Bell Maxey was not an outstanding student. His biographer, Louise Horton, pointed out that Maxey ranked near the bottom of his class in nearly all subjects at West Point. She speculated that this may have been due to the carefree attitude of the Kentucky frontiersman in Maxey. He was liked by his fellow cadets and participated in various extracurricular activities. Although he did well in sciences and languages, he performed poorly in engineering and mathematics. Among his fellow West Point classmates were William B. Franklin and U. S. Grant, seniors in Maxey's plebe year; Winfield Scott Hancock, two years ahead of Maxey; and Edmund Kirby Smith and Fitz John Porter in the class of 1845. Maxey's own class included George B. McClellan, Thomas J. Jackson, George Stoneman, and George Pickett. Ten members of Maxey's class (including Maxey) became Confederate generals; twelve became Union generals in the Civil War.[68]

Maxey graduated next to the last in his class of fifty-nine graduates, ahead only of Virginian George Pickett. Maxey's low class standing meant that he was consigned to the infantry. He was commissioned a brevet second lieutenant in the Seventh Infantry Regiment.[69]

The Seventh Infantry was in Monterrey, Mexico, when Lieutenant Maxey joined it in October 1846. The regiment was part of Zachary Taylor's army that had moved south to the Rio Grande in February 1846. The Seventh had been assigned to occupy the earthen fort that Taylor constructed on the Texas side of the Rio Grande overlooking Matamoros. Its commander, Maj. Jacob Brown, had been killed when the Seventh Infantry engaged in a spirited defense of the fort in early May 1846. When war with Mexico was declared, the Seventh was part of Taylor's army that crossed into Mexico and captured Monterrey in late September 1846.[70]

Maxey's stay in Monterrey was brief. In early 1847 the Seventh Infantry and various other units under the command of Brig. Gen. David E. Twiggs marched to Tampico and joined the forces of Winfield Scott. Under Scott's command they participated in the siege and capture of Vera Cruz. From there Scott's army moved inland through the mountains and marched into the heart of Mexico. In this campaign young Maxey received his initiation in battle, first at Cerro Gordo and later at Contreras and Churubusco. For his gallantry in the latter engagements, Maxey was commended by his superiors and made a brevet first lieutenant. He took part in the battles at Molino del Rey and was present at the capture of Mexico City on September 13-14, 1847. Later he was placed in command of one of five companies that served as security guard for Mexico City.[71]

In the summer of 1848 Maxey and the Seventh Infantry returned to Jefferson Barracks. After his experiences in Mexico, Maxey found garrison duty monotonous and boring. In September 1849 he resigned his commission and returned to his parents' home in Kentucky. He studied law with his father and in April 1851 joined his father's law firm. He was unsuccessful in a race for the Kentucky legislature but in 1852 was elected clerk for the county and circuit courts of Clinton County. In July 1853 Maxey married Marilda Cassa Denton, the daughter of a Clinton County farmer.[72]

In 1857 Sam Bell Maxey and his wife, accompanied by his father's family, moved to Texas. The Kentucky law practice had not been very successful and the Maxeys had received glowing reports about the new state from a relative who had moved to Fannin County. The Maxeys purchased five acres of land near Paris, Texas, and father and son opened a law practice in town. The area was growing and the practice thrived. In 1858 Sam Bell was appointed district attorney to fill out a vacancy; he was elected to the office in 1859. In 1861 he was chosen state senator from Lamar and Hopkins counties, but resigned before taking his seat to join the Confederate army.[73]

Maxey's biographer, Louise Horton, pointed out that there is no correspondence showing Maxey's personal views on the issues dividing the country. His county of residence, Lamar, was one of only eighteen Texas counties in which a majority voted against secession in the popular referendum in Febuary 1861. Nevertheless, Maxey was quick to organize a troop from the county, the Lamar Rifles, that accompanied Col. W. C. Young and the Texas cavalry that moved across the Red River to occupy Federal forts in Indian Territory. In August 1861, Maxey went to Richmond to secure permission to raise a regiment for Confederate service. Although he was unable to see President Davis, as he wished, he was given authority by the War Department to form an infantry regiment.[74]

Once back in Texas, Maxey set to work organizing his regiment. He established Camp Benjamin near Paris and began training his raw recruits. By December he had 1,100 men enrolled in the Ninth Texas Infantry. Later that month he received orders to take the regiment to Memphis, Tennessee, which was on the southern end of Albert Sidney Johnston's line of defense.

After a difficult march the Ninth Texas reached Memphis in early February, but was then ordered to Iuka, Mississippi, to guard the Memphis & Charleston Railroad. Shortly after arriving there, Maxey was appointed brigadier general and assigned to Chattanooga to protect the railroad and river from enemy attack. His old regiment, the Ninth Texas, was ordered to Corinth, where Albert Sidney Johnston was preparing for an attack on Grant's army at Pittsburg Landing. On April 6-7 the Ninth Texas fought in the battle at Shiloh, without its creator, Sam Maxey.[75]

Maxey arrived at Chattanooga on March 15. For the next several weeks the new brigadier was busy organizing troops, guarding bridges and railroads, and obstructing any enemy movement in the area. In late August he attacked the Union garrison at Bridgeport,

Alabama. In this move Maxey's forces captured $30,000 in property, including commissary, ordnance and quartermaster stores. Maxey and his troops were congratulated by army commander Braxton Bragg for "one of the most dashing achievements of the day."[76]

When Bragg began his Kentucky campaign in early September, Maxey and his troops were left behind to protect Chattanooga; however, in mid-September Bragg ordered Maxey to join him. Unfortunately, Maxey had difficulty in moving. Lack of supplies for both men and horses and conflicts between superior officers over jurisdiction delayed his movement. On October 11 he was finally on the way, but four days later he received orders to halt his column as Bragg withdrew from Kentucky.[77]

Maxey joined Bragg at Murfreesboro in late October. There was little action in November as Union and Confederate armies recovered from the intensive campaigning of the two previous months. In early December Maxey and his brigade were ordered to report to Jackson, Mississippi, as part of the 8,000 troops from Bragg's army assigned to John C. Pemberton in the defense of the Mississippi Valley. Maxey and his troops were sent to Port Hudson, the Confederate outpost in Louisiana, about one hundred miles south of Vicksburg. Maxey's Brigade, consisting of the Tenth Arkansas, Fourth Louisiana, Thirtieth Louisiana, Miles' Legion, two consolidated Tennessee regiments, the First Texas Battalion sharpshooters, and three artillery batteries, was placed in the center of the Port Hudson defense line. John Gregg's Brigade was on the extreme right and William N. Beall's Brigade was on the left of Maxey's Brigade.[78]

Maxey's Brigade saw limited action in the early months of 1863. Contact with the Federal army of Nathaniel P. Banks was confined to skirmishes south of Port Hudson and occasional exchanges of artillery fire. Rear Admiral David G. Farragut attempted to run the Port Hudson batteries in March, but only two of his seven vessels were successful. Banks believed his ground forces were not strong enough to challenge the Port Hudson garrison commanded by Maj. Gen. Franklin Gardner.[79]

Upriver from Port Hudson, Union forces commanded by U. S. Grant were more successful. On May 1 Grant's army crossed the Mississippi between Vicksburg and Port Hudson and moved toward Jackson, the rail center for the Confederate army in Mississippi. Alarmed at the propsect of losing Jackson, Lt. Gen. John C. Pemberton, commanding Confederate troops in western Mississippi and eastern Louisiana, ordered Major General Gardner to bring five thousand troops, including Maxey's Brigade, from Port Hudson to Jackson.[80]

The efforts to prevent Federal capture of Jackson were made to no avail. Joseph E. Johnston, Confederate departmental commander, arrived in Jackson on May 13 but evacuated the city the next day. Meanwhile Maxey's Brigade had been delayed at Brookhaven, twenty miles to the south, and did not join Johnston until after the fall of Jackson. Gardner was ordered back to Port Hudson with the rest of the reinforcements.

As part of Maj. Gen. Samuel French's Division, Maxey's Brigade took part in Johnston's futile efforts to link up with Pemberton. After the surrender of Vicksburg on July 4, Johnston's small army, including Maxey's Brigade of approximately 2,600 men, withdrew back into eastern Mississippi.[81]

The failure of the Confederates to concentrate their forces against the enemy disappointed Maxey. He wrote to President Davis requesting that he be transferred west of the Mississippi River. His request was granted and, after a brief assignment at Mobile, Alabama, Maxey reported to Gen. Kirby Smith, commander of the Trans Mississippi Department at Shreveport. On December 11, 1863, Smith appointed Maxey commander of Indian Territory, replacing Brig. Gen. William Steele.[82]

When Maxey assumed command of Indian Territory, he found conditions in a deplorable state. Union troops occupied the northern half of the territory and were poised to drive southward. On paper Maxey had over 8,000 men, but in reality he had fewer than 2,000 present for duty. Slightly over half of his troops were Texans commanded by Richard M. Gano. The others were members of Brig. Gen. Douglas Cooper's Indian Brigade. All were cavalry or horse artillery; none were infantry. Most were poorly equipped, Maxey reporting to General Smith that many of their guns were worthless. Lack of supplies and adequate mounts, poor morale, and internal dissension all contributed to the general despondency.[83]

Maxey established his headquarters on the Red River at Fort Towson, an old military post abandoned by the U.S. Army in 1854.

He immediately set about rebuilding confidence in his command by meeting with various Native American leaders and seeking their support. He organized the native troops into three separate brigades, a step which appealed to the Indian desire for tribal identity and loyalty. In another move, highly popular with the Indians, but less so with some of the Texans, especially Col. Charles De Morse of the Twenty-sixth Cavalry, Maxey ruled that no racial or color line would be used in determining relative rank among officers in his command. Through the use of an old printing press Maxey disseminated information, and propaganda, about Confederate plans for Indian Territory.[84]

While Maxey was completing the reorganization of his department in the spring of 1864, the Union army began a major offensive in the Trans Mississippi. Maj. Gen. Nathaniel P. Banks brought an army of 20,000 men up the Red River into northwestern Louisiana while at the same time Maj. Gen. Frederick Steele marched south from Little Rock with over 10,000 troops. Determined to prevent a linkup between the two Federal armies, Kirby Smith reinforced Richard Taylor's Confederate command in northern Louisiana and Sterling Price's forces in southern Arkansas. To assist Price, Smith ordered Maxey to move into Arkansas with some of his troops. Leaving Douglas Cooper in charge of Indian Territory, Maxey took Tandy Walker's Choctaw Brigade and three regiments of Richard Gano's Texas Brigade to join Confederate forces in Arkansas.[85]

Maxey and his troops joined Sterling Price at Prairie D'Ane in south central Arkansas on April 12. At the time Price's forces were engaged in an artillery duel with Steele's Federals. After a brief skirmish in which Gano's regiments became involved, Steele's army broke off battle and moved east to occupy Camden, an important military center. On the morning of April 18 Confederate cavalry under Brig. Gen. John S. Marmaduke intercepted a large Federal forage train at Poison Spring, fourteen miles west of Camden. When Marmaduke requested reinforcements, Price ordered Maxey and his command to Poison Spring.

Upon arriving at Poison Spring, Maxey found Marmaduke prepared to attack the Union train. As Maxey was senior in rank, Marmaduke tendered command to the Texan, but Maxey declined to issue orders since Marmaduke was more familiar with the terrain and troop dispositions. Marmaduke placed Maxey's Division on the left and the attack began. In less than an hour Union defenders, many of them troops from the First Kansas Colored Infantry, were routed and the entire supply train of 170 wagons was captured.[86]

Once the wagons were in Confederate hands, Maxey, who now assumed command, called off the pursuit of the defeated enemy. Some of his officers, including Marmaduke, questioned the decision, but in doing so Maxey spared the lives of many of the black troops of the First Kansas who were being killed while attempting to flee. Even so, one hundred blacks were killed, many while trying to surrender. Tandy Walker's Choctaws were the worst offenders among the Confederates; "of all those who succumbed to the homicidal frenzy at Poison Spring, none surpassed Col. Tandy Walker's Choctaws for sheer ferocity," according to historian Gregory J. W. Urwin. Anne J. Bailey, another historian who studied the affair, believed "the carnage might have been worse had not Texan Samuel Maxey assumed command over the Missourian Marmaduke."[87]

The defeat at Poison Spring, followed by a similar Confederate capture of a Union supply train on April 25 at Mark's Mill, convinced Steele to abandon Camden and withdraw northward. Maxey wanted to move north to capture Fort Smith and Fort Gibson, but was ordered back to Indian Territory. When he reached Fort Towson he heard that his name had been left off a list of brigadiers that Kirby Smith had recommended for promotion. In anger he submitted a letter of resignation but withdrew it when he was assured that Smith had recommended him for promotion on April 18, the day of the battle of Poison Spring. Although the question of confirmation by the president and the Senate remained an issue, Maxey assumed the title and duties of major general.[88]

With the matter of promotion resolved (at least for the moment), Maxey turned his thoughts to administering affairs in Indian Territory. Although he continued to think about recapturing Forts Gibson and Smith, he did not have the resources to undertake such a campaign. The lack of adequate weapons and shortages of food and clothing for his troops remained as major concerns. He issued appeals through the press to his fellow Texans for contributions of food and clothing, but the response was meager.[89]

Even with limited resources, soldiers under Maxey's command conducted several raids against the enemy in the summer of 1864.

In mid-June Indian troops under Brig. Gen. Stand Watie captured the Union steamboat *J. R. Williams* near Pleasant Bluff on the Arkansas River. In July, Gano's Texas Brigade routed the Sixth Kansas Cavalry in an engagement five miles from Fort Smith. In mid-September Gano and Stand Watie combined forces to attack a large Federal wagon train at Cabin Creek, fifty miles from Fort Gibson. In this, the last major engagement of the war in Indian Territory, Maxey's Confederates captured 130 wagons loaded with supplies.[90]

Despite the success of his command and the strong support of departmental commander Kirby Smith, Maxey found himself in an uncomfortable position in the autumn of 1864. Rumors persisted that Maxey's days as commander of the Indian Territory were numbered. Brig. Gen. Douglas Cooper, former Indian agent to the Choctaw Nation and later Confederate commissioner to the Indian Nations, had been disappointed when Maxey was placed in charge of Indian Territory. Cooper, who led Indian troops from the beginning of the war, had hoped to replace Brig. Gen. William Steele as commander of the Indian Territory when Steele had been reassigned. Although Maxey made attempts to placate Cooper by appointing him commander of the Indian brigades, Cooper wanted to command all troops in the territory, not just the Native Americans.[91]

Although Kirby Smith was opposed to the replacement of Maxey, there was mounting pressure for the appointment of Cooper, a Mississippi planter who had served as an officer with Jefferson Davis during the Mexican War. As secretary of war during the Pierce administration, Davis had appointed Cooper Indian agent. Cooper, in turn, had been a highly popular Indian agent; historian John Waugh said, "Cooper had almost hypnotic sway over the Indians, particularly the Choctaws and Chickasaws." Indian leaders supported Cooper's appointment as commander of the territory almost from the beginning of the conflict. Territorial delegate Elias Boudinot lobbied in Congress for his appointment, and Cooper himself traveled to Richmond to advance his cause.[92]

In August 1864, the War Department directed Kirby Smith to replace Maxey with Cooper. Smith, who opposed the move, procrastinated in carrying out the order. On October 1 Smith wrote the War Department requesting that the order to place Cooper in command be revoked. In his letter Smith praised Maxey for "skill, judgment, and success" in administering his department and warned that "serious injury would result" if the order was enforced. Adj. Gen. Samuel Cooper replied that Cooper's appointment was "deemed imperative and must be carried out." Smith continued to delay implementation, but mounting pressures from Richmond forced him to appoint Cooper on February 26, 1865.[93]

Maxey's removal was unpopular with many of the officers in his command. Cooper might have been well liked by Indian leaders, but he was not liked by the white officers who distrusted him. Maxey himself seemed resigned to the change and accepted appointment as commander of a division of dismounted cavalry created for him. He was assigned to the Houston area, but by this time the war was ending. Discouraged by mass desertions in his new division, Maxey asked to be relieved from command on May 26, 1865. He returned to his home in Paris, where he resumed the practice of law.[94]

Maxey was active in Democratic Party politics during the Reconstruction era. He was nominated judge of the Eighth Judicial District of Texas in March 1873, but declined the commission on the grounds that he was too involved in law cases before the court. Some believe he already had his eyes on a more signficant political position, namely the U.S. Senate. In early 1875 his name, along with John H. Reagan, James W. Throckmorton and others, was put before the state legislature for the Senate seat held by Republican James W. Flanagan. On the first ballot Maxey received a majority of votes.

In his two six-year terms as U.S. senator, Maxey was vitally interested in improving the postal system, establishing a stage route from Fort Worth to Yuma, Arizona, improving Texas harbors, protecting the frontier, and extending the Texas and Pacific Railroad. Although he was an effective representative for Texas in the Senate, he was defeated by John H. Reagan when seeking a third term in 1887. He returned to his law practice in Paris but continued to be involved in politics. When a vacancy occurred on the Interstate Commerce Commission in 1891, friends sought his appointment but were unsuccessful. Early in 1894 he was prostrated by an attack of gastrointestinal disease. When the disease recurred the following year, he went to Eureka Springs, Arkansas, for treatment. He died there on August 16, 1895, and his body was returned to Paris for burial in the Evergreen Cemetery. His home in Paris, built in 1868, has been restored and furnished as a state historic site.[95]

THOMAS GREEN

Thomas Green was probably the most popular of all the Texas generals in the Confederate army. Affectionately called "Daddy" by the men in his command, Green served in the Texas War for Independence, the Mexican War, and Indian campaigns prior to his appointment as colonel of the Fifth Texas Mounted Volunteers in August 1861. In the months that followed, Green demonstrated exceptional ability, first in the New Mexico campaign and later in the recapture of Galveston and the repulse of Banks' army in the Red River campaign, leading Kirby Smith to recommend his promotion to major general in February 1864. His death two months later at Blair's Landing came before his appointment could be confirmed by the president and Senate.

Thomas Green
—Courtesy of Harold B. Simpson Research Center, Hillsboro, Texas

Like many of the early Texas leaders, Tom Green was born (July 8, 1814) in Virginia but spent his youth in Tennessee, where his family moved in 1817.[96] He attended the local school in Winchester and then Jackson College, Tennessee, and Princeton College, Kentucky, prior to graduation from the University of Tennessee in 1834. He studied law with his father, a prominent attorney and member of the Tennessee Supreme Court. The spirit of adventure was strong, however, and in the fall of 1835 he set out to join volunteers fighting for Texas independence from Mexico.[97]

Green arrived in Nacogdoches on Christmas Day, 1835. He

enlisted as a private in the Texas army on January 14, 1836. Although he was only twenty-one years old and still had a boyish countenance, Green was impressive physically, standing over six feet in height and weighing about 200 pounds, with a strong, muscular frame. He joined Sam Houston's army at Gonzales in February 1836 and took part in the withdrawal back to the Brazos and the move to Groce's Plantation. When the Texas army obtained two new six-pounder cannon, known as the "Twin Sisters," from the citizens of Cincinnati, Ohio, Green was made a member of the "corps" created to handle the pieces. He was one of five men who manned the "Twin Sisters" in the Texas victory at San Jacinto on April 21, 1836.[98]

Green was commissioned second lieutenant in the army several days after the battle at San Jacinto. On May 6 he was promoted to major and made aide-de-camp to Gen. Thomas J. Rusk, who succeeded Houston as commander of the Texas army. With independence won, Green resigned from the army on May 30, 1836, and went back to Tennessee. He resumed his law studies there, but in the spring of 1837 returned to Texas. The new Republic offered generous land grants to veterans of the Revolution. Green, who received more than 2,000 acres of land, settled in La Grange in Fayette County. He became county surveyor as well as engrossing clerk in the Texas House of Representatives, a position he held in the First, Second, and Third Congresses. He was elected to the Fourth Congress in 1839, but did not seek reelection in 1840, choosing instead to return to his old position as engrossing clerk. He became clerk of the Texas Supreme Court in 1841, a position he held for the next twenty years. He also served as secretary of the Texas Senate in the Sixth and Eighth Congresses.[99]

Between his clerical duties with Congress and the Supreme Court, Green participated in various military campaigns against the Indians and Mexico. Following a major Indian raid in 1840, Green joined John H. Moore's expedition against the Comanches on the upper Colorado. The following year he served as a captain in another expedition against the Comanches, this time commanded by Maj. M. B. Lewis. When Rafael Vasquez led Mexican troops in a raid against San Antonio in March 1842, Green was captain of the Travis County volunteers assembled to defend the capital city. Vasquez withdrew back into Mexico, but later that year another Mexican force commanded by Adrian Woll captured and held San Antonio for several days. When President Houston ordered Alexander Somervell to organize a force to pursue Woll's army, Green was appointed inspector general.[100]

Somervell's army, consisting of approximately 700 men, marched from San Antonio to Laredo in late 1842. At Laredo, Somervell concluded that it was futile to continue the expedition into Mexico, but 300 of the men, including Tom Green, determined to cross into Mexico. Under the command of Col. William S. Fisher the main body of those continuing the expedition moved south along the east bank of the Rio Grande while a small spy company led by Ben McCulloch, and including Tom Green and Henry McCulloch, moved along the south bank. After seeing a sizable Mexican force being assembled near Mier, members of the spy company advised Fisher not to cross the river. When Fisher refused to follow their advice, the McCulloch brothers, Green, and others in the spy company returned to Texas. Fisher and the other Texans marched on into Mier and disaster.[101]

After his return from the Somervell expedition, Green resumed his duties as clerk of the Texas Supreme Court. When a convention was called to ratify annexation by the United States and to draft a state convention, Green served as secretary of that body.

The completion of annexation led to war between the United States and Mexico in 1846. Green recruited and led a company of Texas Rangers as part of Col. Jack Hays' First Texas Regiment of Mounted Volunteers. The regiment moved with Gen. Zachary Taylor's army toward Monterrey in the summer of 1846. The Rangers played a prominent role in the attacks on Federation and Independence hills the third week in September and in the assault on Monterrey on September 23, 1846. Since the six-month enlistment for most Rangers was up, Hays' Regiment was discharged on October 2, 1846. Some of the Rangers, including Jack Hays and Ben McCulloch, returned to Mexico; however, for Tom Green the war was over.[102]

Green resumed his duties as clerk of the Texas Supreme Court. In January 1849 he married Mary Wallace Chalmers, the oldest daughter of a prominent Austin newspaperman and physician, Dr. John G. Chalmers, who had been killed in a personal altercation earlier in the month. When Mrs. Chalmers died three years later,

Green assumed the responsibilities for rearing his wife's six brothers and sisters in addition to the six children born to him and his wife.[103]

With the coming of the Civil War in 1861, Green found himself with military duties once again. In April, Governor Edward Clark appointed Green as head of one of six newly created military districts charged with recruiting and organizing troops for the Confederate army. A month later Clark created a camp on the San Marcos River for training recruits and named Green as commandant. This appointment proved to be brief. When President Davis authorized Brig. Gen. Henry H. Sibley to organize a brigade for a New Mexico campaign, Green was named commander of one of the new cavalry regiments, the Fifth Texas Mounted Volunteers.[104]

Sibley's Brigade, consisting of Green's Fifth Cavalry, the Fourth Cavalry commanded at first by Col. James Reiley and later by Lt. Col. William R. Scurry, and the Seventh Cavalry commanded by Col. William Steele, began its march from San Antonio to El Paso in late October 1861. After a long and arduous journey the brigade reached Fort Bliss in late December.

Sibley assumed command of all Confederate forces in the area, including a regiment of mounted troops led by John R. Baylor. Sibley then moved his troops along the west side of the Rio Grande into New Mexico Territory. In mid-January the Confederates occupied Fort Thorn, an abandoned Federal post on the river, midway between El Paso and Fort Craig, a strongly defended Union post ninety miles to the north.[105]

In early February, Sibley's army moved toward Fort Craig. Sibley attempted to draw the Federal forces commanded by Col. Edward R. S. Canby out of the fort on to open terrain. When this failed, Sibley, believing the fort too strong to assault from the south, ordered his troops to cross to the east bank of the Rio Grande, move north, and then swing back across the river at Valverde ford about five miles to the north of Fort Craig. Sibley, who was seriously ill at the time, hoped that the crossing would be uncontested but Canby moved troops to oppose the crossing. When the Texans attempted to cross on the morning of February 21, they encountered strong opposition. Bitter fighting went on throughout the day with both sides sustaining heavy casualties. About 1:00 P.M. Sibley, who had been drinking heavily to ease the

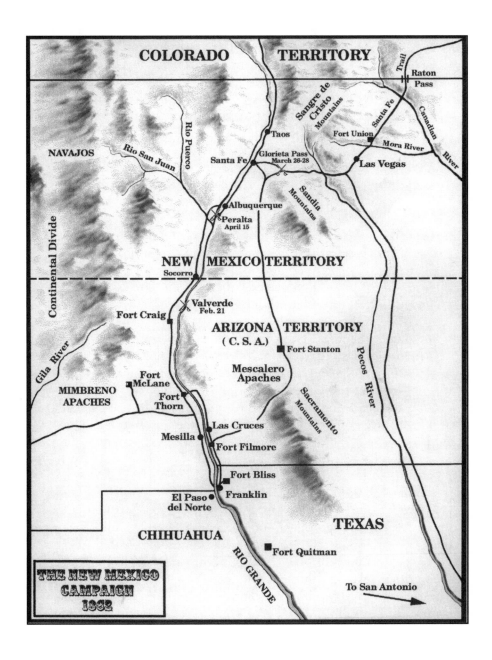

COLORADO TERRITORY

Raton Pass

Santa Fe Trail

Sangre de Cristo Mountains

Santa Fe

Canadian River

Taos

Fort Union

Mora River

NAVAJOS

Rio San Juan

Rio Puerco

Santa Fe

Glorieta Pass
March 26-28

Las Vegas

Albuquerque

Sandia Mountains

Peralta
April 15

Continental Divide

NEW MEXICO TERRITORY

Socorro

Valverde
Feb. 21

Fort Craig

ARIZONA TERRITORY
(C. S. A.)

Fort Stanton

Pecos River

Gila River

Mescalero
Apaches

Fort
McLane

Sacramento Mountains

MIMBRENO
APACHES

Fort
Thorn

Las Cruces

Mesilla

Fort Filmore

Fort Bliss

El Paso
del Norte

Franklin

TEXAS

CHIHUAHUA

Fort Quitman

RIO GRANDE

To San Antonio

THE NEW MEXICO
CAMPAIGN
1862

pain of his illness, became so ill that he relinquished command to Tom Green and retired to an ambulance in the rear. The fierce fighting, highlighted by a costly attack initiated by lancers in Green's regiment, continued during the midafternoon. Finally, the Confederates on the right flank broke through the Union lines, captured a Federal artillery battery, crossed the river, and drove the enemy back to Fort Craig. Exhaustion, confusion over the meaning of a Union flag of truce, and darkness prevented the Confederates from pursuing the retreating Federals.[106]

Valverde was a Confederate victory but at the cost of seventy-two killed and one hundred fifty-seven wounded. The heaviest losses were in Green's regiment, which had twenty killed and sixty-seven wounded. Historian Jerry Thompson noted that the biggest casualty of the battle was the reputation of General Sibley, who relinquished command to Green during the battle. Most of the Texans were convinced that drunkenness and not poor health had necessitated the transfer of command. Tom Green, on the other hand, came out of the battle with his reputation enchanced. His men were impressed with the manner in which he directed the battle, and Sibley praised him for his "coolness under the heaviest fire and interpridity under the most trying circumstances."[107]

In many ways the victory at Valverde was a hollow one. Sibley, who resumed command of the army, attempted to convince Canby to surrender but the Union general refused. Sibley was in a dilemma. His men had won the battle but were so low on supplies that a prolonged siege of Fort Craig was out of the question. Sibley decided to move north toward Albuquerque, where he hoped to find needed supplies. Unfortunately, when Sibley's Brigade reached Albuquerque in early March they discovered most of the stores and provisions had been moved or destroyed.[108]

Sibley believed that the capture of Santa Fe and Fort Union, an important Union supply depot on the Santa Fe Trail, would provide the needed supplies. He ordered several hundred mounted troops under the command of Maj. Charles Pyron to capture Santa Fe and then swing westward through Glorieta Pass toward Fort Union. The Fourth Cavalry and five companies of the Seventh Cavalry commanded by William R. Scurry would move through the Sandia Mountains northwest of Albuquerque to support Pyron's advance. Green and six companies of his cavalry, after making a reconnais-

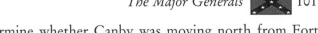

sance to determine whether Canby was moving north from Fort Craig, brought up the rear of Sibley's army.[109]

Confederate occupation of Santa Fe was achieved with little difficulty as Federal authorities withdrew supplies and records eastward to Fort Union. When Confederate troops moved toward Fort Union they encountered a column of Colorado volunteers in Apache Canyon at the western end of Glorieta Pass. In the clash that took place in late March the Confederates pushed the Union troops back; however, while the fighting went on, a detachment of Union troops swung around the Confederate lines and destroyed eighty wagons containing badly needed food, forage, ammunition, and medical supplies.[110]

Tom Green was in Albuquerque when he received news of the battle at Glorieta Pass. Early reports indicated the Confederates had won the battle but were pulling back toward Santa Fe. Green immediately ordered his troops to move for Santa Fe. When he reached Santa Fe on April 3 he found most of Sibley's Brigade there. Sibley still hoped to continue the campaign, but reports from scouts indicated Canby was moving a large force north from Fort Craig. Sibley ordered his brigade south to protect Albuquerque from Canby's army. Green's regiment, which was better mounted than the other Confederates, moved out first, reaching Albuquerque on April 9, only to discover that Canby was falling back toward Fort Craig.[111]

The rest of Sibley's army arrived in Albuquerque on April 10 and 11. Confederate prospects looked gloomy. There were reports that Col. James Carleton was leading several thousand Union troops from California toward New Mexico. Fearing entrapment between superior Federal forces and without adequate food and ammunition, Sibley, in council with Green and other regimental officers, decided to evacuate the territory.[112]

On the morning of April 12 the Confederates began their retreat from Albuquerque. Scurry's Fourth Cavalry and a battalion from the Seventh Cavalry forded the Rio Grande to the west side. Green and his Fifth Cavalry, acting as the army's rear guard, were supposed to follow, but discovered there was too much quicksand for the heavy wagons. Green decided to continue down the east bank to a better crossing at the village of Peralta. By nightfall on April 14, Sibley and the troops west of the river reached the village of Los Lunas. Green and his cavalry reached Peralta, on the east bank approximately three miles north, but instead of fording the river that night Green decided to make camp and cross the river in the morning.[113]

Canby meanwhile had united the Federal forces from Forts Craig and Union. After a forced march the Federals reached the outskirts of Peralta in the evening of April 14. At daylight the next morning they launched an attack on Green's regiment. Although taken by surprise, Green moved quickly to meet the enemy assault. Confederate and Union forces continued firing at each other, mainly with their artillery, throughout the morning. Green received reinforcements led by Lt. Col. William R. Scurry in midmorning, so the danger of a Federal breakthrough was averted. Also, Canby's men were nearly exhausted from the previous day's march. The fighting at Peralta ended about 2:00 P.M. when a howling sandstorm made further operations virtually impossible. That evening, with the wind still blowing furiously, Green's Confederates crossed to the west side of the river and reached Los Lunas before daylight on the 16th. After several hours of rest and reorganization, Sibley's army, now united, resumed its retreat south.[114]

Sibley was now faced with a problem. If the Confederates continued along the Rio Grande, they faced the prospect of being trapped between the pursuing Federals and the garrison that remained at Fort Craig. Several of the officers, including Green, suggested the army bypass Craig by moving west of the river through the mountains and returning to the river south of the fort. After discussing the matter with his staff, Sibley agreed. The detour took the Texans through a wilderness of mountains, brush, and undergrowth. Fortunately for the Confederates, the Union pursuit was poorly coordinated. By early May Sibley's Brigade, including Tom Green and his Fifth Cavalry, was back at Fort Bliss. The retreat continued on to San Antonio, which was reached in early August.[115]

Once back in San Antonio, members of the brigade received sixty-day furloughs with orders to remount and refit themselves. The New Mexico campaign hurt the reputation of some of the officers. Most veterans blamed Sibley for the failure of the campaign, but some were critical of Tom Green as well. Although Green had handled himself well, particularly at Valverde, there were stories that Green, like Sibley, drank excessively. Although these accounts may have been exaggerated, Green was passed over in the promotions that followed the campaign. William R. Scurry and William Steele, both junior to Green, were advanced to the rank of brigadier general while Green remained a colonel.[116]

During the next several months members of the Sibley Brigade gradually recovered from the rigors of the New Mexico campaign. In early autumn the Fifth and Seventh cavalries bivouacked at Hempstead, but were ordered to Houston in December. Green and A. P. Bagby, who succeeded Steele as commander of the Seventh Cavalry, volunteered their troops for Maj. Gen. John B. Magruder's impending campaign to recapture Galveston.[117]

Magruder planned a two-prong assault on the Union forces occupying Galveston. He and William R. Scurry would lead Confederate troops from Virginia Point on the mainland across the railroad bridge to the island and attack the Federals quartered along the waterfront. At the same time two river steamers, *Bayou City* and *Neptune*, which had been converted into gunboats, would steam into Galveston harbor to engage the Union naval vessels supporting the occupation troops. Tom Green and 150 of his Fifth Cavalry would serve as sharpshooters on the *Bayou City* and 100 of Bagby's Seventh Cavalry would perform similar duty on the *Neptune*. Another fifty men of the Seventh would be aboard the tender *John F. Carr*.[118]

The attack on Galveston got under way in the early morning of January 1. Magruder and Scurry led their troops on to the island after midnight. Shortly before dawn Confederate artillery opened fire on the Union troops on Kuhn's Wharf. An effort was made to storm the Federal positions, but fire from Union gunboats forced the Confederates back. At that juncture it appeared the Confederate attack would fail.[119]

Just at that moment the *Bayou City* and *Neptune* came steaming into the harbor. In an exchange with Union warships the *Neptune* was hit by a shell from the *Harriet Lane*, the most powerful of the enemy vessels, and sank in shallow water. Once again the Confederate attack was in danger of failing, but steady rifle fire from Green's sharpshooters on the *Bayou City* forced Union seamen below deck on the *Harriet Lane*. The *Bayou City* rammed the *Lane*, locking the two vessels together. Green's troops, acting as marines, stormed aboard the *Lane*. The *Lane*'s captain and executive officer were killed. The surviving officers surrendered the ship to the Confederates.

Another Union gunboat, the *Owasco*, attempted to aid the *Harriet Lane*, but fire from Green's sharpshooters forced the commander of the *Owasco* to pull away. Meanwhile, another Union vessel, the *Westfield*, ran aground and was scuttled by her captain, who was killed in the explosion. The ranking Union naval officer in the area, believing the Confederates were much stronger than they actually were, gave orders for other Union naval vessels to withdraw from the harbor. More than 200 Union soldiers on the waterfront surrendered to General Scurry as the Union fleet sailed away.[120]

The recapture of Galveston was hailed as a great Confederate victory. President Davis and Texas Governor Lubbock both praised Magruder for his achievement. In his report of the battle Magruder lauded Tom Green for "most ably and gallantly" serving in the action against the *Harriet Lane* and *Owasco*.[121]

Green and other members of the Sibley Brigade had two weeks to enjoy their victory at Galveston. In mid-January the brigade was ordered to join Richard Taylor's army in the Louisiana bayou country. Taylor hoped to use Sibley's Brigade in a campaign along Bayou Teche and Bayou Lafourche to relieve the pressure being placed on Port Hudson by Federal troops commanded by Nathaniel P. Banks. Unfortunately for the Confederates, Banks had a heavy numerical superiority over Taylor. In battles fought at Bisland and Irish Bend in April the Confederates were defeated and driven from the field. Green, who commanded the extreme right flank of the Confederate troops, handled his command well and was praised by Taylor for his "great coolness and steadiness." Sibley, on the other hand, made a number of serious errors at Bisland. Shortly after the battle, Taylor removed Sibley from command and named Green as his successor. On May 20, 1863, Green was promoted to brigadier general.[122]

Though defeated at Bisland and Irish Bend, Taylor was determined to continue the attacks upon Union forces in the bayou country. With the combined brigades of Tom Green, James P. Major, and Alfred Mouton, Taylor attacked Brashear City, a Union stronghold on Bayou Teche and Berwick Bay. After a brief resistance, the surprised Federals surrendered, netting the Confederates 1,700 prisoners, twelve heavy artillery pieces, and more than two million dollars' worth of supplies. The Confederates then moved east, Mouton capturing Thibodaux on Bayou Teche and Green moving north to Donaldsonville, at the juncture of the Teche with the Mississippi. Although Green failed in an attack upon an enemy earthwork, Fort Butler, he was able to place artillery along the Mississippi so as to interrupt river traffic.[123]

Although the Lafourche district was now in his control, Taylor was unable to break the Union grip on Port Hudson. In early July Vicksburg surrendered, followed the next week by Port Hudson. With Banks' large army now free from duty at Port Hudson, Taylor was forced to abandon the Lafourche district. As Taylor's forces fell back toward Bayou Teche, Green's Brigade fought an important delaying action near Donaldsonville on July 13. Outnumbered four to one, Green launched a vigorous attack that drove the enemy back, capturing 200 prisoners and several enemy artillery pieces in the process. Green's heroics could only slow the enemy. Although elated at the success of the "gallant noble Green," Taylor moved his forces up the Teche toward Vermillionville, abandoning the Lafourche district and the southern Teche to the enemy.[124]

There was little activity in southern Louisiana during the month following the Confederate withdrawal from the Lafourche region. Morale in the Southern forces was low. Desertion rates were high, particularly in the Texas regiments as men desired to return home. The lull ended in late September. Embarrassed by their failure at the Battle of Sabine Pass on September 8, 1863, the Federals were determined to move against Texas. General Banks considered a direct march from Brashear City toward Sabine Pass but decided that an advance up the Teche toward the Red River was a more likely way to get into Texas. In late September Banks ordered Maj. Gen. William B. Franklin to move up the Teche with the Nineteenth Army Corps and elements of the Thirteenth Army Corps.[125]

Tom Green, now commanding a division consisting of Major's Brigade and the old Sibley Brigade commanded by A. P. Bagby, played a significant role in impeding Franklin's advance up the Teche. On September 26 Green's Division and Mouton's Brigade struck a Union outpost at Morgan's Ferry on Bayou Fordoche and captured 450 prisoners. Green's cavalry harassed Franklin's army as it slowly moved up the Teche. On November 3 Green's Division and three Texas infantry regiments from John G. Walker's Division attacked the rear guard of Franklin's army at Bayou Bourbeau several miles south of Opelousas. The Federal troops fought tenaciously but were driven back a mile and a half. Following the battle Franklin withdrew his troops back to New Iberia for the winter.[126]

Green and his cavalry returned to Texas in December. Federal troops had landed at the mouth of the Rio Grande and occupied Brownsville in early November. John B. Magruder, Confederate commander in Texas, was fearful that other Union landings might be attempted on the middle Texas coast. Magruder requested that Green's cavalry be returned to aid in the defense of Galveston.

While Green was in Texas, Kirby Smith recommended that Green be promoted major general. In making the recommendation, Smith described Green as "a rising officer" who "has displayed greater ability and military genius than any officer of his grade in the department." Green received news of the recommendation on February 14, 1864, and, as was the custom in the Trans Mississippi, assumed his duties as major general at once.[127]

In March Green was ordered back to Louisiana to assist Richard Taylor in blocking a major Union offensive by Nathaniel P. Banks up the Red River. Taylor believed he must attack Banks as early as possible. Once Green and his cavalry joined him, Taylor planned a full-scale assault on the advanced elements of Banks' army.

The first of Green's cavalry reached Taylor near Mansfield, Louisiana, on April 4, with other units arriving during the next two days. On the afternoon of April 8, Taylor attacked Banks at Sabine Crossroads near Mansfield. In the attack Green's cavalry division, consisting of brigades led by James P. Major and William P. Hardeman, was on the extreme Confederate left. The battle itself was a major Confederate victory as Taylor's troops swept the field and Union forces retreated toward Pleasant Hill.[128]

The Confederates pursued Banks' army as it fell back to Pleasant Hill, fifteen miles away. Late in the afternoon on April 9, Taylor attacked once again. The initial Confederate assault was successful as the Union left flank gave ground, but resistance stiffened as the battle continued. In the fighting on the Confederate left, regiments of Green's cavalry commanded by Xavier Debray and August Buchel encountered heavy enemy fire. Buchel wanted to pull his troops back to avoid heavy casualties, but Green, believing the enemy was retreating, ordered the attack to continue. Dozens of Confederate cavalrymen, including Buchel, were killed or mortally wounded in the charge.[129]

It still appeared that Taylor's troops would triumph again when Union reserves struck at the Confederate right flank. The outnumbered Rebels gave ground, leaving their left flank exposed. Only fierce fighting by Horace Randal's and Thomas Waul's brigades prevented a major defeat. As darkness approached, the Confederates withdrew from the field. The Federals, themselves exhausted, made no attempt to pursue.[130]

Although he had held his ground at Pleasant Hill, Banks determined to continue his withdrawal back to the Red River. Richard Taylor wanted to resume the attack the next day but Kirby Smith, his departmental commander, was more concerned about the advance of Union forces into southern Arkansas. To meet this threat Smith ordered two of Taylor's three infantry divisions north to Arkansas. With the forces left to him, Polignac's infantry division and Green's cavalry, Taylor attempted to prevent Banks' withdrawal down the river. On April 12 Texas cavalry and a small artillery battery commanded by Green opened fire on Union gunboats at Blair's Landing on the river. In a two-hour exchange of fire, both Confederates and Federals suffered numerous casualties. Among the Confederate dead was Tom Green, hit by a piece of grapeshot which tore away part of his skull, killing him instantly. As darkness fell the Confederates, now led by James P. Major, withdrew from the field.[131]

The death of Tom Green was a serious blow to the Confederates. General Taylor described his death as "a public calamity and mourned as such by the people of Texas and Louisiana." He would also note of Green: "His men adored him and would follow him wherever he led." Taylor wrote in his memoirs another description of Tom Green: "Upright, modest, and with the simplicity of a child, danger seemed to be his element and he rejoiced in combat." At his funeral held in the State Capitol, Governor Pendleton Murrah praised Green as the savior of Texas.[132]

Green, veteran of San Jacinto, Indian campaigns, the Mexican War and the Civil War, and most beloved of all Texas Confederates, was buried in the family plot in Oakwood Cemetery at Austin as he had earlier requested. Tom Green County was later named for him.

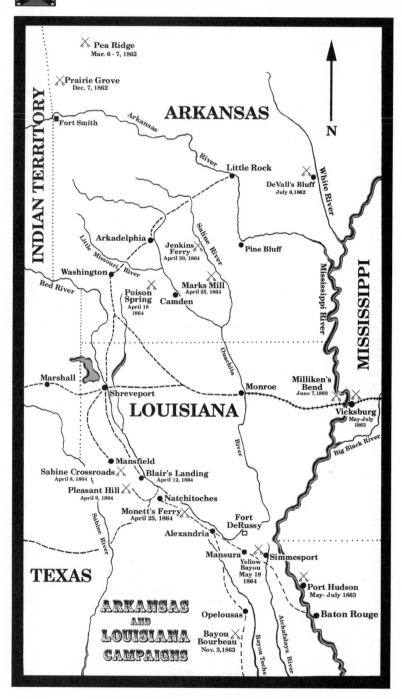

ARKANSAS

Pea Ridge
Mar. 6 - 7, 1862

Prairie Grove
Dec. 7, 1862

Fort Smith

Arkansas

River

Little Rock

DeVall's Bluff
July 6, 1862

White River

INDIAN TERRITORY

Arkadelphia

Jenkins
Ferry
April 30, 1864

Sabine River

Pine Bluff

Little Missouri River

Washington

Red River

Poison
Spring
April 18
1864

Marks Mill
April 25, 1864

Camden

Ouachita

Mississippi River

MISSISSIPPI

Marshall

Shreveport

Monroe

Milliken's
Bend
June 7, 1863

Vicksburg
May-July
1863

LOUISIANA

River

Big Black River

Mansfield

Sabine Crossroads
April 8, 1864

Blair's Landing
April 12, 1864

Pleasant Hill
April 9, 1864

Natchitoches

Monett's Ferry
April 23, 1864

Fort
DeRussy

Alexandria

Sabine River

Mansura

Yellow
Bayou
May 18
1864

Simmesport

TEXAS

Port Hudson
May- July 1863

ARKANSAS
AND
LOUISIANA
CAMPAIGNS

Opelousas

Bayou
Bourbeau
Nov. 3, 1863

Bayou Teche

Atchafalaya River

Baton Rouge

ARTHUR PENDLETON BAGBY

Arthur Pendleton Bagby was the sixth Texan to be appointed major general in the Civil War. Bagby, born on May 17, 1833, in Claiborne County, Alabama, was the only individual named first to the rank of brigadier general and then to major general by Edmund Kirby Smith but never approved for either rank by President Davis or the Confederate Senate.

Arthur Pendleton Bagby
—Courtesy of Harold B. Simpson
Research Center, Hillsboro, Texas

Bagby's father, a native of Virginia, was a prominent political leader in Alabama who served several terms in the state legislature prior to his election as governor in 1837. In 1841 the elder Bagby was elected to the United States Senate, taking his family with him to the nation's capital. In 1848 President Polk named the senior Bagby as minister to Russia. That same year young Arthur Bagby was appointed to the United States Military Academy.

Bagby graduated from West Point near the bottom of his class in his nineteenth year, 1852. As a second lieutenant in the infantry he served at Fort Columbus, New York, from 1852 to 1853. He was stationed briefly at Fort Chadbourne, Texas, in 1853, but resigned from the army in September. He returned to Alabama, where he studied law. He was admitted to the Alabama bar in 1855 and began his practice in Mobile, where his father then resided. In 1858, apparently due to despondency over the death of his father, Bagby moved to Gonzales, Texas. There he married Frances Taylor in June 1860.[133]

With the outbreak of the Civil War, Bagby raised a company of volunteers in Lavaca and Victoria counties. When Henry H. Sibley formed his brigade in October 1861, Bagby became a major in the Seventh Texas Mounted Volunteers commanded by another West Point graduate, William Steele (class of 1840). Bagby remained in San Antonio with Colonel Steele as the regiment completed its organization in October and November. On December 15 Bagby led the last four companies of the regiment out of San Antonio on the march to New Mexico.[134]

Bagby saw little fighting in the New Mexico campaign. While the Fourth and Fifth Cavalry and several companies of the Seventh marched north toward Albuquerque and Santa Fe, Bagby remained with Steele and four companies guarding the Mesilla Valley. Following the death of the regiment's executive officer, Lt. Col. John Sutton, at Valverde, Bagby was promoted to the rank of lieutenant colonel on April 4, 1862.

Occupation duty in New Mexico was boring to Bagby and other Confederates. Many of the officers turned to alcohol to relieve the tedium and monotony. On April 16, two weeks after his promotion, Bagby became so intoxicated while serving as officer of the day at the camp near Dona Ana that he could not perform his duties. While in this condition he drew his pistol on another officer. The officer subsequently filed charges against Bagby for drunkenness and misconduct while on duty. When Bagby sobered up he submitted his resignation, rather than face the embarrassment of a court-martial.

Bagby's commanding officer, Colonel Steele, authorized Bagby to return to Gonzales while he awaited action by President Davis concerning the resignation. In August 1862 the War Department informed Bagby that his resignation was not accepted and that he must face a court of inquiry. This court, with Tom Green as presiding officer, met in Austin on September 15, 1862. After hearing the evidence the court found Bagby not guilty of the charges and ordered him reassigned to his regiment.[135]

The charges against Bagby did not hurt his army career. After Colonel Steele was promoted to brigadier general in the autumn of 1862, Bagby was promoted to colonel and commanding officer of the Seventh Cavalry. Along with Tom Green, commander of the Fifth Cavalry, Bagby volunteered his regiment for service in Magruder's attack on Federal forces occupying Galveston. Although he and 100 of his men were on board the *Neptune* when she was hit by fire from the *Harriet Lane*, Bagby was uninjured. Bagby, like Green, was praised by General Magruder in his official report of the battle.[136]

In mid-January, 1863, Bagby's regiment, along with other units of the Sibley Brigade, was ordered to join Richard Taylor's army in the Louisiana bayou country. Bagby and his cavalry received praise for their performance in the battles at Bisland and Irish Bend. In the fighting on April 13, Bagby and his troops defended the left flank of Taylor's line against a powerful enemy assault. Although heavily outnumbered, the Texans held the line until dusk, allowing the Confederates time to withdraw from the field. Bagby, who was wounded in the arm, was lauded by both Generals Taylor and Alfred Mouton. In his official report Mouton, who commanded the left side of Taylor's army, cited "the gallant and chivalric Bagby" and his "handful of heroes" for preventing a major Union victory.[137]

In the early summer of 1863 Bagby was in command of the Confederate post at Shreveport while he recovered from his wound. He rejoined Taylor's army later that summer and participated in the autumn campaigns along the Bayou Teche. When Tom Green was given command of the cavalry division under Taylor, Bagby succeeded Green as commander of the old Sibley Brigade. In the Confederate victories at Stirling's Plantation and Bayou Bourbeau, Bagby led his brigade in what Richard Taylor described as "brilliant charges."[138]

The threat of a Union attack on the coastline brought Bagby and his brigade back to Texas in December 1863. The brigade returned to Louisiana in early April to meet Banks' advance up the Red River. In the battle at Mansfield the brigade fought dismounted on the left flank as part of a division commanded by James P. Major. The following day at Pleasant Hill, Bagby and his troops were again on the left wing of the army. When Banks continued his withdrawal toward the Mississippi, Bagby was ordered to attack the Union fleet at Grand Bayou; however, the Union vessels passed before Bagby arrived. Bagby hoped to join Tom Green in an atttack on the Union fleet at Blair's Landing the following day, but the lack of a pontoon bridge delayed Bagby at Bayou Pierre. He reached Blair's Landing after Green was killed and the fighting had ended.[139]

General Taylor remained determined to prevent the withdrawal of Banks' army. He planned to attack as Banks attempted to cross the Cane River at Monett's Ferry. He ordered Brig. Gen. Hamilton P. Bee, with cavalry brigades commanded by Bagby, Major, and Debray, to move downstream past Banks' army and occupy the bluffs on the south side of the Cane River commanding the crossing at Monett's Ferry. Bee was to delay the Federals while Taylor brought the rest of his army up to attack Banks from the rear.

Bagby's Brigade was on the right of Bee's forces at Monett's Ferry. Major held the center and Debray commanded the left flank. When the Union army made a major assault on the left flank, Bee, apparently supported by his senior brigade commanders Bagby and Major, ordered a withdrawal, allowing Banks' army to continue its move toward Alexandria.[140]

General Taylor blamed Bee for the escape of the Union army. In early May he relieved Bee of his command and appointed Bagby to succeed him. Bagby, who had been named brigadier general by Kirby Smith on April 13, led the division in continuing attacks on the Federals as they marched toward Simmesport. On May 18 the division took part in two unsuccessful assaults on the Union army at Yellow Bayou.[141]

During the summer of 1864, Bagby's cavalry defended the Atchafalaya line from Union attack. In late August Bagby was ordered to southwestern Arkansas to support Sam Maxey's forces defending the region while Sterling Price led other Confederate cavalry in a major raid into Missouri. Following Price's return to Arkansas, Bagby and his cavalry resumed their duties in northern Louisiana. Bagby made his headquarters near Alexandria during the winter months of 1864-1865. In April the division fell back toward Natchitoches in western Louisiana, where it remained until the final surrender.[142]

Although Bagby acted as a brigadier general for more than a year, his promotion was never approved by the Richmond government. On May 16, 1865, two weeks before the Trans Mississippi Department surrender, Kirby Smith named Bagby, still technically a colonel, major general. Like the earlier promotion to brigadier, this promotion had no official sanction of the (now defunct) Confederate government.[143]

Bagby resumed his law practice after the war. He worked briefly as assistant editor of the *Victoria Advocate* as well. When he died at Hallettsville in his eighty-eighth year on February 21, 1921, he was one of the last surviving Confederate generals. He was buried in Hallettsville City Cemetery.[144]

CHAPTER FOUR

Brigadiers of the
Trans Mississippi

TWENTY-ONE OF THE thirty-six Texans who served as brigadier generals during the Civil War performed their primary military service west of the Mississippi River.[1] Fifteen of these twenty-one individuals served their entire Civil War careers in the Trans Mississippi; six others (Richard Gano, Elkanah Greer, Joseph Hogg, Walter P. Lane, Sam Maxey, and Thomas N. Waul) saw some duty east of the Mississippi but spent more of their time in the Trans Mississippi. Three of these western brigadiers, Arthur P. Bagby, Tom Green, and Sam Maxey, were appointed major general by departmental commander Kirby Smith but not confirmed by the Confederate president and Senate.[2]

Three other Texans, John A. Wharton, M. D. Ector, and Lawrence S. Ross, served part of their Civil War careers west of the river but are best known for their activities in the Confederate heartland between the Mississippi and the Carolinas.[3]

ARTHUR PENDLETON BAGBY

(See Chapter Three for biographical information.)

114

HAMILTON PRIOLEAU BEE

Hamilton Prioleau Bee, successful planter and longtime public servant in Texas, is remembered primarily by Civil War students for

Hamilton Prioleau Bee
—Courtesy of Harold B. Simpson Research Center, Hillsboro, Texas

his role in the battle at Monett's Ferry, Louisiana, on April 23, 1864. Heavily outnumbered by Federal forces, Bee withdrew from a strong position over-looking the Cane River crossing. His action al-lowed Union troops under Nathaniel P. Banks to con-tinue their retreat toward the Red River and spoiled Richard Taylor's plans for a major assault. Taylor, commander of Confeder-ate forces in western Lou-isiana, blamed Bee for the escape of Banks' army. Bee was relieved of his com-mand and returned to Texas. Although he was later reassigned to com-mand a brigade in Indian Territory, Bee spent the rest of the war under a cloud of suspicion.[4]

The son of Anne and Barnard E. Bee, Hamilton P. Bee was born in Charleston, South Carolina, on July 22, 1822. His father was active in South Carolina politics prior to moving to Texas in 1832. The family joined the father in Texas several years later. Barnard Bee held several offices in the Republic of Texas. Young Hamilton, then only seventeen, was almost immediately involved in public affairs, being appointed secretary of the commission to determine the boundary between Texas and Louisiana. Four years later Bee was one of three commissioners named by President

Houston to convene a peace council with the Comanches. Bee's father returned to South Carolina after the annexation of Texas, but Hamilton remained in Texas. In 1846 he became secretary of the Texas Senate.[5]

During the Mexican War, Bee served briefly as a private in Ben McCulloch's company in Jack Hays' First Regiment, Texas Mounted Volunteers. He transferred as a lieutenant to Mirabeau B. Lamar's Texas cavalry in October 1846. After the war, Bee settled in Laredo as a merchant. He served in the Texas House of Representatives from 1849 to 1858. In 1855-1856 he was Speaker of the Texas House.

He married Mildred Tarver of Alabama in 1854; the couple had six children. Bee retired from politics in 1858 and settled at Woodstock, a plantation on the San Antonio River in Goliad County. In 1860 he possessed slightly more than $100,000 in property, including sixty-seven slaves.[6]

With the outbreak of the Civil War, Bee was almost immediately involved with military duties. In June 1861 Governor Clark appointed him brigadier general in the state militia, with responsibilities for the 29th Militia District, a ten-county area in South Texas. Later that summer Clark named Bee as one of six purchasing agents charged with procuring arms for Texas troops. Bee succeeded in making contracts with two firms in Mexico, but the state's inability to use U.S. bonds for the purchase negated the sale.[7]

On March 6, 1862, Bee was appointed brigadier general in the Confederate army with date of rank on March 4. As his military experience was limited, the appointment to general officer rank at this early date was probably due to his political connections. He was assigned as commander of the Rio Grande military sub-district, a vast area which included all of Texas south of San Antonio. Bee made his headquarters at Brownsville, where he used his familiarity with the people, their customs and language in an effort to bring some order to the region. Bee struggled to regulate the export of cotton in exchange for imported weapons and ammunition while at the same time providing military defense for the sub-district, which "had become a swirling mass of speculators, bandits, Unionists, deserters, spies, and Confederate agents."[8]

Life in South Texas changed abruptly in the autumn of 1863. On November 3 the first of 7,000 Union troops under the command of Nathaniel P. Banks landed at the mouth of the Rio Grande.

Bee, who had only a handful of men to assist him, ordered evacuation of Brownsville. Under his supervision forty-five wagons of valuable supplies were moved into the interior, saving millions of dollars for the Confederacy. Cotton and other goods that could not be moved were set afire as the Confederates withdrew. The fire grew out of control and burned an entire block of buildings along the river.[9]

Bee was relieved of his duties as sub-district commander in January and given command of a newly formed Texas cavalry brigade. Later that month the new brigade was ordered to join Richard Taylor's army in northwestern Louisiana. Bee and his cavalry arrived in Louisiana in early April. Because of his early date of rank, Bee was given command of a cavalry division consisting of brigades headed by Xavier Debray and August Buchel, both more experienced in military matters than Bee.

The new division saw action almost immediately. As Banks' Union army moved toward Shreveport, Taylor planned a major assault. Bee's cavalry skirmished with the advanced units of the Federal forces near Pleasant Hill on April 7 while Taylor prepared his troops to meet the Union army at Mansfield the next day. In the battle that took place near Mansfield on April 8, Bee's cavalry was on the extreme right flank next to Walker's infantry division. Gen. Alfred Mouton's infantry began the Confederate attack on the left. Then Walker moved forward while Confederate cavalry under Tom Green on the left and Bee on the right attempted to swing around the Federal flanks. After being repulsed several times, the Confederates broke the Union lines and pushed Banks' army back. Darkness and the arrival of fresh Federal troops halted the Confederate advance near a small orchard known as Pleasant Grove.[10]

During the night Banks withdrew his army from Pleasant Grove. Taylor ordered his troops to pursue the Federals. Late on the afternoon of April 9, Taylor attacked Banks at Pleasant Hill, fourteen miles south of Mansfield. This time Bee's cavalry and Walker's infantry were on the Confederate left. After the Confederates under Thomas Churchill opened the attack on the Union left, Walker's infantry advanced while Bee, with Debray's and Buchel's cavalry, charged from the north. Bee took command of Buchel's cavalry when Buchel was mortally wounded. Bee had two horses shot from under him and was wounded in the face, but continued to fight until it was apparent the Confederate attack would not succeed.[11]

That night most of Taylor's army fell back several miles to where they could find water and forage. Taylor and Bee, with part of Debray's cavalry, remained near the battlefield, and were joined later that evening by departmental commander Kirby Smith. The three men had coffee at Bee's campfire and discussed the next course of action.[12]

Bee was pleased with himself. He had led troops in battle for two days and handled himself with what General Taylor described as "coolness and pluck." In addition, he had discussed high strategy and tactics with the two senior generals when Kirby Smith visited his camp. Although Gen. John Walker would later criticize Bee severely for his failure to advance more rapidly at Mansfield and Pleasant Hill, Bee was convinced that he and his men had performed well.[13]

Even though Banks held off the Confederates at Pleasant Hill, the Union army continued to fall back toward Alexandria. Taylor, whose army was reduced in size by the transfer of Walker's and Churchill's infantry divisions to Arkansas, attempted to prevent Banks' withdrawal. When Tom Green was killed at Blair's Landing on April 12, command of the cavalry corps passed temporarily to Bee until John A. Wharton arrived and assumed command.

Banks' army, meanwhile, was moving south. Taylor planned to attack the Federals from all sides as they attempted to cross the Cane River at Monett's Ferry. Bee, with 2,000 cavalry and four batteries of artillery, was ordered to move downstream past Banks' army and occupy the south side of the Cane River commanding the crossing at Monett's Ferry. Taylor hoped that Bee, holding a strong position, could delay Banks' troops until other Confederates attacked from the rear. It was here, on April 23, that Bee, heavily outnumbered and fearing that he was being outflanked, ordered a retreat. As a result Banks' army crossed the Cane and continued its withdrawal to the south.[14]

Although the Confederate cavalry continued to harass Banks' retreating army in late April and early May, Bee's days as cavalry commander under Taylor were numbered. Taylor blamed Bee for allowing Banks to escape. While acknowledging Bee's "great personal gallantry," Taylor faulted Bee for failing to construct breastworks, for massing his forces in the center instead of on the flanks, and for sending A. W. Terrell's Brigade to look after the supply base when this had already been taken care of. On May 14 Bee was relieved of his command and ordered to report to departmental headquarters at Shreveport.[15]

Bee was stunned by Taylor's action. He believed that the enemy force at Monett's was so large that his cavalry would have been overrun had he attempted to hold his position. In this opinion he was supported by other cavalry officers, including John A. Wharton, A. P. Bagby, and James P. Major, who expressed their willingness to make public statements supporting Bee's actions. Bee wrote Kirby Smith requesting a court of inquiry to investigate his actions at Monett's Ferry. Smith, who disagreed with Taylor on a number of military matters, was sympathetic to Bee but dismissed the need for a court of inquiry.[16]

Bee never received his court of inquiry. He returned to Texas, where he served as an area commander during the summer and fall of 1864. In February 1865 he was assigned to command a cavalry division under John A. Wharton. In April he was given an infantry brigade in a new division created for Sam Maxey. In the closing days of the war Bee was assigned to command a cavalry corps.[17]

After the war Bee and his family moved to Mexico, where they lived until 1876 when they relocated in San Antonio. Bee died from heart disease on October 2, 1897, and was buried in the Confederate cemetery in San Antonio.[18]

XAVIER DEBRAY

Xavier Debray, who commanded one of Bee's cavalry brigades in the Louisiana campaigns, was born on January 25, 1818, in Epinal, France. Information on his early life, based on what he told contemporaries, is sketchy and contradictory. In her 1940 book *Foreigners in the Confederacy*, Ella Lonn stated that Debray attended the prestigious French military academy St. Cyr and that he later served in the French diplomatic corps. Bruce Allardice, author of *More Generals in Gray*, doubted he did either. He does believe that Debray attended a national college in Paris and that during the Revolution of 1848 wrote political pamphlets which angered the government, forcing him to immigrate to the United States.[19]

According to his own account, Debray landed in New York City on September 25, 1848. He arrived at San Antonio sometime later, published a Spanish newspaper, *El Bejareno*, and was naturalized. He moved to Austin, where he worked as a translator of Spanish documents for the General Land Office. In the late 1850s he established and operated an academy.[20]

When Texas seceded from the Union, Debray joined the Tom Green Rifles, a Travis County company of volunteers, as first lieutenant. In early summer Governor Clark made Debray a military aide on his staff. In August 1861 Debray was chosen as

Xavier Debray
(photo taken after war)
—Courtesy of Harold B. Simpson
Research Center, Hillsboro, Texas

major of the newly formed Second Texas Infantry, commanded by Col. John C. Moore. When a new cavalry battalion lost its commander in December, Debray replaced him. Debray was chosen its colonel when the battalion was expanded to regiment strength (the Twenty-sixth Texas Cavalry).[21]

Debray's regiment spent the spring and summer of 1862 on garrison duty along the middle Texas coast. On two occasions the regiment was alerted to move, first to the Mississippi and later to New Mexico, but the fall of New Orleans to the Federal fleet and the failure of Sibley's New Mexico campaign caused both movements to be canceled. The regiment was camped along the San Bernard River during much of the summer. As Debray later wrote, "nothing happened for several months to break the monotony of camp life, except patrols on the coast on which duty landing parties from the blockading squadron in search of fresh meat, were captured or otherwise punished."[22]

In July 1862 Debray was appointed commander of the military sub-district of Houston. During the next several months he shifted forces around to deal with the increased number of Union naval raids. In December Debray assisted the newly arrived commander of the Texas district, Maj. Gen. John B. Magruder, in planning the recapture of Galveston. When Magruder launched his assault on the morning of January 1, Debray led his Twenty-sixth Texas in the attack along the waterfront. In his official report, Magruder cited Debray for his "coolness and courage" under enemy fire.[23]

Debray spent most of 1863 as commander of the Galveston defenses. Magruder was concerned that the Union would make an effort to recapture the island, so extensive efforts were made to strengthen the city's defenses. Debray and Magruder apparently worked well together; in May, Magruder appointed Debray acting brigadier general while seeking confirmation of the promotion by the Confederate government. When Federal troops occupied the lower Texas coast in November 1863, Magruder appointed Debray commander of a cavalry brigade stationed near the mouth of Caney Creek.[24]

Magruder fully expected the Union army to make a major assault near Caney Creek early in 1864. Suddenly, the Union threat disappeared. The Federal high command shifted its attention from the Texas coast to a move up the Red River in Louisiana. Union troops that had occupied Brownsville, Indianola, and Matagorda island in the winter months were transferred to General Banks' army in Louisiana. To meet the Union threat there, the Confederate command stripped Texas of most of its troops and sent them to Louisiana.

Debray and his brigade, consisting of the Twenty-third, Twenty-sixth, and Thirtieth cavalry regiments, were ordered to Louisiana. Debray reached Taylor's army on April 2. For the next several days Debray's cavalry, along with a brigade of fellow Texans commanded by A. P. Bagby, skirmished with the enemy. On April 8 Debray's Brigade, now part of Hamilton Bee's Division, was on the right wing of Taylor's army in the Battle of Mansfield. The following day at Pleasant Hill the brigade was under heavy fire as Debray led them in a charge along the Mansfield Road. Debray's right leg was injured and he lost a boot when his horse was killed in the charge. As Debray limped back to the Confederate line, he met General Taylor. "Why, Colonel, are you wounded?" inquired the General.

"No, General," answered Debray, "I am slightly hurt, but as you may see, I was sent on a bootless errand."

"Never mind your boot," said Taylor, "You have won your spurs."[25]

On April 13, 1864, four days after the Battle of Pleasant Hill, Kirby Smith assigned Debray duties as brigadier general. Although the appointment was never confirmed by the Davis administration, Debray peformed duties as brigadier general for the rest of the war. His brigade was part of Bee's cavalry division as the Confederates harassed Banks' retreating army in late April and May. The brigade was on the left flank of Bee's cavalry at Monett's Ferry, when ordered to fall back after Union troops crossed upriver. The brigade was on the Confederate right in the futile Confederate attack at Yellow Bayou on May 18.

After the end of the Red River campaign, Debray and his brigade moved about in western Louisiana, camping wherever food for man and forage for horses could be found. In October the brigade was assigned to guard the Confederate line along the Atchafalaya River. There, according to Debray, "bad rations, scanty forage, malarial fevers and camp diseases, the absence of medical stores, and worn out clothing and blankets caused much suffering and misery, nearly destroying the efficiency of the brigade."[26]

Debray received orders in December 1864 to lead his brigade back to Texas, where more food and forage could be found. The brigade moved slowly through East Texas, reaching the Brazos near Richmond at the end of March. In the closing days of the war the brigade was ordered to Houston.

Debray remained in Houston for two years after the war. In 1867 he moved to Galveston, where he served as an accountant for the Produce Exchange. In 1871 he was elected as a delegate to the Tax Payers' Convention in Austin. After serving a term as city councilman in Galveston, he moved to Austin in 1877 and resumed his old job as translator of Spanish documents for the General Land Office. He died January 6, 1895, and is buried in the Texas State Cemetery.[27]

RICHARD MONTGOMERY GANO

Born in Bourbon County, Kentucky, on June 17, 1830, Richard Montgomery Gano was one of two Texas physicians who became Confederate generals. Gano received his medical training at Louisville University Medical School. He practiced medicine in Kentucky and Louisiana for eight years. In 1853 he married Martha J. Welch of Crab Orchard, Kentucky. The couple had twelve children, nine of whom lived to maturity.

Richard Montgomery Gano
—Courtesy of Harold B. Simpson Research Center, Hillsboro, Texas

In 1859 the Gano family moved to Texas and settled in Grapevine Prairie in Tarrant County, where Gano farmed, raised horses and cattle, and practiced medicine. When Indians raided the area, Gano helped raise a company of volunteers and led them in pursuit of the raiders. In 1860 he was elected to the state legislature representing Tarrant County.[28]

At the beginning of the Civil War, Gano organized two companies of Texas cavalry at the request of his friend Albert Sidney Johnston. The two companies, known as Gano's Texas Cavalry Battalion or Gano's Squadron, were ordered to Chattanooga for service with John Hunt Morgan. Gano, then a major, joined Morgan in time to participate in the Kentucky raid of July 4-28, 1862 (Morgan's 1st Raid), in which the Confederate cavalry covered over 1,000 miles, captured and paroled more than 1,200 prisoners, and did much damage to Federal morale. In the course of the raid Gano's cavalry played a key role in destroying the bridge on the Kentucky Central Railroad to prevent Union troops from Cincinnati reaching Lexington. Gano and his cavalry also took part in an engagement at Cynthiana, in which the enemy was driven from the town and the Confederates took more than 400 prisoners.[29]

During the late summer and fall Morgan's Brigade continued to make raids on Union supply lines in Tennessee and Kentucky. Gano's cavalry was in the thick of the fighting. After an engagement at Gallatin, Tennessee, in late August, Morgan lauded the Texans as "a small body of men commanded by Major Gano, of whom I cannot speak too highly, as they have distinguished themselves ever since they joined my command, not only by their bravery, but their good, soldier-like conduct."[30]

Gano was promoted to colonel following the fighting at Gallatin and named commander of the Seventh Kentucky Cavalry, which included his two Texas companies. In October Gano's regiment was part of Morgan's cavalry that moved into Kentucky with Braxton Bragg and Kirby Smith. Morgan's assignment was to delay the movement of Don Carlos Buell's Union army by disrupting transportation and communication. Gano's regiment was particularly effective in this campaign, burning several bridges along the Louisville and Nashville and the Edgefield and Kentucky railroads.[31]

In December Morgan led his raiders in what came to be known as "the Christmas raid." Once again the objective was the line of supply and communication for the Union army in Tennessee, now commanded by William S. Rosecrans. And once again Morgan's troopers, now organized into two brigades, did an effective job in destroying enemy property.

Gano's service with Morgan came to an end in late spring, 1863. His health had been poor throughout the winter months; in April he was diagnosed as having "valvular heart disease with hypertrophy" and pronounced unfit for active duty. Gano returned to Texas to recuperate. Basil W. Duke, who was second in command to Morgan, lamented Gano's departure. "[N]o officer had won more and better merited distinction, and his popularity was justly very great," wrote Duke.[32]

Gano recovered sufficiently from his illness so that in July 1863 he accepted assignment as commander of all Texas state cavalry. General Magruder, Confederate commander in Texas, was delighted that Gano was willing to take command of the mounted state troops who had been called into service by Governor Lubbock to supplement Confederate forces defending the state.[33]

Gano's service in organizing and training state troops was brief. In October 1863 he was given command of a brigade of Texas Confederate cavalry and ordered to report to Brig. Gen. William Steele in Indian Territory. Confederate authorities hoped that Gano and his brigade could help Steele recover some of the Indian Territory lost earlier in the year to Union forces commanded by Maj. Gen. James G. Blunt. Unfortunately, the Texas brigade, which was in a rebellious state when Gano took command, was in no condition to be of much military value. Many of the troops were unarmed and all were poorly fed and clothed. Much of Gano's time in November and December was spent in attempting to correct these problems. In addition, desertion and illness reduced the numbers of men available. Although he left Texas with 1,500 men, Gano reported only 946 present for duty on December 31, 1863.[34]

The new year brought new hopes as well as new challenges. Sam Maxey, a fellow North Texan, replaced Steele as Indian Territory commander. More enthusiastic and vigorous than his predecessor, Maxey took up the task of improving Confederate fortunes in Indian Territory. In spring 1864 Maxey was called upon to assist Sterling Price in blocking Union movements in southern Arkansas. Maxey, two regiments of Indian troops, and Gano's Brigade joined Confederate forces in southern Arkansas near Prairie D'Ane in early April. On April 18, Maxey and Missouri general John S. Marmaduke defeated Union forces at Poison Spring, just west of Camden. Charles DeMorse, colonel of the Twenty-ninth Texas Cavalry, commanded the brigade in the fighting at Poison Spring in place of Gano, who had been wounded several days earlier in a skirmish at Munn's Mill.[35]

With the Union threat to Arkansas checked, Maxey and Gano returned to their duties in Indian Territory. In September 1864 Gano commanded a large cavalry force consisting of his own brigade, Stand Watie's Indian Brigade, Daniel McIntosh's Brigade, and a Seminole Indian battalion, in what Maxey called "one of the most brilliant and skillfully managed cavalry raids of the war." After crossing the Canadian and Arkansas rivers, Gano's troops destroyed tons of hay being cut and stacked for Federal livestock near

Fort Gibson. Then, learning that a large Union supply train was in the northeastern corner of the Indian Territory, Gano and Stand Watie moved their horsemen to Cabin Creek, where they quietly encircled the Union wagons. In the early morning of September 19 the Confederates attacked the surprised Federals. One hundred twenty Union wagons loaded with supplies valued at more than a million dollars were captured. Dozens of other wagons were burned. Confederate losses were minimal, but Gano's left arm was broken by an enemy bullet.[36]

The Cabin Creek raid was Gano's most successful, and last, large operation. In October his brigade was ordered into the southeastern corner of Indian Territory to support Sterling Price's troops as they retreated from their unsuccessful raid into Missouri. In late January 1865 the brigade was transferred, over Maxey's protest, from Indian Territory and placed under Hamilton P. Bee in Rusk, Texas. On March 18, Gano, who had been assigned duties as a general officer for a year, was officially promoted to brigadier general.[37]

After the war Gano moved back to his native Kentucky for a brief period, but returned to Texas in 1866. He became a minister in the Christian Church, serving in that capacity for forty-five years. He raised and imported livestock as well and was president of the Estado Land and Cattle Company. He was active in the United Confederate Veterans and the prohibition movement. He died in Dallas of uremic poisoning on March 27, 1913, and is buried in the Oakland Cemetery of Dallas.[38]

THOMAS GREEN

(See Chapter Three for biographical information.)

ELKANAH BRACKIN GREER

Elkanah Brackin Greer was born on October 11, 1825, in Paris, Tennessee. His family moved to Mississippi when he was still a youth and Greer grew up in that state. When the Mexican War began, he joined the First Mississippi Rifles commanded by Jefferson Davis. He participated in the battles of Monterrey and Buena Vista

Elkanah Brackin Greer

—Courtesy of Harold B. Simpson
Research Center, Hillsboro, Texas

and after the war was a general officer in the Mississippi militia. In 1848 Greer moved to Marshall, Texas, where he became a merchant, planter, and lawyer. In 1851 he returned briefly to Tennessee, where he married Anna Holcombe; the couple subsequently had four children.

An ardent states' rights Democrat, Greer became Grand Commander of the Texas Knights of the Golden Circle in 1859. He organized support for the filibustering program of the Knights and in February 1860 offered Governor Sam Houston a regiment of mounted volunteers for a projected invasion of Mexico. As a delegate to the Democratic national convention in Charleston, he bolted the party rather than support Stephen A. Douglas. He worked for John C. Breckinridge's election as president, and when Abraham Lincoln was elected he spoke out in favor of secession.[39]

Once Texas seceded from the Union, Greer traveled to Montgomery, Alabama, where he received one of the first colonelcies from the Confederate provisional government. He then returned to Texas to recruit and organize a cavalry regiment. Greer intended the unit to be used to liberate Kansas from abolitionist control; thus the regiment was called the South Kansas-Texas Cavalry. Made up of men from East Texas, the regiment was mustered into Confederate service at Dallas in June 1861, and officially became the Third Texas Cavalry. Serving under Greer as officers were two future Confederate generals—W. P. Lane and M. D. Ector. A third officer, Hinche P. Mabry, was acting general in the later stages of the war.[40]

In July 1861 the Third Texas rode north to join Ben McCulloch's Army of the West near Fort Smith, Arkansas. When McCulloch's army moved into southern Missouri to support Sterling Price, Greer and the Texans rode ahead as the vanguard of the army, reaching Wilson's Creek on the evening of August 7. In the battle that took place on August 10, the Third Texas was on the left flank of the Confederate line. About 10:00 A.M. as the battle raged, Greer's mounted troops slipped around the Federal line and charged. There was much confusion as a result of the dense undergrowth of the terrain. Although Greer and his men were driven back, the charge did divert Federal attention long enough to give the Confederate infantry time to regroup for a new assault on the Union lines. By noon the Union army was beaten and retired toward Springfield.[41]

There was little fighting for Greer and the Third Texas for the next three months. McCulloch initially planned to move the army against the Kansas Jayhawkers, but lack of supplies, a measles epidemic, and renewed Federal activity in Missouri led him to abandon the Kansas move. In November McCulloch went to Richmond to confer with Confederate authorities. Believing there would be no further campaigning that year, Greer took a leave of absence to visit his family. While Greer was on leave, the Third Cavalry was involved in a December attack on the Creek stronghold at Chustenahlah.[42]

Greer and the Third Texas were in McCulloch's Division in the Battle of Pea Ridge, March 7-8, 1862. In the battle Maj. Gen. Earl Van Dorn, who now commanded both McCulloch's and Price's forces, divided his army for an assault against the Union army of Samuel R. Curtis. McCulloch's Division charged the Union left near Leestown while Price followed with an attack on the Union right at Elkhorn Tavern, two miles to the northeast. Although McCulloch drove the enemy back that morning, Union resistance stiffened. Meanwhile, Greer and the Third Texas waited in the rear for orders to charge. Later that afternoon Greer learned that McCulloch and Brig. Gen. James McIntosh had been killed and Col. Louis Hebert, the third ranking officer in the division, was missing and presumed dead. Albert Pike, the next ranking officer, had taken part of the

division toward Elkhorn Tavern. Greer was the senior officer left
on the field. Although he had never commanded anything larger
than his regiment, Greer did the best he could to bring some order
out of the chaos. He soon determined he could not continue the
offensive, and decided to withdraw from the field.[43]

The fighting resumed the next morning. Under orders from
Van Dorn, Greer marched the fragments of McCulloch's Division
to Elkhorn Tavern during the night. However, they arrived in such
poor condition they contributed little to the battle. After a spirited
Union attack in midmorning, Van Dorn broke off the engagement
and retreated southward into the Boston Mountains. Soon thereafter Van Dorn reorganized what remained of his army. McCulloch's Division and Price's Division were merged into one division
under Sterling Price. The division contained four infantry brigades
and two cavalry brigades, one commanded by Greer.[44]

On March 19 Van Dorn received orders to bring his army to
Corinth, Mississippi, where Confederates under Albert Sidney
Johnston were concentrating for an offensive against the Union
army. On March 21 Greer started his troops on the 500-mile journey to Corinth. Because of the need for infantrymen and the lack
of space on the riverboats taking the army across the Mississippi,
Van Dorn ordered his cavalrymen to give up their horses. Although
Greer's Texans regarded this as a breach of contract there was little
they could do. For the time being, at least, the Third Texas Cavalry
was dismounted.

Van Dorn's troops arrived too late to take part in the bloody
fighting at Shiloh, but their presence at Corinth was needed. The
defeated Confederates, now under P. G. T. Beauregard, were falling
back toward the city and required all the assistance they could find.
Van Dorn's army, including the Third Texas, reached Corinth in late
April. Conditions were deplorable as 50,000 men, many wounded at
Shiloh, crowded into the small town. Dysentery and typhoid raged
throughout the camps, and thousands died from disease.[45]

Because a recently passed Confederate law allowed men too
old or too young for conscription to return home, the Third Texas
and other Confederate units at Corinth underwent extensive reorganization in late April and May. More than 200 men of the Third
Texas availed themselves of the opportunity for discharge. In addition a number of officers resigned due to dissatisfaction or ambi-

tion for other commands. Elkanah Greer was one of these. Historian Douglas Hale believed that Greer was unhappy with Van Dorn's self-serving report on the Battle of Pea Ridge. Also, Greer was keenly interested in promotion which was not possible in his present position. Greer left the army and went home. The action must have had some effect; on October 8, 1862, Greer was promoted to brigadier general.[46]

Greer spent the rest of the war as a desk soldier. On June 3, 1863, he was appointed commandant of conscripts for the Trans Mississippi Department with headquarters initially at Shreveport, and later at Marshall. For the next twenty months Greer struggled to administer Confederate conscription laws efficiently and fairly. He enountered a variety of difficulties, particularly in dealing with Texas state officials. Texas enrolled individuals subject to Confederate conscription in the state militia. Greer and District Commander John B. Magruder objected, contending that Confederate laws superseded state laws. Texas Governor Pendleton Murrah was determined to uphold state sovereignty. Department Commander Kirby Smith, who wished to avoid conflict, proposed a compromise whereby the state would retain militiamen already enrolled, provided they be subordinated to Confederate authority in an emergency. Murrah agreed in substance, but refused to concede in the case of militiamen who served in frontier defense companies. In the summer of 1864 Greer attempted to control conscription in these counties, but state authorities refused to budge. Smith agreed to submit this matter to President Davis for a decision, but the war ended before the issue was resolved.[47]

Greer also encountered opposition in his efforts to reduce the number of exemptions Confederate and state officials received for their employees. This resulted in a steady stream of correspondence from quartermasters and others seeking to protect their clerks and agents from conscription. "To add to his unpopularity," wrote Anne J. Bailey, "Greer also had the task of collecting slaves for Confederate use." In December 1864, Kirby Smith requested Greer to furnish four to five thousand slaves for labor on defensive works, an action that did not endear Greer to planters of the region.[48]

Although the inspector general declared that "General Greer appears to be an officer of energy and capacity," the Confederate War Department appointed Francis T. Nicholls to replace the embattled Greer. Kirby Smith objected to the removal, declaring that Greer had "labored zealously, industriously, and intelligently in the discharge of his duties." Smith admitted that Greer had made enemies but argued that in spite of many difficulties his department was a success. "To relieve him by his junior at the moment he is reaping the reward of many months of labor and industry," Smith believed would be unjust.[49]

Unjust or not, the Confederate War Department was insistent that Greer be relieved. In March 1865, Greer was reassigned as commander of the Reserve Corps of Texas, replacing Brig. Gen. Jerome B. Robertson. Kirby Smith expressed his appreciation to Greer for discharge of the onerous duties of the Conscription Bureau, "which, from a state of utter disorganization and confusion, has under his administration been thoroughly and completely systematized."[50]

With the end of the war Greer returned to his home in Marshall. He died while visiting his sister at DeVall's Bluff, Arkansas, on March 27, 1877, and was buried next to his parents at Elmwood Cemetery in Memphis, Tennessee.[51]

WILLIAM POLK HARDEMAN

William Polk Hardeman, known to family and friends as "Gotch," was born in Franklin, Tennessee, on November 4, 1816. His father, Thomas Jones Hardeman, was a veteran of the Battle of New Orleans, a lawyer, and a politician. His mother, Mary Ophelia Polk Hardeman, was an aunt of future U.S. President James K. Polk. Young Hardeman attended the University of Nashville in 1834, but migrated to Texas with his family to settle on Caney Creek in Matagorda County in October 1835.

"Gotch," his four brothers, his father, and uncle were all involved in the Texas Revolution. "Gotch" and his uncle, Bailey Hardeman, joined a group that brought a cannon from Dimitt's Landing to the Texans at Bexar in December 1835. Later "Gotch" and a brother participated in an unsuccessful effort to reinforce the Alamo garrison. Because of an illness young Hardeman missed the Battle of San Jacinto but was in the Texas army during May and June 1836. He later joined "Deaf" Smith's Ranger company in frontier service and was with Col. John H. Moore in his campaign against the Comanches. He was also a member of the Somervell expedition to Laredo in 1842.[52]

With the outbreak of the Mexican War, Hardeman enlisted as a private in Ben McCulloch's spy company. After service in the Monterrey and Buena Vista campaigns he returned to Texas and became a farmer. In February 1848 he married Rebecca A. F. Wilson, the widow of his deceased uncle, Bailey Hardeman. Rebecca died in November 1854, and Hardeman married Sarah Ann Hamilton in December 1857. He had two children by his first wife and five by his second.[53]

William Polk Hardeman
—Courtesy of Harold B. Simpson Research Center, Hillsboro, Texas

Hardeman was a prosperous farmer during the pre-Civil War decade. In 1850, as a resident of Caldwell County, he had property valued at $14,500 and owned sixteen slaves. Ten years later he was living near Seguin in Guadalupe County with real property valued at $25,005 and personal propery at $39,410, including thirty-one slaves.[54]

Like many Texans Hardeman supported secession in 1861. He served as a delegate from Guadalupe County in the Texas convention and voted to separate from the Union. Soon thereafter Hardeman organized a cavalry company composed of men from Guadalupe and Caldwell counties. This unit, subsequently designated as Company A, Fourth Texas Cavalry, and captained by Hardeman, became the first company to join Henry H. Sibley in his efforts to occupy New Mexico. In the Battle of Valverde fought on February 21, 1862, Hardeman and his company took part in the successful charge by the Fourth Cavalry that broke the enemy line. Although slightly wounded at Valverde, Hardeman led his company as it rode north with Sibley's Brigade. Promoted to lieutenant colonel on March 28, Hardeman was in command at Albuquerque in early April when Union general E. R. S. Canby attempted unsuccessfully to drive the Confederates from the town. Later, when Sibley's Brigade retreated from New Mexico, Hardeman led the Fourth Texas on its long journey back to Texas.[55]

After the New Mexico campaign the units of the Sibley Brigade were stationed on the Texas coast. William R. Scurry, commander of the Fourth Texas, was promoted to brigadier general, and Hardeman, promoted to colonel, was given command of the regiment.

Hardeman and the regiment served with Magruder's troops in the Battle of Galveston on January 1, 1863. Soon thereafter the Fourth Texas and other regiments of the Sibley Brigade were ordered to Louisiana to strengthen Richard Taylor in his campaign in the bayou country. In the summer and autumn of 1862 Hardeman and his men participated in battles at Bisland, LaFourche, Fordache, and Bayou Bourbeau. In December the old Sibley Brigade, now commanded by Hardeman, was ordered back to Texas.[56]

Hardeman's Brigade, along with other cavalry commanded by Tom Green, was sent back to Louisiana in March 1864 to assist Richard Taylor in the Red River campaign. In the Battle of Mansfield on April 8 the brigades of James P. Major and Hardeman were in Green's cavalry division on the Confederate left. The following day at Pleasant Hill, Hardeman's cavalry was on the Confederate left. Hardeman's troopers played a key role in preventing Union forces under A. J. Smith from outflanking Mosby Parsons' Missouri Infantry Brigade. In his report of the battle, Parsons expressed his gratitude to "Colonel Hardeman and his gallant band of Texans for their heroic efforts to prevent the enemy from finally flanking my right."[57]

Along with other Confederate cavalry, Hardeman and his men continued to harass Banks' forces as they retreated southward. On May 5 Hardeman's and W. P. Lane's brigades attacked the Union fleet on the Red River near Fort DeRussy, blowing up a gunboat and capturing another gunboat and transport vessel. Four days later a squadron of Hardeman's Brigade skirmished with the northern cavalry south of Alexandria, driving the Federals from the field and taking prisoners.[58]

Hardeman's service in Louisiana earned him the praise of both Generals Taylor and Smith. In late October 1864 Smith recommended Hardeman be promoted to brigadier general, declaring the promotion "is deserved and will give satisfaction." Smith concluded that Hardeman, Xavier Debray, and Walter P. Lane were "the best brigade commanders in the Trans Mississippi."[59]

That October, Hardeman's Brigade was sent to Arkansas to relieve other Confederate cavalry taking part in Sterling Price's raid into Missouri. In late December President Davis approved Hardeman's promotion to brigadier general. Final confirmation by the Confederate Senate came on March 18, 1865, with date of rank from the previous day.[60]

Hardeman and his brigade were ordered to Hempstead, Texas, in late February 1865 as part of an effort to find food and forage for men and horses. After the war ended, Hardeman joined a group of fellow Confederates in Mexico, where he served briefly in Maximilian's army. He returned to Texas in 1866. After farming several years, Hardeman became assistant sergeant-at-arms in the Texas House of Representatives, then state inspector of railroads, and finally superintendent of public buildings and grounds in Austin.

Hardeman died in Austin of Bright's disease on April 8, 1898. He was buried in the Texas State Cemetery.[61]

JAMES EDWARD HARRISON

James Edward Harrison, public official, Confederate general, and prominent Baptist layman, was born in Greenville District, South Carolina, on April 24, 1815. Soon after James' birth the family moved to Jefferson County, Alabama, where his brother, future brigadier general Thomas Harrison, was born. In 1829 the family moved to Monroe County, Mississippi, where Harrison later served two terms in the state senate. In Mississippi he met Mary Evans, whom he married in 1841. Harrison moved to Texas in 1857, settling near Waco. Fluent in the Creek and Choctaw languages, he became Indian commissioner in Texas.[62]

With the outbreak of the Civil War Harrison entered Confed-

James Edward Harrison
(photo taken after war)
—Courtesy of Harold B. Simpson
Research Center, Hillsboro, Texas

erate service as a major in Lt. Col. Joseph W. Speight's First Texas Infantry Battalion. He became a lieutenant colonel in 1862 when the battalion was expanded to become the Fifteenth Texas Infantry. The regiment was assigned to Col. Horace Randal's Brigade. When Speight was named commander of the brigade, Harrison became regimental commander.[63]

The Fifteenth Texas, consisting largely of farmers recruited in Central Texas, marched to Arkansas in the summer of 1862. The regiment and other units of the brigade spent the late summer and autumn in the Little Rock vicinity, but in January 1863 was ordered to join Brig. Gen. William Steele in Indian Territory. The brigade spent the early months of 1863 there. The men of the brigade had little contact with the enemy but suffered from inadequate food, poor clothing, bitterly cold weather, and a variety of illnesses. In an effort to find food and housing, the brigade was constantly on the move.[64]

In April 1863 Speight's Brigade received orders to join Richard Taylor in Louisiana. When the brigade reached Shreveport the condition of the men was so poor that two regiments were held there for additional training, but Harrison's Fifteenth Texas and Lt. Col. George Guess' Thirty-first Texas were sent on to join Taylor in the bayou country. In July Colonel Speight was placed under arrest after a controversy with another officer, and Harrison temporarily became brigade commander.

Under Harrison's leadership, the brigade, strengthened by the addition of Ashley W. Spaight's battalion from the Beaumont area to replace units held at Shreveport, took an active part in Taylor's autumn campaign in the Lafourche district. The brigade suffered heavy casualties in a successful charge on the Federal outpost at Stirling's Plantation in late September. In his official report Tom Green, who directed the operation, praised Harrison for his role in the Confederate victory.[65]

In October 1863, Col. Joseph W. Speight resumed command of the brigade. His command was only brief, however, as the small brigade was soon merged with another brigade led by Camille Armand Jules Marie, Prince de Polignac, a French officer serving in the Confederate army. Polignac was given command of the consolidated brigade and Speight, who was in poor health, returned to Texas.[66]

Harrison resumed his duties as commander of the Fifteenth Texas Infantry. The regiment was separated from the new brigade briefly in November when ordered to join units from John G. Walker's Division and Tom Green's cavalry in an attack on a Federal camp at Bayou Bourbeau. Once again Harrison performed admirably, leading his infantry in the successful assault on the enemy. The regiment rejoined the brigade soon thereafter and spent the winter months in northern Louisiana.[67]

The Fifteenth Texas was part of Richard Taylor's army in the Red River campaign of 1864. Harrison himself was on leave in Texas and missed the battles of Mansfield and Pleasant Hill, but returned shortly thereafter to lead his regiment as the Confederates attempted to prevent Banks' withdrawal southward. When Polignac became division commander following the death of Alfred Mouton at Mansfield, members of the brigade requested that Harrison, who had recently been promoted colonel, be named brigade commander. Confederate authorities, however, appointed Wilburn H. King, former colonel of the Eighteenth Texas in Walker's Division, to command the brigade. When King was unable to assume command due to serious injuries received at Mansfield, the brigade was left under its senior colonel, Robert D. Stone of the Twenty-second Texas.[68]

Harrison was disappointed that he was not placed in command. Historian Alwyn Barr, who carefully chronicled the story of the brigade, noted that "Harrison subdued his own unhappiness at the decision and restrained another petition on his behalf by the brigade." When Stone, temporary commander of the brigade, was killed in the fighting at Yellow Bayou on May 18, Harrison assumed temporary command. He remained in command of the brigade throughout the summer and into the early fall when the brigade was ordered into southern Arkansas.[69]

Even the patient Harrison must have been preplexed in mid-October 1864, when for the second time Wilburn H. King was named brigade commander. Although Kirby Smith recommended that Harrison be appointed brigadier general, he believed another command should be found for him. According to Alwyn Barr, "Harrison had finally reached the end of his patience." Armed with letters of support from fellow officers, he went to Richmond, ostensibly to discuss Indian affairs. His visit must have had some impact, because Harrison was appointed brigadier general to rank from December 22, 1864.[70]

Harrison's service as a general officer in the closing months of the war was spent in Texas. He was ordered to take command of a new brigade being formed from infantry and dismounted cavalry in East Texas. This brigade, which included Harrison's old Fifteenth Texas Infantry, and was part of Sam Maxey's Division, was under the overall command of John A. Wharton. While accompanying Wharton in Houston, Harrison attempted unsuccessfully to separate Wharton and George W. Baylor in an altercation in which Wharton was killed.[71]

When the war ended, Harrison returned to Waco. He was very active in Baptist affairs during the next decade. As a trustee of Baylor University, Harrison was among those who worked for the consolidation of Baylor and Waco universities. In 1873 he had what his physician brother called "rheumatic paralysis." As a result he was able to walk only with difficulty the last two years of his life. He died February 23, 1875, at Waco, and was buried in the First Street Cemetery, Waco.[72]

JOSEPH LEWIS HOGG

Joseph Lewis Hogg, lawyer, planter, public official, and father of future Texas Governor James Stephen Hogg, was born in Morgan County, Georgia, on September 13, 1806. In 1818 he moved with his family to Tuscaloosa County, Alabama, where his father established a plantation and where young Hogg studied law and served as a colonel in the militia. He married Lucanda McMath in Alabama; the couple had three sons and two daughters.

Joseph Lewis Hogg
—Courtesy of Harold B. Simpson Research Center, Hillsboro, Texas

In 1839 Hogg moved to Cherokee County, Texas, where he opened his law office. He served in the House of Representatives of the Eighth Congress of the Republic, the Convention of 1845, and the Senate of the first state legislature. At the outbreak of the Mexican War he sought election as colonel of the Second Regiment of Texas Volunteers but was defeated by George T. Wood. He remained with the regiment as a private soldier and participated in the capture of Monterrey.[73]

Hogg was a successful businessman and planter during the 1850s. In 1860 he owned $9,000 in real property, $22,000 in personal property, and twenty-six slaves. Although he was a good friend of Sam Houston, Hogg supported secession and as a delegate to the secession convention voted for immediate separation from the Union. When Texas joined the Confederacy, Hogg ran for a seat in the Confederate Congress but was defeated by Franklin B. Sexton.[74]

Hogg was one of six Texans appointed by Governor Edward Clark to head military districts for the purpose of recruiting and organizing military units. He was elected captain of the Lone Star

Defenders, which became Company C of the Third Texas Cavalry, but later resigned from the company to accept a colonel's commission from Governor Clark. When the Lone Star Defenders left Rusk in June 1861, Hogg delivered the farewell address. Sam Barron, one of the men in the company, remembered Hogg as "a fine specimen of the best type of Southern manhood—tall, slender, straight as an Indian, and extremely dignifed in his manner. . . . We venerated, admired, and loved him."[75]

On February 14, 1862, Hogg was appointed brigadier general in the Confederate army with orders to report to Ben McCulloch's Army of the West near Fayetteville, Arkansas. He arrived shortly after McCulloch's death at Pea Ridge. Earl Van Dorn appointed Hogg as commander of a brigade consisting of the Third, Tenth, and Eleventh Texas Cavalry regiments, a Texas dismounted cavalry battalion, an Arkansas infantry battalion, and John J. Good's Texas artillery battery.[76]

Hogg's Brigade was ordered to Corinth, Mississippi, in late April 1862 to join Beauregard's army. Soon after his arrival at the disease-ridden camps at Corinth, Hogg fell victim to dysentery. He was removed to a private home several miles from camp and nursed by his African-American body servant. A doctor was with him much of the time, but Hogg died on May 16, 1862. His Confederate service was so brief that some sources say he died never having donned a Confederate uniform. Extant photographs of him in uniform, however, demonstrate such statements are incorrect.[77]

Hogg was first buried near Mount Holly School House, but in 1918 his remains were moved to the Confederate cemetery at Corinth.

WILBURN HILL KING

Wilburn Hill King, referred to frequently in the *Official Records of the War of the Rebellion* as William H. King, was the youngest Texan to be named a general officer in the Civil War. Born in Cullondenville, Georgia, on June 10, 1839, King was only twenty-four years old when appointed brigadier general by Edmund Kirby Smith.

Educated at Americus, Georgia, where he studied law and

medicine, King visited Texas in 1856 and settled in Cass County four years later. King was in Missouri on business during the secession crisis and enlisted in the Missouri State Guard under Sterling Price. He became captain of his company in the summer of 1861 and led the company in the Battle of Wilson's Creek on August 10. Seriously wounded in the battle, King resigned when the Missouri State Guard was not accepted into Confederate service. He returned to Texas, where he enlisted in the Eighteenth Texas Infantry. When the regiment was mustered into Confederate service in May 1862, King was elected major.[78]

Wilburn Hill King

—Courtesy of Harold B. Simpson Research Center, Hillsboro, Texas

In June 1862 the Eighteenth Texas, under the command of Col. William B. Ochiltree, was ordered to march to Little Rock, Arkansas. There it was assigned to Col. Overton Young's Brigade in a division commanded by Brig. Gen. Henry E. McCulloch. In January 1863 Maj. Gen. John G. Walker assumed command of the division. In April the division, including the Eighteenth Texas, was ordered to join Richard Taylor's army at Alexandria, Louisiana. By this time King had been promoted to lieutenant colonel of the regiment. The Eighteenth Texas saw its first action in an engagement near Richmond, Louisiana, on June 15. There the regiment, commanded by Col. David B. Culberson, beat back enemy attacks until the weight of the enemy numbers forced the Texans to withdraw.[79]

In the autumn of 1863 the regiment, now commanded by King, who had been promoted again, was one of the major components in the Confederate attack at Bayou Bourdeau. In the three-hour engagement King's regiment was in the center of the Confederate attackers who drove the enemy back and captured 600 prisoners. The regiment suffered the highest casualties of any Confederate unit in the fighting, approximately eighteen percent.[80]

The Eighteenth Texas was assigned to Thomas N. Waul's Brigade in February 1864. The brigade was in the center of Taylor's army in the Battle of Mansfield. King was severely wounded while leading the regiment in one of the last assaults of the day.[81]

Two weeks after the Battle of Mansfield, King was appointed commander of Polignac's Texas Brigade to replace Polignac, who had become division commander. Because of his injuries at Mansfield, however, King was unable to assume command at that time. Six weeks later, King, still recovering from his wound, was made temporary commander of the division, replacing John G. Walker, who had been named to succeed Richard Taylor as district commander. Kirby Smith appointed King, only twenty-four years of age, brigadier general with date of rank April 8, 1864 (the date of his injury at Mansfield). Although the appointment was never approved by President Davis, King served as a general officer the rest of the war.[82]

King was relieved of his duties as division commander in October 1864, when Maj. Gen. John H. Forney arrived to assume command. King then took command of Polignac's Brigade. As noted earlier, this was not a popular move as men in the brigade supported the appointment of Col. James E. Harrison, veteran commander of the Fifteenth Texas. At the time, the brigade, part of Forney's Division, was camped near Camden, Arkansas.[83] Shortly after King became brigade commander, the division was ordered back to Louisiana. By late November 1864, the brigade was in winter quarters near Minden, Louisiana. Although he was not the first choice of the men as brigade commander, King soon won the respect and admiration of the soldiers in the brigade, in part because of improvements in rations and health.[84]

In February 1865 shortage of forage for his mounts forced Kirby Smith to dismount nine cavalry regiments. Two new infantry brigades were to be created from the dismounted regiments and parts of King's Brigade. King was given command of one of the new brigades, consisting of the Sixteenth and Eighteenth Infantry, the

Twenty-eighth and Thirty-fourth Dismounted Cavalry, and John Wells' Dismounted Cavalry. The new brigade was assigned to Forney's Texas Division. In March the division received orders to march to Texas. In mid-April the division made its last camp near Hempstead, Texas. When Forney was relieved of command, King once again took over the division. In late May, King disbanded the division and the men headed home.[85]

King established a sugar plantation in Central America after the war. Early in 1867 he went to New Orleans, where he met and married Lucy Furman. The couple moved to King's plantation in Central America. After the death of his wife and infant child a year later, King returned to Texas. He lived briefly in Jefferson and then moved to Sulphur Springs, where he practiced law. He was mayor of Sulphur Springs, a state representative for two terms, and adjutant general of the state from 1881 to 1891. After 1891 he retired in Sulphur Springs, where he devoted his attention to writing Texas history and working with the Masonic Order. He died on October 12, 1910, in Sulphur Springs, and was buried in Oakwood Cemetery, Corsicana.[86]

WALTER PAYE LANE

Soldier, adventurer, merchant, and a legend in his own time, Walter Paye Lane was born on February 18, 1817, in County Cork, Ireland. He came to the United States with his parents when he was only four. The family settled at Fairview, Guernsey County, Ohio, but young Lane moved to Louisville, Kentucky, as a teenager. There he met Stephen F. Austin, who persuaded him to join the Texans in their struggle for independence from Mexico. He arrived in Texas on March 1, 1836, joined the Texas army, and fought in the Battle of San Jacinto with Henry W. Karnes' cavalry. Promoted to second lieutenant for his gallantry, Lane later served aboard the privateer *Thomas Toby* in raids against the Mexican coast. After Texas gained its independence he took part in several battles with the Indians. He was wounded by a Mexican lance at San Jacinto and by a bullet in a fight with the Kickapoos.[87]

Lane lived in San Augustine County, 1838-1843, and then moved to San Antonio, where he joined John C. Hays' Ranger

Walter Paye Lane
(photo taken after war)
—Courtesy of Harold B. Simpson
Research Center, Hillsboro, Texas

company on several expeditions. When the Mexican War began, Lane was elected first lieutenant in the First Regiment of the Texas Mounted Riflemen. He fought at Monterrey and Buena Vista and was promoted to the rank of major. During the war he recovered the remains of Texans executed in the Mier expedition, which were taken to La Grange for reinterment.[88]

Lane went to California during the gold rush. He mined there and in Nevada and Peru for several years, then returned to Marshall, where he and his brother George opened a store. After the Gadsden Purchase in 1854 he went to Arizona, where he prospected and ranched. He went back to Marshall in 1858 to resume his mercantile business.

When the Civil War began, Lane was among the first to issue a call for arms. His reputation was such that the first volunteers enrolled in Harrison County designated themselves the "W. P. Lane Rangers." Lane himself was elected lieutenant colonel in Col. Elkanah Greer's Third Texas Cavalry. Douglas Hale, who wrote a splendid account of the regiment, noted that Lane's exploits in the Mexican and Indian campaigns were well known. He was "a colorful fellow," noted Hale, "full of blarney and bombast, but his courage and resourcefulness under fire would vindicate his own high opinion of himself."[89]

The Third Texas joined Ben McCulloch's Army of the West in Arkansas in July 1861. In the Battle of Wilson's Creek, fought on August 10, Lane had his horse shot out from under him but continued the fight on foot until another mount was found. When Colonel Greer went on leave in late autumn, Lane commanded the regiment during his absence. In the battle against the Creeks at Chustenahlah, Lane led five companies of the regiment in the attack. In his report of the fighting Col. James McIntosh, who commanded the Confederates in the campaign, declared that Lane's cavalry "rushed over its rugged side with the irresistable force of a tornado, and swept everything before it." Three months later at Pea Ridge, Lane joined in the charge against the Federal position at Sturdy's Farm.[90]

In late March 1862 the Third Texas, led by Lane, who replaced Greer (now commanding the brigade) was ordered to cross the Mississippi and join the Confederates at Corinth. Because of shortages of forage and limited space on the riverboats the regiment was forced to leave its horses behind. This caused considerable resentment among the Texans. Lane decided to return to Texas and organize a new mounted regiment, but at the request of the men of the Third Texas he agreed to stay on until his replacement could be found. During the interim he commanded troops in the battle at Farmington, Mississippi, where enemy forces were routed. For this action Lane received the praise of General Beauregard. In general orders the general called the attention of the army "to the brave, skillful, and gallant conduct of Lieutenant Colonel Lane, of the Third Regiment of Dismounted Cavalry, who with 246 men, on the 29th ultimo, charged a largely superior force of the enemy, drove him from his position, and forced him to leave a number of his dead and wounded on the field. The conduct of this brave regiment is worthy of all honor and imitation."[91]

Lane returned to Texas in late summer of 1862 and organized a new regiment called the First Texas Partisan Rangers. The Rangers, assigned to Douglas Cooper's Brigade in Indian Territory, took part in the Battle of Prairie Grove, Arkansas, in December 1862, but Lane, who was ill, was not with the regiment at the time. After the battle the Rangers received permission to withdraw to the Red River for refitting and collecting absentees, but crossed back into Texas. In April and May 1863, William Steele, commander of Indian Territory, wrote plaintively to Lane, who was in Jefferson, urging him to bring his regiment back to Indian Territory. Lane apparently had no wish to return. He sought and secured transfer of the regiment to Louisiana, where, in the summer of 1863, the Rangers were assigned to James P. Major's command.[92]

Lane and the Rangers served in the campaigns in the bayou country throughout the late summer and autumn of 1863. In the spring of 1864 Lane commanded one of three cavalry brigades in Major's Division. At the Battle of Mansfield the division was on the extreme Confederate left. While leading his brigade across the open field, Lane was shot through the thigh and six bullets passed through his coat. George W. Baylor, who assumed command when Lane fell, reported later that Lane "led us with his accustomed coolness and bravery," and had been in the front rank "encouraging his men by his voice and example." Baylor concluded that members of the brigade could "wish for no braver or experienced officer to lead us."[93]

Although Lane rejoined the brigade after recovering from his wound, this was his last major battle. In October 1864, Kirby Smith recommended Lane for promotion to brigadier general, declaring Lane to be one of the best brigade commanders in the Trans Mississippi. Although President Davis approved Lane's promotion in December, it was not until March 18, 1865, that the Senate confirmed the appointment.[94]

The old soldier resumed his mercantile business in Marshall after the war. In the next decade he served as a federal marshal, helped established the Texas Veterans Association, and was active in the restoration to power of the Democratic Party. In 1887 he published his memoirs entitled *The Adventures and Recollections of Walter P. Lane*. Lane, who never married, died at Marshall on January 18, 1892. He was buried in the Old Marshall Cemetery.[95]

SAMUEL BELL MAXEY

(See Chapter Three for biographical information.)

BEN McCULLOCH

Ben McCulloch, the first Texan to be appointed a general officer in the Civil War, the first general appointed from civil life in the

Confederacy, and the first Texas general to die in the war, was the personifica-tion of the nineteenth-century American frontier soldier. Lacking any for-mal education or military training, McCulloch was a born leader of men, as he demonstrated in the Texas Revolution, Indian cam-paigns, the Mexican War, and two major battles of the Civil War. Admired by his men and feared by his enemies, McCulloch had a national reputation due to his many colorful exploits along the southwestern border. His death while leading the charge at Pea Ridge in March 1862 was a shock to Texas and the South.[96]

Ben McCulloch
—Courtesy of Harold B. Simpson Research Center, Hillsboro, Texas

Ben McCulloch was, according to his biographer Thomas W. Cutrer, "at once the son of the eastern aristocratic establishment and a child of the ever shifting western frontier." His mother, Frances LeNoir, was the daughter of a prominent Virginia planter. His father, Alexander McCulloch, was a graduate of Yale and an officer on Andrew Jackson's staff in the Creek Wars. The McCul-lochs were once a prosperous North Carolina family, but Alexander squandered away his inheritance. Trying to reestablish himself in society, he moved his family several times between 1812 and 1830, finally settling at Dyersberg, Tennessee, where David Crockett was a neighbor and family friend. Ben, born on November 11, 1811, in Rutherford County, Tennessee, was one of thirteen children.[97]

If not for a case of measles, Ben McCulloch may have been one of the martyred heroes of the Alamo like his Tennessee hunting companion David Crockett. McCulloch and his younger brother

Henry agreed to follow Crockett to Texas in 1835. The brothers planned to meet Crockett at Nacogdoches on Christmas Day, 1835, but were late reaching the rendezvous. Ben decided to go on to find Crockett, who was on his way to San Antonio, but persuaded Henry to return to spend time with his parents in Tennessee. On his way to join Crockett, Ben was struck with measles. By the time of McCulloch's recovery, Crockett had died at the Alamo.[98]

McCulloch recovered from his illness in time to join Sam Houston's army as it retreated to East Texas. Although he had never fired a cannon, McCulloch was named commander of the "Twin Sisters," the two artillery pieces given the Texans by the citizens of Cincinnati, Ohio. At the Battle of San Jacinto, McCulloch displayed such courage and ability that he was promoted to first lieutenant. After the War for Independence, McCulloch returned to Tennessee to learn surveying from his father. He went back to Texas in 1838, settling in Gonzales, where he earned his living as a surveyor. His brother Henry soon joined him.[99]

McCulloch was called upon to help protect the Guadalupe valley from Indian raiders. He joined the Texas Rangers and for the next decade was almost constantly in the saddle, fighting Indians and Mexicans as the occasion demanded. He battled Comanches at Plum Creek (1840), served as a scout against the Vasquez and Woll raiders, and was a member of the Somervell expedition to the Rio Grande (1842). When the Mexican War began, McCulloch raised a company which served in Jack Hays' First Regiment, Texas Mounted Volunteers. He was later named as chief of scouts by Gen. Zachary Taylor, who praised him for his reconnaissance expeditions. He distinguished himself while leading his company in the battle for Monterrey. His scouting saved Taylor's army at Buena Vista, and for his actions there McCulloch was promoted to major of volunteers. His exploits were so publicized by George Wilkins Kendall, editor of the *New Orleans Picayune*, and Samuel Reid, who wrote a popular account of the war, that McCulloch gained a national reputation.[100]

Although McCulloch resumed surveying when he returned to Texas after the Mexican War, his main ambition was a military career. He spent much time reading books on military history and strategy and in writing and talking to friends in hopes of obtaining a regular commission in the U.S. Army. He soon discovered, however, that in spite of his new fame and reputation, most such commissions went to West Point graduates. After serving briefly as a scout for Brig. Gen. David Twiggs, McCulloch headed for the California gold fields. He had little success in mining, but was elected sheriff of Sacramento County.

In late 1851 McCulloch returned to Texas, where his friends in Congress, Sam Houston and Thomas J. Rusk, were pushing his candidacy for colonel of the newly created frontier cavalry regiment. The appointment went instead to West Pointer Albert Sidney Johnston. Disappointed over the failure to secure the colonelcy of the Second Cavalry, McCulloch accepted appointment as federal marshal for the Eastern District of Texas.[101]

In 1858 President James Buchanan named McCulloch as one of the two peace commissioners to negotiate with Brigham Young and the Mormons, who were challenging the authority of the Federal government. McCulloch and his fellow commissioner, Lazarus W. Powell of Kentucky, set out for Utah at once. In Salt Lake City they successfully negotiated an agreement in which Mormon leaders agreed to accept civil officers appointed by President Buchanan, thus avoiding a possible military clash between the Federal government and the Mormons.

Once the Utah mission was completed, McCulloch returned to Texas. In March 1859 he resigned as U.S. marshal. During the next year he traveled to the East Coast and while there he purchased interest in a newly patented carbine, a modification of the Springfield rifle by George W. Morse. For the next several months he traveled through the country demonstrating the new weapon. At the same time he followed the growing controversy between the North and South. Although he was not a delegate, he attended the Democratic conventions at Charleston and Baltimore in 1860.[102]

When Texas seceded from the Union in early 1861, the Committee on Public Safety commissioned McCulloch colonel and instructed him to demand the surrender of Federal property in the state. McCulloch accomplished this in a bloodless confrontation in San Antonio on February 16 with Gen. David Twiggs, the U.S. commander in Texas.[103]

In May 1861, McCulloch was appointed brigadier general in the Confederate army by President Jefferson Davis. The appointment came as something of a surprise because it was Davis who, as secretary of war in the Pierce administration, appointed Albert Sidney Johnston rather than McCulloch to command the Second U.S. Cavalry. It was also well known that Davis preferred West Point men to command the Confederate army. McCulloch was the first non-West Pointer Davis appointed as a general officer. McCulloch was also the first Texan chosen as a general.[104]

McCulloch was assigned command of Indian Territory with instructions to defend the area against Union invasion from Kansas. During the early summer of 1861, McCulloch worked diligently to find men and materials necessary to carry out the task. With the assistance of Albert Pike, McCulloch, the old Indian fighter, made a series of alliances with various Cherokee, Creek, and Choctaw leaders to assure their loyalty to the Confederacy. When it appeared that the main threat to Indian Territory was coming from Federal troops in Missouri, McCulloch led his Army of the West into southwestern Missouri to support Sterling Price's Missouri Confederates. On August 10, 1861, the combined forces of McCulloch and Price defeated Union troops led by Nathaniel Lyon at Oak Hill, or Wilson's Creek. Although McCulloch, the seasoned scout, was surprised by the initial Union attack, he fought sufficiently well to win the battle and enhance his reputation as a military leader.[105]

The Confederates failed to capitalize on their victory at Wilson's Creek. Logistical problems, lack of adequate weapons, and differences over strategic objectives plagued Confederate forces in the Trans Mississippi during the autumn of 1861. Sterling Price favored a major offensive to drive Federal troops from Missouri. McCulloch believed the Confederates were not strong enough to achieve such objectives and favored a more cautious approach. The two men did not care for each other personally. McCulloch considered Price to be pompous and overbearing; Price believed the Texan to be lacking in initiative. Their inability to come to terms led President Davis in January 1862 to appoint Earl Van Dorn to command both the armies of McCulloch and Price.[106]

Van Dorn, described as "a romantic warrior, not a military intellectual," was more in agreement with Sterling Price than McCulloch concerning strategy. Combining the troops of Price and McCulloch in a single army under his command, Van Dorn launched a campaign to capture St. Louis. Moving northward, Van Dorn's Confederates encountered Union forces commanded by Samuel R. Curtis near Pea Ridge in northwestern Arkansas.

Van Dorn divided his troops for an attack. McCulloch, commanding a division of Texans, Arkansans, Louisianians, and Indians, opened the battle with a spirited assault on the Union forces near Leetown, while Van Dorn and Price followed with an attack on the Union right near Elkhorn Tavern, two miles to the north. McCulloch's men drove the Federal troops back in the initial assault, but Union resistance stiffened in late morning. McCulloch rode forward through the brush and trees to reconnoiter the Federal position before ordering an all-out assault on the enemy. As he rode along the front lines he was fired upon by riflemen from the Thirty-sixth Illinois. He fell from his horse, a bullet in the heart killing him instantly. Brig. Gen. James McIntosh, who succeeded McCulloch in command, was killed a few minutes later while leading a charge to recover McCulloch's body. Louis Hebert, the division's senior colonel, was captured in the same charge. Col. Elkanah Greer, commander of the Third Texas Cavalry, assumed temporary command. The fighting centered around Elkhorn Tavern the next morning, but at midday Van Dorn broke off the engagement and retreated.[107]

Many Texans were convinced that McCulloch's death prevented the Confederates from winning a victory at Pea Ridge. The colorful and often flamboyant Walter P. Lane, who took part in the charge at Pea Ridge, was astonished that Van Dorn retreated. "If Gen. McCulloch had not been killed so early in the fight at Elk Horn we would have whipped that battle for his men had confidence in his leadership," wrote Lane.[108]

McCulloch was first buried on the field where he fell but was reinterred in Bentonville, Arkansas. Several days later the body was disinterred again and taken back to Texas for burial. The body lay in state in the State Capitol for a day and then was buried in the Texas State Cemetery.

McCulloch, who never married, left most of his possessions to his brother Henry. At the time of his death McCulloch, who seldom wore a uniform, was wearing the black velvet suit he so often wore on the field of battle. Ever popular, he was always remembered as "Old Ben" to the men who served under him.[109]

HENRY EUSTACE McCULLOCH

Henry Eustace McCulloch, younger brother of Ben McCulloch, was born on December 6, 1816, in Rutherford County, Tennessee. As mentioned earlier he accompanied his brother to Texas in 1836 but returned home to care for his parents. In 1838 he joined Ben at Gonzales, where he served first as county assessor and later as sheriff. Like his brother Ben, to whom he was deeply attached, Henry served in the Texas Rangers, fought in various Indian campaigns, and commanded a Ranger company in the Mexican War. He married Jane Isabella Ashley in 1840 and shortly thereafter moved to Seguin, where he engaged in merchandising and continued Ranger service. He represented Guadalupe County in the Texas House of Representatives, 1853-1854, and

Henry Eustace McCulloch
(photo taken after war)
—Courtesy of Harold B. Simpson
Research Center, Hillsboro, Texas

the Texas Senate, 1855-1859. When his brother Ben resigned as U.S. marshal in 1859, Henry was appointed as his successor.[110]

When Texas seceded in 1861, Henry McCulloch was appointed colonel by the Committee on Public Safety, placed in command of the northwestern district of the state, and directed to secure the surrender of Federal property from the Colorado to the Red River. Pursuant to instructions, McCulloch obtained the surrender of Forts Mason and Chadbourne and Camp Cooper without resistance. McCulloch also raised and commanded volunteers that formed the First Regiment of Texas Mounted Rifles. In September

1861, Earl Van Dorn, who had served as commander of the Texas district and was being transferred elsewhere, appointed McCulloch to serve as district commander until the arrival of his successor, Brig. Gen. Paul O. Hebert. In appointing McCulloch as his temporary successor, Van Dorn stated "there is not a more reliable soldier and pure gentleman in the Army of the Confederacy."[111]

After Hebert's arrival, McCulloch was assigned to command the military sub-district of the Rio Grande. He was appointed brigadier general on March 18, 1862. Although he hoped to join Ben McCulloch's old command in Mississippi, he was placed in charge of the eastern sub-district of the state in June 1862. When the threat of Union conquest of Arkansas developed later that summer, McCulloch was directed to proceed to Little Rock with all available forces. There McCulloch and another Texas brigadier, Allison Nelson, were assigned to command divisions under the overall direction of Trans Mississippi departmental commander Theophilus H. Holmes.[112]

Although the sixteen regiments of Texas infantry under McCulloch and Nelson did comparatively little fighting that autumn, their presence saved the fertile Arkansas River Valley from Federal occupation. When Confederate authorities instructed Holmes to send McCulloch's Division to Vicksburg in December, Holmes objected. Such a movement, Holmes protested, would be the "equivalent to abandoning Arkansas." Holmes' objections apparently carried some weight because McCulloch's Division was allowed to spend the winter of 1862 in Arkansas. McCulloch, however, no longer commanded the division. In an effort to bring more experienced leadership to the Trans Mississippi the Confederate War Department assigned Maj. Gen. John G. Walker, a veteran officer from the Army of Northern Virginia, to the department. In December 1862 Walker was appointed division commander, and McCulloch was relegated to command the brigade in the division previously led by George M. Flournoy.[113]

In the spring of 1863, McCulloch's Brigade, consisting of the Sixteenth, Seventeenth, and Nineteenth Texas Infantry, the Sixteenth Texas Dismounted Cavalry, and an artillery battery, was ordered to Louisiana with the rest of Walker's Division. In May and early June the division attacked Federal forces along the west bank of the Mississippi in an effort to impede Grant's move around

Vicksburg. In a fierce assault on Milliken's Bend, McCulloch's Brigade attacked a strong Union position along the river levee but was driven off the field by fire from enemy field artillery and gunboats. In hand-to-hand fighting some of McCulloch's men gave no quarter to Union black troops, killing a number of wounded before being forced to fall back. In his report of the battle McCulloch made no mention of the incident but praised his men for their courage and gallantry. General Walker agreed that McCulloch's men had shown gallantry but attributed the failure of the attack upon want of local knowledge and the strength of the enemy defenses. General Taylor, the overall commander of Confederate forces in Louisiana, was more critical, reporting that "in this affair General McCulloch appears to have shown great personal bravery, but no capacity for handling masses."[114]

Although he did not know it at the time, Henry McCulloch had fought his last Civil War battle. In late July 1863, he was relieved of his duties in the District of Louisiana and ordered to report to Maj. Gen. John B. Magruder in Texas. After a brief visit to his home in Seguin, McCulloch was assigned to command the northern sub-district of Texas with headquarters at Bonham.[115]

McCulloch assumed his new duties in mid-September. He soon discovered that the problems he faced were vast and the resources available to him were few. The threat of Indian raids and Federal invasion from Indian Territory was always present, but often McCulloch had fewer than a thousand troops available to patrol a frontier running hundreds of miles. Most pressing was the growing number of deserters, draft dodgers, Jayhawkers, and bushwhackers in the region. Historian David Paul Smith pointed out that McCulloch first attempted to use the olive branch in dealing with this problem but gradually turned to harsher measures.

Edmund Kirby Smith, now commander of the Trans Mississippi Department, urged McCulloch to make use of the guerrilla chieftain William Clarke Quantrill, who had established a winter camp northwest of Sherman, Texas, to seek out deserters and draft dodgers. McCulloch reluctantly did so but was appalled at Quantrill's ruthlessness in killing rather than taking prisoners. In February 1864, McCulloch complained to district commander John B. Magruder: "Quantrill will not obey orders, and so much mischief is charged to his command here that I have determined to disarm, arrest, and send his entire command to you or Gen. Smith." Quantrill's men "regard the life of a man less than you would that of a sheep-killing dog." When complaints from local citizens in Sherman and Bonham about acts of violence continued, McCulloch ordered Quantrill's arrest; however, the wily guerrilla leader and his men fled to Indian Territory.[116]

Quantrill's departure did not end McCulloch's problems in dealing with lawless elements. In the spring of 1864 a suspected conspiracy involving deserters, draft evaders, and unionists led to the arrest of several suspects and the hanging of an officer of state troops. Rumors of other conspiracies and uprisings abounded. Col. James Bourland, commander of the Frontier Regiment and one of McCulloch's subordinates, was particularly zealous in rounding up unionists and deserters. Stories circulated that Bourland and his men murdered suspects while holding them prisoner. McCulloch, ever fair-minded, was critical of Bourland's methods. In September he advised Bourland to concentrate on the Indian problem and leave internal security matters to state authorities. A new rash of deserters and bushwhackers in October, however, forced McCulloch to modify his previous instructions and allow Bourland a free hand in hunting down deserters.[117]

In addition to problems associated with deserters and unionists, McCulloch was concerned with the threat of Indian raids. In October 1864 several hundred Comanche and Kiowa warriors crossed the Red River near present-day Burkburnett, divided into several groups, and attacked ranches and farms along Elm Creek, a tributary of the Brazos. Confederate troops from McCulloch's district and state troops from the First Frontier district rode to the assistance of the settlers but arrived after the Indians had withdrawn. The Elm Creek raid caused great concern all along the Red River and led McCulloch to request additional troops to protect the area.[118]

McCulloch desired a return to field command, but his petitions were ignored by Confederate officials. He was still in charge of the northern sub-district of Texas when the war ended in 1865. He returned to his home in Seguin, where he farmed and ranched. In 1876 he was appointed superintendent of the Texas Asylum for the Deaf and Dumb, a position he held for three years. He then retired to his farm at Seguin. He died in Rockport, Texas, on March 12, 1895, and was buried in San Geronimo Cemetery in Seguin.[119]

ALLISON NELSON

Lawyer, politician, and soldier, Allison Nelson was born on March 11, 1822, in Fulton County, Georgia. When he was only twenty-four years of age he recruited a company of volunteers

which he led during the Mexican War. He later served in the Cuban war for independence and was appointed brigadier general by Narcisco Lopez. He was elected to the Georgia legislature in 1848 and as mayor of Atlanta in 1855. A staunch supporter of slavery and states' rights, he traveled to Kansas and became involved in the controversy there. In 1856 he moved to Meridian, Texas, in Bosque County. During the later 1850s he served alternately as an Indian agent and an Indian fighter under Lawrence Sullivan Ross. He was elected to the Texas legislature in 1859 and to the secession convention in 1861.[120]

Allison Nelson
(photo taken before war)
—Courtesy of Harold B. Simpson
Research Center, Hillsboro, Texas

At the outbreak of the Civil War, Nelson helped raise the Tenth Texas Infantry and was elected its colonel. In the summer of 1862 Nelson and his regiment were ordered to report to Thomas C. Hindman in Arkansas. Apparently the regiment was well drilled and equipped, for Hindman later wrote that Nelson, "a most excellent officer, arrived at Little Rock from Texas with his well armed and finely disciplined regiment of infantry."[121]

Nelson and his men were ordered to Devall's Bluff, where they harassed Union gunboats on the White River. Nelson was reinforced by an additional regiment, a battalion of infantry, and three artillery batteries. During the late summer his force turned back several Union gunboats before they could reach Devall's Bluff. On recommendation of departmental commander Theophilus H. Holmes, Nelson was promoted to brigadier general on September 26, 1862, and assigned command of Holmes' Second Division consisting of his own and George Flournoy's brigades. Fellow Texan Henry E. McCulloch commanded the other division in Holmes' army.[122]

What appeared to be a promising Civil War career was soon cut short. Nelson developed typhoid fever three days after his promotion and died at Camp Hope near Austin, Arkansas, on October 7. He was buried in the Mount Holly Cemetery in Little Rock. General Holmes described Nelson's death as "an irreparable loss."[123]

HORACE RANDAL

Horace Randal was one of five Texans assigned as brigadier general by Edmund Kirby Smith but never approved by President Davis and the Confederate Senate. Born on January 4, 1833, in McNairy County, Tennessee, Randal came to Texas with his parents, who settled near San Augustine in 1838. In 1849 young Randal, the son of an army surgeon, was one of the first Texans appointed to the U.S. Military Academy at West Point. Because of academic difficulties Randal did not graduate until five years later, forty-fifth in a class of forty-six. Among his fellow graduates were J. E. B. Stuart, Stephen D. Lee, and Oliver O. Howard.[124]

Upon graduation Randal was posted first to the infantry, but, a talented horseman, was transferred to the Second Dragoons in 1855. For the next five years he served at frontier forts in Indian Territory, New Mexico Territory, and Texas. He saw action against the Apaches on at least three different occasions. In 1857 Secretary of War Jefferson Davis recommended Randal receive a brevet promotion for "gallant and meritorious conduct in affairs with the

Horace Randal

—Courtesy of Harold B. Simpson
Research Center, Hillsboro, Texas

Apache Indians." Randal was in Washington, D.C., the week before Lincoln's inauguration, and apparently was offered a majority if he would remain in the U.S. Army. Randal declined the offer and accepted a commission as a first lieutenant in the Confederate army. He served briefly on the staff of Braxton Bragg in Pensacola, Florida, and later in Virginia as aide-de-camp to his brother-in-law, Gustavus W. Smith. Much was expected of Randal; a fellow officer, John Cheves Haskell, said that Randal's classmates, including John Bell Hood, "predicted that he would be the cavalry leader of the war if he got the chance."[125]

Randal got his opportunity for mounted service when he was commissioned colonel of cavalry and given command of the Twenty-eighth Cavalry recruited in and around Marshall. On July 9, 1862, the regiment left Marshall for service in Arkansas, where, to the displeasure of the men, it was dismounted and became part of Henry McCulloch's (later Walker's) Texas Division. In September 1862, Randal was appointed commander of the division's Second Brigade, consisting of Randal's regiment and the Eleventh, Fourteenth, and Fifteenth Texas infantry regiments. In late spring of 1863 the division moved to Louisiana to serve under Richard Taylor. The brigade was in reserve at Milliken's Bend when McCulloch's Brigade attacked a strong Union position. Randal brought his brigade up when McCulloch requested reinforcements but arrived too late to take part in the battle. The brigade remained in

Louisiana the rest of 1863 and participated in Tom Green's campaign in the bayou country.[126]

At the Battle of Mansfield on April 8, 1864, Randal's Brigade was in the center of the attack that drove the Union forces back. At Pleasant Hill the next day the brigade was under heavy enemy fire. When Banks' army threatened to outflank William R. Scurry's Brigade, the brigades of Randal and Thomas N. Waul fought tenaciously to stem the Federal advance. Randal so impressed departmental commander Kirby Smith that four days later Smith appointed Randal brigadier general, to date from April 8, the day of the Battle of Mansfield.[127]

Randal had little time to enjoy his promotion. To stop the advance of Frederick Steele's Union army in southern Arkansas, Kirby Smith ordered Walker's Division to the assistance of Sterling Price. When Walker's Division reached the Camden area, Steele was already withdrawing toward Little Rock. In a battle fought on April 30, 1864, at Jenkins' Ferry, Walker attacked the retreating Federals. In the savage fighting that took place all three of Walker's brigade commanders were wounded; two of them, Randal and W. R. Scurry, mortally. Scurry died on the field of battle, but Randal lived until May 2.

Randal was first buried near the battlefield but his remains were later moved to the Old Marshall Cemetery in Marshall, Texas. Randal left a wife, Nannie E. Taylor, and one son, Horace Randal, Jr., born in December 1863. Randal's first wife, Julia S. Bassett, had died in 1860 after a marriage of two years.[128]

Randall County, Texas, is named for him, though spelled incorrectly.

WILLIAM READ SCURRY

Soldier, lawyer, and politician, William Read Scurry was mortally wounded while leading his brigade at Jenkins' Ferry the same day as Horace Randal. An orator, poet, and born fighter, Scurry was an ardent defender of Southern rights who traveled extensively throughout the state speaking for secession, earning the sobriquet "Dirty Shirt" because of his stained garments.[129]

William R. Scurry was born in Gallatin, Summer County,

William Read Scurry

—Courtesy of Harold B. Simpson
Research Center, Hillsboro, Texas

Tennessee, on February 10, 1821. After studying law in Tennessee, he moved to San Augustine, Texas, in 1839 to join his brother Richardson Scurry, a veteran of San Jacinto, in the practice of law. Not yet twenty-one years of age, Scurry became district attorney of the Fifth Judicial District in 1844. He served briefly as aide-de-camp to Gen. Thomas J. Rusk, moved to Clarksville, and became a member of the Ninth Congress of the Texas Republic. With the outbreak of the Mexican War he enlisted as a private in George T. Wood's Second Regiment, Texas Mounted Volunteers. He was promoted to major of the regiment in July 1846 and took part in the Battle of Monterrey.[130]

After the Mexican War, Scurry settled in Brenham, where he married Jennette B. Sutton; the couple subsequently had seven children. Scurry later moved to Austin, where he purchased an interest in the *Texas State Gazette*, one of the state's most influential newspapers. He served as co-editor of the paper from November 1853 through mid-August 1854. In 1854 he sold his interest in the *Gazette* and moved to Victoria County.

In 1858-1859 he was a commissioner for the state in determining the Texas-New Mexico boundary line. The 1860 Federal census returns show Scurry living in Victoria, with his wife and (at that time) five children. Neither personal nor real property are listed, nor are slaves enumerated for him in the county even though he earlier owned two mulatto slaves. He moved to Clinton in DeWitt County in late summer of 1860. He strongly supported Southern rights and as a member of the 1861 state convention voted to secede from the Union.[131]

Scurry was an eager volunteer when the Civil War began. In the late summer of 1861 he was commissioned lieutenant colonel in the newly formed Fourth Regiment of Texas Mounted Volunteers. A mixture of recruits from South Central and East Texas, the Fourth Texas was one of three cavalry regiments formed to serve under Brig. Gen. Henry H. Sibley in his campaign to occupy New Mexico Territory. Col. James Reily, commander of the Fourth Texas, was a veteran diplomat, politician, and public servant whom Sibley sent on a mission to the northern Mexican states of Chihuahua and Sonora in an effort to gain support for Sibley's campaign. Consequently, leadership of the Fourth Texas throughout the New Mexico campaign fell upon Scurry, the regiment's executive officer.[132]

Scurry played an active role in the New Mexico campaign. In the battle with Federal forces at Valverde on February 21, his regiment made the initial assault on enemy troops defending the river ford. When Union forces fell back under heavy pressure, Scurry led the Confederates across the river in pursuit of the enemy. He halted only when the Federal commander dispatched a flag of truce. Half of the regiment's horses were killed in the attack. After the battle the men who still had mounts agreed to give up their horses so that the whole regiment was dismounted.[133]

For his performance at Valverde, Scurry was promoted to colonel in late March 1862. He was in command of Confederate forces in the last day of the battle at Glorieta Pass, described by some historians as "the Gettysburg of the West." In six hours of bitter fighting the Texans drove John P. Slough's Federals from the field. In the course of the battle Scurry's cheek was grazed twice by minié balls and his clothes torn by Federal bullets. Although Scurry later praised his troops in an address in which he compared them to the heroes of San Jacinto, the outcome of the battle was disappointing. The Federals had been pushed back from Pigeon's Ranch, but they still blocked the Confederate effort to move along the Santa Fe Trail toward the objective, Fort Union.[134]

Even before the fighting at Pigeon's Ranch ended, the Confederates heard reports, later confirmed, that while the battle raged Union troops commanded by Col. John Chivington had swung around the Confederate lines and destroyed Scurry's supply train at Johnson's Ranch. Already short on food and ammunition, and having suffered more than one hundred casualties at Pigeon's Ranch, Scurry ordered a retreat to Santa Fe to join the rest of Sibley's Brigade. He still hoped that the campaign could be continued after his troops were resupplied, but reports that additional Union troops were approaching convinced General Sibley to retreat to Texas.

For Scurry the New Mexico campaign was a mixed success. He handled his regiment well at Valverde and pushed the Union forces back at Glorieta Pass. He had won the respect of the men who served with him. A. B. Peticolas, a young lawyer in Company C of the Fourth Cavalry, praised Scurry as "the best officer, most polished gentleman, most sociable gentleman, and the most popular Colonel in the whole outfit." However, the failure to provide an adequate force to guard the supply train at Glorieta was, according to historian Jerry Thompson, "one of the worst mistakes of the campaign."[135]

Confederate authorities apparently were pleased with Scurry's performance in the New Mexico campaign. On September 26 he was promoted to brigadier general, with date of rank September 12, 1862. The Fourth Cavalry, which Scurry now commanded, was stationed in the Houston area along with other regiments of the old Sibley Brigade in the autumn of 1862. When the newly appointed commander of the Texas district, John B. Magruder, determined to recapture Galveston Island, units of the brigade became involved. The Fifth and Seventh cavalries, commanded by Tom Green and A. P. Bagby, for the moment became horse marines and served on the *Bayou City* and *Neptune* in the naval attack. Magruder appointed Scurry commander of the ground forces that included his Fourth Cavalry and assorted other units. As ground commander Scurry led troops around the railroad bridge and opened fire on Federal forces garrisoned at Kuhn's Wharf. When the Union troops capitulated following the departure of the Union navy, Scurry took the surrender, gallantly declining to take the Federal commander's sword.[136]

Magruder praised Scurry for his role in the recapture of Galveston. He was so impressed that in early January he wrote directly to President Davis requesting Scurry's promotion to major general. The promotion never came, but Magruder did give Scurry additional duties and responsibilities as commander of the eastern sub-district of Texas. Under Scurry's direction additional fortifications at Galveston and on the Sabine River were constructed by engineers Col. Valey Sulakowski and Maj. Getulius Kellersberger. When Union forces moved into the bayou country of Louisiana in early 1863, Scurry arranged for the transfer of troops from Texas to help Richard Taylor meet the Federal threat.[137]

In September 1863, Scurry was ordered to Louisiana to assume command of Henry McCulloch's Brigade in Walker's Texas Division. J. P. Blessington, a member of the brigade, noted that Scurry was generally known to men in the division owing to his experiences at Valverde, Glorieta, and Galveston. "We believe, to him," wrote Blessington, "is mainly due the credit for saving, after its capture, the celebrated Valverde battery, which has made itself heard and felt by the Yankee invaders on more than one occasion." Another Texan, Capt. E. P. Petty, noted the arrival of Scurry: "I am well pleased with him. I knew him well in Texas. He is a fighter and those who follow him will go to the Cannon's Mouth."[138]

For the next seven months Scurry was with the brigade in Louisiana. The brigade saw little action during the late fall and winter, but with the coming of spring the situation changed. In the critical battle at Mansfield on April 8, Scurry's Brigade, one of three in Walker's Division, was on the Confederate extreme right. In the afternoon fighting Scurry's Brigade broke through the Union line and forced the Federals to fall back. The following day at Pleasant Hill Walker's Division was on the left side of the Confederate line. Scurry's Brigade was on the right wing of the division, in the center of the Confederate line next to Churchill's Division which formed the Confederate right. In the bitter fighting Churchill's Division gave ground, leaving Scurry's Brigade exposed to brutal enemy crossfire. The brigade suffered heavy casualties but held until Walker's other two brigades checked the Federal advance. In the closing minutes of the battle Scurry, who was at the front rallying his men, was grazed by a minié ball but refused to leave the field until the fighting ended.[139]

After Banks' army began to withdraw back down the Red River, Kirby Smith ordered Walker's Division, including Scurry and his men, to move north to Arkansas to help repulse Frederick Steele's Union army. At the Battle of Jenkins' Ferry, fought on April 30, 1864, Scurry and fellow brigade commander Horace Randal were severely wounded. Scurry once again refused to leave the field and lay unattended for two hours while the fighting went on. He died in the closing moments of the battle after he was assured the Confederates had won the day.

His body was taken back to Texas for burial in the Texas State Cemetery in Austin. Scurry County is named for him.[140]

WILLIAM STEELE

William Steele was born in Watervliet, in upstate New York, on May 1, 1819. A graduate of the Military Academy at West Point in 1841 (thirty-first in a class of forty-two), Steele served in the U.S. Army for twenty years before resigning to accept a commission in the Confederate army. During that time he fought in the Seminole and Mexican wars. In the Mexican War, he saw action at Palo Alto, Monterrey, Cerro Gordo, Contreras, Churubusco, and Molino del Rey. He was cited for meritorious conduct at Contreras and Churubusco and received a brevet for captain. Following the Mexican War he was stationed in Mississippi and then later at Fort Martin Scott at Fredericksburg, Texas. He married Annie E. Duval, daughter of the former governor of Florida Territory and sister to John C. Duval, one of the survivors of Goliad. The Steeles had one child. During the 1850s Steele, a cap-

William Steele
(photo taken after war)
—Courtesy of Harold B. Simpson
Research Center, Hillsboro, Texas

tain in the Second Dragoons, served in various western posts and fought Apaches in New Mexico and Sioux in Dakota Territory.[141]

When the Civil War began, Steele resigned his commission in the U.S. Army, returned to his adopted state, Texas, and accepted a commission in the Confederate army. With twenty years of active duty, Steele had more regular army experience than any other Texan with the possible exception of Albert Sidney Johnston. In August 1861, Steele became colonel of the Seventh Texas Cavalry, one of the three regiments commanded by another veteran of the Second Dragoons, Henry H. Sibley. The Seventh Cavalry was the last of Sibley's regiments to be organized and brought up the rear in the march to New Mexico. During the campaign Steele and part of the regiment remained at Mesilla, while Sibley and the rest of the brigade marched north to Albuquerque and Santa Fe. When the Confederates retreated after the battle at Glorieta, Steele and his regiment served as the rear guard, arriving back in Texas in late summer.[142]

In early October 1862, Steele was promoted to brigadier general. He was assigned to the Trans Mississippi Department as commander of Indian Territory, but was delayed by business matters in San Antonio, not arriving at Fort Smith until early January 1863. He soon discovered that affairs in Indian Territory were chaotic. Later he wrote in his report that "on my arrival at Fort Smith the appearance of everything was of the most gloomy description." Inadequate clothing, poor food, shortages of arms and ammunition, and incompetent staff officers were among the difficulties Steele faced. To add to his problems Douglas H. Cooper, former Indian agent and commander of the Indian Brigade, believed that he, not Steele, should be the head of the territory. Cooper had powerful friends both among the Indian tribes and Richmond politicians. He made Steele's role even more difficult and eventually caused his resignation.[143]

For a year Steele struggled to bring about some order in the territory while trying to hold a defensive line along the Arkansas River. In July 1863, Union troops commanded by Maj. Gen. James Blunt pushed southward, attacking the Confederate supply depot south of the Arkansas River near Honey Springs (or Elk Creek). In the largest battle fought in Indian Territory, Blunt's army drove the Rebels back. The Confederates retreated across the Canadian River, leaving the northern half of the territory in Federal hands.

In late summer Steele attempted to put together sufficient

force to clear Indian Territory of Union troops, but a variety of problems thwarted Steele's plans, including massive desertions in William Cabell's Arkansas Brigade and the inability of Brig. Gen. Smith P. Bankhead to bring up reinforcements from Texas. He attempted to bring W. P. Lane's regiment back from Texas, but Lane managed to secure transfer to Louisiana. Steele also found it difficult to work with Indian troops. An old-line professional, he was intolerant of the lack of discipline among the Native Americans. Experience convinced him "that, with a few exceptions, the Indians are wholly unreliable as troops of the line." Steele wrote, "The officers, as a general rule, are ignorant, void of moral tone of character, and indisposed to enforce discipline among their men."[144]

Frustrated in his inability to receive proper support, Steele requested and was granted release from his assignment in Indian Territory in December 1863. In reassigning Steele, departmental commander Kirby Smith noted the difficulties Steele faced and expressed "satisfaction with the manner in which that officer [Steele] has conducted the affairs of the Indian Territory amid all the embarrassments that surround him, and in assigning him to other duty, does so with unbated confidence in his ability and patriotism." Smith requested that Steele remain in a secondary capacity until his successor, Samuel B. Maxey, familiarize himself with the command. Steele, embittered over his treatment by Cooper and his friends, declined to stay, saying, "the slanders that have been industriously circulated through the Indian country and Northern Texas not only make it extremely disagreeable for me to serve here, but it impairs my usefulness." He concluded: "notwithstanding the fact that all the property I owed at the beginning of this war was at the North, and that I resigned from the army and cast my lot with the South, I am looked upon with suspicion as a Yankee, and am told that people will not believe that I am not a brother of the Federal general [Frederick Steele] of the same name, that being one of the reports circulated."[145]

In February 1864 Steele reported to General Magruder in Texas. The next month he relieved James P. Major in command of the defenses of Galveston. Three months later he was ordered to Louisiana and there was assigned a cavalry division under John A. Wharton, who had succeeded the deceased Tom Green as chief of cavalry under Richard Taylor. The Louisiana cavalry brigade assigned to Steele never arrived, however, so Steele's Division during the late spring consisted only of Col. William H. Parsons' Brigade. Wharton, Steele, and Parsons participated in the latter stages of the Red River campaign as Taylor attempted to prevent Banks' army from retreating. Parsons' Brigade, commanded by Steele, was on the extreme Confederate left in the unsuccessful Confederate attack at Yellow Bayou on May 18, 1864. Although the brigade showed heroism and courage in the attack, it and other Confederate units were driven back by the superior firepower of Banks' army.[146]

At the end of the Red River campaign, Steele's cavalry was ordered to southern Arkansas. By late September Steele had Parsons' Twelfth Cavalry, Charles Morgan's Cavalry Battalion, Ben Watson's Nineteenth Cavalry, and DeWitt Giddings' Twenty-first Cavalry under his command. In November 1864 Steele was ordered to Nacogdoches, Texas, where he was given command of a cavalry corps of two brigades, one commanded by Parsons and the other by Walter P. Lane. Steele's Corps was with Wharton's command in the Hempstead area when the war ended.[147]

In many ways the war was a disappointment for William Steele. One of the most experienced soldiers in the Confederacy when the war began, Steele was never in command in a major battle of the war. He was in Mesilla when other units of Sibley's Brigade fought at Valverde and Glorieta. He spent a year of frustration in Indian Territory and arrived in Louisiana just after the battles of Mansfield and Pleasant Hill. Although a West Point graduate with brevets for distinguished service in Mexico and experience in fighting the Apache and Sioux, Steele never advanced beyond the rank of brigadier general.

After the war, Steele made his home in San Antonio. In 1874 he moved to Austin, where he became the state adjutant general. While in this position he reorganized the Texas Rangers for greater efficiency. Unfortunately, he also caused resentment when, in order to save costs, he retired the famed Texas Ranger captain L. H. McNelly, who was dying of tuberculosis. Steele himself died at San Antonio on January 12, 1885, after suffering from a stroke the previous day. He was buried in Oakwood Cemetery in Austin.[148]

ALEXANDER WATKINS TERRELL

Alexander Watkins Terrell, the last Texan appointed general officer in the Civil War, is probably better remembered as a jurist, legislator, and author of the Terrell election laws which (with amendments) govern Texas elections.

Alexander Watkins Terrell
(photo taken after war)
—Courtesy of Harold B. Simpson
Research Center, Hillsboro, Texas

Born in Patrick County, Virginia, on November 3, 1827, Terrell moved with his family to Boonville, Missouri, when he was only four years old. He was educated in primary school there and at the University of Missouri, then studied law and was admitted to the bar in 1849. He practiced law in St. Joseph, Missouri, for several years. Terrell married Ann Elizabeth Boulding, who bore him five children before her death in July 1860. He had moved his family to Austin, Texas, in 1852, in the futile hope that the warmer climate would help his wife, who had consumption.[149]

Terrell practiced law in Austin until his election as district judge in 1857. He became a good friend of Sam Houston, and like Houston opposed secession. When Texas did secede, Terrell turned down a military commission, but in February 1862 he visited Richmond, Virginia, carrying a message from Governor Francis Lubbock to Secretary of War Judah P. Benjamin. In June 1862, Terrell accepted appointment as a volunteer aide-de-camp to Henry E. McCulloch with the rank of captain. Terrell accompanied McCulloch to Arkansas later that year and remained on his staff until McCulloch was replaced as division commander.

On March 31, 1863, Terrell was commissioned lieutenant colonel by John B. Magruder with instructions to take command of a battalion being formed for frontier service. The battalion was enlarged to regimental size in June, with Terrell made colonel and commander. The regiment was sometimes referred to as the "Thirty-fourth Texas Cavalry," but more often as "Terrell's Texas Cavalry."[150]

Terrell's regiment remained in Texas during 1863. After initial training at Hempstead the unit moved to Galveston, where it was temporarily dismounted. Terrell was in Houston at the time discussing a proposal by Kirby Smith that he (Terrell) become head of the Texas Cotton Bureau. While Terrell was away, several officers led by Capt. C. G. Murray staged a mutiny over the dismounting of the regiment. When Terrell, who turned down the proposal to head the Cotton Bureau, returned to the regiment, he ordered the arrest of Murray and several others. After a military trial Murray and one other officer were imprisoned, and the others returned to duty. The orders for dismounting the regiment were rescinded, and harmony was restored.[151]

In the fall of 1863 Terrell's regiment was ordered to the middle Texas coast as part of General Magruder's buildup of forces to meet a possible Union invasion. At the end of the year the regiment was assigned to Col. Xavier Debray's Brigade at Gulf Prairie near the mouth of Caney Creek. After a brief stay at Galveston in February 1864, the regiment was ordered to report to Richard Taylor in Louisiana. On the morning of April 8, 1864, Terrell's troops skirmished with Federal cavalry near Mansfield while Taylor prepared his infantry for an all-out attack. That afternoon the regiment was on the army's right flank, fighting as dismounted cavalry when the battle began. During the course of battle the regiment was shifted toward the center of the field in the assault against the enemy position. At Pleasant Hill the next day, Terrell's regiment was again on the far right of the Confederate line. In the confused fighting on rough terrain, Terrell and one company were cut off from the rest of the regiment and spent the evening making their way back to the Confederate lines.[152]

Terrell and his regiment took part in the final phases of the Red River campaign, but saw less action than some other cavalry units. At Monett's Ferry the regiment was guarding the wagon train and missed the fighting. At Yellow Bayou the regiment was in reserve but became involved when George W. Baylor's cavalry needed support to avoid being encircled.

In early September 1864, Terrell was made head of a brigade formerly commanded by A. P. Bagby, who had been elevated to division command. Terrell's Brigade, consisting of his own regiment, William O. Yager's First Texas Cavalry, and James B. Likens' Thirty-fifth Texas Cavalry, was engaged in several skirmishes with Union forces along the Atchafalaya River in September, but was forced to give ground due to vastly superior Federal numbers. The brigade spent the late fall encamped on Bayou Boeuff, but went into winter quarters near Alexandria in December.[153]

In early spring, 1865, Terrell's troops moved to Grand Ecore, where they remained until orders were received returning the brigade to Texas. The brigade was disbanded on May 14 at Wild Cat Bluff, a small community on the Trinity River. Terrell himself returned to Trans Mississippi Department headquarters in Shreveport, where, on May 16, Kirby Smith issued orders promoting him to brigadier general. Smith then departed for Houston, where he made his headquarters prior to the surrender of the department at Galveston on June 2, 1865. Terrell rode back to Austin, where he joined a group of Confederates heading for Mexico.[154]

Terrell remained in Mexico for five months. During this time he met Emperor Maximilian and was appointed *"chef d'battalion"* (a rank comparable to colonel) in the French occupation forces. When the French withdrew from Mexico, Terrell resigned his commission and returned to Texas.[155]

Back in Texas, Terrell practiced law. His second wife, the former Sallie D. Mitchell, died in 1871. In 1874 he was chosen as reporter for the Texas Supreme Court. In 1875 he was elected to the Texas Senate, and served until 1884, when he was elected to the Texas House of Representatives. In the legislature he authored numerous important measures, including the Terrell election laws, an enabling act for the Texas Railroad Commission, and an act pledging three million acres of land to the Capitol Syndicate to construct a new state capitol. He served as U.S. ambassador to Turkey, 1893-1897, was appointed a regent of the University of Texas in 1909, and was president of the Texas State Historical Association in 1912. With his law partner Judge A. S. Walker, he reported and annotated thirteen volumes of Texas Supreme Court decisions and later reported an additional eleven volumes himself. He married his third wife, Mrs. Ann Holliday Anderson Jones, in 1883.

Terrell died on September 9, 1912, at Mineral Wells and was buried in the Texas State Cemetery in Austin.[156]

RICHARD WATERHOUSE

Richard Waterhouse, the regimental commander who led the 1862 assault against Milliken's Bend, was born in Rhea County, Tennessee, on January 12, 1832. As a teenager he ran away from home to take part in the Mexican War. He rejoined his family after the war and moved with them to San Augustine, Texas, in 1849. There he went into the mercantile business with his father. When Texas seceded he helped form the Nineteenth Texas Infantry and became its colonel in May 1862.[157]

The Nineteenth Texas was ordered to Arkansas in the summer of 1862. In October the regiment was assigned to George Flournoy's Brigade in Henry McCulloch's Division camped near Austin, Arkansas. When McCulloch was replaced as division commander by John G. Walker, McCulloch became the brigade commander. The first major engagement for Waterhouse and his men was at Milliken's Bend, Louisiana, on June 7, 1863. The Nineteenth Texas spearheaded the Confederate

Richard Waterhouse
—Courtesy of Harold B. Simpson Research Center, Hillsboro, Texas

assault on the Union troops who were protected by a river levee. In the attack Waterhouse led the Texans who drove the Federal defenders back to the river. In the melee a number of black troops were killed by Waterhouse's men, leading Union officials to charge that the Confederates had deliberately massacred African Americans.[158]

Henry McCulloch, the brigade commander, admitted the enemy had fought stubbornly but denied Waterhouse's men killed black troops trying to surrender. McCulloch praised Waterhouse, declaring "in the charge Col. [Richard] Waterhouse with his regiment distinguished themselves particularly, not only by a gallant and desperate charge over the levee, but they drove the enemy (leaving the camp covered with the dead) to the very bank of the river, and within short and direct range of the gunboats of the enemy." McCulloch concluded that Waterhouse "behaved in the most gallant manner, and his officers and men seemed to catch the enthusiasm of their commander, and did their duty nobly and gallantly upon every portion of the field."[159]

Waterhouse and the Nineteenth Texas remained with Walker's Division in Louisiana for the rest of the year. In late summer of 1863, William R. Scurry replaced Henry McCulloch as brigade commander, a move welcomed by members of the brigade. Waterhouse's regiment served under Scurry in the bayou country during the fall of 1863 and in the Red River campaign of 1864. At Mansfield the brigade was on the right flank of the army as the Confederates drove the enemy from the field. At Pleasant Hill the next day, Walker's Division was on the left side of the Confederate line with Scurry's Brigade on the division's right next to Churchill's Division to the south. When Churchill's Division gave ground under a furious Union attack, Scurry's Brigade was unprotected on its right flank. Waterhouse, whose regiment was on the brigade's right, was able to hold the line until the brigades of Randal and Waul could stabilize the front. O. M. Roberts, future governor of Texas and a colonel in Randal's Brigade, later reported that General Taylor praised both Scurry and Waterhouse for preventing "the confusion on the right side from becoming disastrous."[160]

Scurry's Brigade, including Waterhouse's regiment, marched north with Walker's Division in late April as part of Kirby Smith's efforts to stop the Union drive in southern Arkansas. When Scurry was mortally wounded at Jenkins' Ferry on April 30, 1864, Water-house assumed command of the brigade. On May 13, Kirby Smith appointed Waterhouse brigadier general, with date of rank April 30. When the Confederate government failed to confirm his action, Smith wrote to Adjutant General Cooper in late October request-ing approval, but no action was forthcoming. On March 16, 1865, Smith wrote Confederate authorities on the matter once again. On March 18, 1865, the last day the Confederate Senate met, Water-house's promotion was approved. Promotions for Richard Gano, William P. Hardeman, and Walter P. Lane were approved at the same time.[161]

Waterhouse returned to East Texas after the war. He speculat-ed in land in both San Augustine and Jefferson. While in Waco, Texas, dealing with some land matters, Waterhouse fell down the hotel stairs, dislocating his shoulder. He contracted pneumonia and died two days later, on March 20, 1876. He was buried in Oakwood Cemetery in Jefferson.[162]

THOMAS NEVILLE WAUL

Thomas Neville Waul was one of three Texans who served in the Confederate Congress before becoming a general in the Confederate army. Born January 5, 1813, near Statesburg in the Sumter District of South Carolina, Waul attended South Carolina College, taught briefly in Florence, Alabama, and then studied law in Vicksburg, Mississippi. He was admitted to the bar in 1835, and married America Simmons in November 1837. He moved to Texas before 1850 and established a cotton plantation on the Guadalupe River in Gonzales County. A staunch defender of the institution of slavery, he became active in the Democratic Party in Texas and campaigned against the Know-Nothing Party. He ran for Congress in 1859 but was narrowly defeated by the more moderate A. J. Hamilton. In 1860 he owned $55,000 in property, including forty-five slaves.[163]

As a defender of states' rights and slavery, Waul supported secession of Texas from the Union following Lincoln's election as president. After the state convention voted to secede, Waul was selected as one of Texas' delegates to the Confederate Provisional

Thomas Neville Waul
(photo taken after war)
—Courtesy of Harold B. Simpson
Research Center, Hillsboro, Texas

Congress meeting in Montgomery, Alabama. Waul was an active member of the congress, supporting a constitutional guarantee to allow importation of slaves from anywhere other than Africa and introducing legislation to strengthen defense of the Texas frontier. He was one of three nominees considered by the state legislature for the seat from the Texas western district in the first regular Confederate Congress but was not chosen.[164]

Waul returned to Texas after the provisional congress completed its work. In the spring of 1862 he raised a military unit known as Waul's Legion. The Legion, of which Waul became the colonel, originally consisted of twelve companies of infantry, six companies of cavalry, and a six-gun light artillery battery with a total complement of 2,000 men. The Legion was first sent to Arkansas, but in October 1862 was ordered to join Maj. Gen. W. W. Loring's Division in Mississippi. In February 1863, Waul and his troops were ordered to Fort Pemberton, a hastily constructed breastworks near the juncture of the Tallahatchie and Yazoo rivers, approximately sixty miles northeast of Vicksburg. For the next four months Waul and the Legion labored on the fortifications while beating off Union attacks. For his efforts Waul was praised by Loring "for his energy, promptness, and good judgment in the discharge of his duty. . . ."[165]

When Grant moved his army to the south and crossed the Mississippi below Vicksburg, Waul and the Legion, consisting then of eleven companies of infantry, one company of artillery, a detachment of mounted scouts and a battalion of Louisiana Zouaves attached to his command, were ordered to the outer limits of the Vicksburg defenses. Assigned to Stephen D. Lee's Brigade in Carter Stevenson's Division, Waul's Legion was in the center of the Confederate defense line. The Legion distinguished itself on May 22, when it recaptured the railroad redoubt which Grant's troops had taken in a major assault. Of this action brigade commander Stephen D. Lee wrote "a more daring feat has not been performed during the war and too much praise cannot be awarded to every one engaged in it." Lee lauded Waul for his "dashing gallantry and coolness" which "inspired every one around him with confidence."[166]

After the failed attack on May 22, Grant lay siege to Vicksburg. During the next six weeks, constant artillery bombardment, illness, hunger, and exposure took its toll on the Confederate defenders. When bacon and beef had all been eaten, the Confederates slaughtered their mules. Teamsters in Waul's Legion dried the mule meat to render it into a form of jerky. By the end of June conditions inside Vicksburg were desperate. On July 4 Lt. Gen. John C. Pemberton, commanding the Vicksburg garrison, surrendered. Waul's Legion, along with thousands of other Confederates, was paroled pending exchange. This exchange occurred in September 1863. Waul was promoted to brigadier general on September 19 and ordered to report to Kirby Smith for assignment in the Trans Mississippi.[167]

Waul arrived at Kirby Smith's headquarters in Shreveport on November 17, 1863. The following day he was ordered to proceed to Texas for service with John B. Magruder. Delighted to have Waul and his Legion serve under him, Magruder assigned Waul to command the Second Infantry Brigade consisting of his Legion, the Second Texas Infantry, Hobby's Infantry Regiment, and H. Willke's artillery battery. After a short leave home, Waul was instructed to advance to Brazoria with his command to meet the expected Union attack on the middle Texas coast. For Waul this assignment was short-lived. The threat to the Texas coast evaporated when Banks began his Red River campaign. In February Waul was directed to report to Richard Taylor in Louisiana, where he was given command of the First Infantry Brigade in John G. Walker's Texas Division.[168]

As commander of the First Brigade, Waul participated in the battles of Mansfield and Pleasant Hill. In these engagements Waul's

Brigade was in the center of the Confederate battle line. On both occasions the brigade, consisting of the Twelfth, Eighteenth, and Twenty-second Texas Infantry and the Thirteenth Dismounted Texas Cavalry, performed well. At Mansfield the brigade supported Scurry's Brigade in breaking the center of the Federal line; at Pleasant Hill the brigade helped stem the Federal breakthrough on the right that threatened to flank Scurry's Brigade.[169]

After the battles at Mansfield and Pleasant Hill, Walker's Division, including Waul's Brigade, was ordered to Arkansas to support Sterling Price's efforts to stop Frederick Steele's advance southward. When Walker's Division reached Camden, Steele was already in retreat. The Confederates attacked the Federals at Jenkins' Ferry as they attempted to cross the Saline River. In the fighting described as "a nightmare to both armies," all three of Walker's brigade commanders were wounded. Horace Randal and William R. Scurry were mortally wounded; Waul was severely wounded and his left arm broken, but he remained on the field until loss of blood forced him to withdraw.[170]

Waul went home to recover from his wounds. He returned to the army late in the year, taking command of his old brigade, then in Louisiana. The brigade moved to East Texas in the spring of 1865, but Waul received a medical leave as the bones in his arm had not yet reunited.[171]

After the war, Waul returned to his plantation in Gonzales County. He was elected as a delegate to the Texas Constitutional Convention in 1866. Soon thereafter he moved to Galveston, where he practiced law. He died on his farm near Greenville in Hunt County on July 18, 1908. He was buried in the Oakwood Cemetery in Fort Worth.[172]

CHAPTER FIVE

Brigadiers
East of the Mississippi

FIFTEEN TEXANS WHO SERVED as brigadier general in the Confederate army performed their primary military service east of the Mississippi River. Three of these, John Bell Hood, Thomas Rosser, and John A. Wharton, were later promoted to higher rank and their biographies are included in earlier chapters. Biographies of the other twelve are included in this chapter. Three of this group, Matthew D. Ector, Lawrence Sullivan Ross, and John Whitfield, served on both sides of the river but their most significant roles were played east of the Mississippi. Except for brief periods in recruiting and organizing, five other Texas generals, Hiram Granbury, Tom Harrison, Adam Johnson, John Moore, and William H. Young, spent their military service in the vast heartland area between the Mississippi and the Carolinas. Three Lone Star generals, John Gregg, Jerome B. Robertson, and son Felix Robertson, fought in both the heartland and Virginia. Louis T. Wigfall spent his brief military service entirely in Virginia.

MATTHEW DUNCAN ECTOR

Like Nathan Bedford Forrest, Matthew Duncan Ector enlisted as a private soldier in the Confederate army and rose to the rank of general officer. Born in Putnam County, Georgia, on February 28,

Matthew Duncan Ector
(photo taken after war)

—Courtesy of Harold B. Simpson
Research Center, Hillsboro, Texas

1822, Ector was educated at Centre College in Danville, Kentucky. He later studied law at Greenville, Georgia, and served one term in the Georgia legislature. He married Louise Phillips in 1842, gave up his law practice, and farmed for several years. After his wife's death in 1848, he traveled to California but soon thereafter settled in Henderson, Texas. Ector resumed the practice of law and in 1851 married Letitia M. Graham. He was elected to the state legislature in 1855, and was listed in the 1860 census returns as having $29,000 in property and owning twenty slaves.[1]

When the Civil War began, Ector joined the Third Texas Cavalry. He was soon promoted to lieutenant and made regimental adjutant. He participated in the battles at Wilson's Creek, Chustenahlah, and Pea Ridge, winning the praise of regimental commander Elkanah Greer for his "gallant bearing and conduct." When the regiment moved to Corinth, Mississippi, in spring of 1862, he became adjutant for brigade commander Joseph L. Hogg. In May Ector was chosen as colonel of the Fourteenth Texas Dismounted Cavalry. His regiment was part of a new brigade commanded by Arkansas Col. Thomas H. McCray that was sent to join Edmund Kirby Smith in eastern Tennessee. In late summer the brigade moved with Smith's army in the cooperative effort with Braxton Bragg to liberate Kentucky. On August 30, 1862, the brigade made what Kirby Smith described as a "well timed and dashing charge" at Richmond, Kentucky, which broke the enemy line and allowed Confederates to push across the Kentucky River. In his report of the action Colonel McCray praised Ector and several others who "particularly distinguished themselves being in the front of battle and cheering their men during the entire engagement."[2]

Although the Kentucky campaign achieved little, Ector was promoted to brigadier general on September 27. In October he was named commander of the second brigade in Maj. Gen. J. P. Mc-Cown's Division. At the time the brigade consisted of the Tenth, Eleventh, Fourteenth, and Fifteenth Texas dismounted cavalries, plus Capt. James Douglas' Texas artillery battery. Later the Ninth Texas Infantry replaced the Eleventh Texas Cavalry, and the Twenty-ninth and Thirty-ninth North Carolina infantries were added to the brigade.[3]

Ector's Brigade played a prominent role in the Battle of Murfreesboro, or Stone's River. The brigade and another from McCown's Division made the initial assault on the Union army on the morning of December 31, 1862. In the attack Ector led his troops against the Union right flank, driving the enemy back over two miles before Federal artillery stopped the advance. The fighting raged throughout the day as casualties mounted on both sides. Ector's Brigade sustained more than 300 casualties (approximately one-third of the brigade), including the death of Col. John C. Burks, the popular commander of the Eleventh Texas. Although the battle ended in a stalemate, General McCown praised Ector and his other two brigade commanders for their "cool and dauntless courage, as well as skill, in handling of their commands."[4]

In the summer of 1863 Ector's Brigade was sent to central Mississippi to join Joseph E. Johnston in his efforts to relieve the Confederate garrison at Vicksburg. The brigade remained in Mississippi throughout the summer as Johnston attempted unsuccessfully to put together sufficient forces to challenge Grant's army. Although there was considerable movement, the brigade, now part of W. H. T. Walker's Division, saw little action. After the fall of Vicksburg, Ector's Brigade returned to the Army of Tennessee in time to participate in the Battle of Chickamauga, September 19-20, 1863. Walker's Division was assigned to reserve duty, but during the fighting on the first day Ector's Brigade was called upon to assist Forrest's cavalry on the Confederate right. Historian Peter Cozzens pointed out that "Ector was a man whom Forrest could understand." Like Forrest, both had come up from the ranks. Both men had talents too obvious to go unnoticed, and both were bold and courageous. Forrest welcomed Ector's support. In his report of the battle, Forrest stated that "the superior force of the enemy compelled us to give back until re-enforced by General Ector's brigade, when the enemy was driven back away." In the fighting on September 20 Ector's Brigade was called upon to support South Carolina and Georgia troops in their attack against Union troops along the La Fayette road. Once again Ector and his troops helped achieve the Confederate objective, but the losses were high. In two days of fighting Ector sustained 536 casualties in a brigade that entered the battle with an effective strength of approximately 1,300 men. Ector himself was hit four times in the battle but did not leave the field.[5]

After the Battle of Chickamauga, Ector's Brigade was ordered back to central Mississippi to rejoin Joseph E. Johnston's Army of Mississippi. In October the brigade was assigned to Maj. Gen. Samuel French's Division near Brandon, Mississippi. There the division remained until late January 1864, when William T. Sherman moved his army from Vicksburg across the state, forcing the Confederates, now under the command of Leonidas Polk, to withdraw into Alabama. When it appeared Sherman would turn south toward Mobile, part of French's Division was moved there by rail. Ector's Brigade was prepared to make the move, but when Sherman pulled back toward the Mississippi, Polk, who reoccupied eastern Mississippi, retained Ector and his brigade. In late February the brigade was camped near Meridian, Mississippi.[6]

In May 1864, French's Division, including Ector's Brigade, was ordered to northern Georgia to join the Army of Tennessee now commanded by Joseph E. Johnston. The brigade took part in several battles as the Confederates fell back toward Atlanta. Ector himself was slightly wounded in the fighting at New Hope Church in late May. In June the brigade was on the front line in the battle at Kennesaw Mountain in which the Confederates repulsed the Union attack. In the early battles for Atlanta fought on July 20 and 22, the brigade was on the west side of the city and escaped the major fighting. When Sherman's army swung west of Atlanta, however, the brigade was heavily engaged. On July 27 Ector was severely wounded when a piece of exploding shell tore into his left leg above the knee. An operation was performed that evening in which the damaged leg was amputated at midthigh.[7]

As Ector had been wounded, Col. William H. Young, commanding the Ninth Texas, took over direction of the brigade during the fighting. In his report of the battle Young praised Ector, who "by his patriotic zeal, his tireless energy, his undaunted bravery . . . was able to conduct his brigade through every contest and trial with great credit and honor."[8]

Ector returned to Texas to convalesce after the operation. Although he was scheduled to rejoin his brigade in the defense of Spanish Fort near Mobile in April 1865, he apparently was unable to do so.[9]

A widower since the death of his second wife in 1859, Ector married Sallie P. Chew of Mississippi in 1864. The couple made their home in Henderson, Texas, following the war. Ector was elected district judge in 1867, but was removed by Gen. J. J. Reynolds as an impediment to Reconstruction. The Ectors moved to Marshall, where he opened a law practice. He became judge of the district court again in 1874, and in 1875 was elected to the Texas Court of Appeals. In 1876 he was chosen presiding judge of the appeals court, a position he held until his death in Tyler on October 29, 1879. His grave is in the Greenwood Cemetery in Marshall.[10]

HIRAM BRONSON GRANBURY

Hiram Bronson Granbury, one of the most outstanding Texas brigadier generals in the Civil War, was born on March 1, 1831, in Copiah County, Mississippi. The son of a Baptist minister, Granbury was educated at Oakland College in Rodney, Mississippi. He moved to Waco, Texas, in the early 1850s, studied law, and was admitted to the bar. From 1856 to 1858 he served as chief justice of McLennan County. On March 31, 1858, he married Fannie Sims of Waco. The couple had no children.[11]

Following Texas' secession from the Union, Granbury organized the Waco Guards, which became a part of the Seventh Texas Infantry. Although he had no previous military experience, Granbury was elected major in the regiment, commanded by Col. John

Hiram Bronson Granbury
—Courtesy of Lawrence T. Jones III

Gregg. In the fall of 1861 the Seventh Texas was ordered to join units of Albert Sidney Johnston's army at Clarksville, Tennessee. After serving under Brig. Gen. Lloyd Tilghman on the Tennessee River for two months, the regiment was assigned to the division commanded by Tennessee lawyer Gideon Pillow and ordered to report to Fort Donelson on the Cumberland River. In February 1862 the Confederate garrison at Donelson, including the Seventh Texas, was surrounded by Union troops commanded by Brig. Gen. U. S. Grant. For their part in the attempted Confederate breakout from Union encirclement on February 15, 1862, both Granbury and Gregg were commended by brigade commander Col. John M. Simonton. In his own report Gregg acknowledged the effective assistance of Granbury in managing the regiment during the fighting.[12]

After the failure of the attempted breakout, the Confederate commanders at Donelson agreed to surrender the garrison. Under Grant's unconditional surrender terms the Confederate defenders were sent north as prisoners of war. Enlisted men and company officers were taken to prisons in Ohio and Illinois, but senior personnel, including Granbury and Gregg, were sent to Fort Warren in Boston harbor. Although the prison was cold and barren and most of the officers became ill at one time or another, confinement at Fort Warren was more pleasant than the usual Civil War imprisonment. The food was generally good and camaraderie between officers and political prisoners provided intellectual and social stimulation. Prison records indicate that Granbury was given a pass in July 1862 to be with his wife, who had undergone surgery in Baltimore. Regimental commander John Gregg's wife apparently stayed with him during part of his captivity.[13]

In late August 1862, Gregg, Granbury and other Donelson prisoners were exchanged. Promotions for several of the officers were soon forthcoming. Granbury was elevated to regimental commander with the rank of colonel to replace Gregg, who was made brigadier general and given his own brigade.

For several months the Seventh Texas was stationed in northern Mississippi as part of Maxey's Brigade, but in early 1863 the regiment was made part of Gregg's Brigade and ordered to Port Hudson, Louisiana. Granbury and his regiment took part in defense of Port Hudson in March, when Rear Admiral David Farragut attempted to pass the batteries with the Union fleet. In late April 1863, Granbury and his Texans were sent on temporary duty to Woodville, Mississippi, in an unsuccessful effort to intercept Union raiders led by Col. Benjamin Grierson.[14]

Following the failure to capture Grierson and his cavalry, Granbury and the Seventh Texas rejoined Gregg's Brigade near Jackson, Mississippi. Grant had moved his army across the Mississippi River and was heading toward Jackson and Vicksburg. On May 12 Gregg's Brigade attempted to block the advance of Grant's army at Raymond, Mississippi. In the fighting Gregg's Brigade was pushed back by a much larger Union force spearheaded by Maj. Gen. John A. Logan's Division. In the battle the Seventh Texas held its position for over an hour until, according to Granbury, "the men had exhausted their own ammunition and emptied the cartridge boxes of the dead of the enemy and of our killed and wounded." The regiment sustained 158 casualties, including twenty-two men killed.[15]

The brigade fell back to Jackson after the battle at Raymond. Gen. Joseph E. Johnston arrived on the night of May 12. He hoped to put together a large enough force so that he could aid John C. Pemberton and the Confederates at Vicksburg, but was unable to do so. After the fall of Vicksburg in early July, Johnston and the forces under his command retreated toward Meridian, Mississippi. Granbury and the Seventh Texas spent the next two months bivouacked at Enterprise, Mississippi. There they recuperated from their losses at Raymond and prepared for the next campaign.[16]

In early September Gregg's Brigade was ordered to northern Georgia to join Braxton Bragg's army. The brigade, including Granbury and the Seventh Texas, was part of Maj. Gen. Bushrod R. Johnson's Division in the Battle of Chickamauga, fought later that month. In the fighting on that afternoon Granbury was wounded by a bullet that struck his lower abdomen. The velocity of the bullet was not fast enough to break the skin but did cause a painful bruise that forced Granbury out of the battle. The regiment, under command of Maj. K. M. Van Zandt, continued fighting the next day as the Confederates pushed the Union troops back to Chattanooga.[17]

After the battle at Chickamauga there were numerous organizational changes made in Bragg's army. John Gregg, the brigade commander, had also been wounded at Chickamauga. After his recovery he was transferred to the Army of Northern Virginia. Granbury and the Seventh Texas were transferred to Brig. Gen. James A. Smith's Brigade in Patrick Cleburne's Division, replacing an Arkansas regiment that was moved elsewhere. The brigade remained with Bragg's army, which lay siege to Chattanooga throughout October and early November.[18]

In late November Union forces launched a major assault on Bragg's army occupying Missionary Ridge overlooking Chattanooga. Smith's Brigade was posted on Tunnel Hill on the Confederate right flank when the battle began. In the fighting Brigadier General Smith was wounded. As senior colonel Granbury assumed command of the brigade. Although Cleburne's Division and Smith's Brigade held their own, Union forces broke through the center of the line, necessitating a Confederate withdrawal back into Georgia. Under Granbury's command the brigade played a signficiant role in preventing the capture of Confederate wagons and artillery at Ringgold, Georgia. For his performance in the Chattanooga-Ringgold campaign Granbury later received the thanks of Pat Cleburne, the division commander, and promotion to brigadier general commanding the brigade.[19]

Granbury was not present in early January 1864 when Cleburne presented a proposal that slaves be enlisted in the Confederate army, in return for which they would be granted their freedom. Before giving the proposal to army commander Joseph E. Johnston, Cleburne invited as many of his officers who so wished to sign the plan. Two brigade commanders, Daniel Govan and Mark P. Low-rey, and their officers did so. Granbury and Lucius Polk, the other brigade commander, were not on hand when the copy was ready for signature. Cleburne's biographer, Craig L. Symonds, stated that both would have signed had they been present and both gave Cleburne permission to express their support. The proposal was so controversial, however, that Johnston refused to forward Cleburne's plan to Richmond authorities. A copy did reach the desk of President Davis, but the chief executive ordered suppression of the proposal.[20]

Meanwhile, Cleburne's Division was sent to Mississippi for a brief period in mid-Feburary to meet an expected Federal advance. Before the end of the month the division was back in Georgia with the Army of Tennessee. Granbury's Brigade remained in Georgia for the next seven months as Joe Johnston and his successor John B. Hood attempted to halt the southward movement of William T. Sherman's army. At Dug Gap, near Dalton, Georgia, on May 8, Granbury's Brigade routed enemy attackers. Three weeks later as the armies drew closer to Atlanta, Granbury and his Texans were called upon to carry out a night attack against the Federals near Pickett's Mill. With fixed bayonets, Granbury's men moved across an open field, capturing more than 200 Union troops. Cleburne lauded Granbury and his men, declaring "it needed but the brilliancy of this night to add luster to the achievements of Granbury and his brigade in the afternoon. I am deeply indebted to them both." The next morning army commander Joe Johnston, elated at Granbury's performance, congratulated the Texan and told Granbury "this shall no longer be called Granbury's, but shall be known as Johnston's brigade."[21]

Unfortunately for Joe Johnston, the success at Pickett's Mill did not stop Sherman from moving closer and closer to Atlanta. On July 17 President Davis, exasperated by Johnston's constant retreating, removed him from command and replaced him with John B. Hood. Hood almost immediately went on the attack. Granbury's Brigade played little part in the Battle of Peachtree Creek on July 20, 1864, but was involved in the fighting east of Atlanta the next two days. Granbury was ill at the time and James A. Smith once again commanded the brigade. Smith was wounded, and many of the Texans in the brigade's Seventeenth-Eighteenth Consolidated

Regiment were captured in a Federal counterattack on July 22. The brigade sustained 311 casualties in the fighting.[22]

Granbury returned from sick leave as the fighting north and east of Atlanta was coming to an end. Sherman now shifted his army around the west side of Atlanta and moved southward to cut the railroads bringing necessary supplies to the city. In the Battle of Jonesboro, fought south of Atlanta in late August, Granbury's Brigade was on the extreme left side of the line as the Confederates attempted to drive the Union troops back to the Flint River. As planned, Granbury's Brigade led off the Confederate attack, but instead of swinging to the right against the flank of the Federal infantry the Texans moved directly ahead against Judson Kilpatrick's Union cavalry. Granbury forced Kilpatrick to fall back across the river but failed to attack the entrenched Union troops to his right. Brig. Gen. Mark Lowrey, temporarily commanding the division, later criticized Granbury's troops as being "too full of impetuosity" and pursuing the Federal cavalry "contrary to instruction." Granbury defended the actions of his brigade, reporting that his orders "were to drive all opposing forces beyond the Flint River."[23]

Elsewhere, other Confederate units in the attack at Jonesboro were unsuccessful, forcing the area commander, General Hardee, to order a withdrawal to Lovejoy's Station. Two days later, Hood evacuated Atlanta.

Granbury's Brigade marched with Hood's army in the Tennessee campaign in autumn of 1864. When Hood attacked the Union forces of John Schofield at Franklin, Tennessee, on November 30, Granbury's Texas Brigade was in the center of the Confederate line. Although the initial assault pushed the Federals back, the Union center rallied and held. In the bitter fighting, described by one Texan as the "bloodiest battle I have ever seen," division commander Pat Cleburne was hit in the chest and killed instantly. Granbury, leading his brigade, was hit in the eye about the same time. The bullet passed through his brain and exploded at the back of his head. He threw his hands up to his face and fell dead instantly.[24]

The bodies of Granbury, Cleburne, and Confederate brigadiers John Adams and Otto French Strahl were taken to Carnton, the McGavock plantation house, just a mile away and lay there on the porch until taken away for burial. Granbury was first buried near Franklin, but his body was later reinterred at the Ashwood

Church Cemetery south of Columbia, Tennessee. Twenty-nine years later, on November 30, 1893, his remains were moved to Granbury, Texas, a town named in his honor.[25]

JOHN GREGG

John Gregg, killed while leading Hood's Texas Brigade south of Richmond seven weeks before his former subordinate Hiram Granbury died in the attack at Franklin, Tennessee, was one of the finest combat officers in the Confederate army. His bravery, courage, and leadership ability were demonstrated at Fort Donelson, Chickasaw Bluffs, Raymond, and Chickamauga before his appointment to command Hood's Brigade and shown again in his leadership of the Brigade in the Wilderness, Spotsylvania, and Petersburg campaigns.

Historian William C. Davis believed Gregg was admirably suited to command the Texas Brigade. "A rugged and unrelenting fighter, he was personally without fear," wrote Davis, "even looking the role of a rugged frontiersman with his 'spade' beard, high forehead, and fierce gaze." In his biography of Robert E. Lee, Douglas Southall Freeman noted that one of Lee's staff officers, Richard W. Corbin, said that "Lee regarded Gregg as the best brigadier in his army" and was considering him for division command when Gregg was killed on the Charles City Road on October 7, 1864.[26]

John Gregg
—Courtesy of Harold B. Simpson Research Center, Hillsboro, Texas

John Gregg was born on September 28, 1828, in Lawrence County, Alabama. He graduated from La Grange College in Georgia in 1847, taught mathematics and languages there for a year, and then studied law in Tuscumbia, Alabama. He moved to Fairfield, Texas, in 1852. After his first wife, Mollie Winston, died in 1855, he married Mary Frances Garth; the couple had two children.[27]

Gregg practiced law for several years and began the first newspaper in the county, the *Freestone County Reporter*. He was elected district judge in 1855, became a successful farmer and small slaveholder, and was a recognized leader in local affairs. A staunch supporter of states' rights, he was elected as a delegate to the Texas secession convention. At the convention Gregg worked for immediate separation from the Union. He opposed any delay in seceding; on the fourth day of the convention he moved to defeat a proposed requirement that the secession ordinance be submitted to the people for ratification. His motion lost by a 145-to-29 vote, but the action marked Gregg as a leader among the convention's most ardent secessionists. He was one of three convention members chosen to be a delegate to the Montgomery convention that created the Confederate States of America. He was the first Texas delegate to arrive at the convention and remained in the provisional congress when it moved to Richmond, Virginia. He stayed in the congress until after the Battle of Manassas, when he resigned his seat and went home to form an infantry regiment.[28]

The Seventh Texas Infantry, organized by Gregg in October 1861, consisted of 746 men recruited in ten East Texas counties. Gregg was elected colonel, J. J. Clough, the district attorney of Harrison County, was chosen lieutenant colonel, and Hiram B. Granbury became major of the regiment. The Seventh Texas was assigned to duty at Fort Donelson, Tennessee. When the fort surrendered to U.S. Grant, Gregg and other members of the regiment became prisoners of war. As noted earlier, senior officers captured at Donelson were imprisoned at Fort Warren in Boston harbor. Confinement at Warren was not as unpleasant as it was at most Civil War prisons. Gregg's wife, Mary, was allowed to stay with him during some of his captivity.[29]

Gregg and other Donelson prisoners were exchanged in August 1862. Gregg was promoted to brigadier general on September 27, with date of rank August 29, 1862. He was given command of a brigade consisting of the Seventh Texas, the Third, Tenth, Fifteenth, Thirtieth, and Forty-first Tennessee infantry regiments, and a battery of light artillery. The brigade was sent to the Vicksburg area, where in late December Gregg and his men took part in repulsing William T. Sherman's Corps at Chickasaw Bluffs. Later the brigade was transferred to the defense of Port Hudson, remaining there until ordered to Raymond, Mississippi, in early May. At Raymond on May 12, Gregg's Brigade made a desperate but unsuccessful effort to block the advance of Grant's army toward Jackson. Although his brigade faced an entire Union Corps commanded by James McPherson, Gregg held up the Federal advance for several hours before giving ground to the superior enemy numbers. The brigade fell back toward Jackson, where Gregg joined Confederate forces commanded by Joseph E. Johnston. When Johnston withdrew from Jackson on May 14, Gregg commanded the rear guard of the retreating Confederate forces.[30]

After the evacuation of Jackson, Gregg's Brigade withdrew to Meridian, Mississippi. For the next three months the brigade was not involved in any heavy fighting as Johnston attempted unsuccessfully to put together sufficient forces to challenge Grant's control of western and central Mississippi. In September the brigade was transferred to Braxton Bragg's Army of Tennessee. In mid-September the brigade was in the bloody Battle of Chickamauga. On the first day of the fighting Gregg rode in front of the brigade to reconnoiter the Federal position but found himself in the Union skirmish line. The Federals called upon him to surrender, but Gregg turned his horse and attempted to ride to safety. The Union troops fired and Gregg fell from his horse with a bullet in his neck. Federal troops gathered around to scavenge. They removed his sword and spurs before being driven off by Texans from Jerome B. Robertson's Brigade (Hood's old Texas Brigade) who were nearby. Although the wound was serious, Gregg recovered. Historian Harold B. Simpson noted that "little did the men of Robertson's command realize that the officer they had saved would command their brigade within a few months and die a hero's death leading them into battle within a year."[31]

Gregg's appointment to command the Texas Brigade of the Army of Northern Virginia came through a series of unforeseen circumstances. Jerome Robertson, who commanded the brigade at

Chickamauga, had incurred the displeasure of corps commander James Longstreet and Micah Jenkins, who assumed temporary command of the division when John B. Hood, like Gregg, was wounded at Chickamauga. As a result Robertson was relieved of brigade command and transferred to Texas. Meanwhile, Gregg, who had recovered from his wounds, was without a command as his old brigade had been reorganized. On January 11, 1864, he was ordered to report to Russellville, Tennessee, to fill the vacancy created by Robertson's dismissal as commander of the Texas Brigade.[32]

Gregg had barely assumed command of his new brigade when Longstreet's Corps was ordered back to Virginia. Charles Field, a Kentuckian and West Point graduate, had been appointed division commander in place of Micah Jenkins. Field and Gregg got along well together and soon won the support of the men under their command, although Gregg, a serious-minded and stern individual, was more respected than liked by his troops.[33]

Gregg's first opportunity to lead the Texas Brigade in battle came in the Wilderness in May 1864. Grant attempted to move the Army of the Potomac through the heavily forested area before Lee could react. But once again, as in the previous year at nearby Chancellorsville, Lee ordered his army to attack. Longstreet's Corps, including Gregg's Brigade, entered the battle from the west after the other two corps of the army were engaged. Gregg and his Texans arrived on the scene just as units from A. P. Hill's Corps were giving way under strong enemy pressure.

As Gregg formed his brigade in line to enter the battle, General Lee arrived on the scene. Unfamiliar with Gregg, who had served in the western armies, Lee inquired, "Who are you, my boys?" "Texas boys," was the response. For once, according to Lee's biographer Douglas Southall Freeman, "the dignity of the commanding general was shattered; for once his poise was shaken." "Hurrah for Texas," Lee shouted, waving his hat and repeating "hurrah for Texas." Lee turned to Gregg and instructed him to give the enemy the cold steel of the bayonet. Gregg then ordered his men to charge with the admonition "the eyes of General Lee are upon you." As the men moved out, Lee again waved his hat and exclaimed, "Texans always move them." As Lee's words were passed along the line, Gregg's men cheered and moved forward. Lee himself, deeply moved by the response, rode ahead as if to lead the brigade in the attack. The Texans, fearing an injury to their commander, began crying "Lee to the rear" and "Lee go back." According to some accounts, one of Gregg's men seized the bridle of Lee's horse, Traveller, and several staff officers escorted Lee to a place where he could observe the attack in safety.[34]

As Lee watched, Gregg and his brigade advanced across the open field and drove the enemy back through the woods until Federal artilley fire forced them to fall back and regroup. Once again, the Texas Brigade charged, stopping Winfield Hancock's Corps at it attempted to move forward. After heavy fighting Gregg and his Texans were relieved by other brigades. The Union advance was halted and some lost ground regained. Casualties were high; in Gregg's Brigade between 450 and 550 out of the 700-800 who were engaged. Gregg was not wounded but had three horses shot out from under him in the fighting.[35]

Although Grant was defeated in the Wilderness, he did not retreat. He swung his army to Lee's right and moved toward Spotsylvania Court House. Field's Division was one of the first Confederate units on the scene and began entrenching immediately. The Union army made several assaults on the Confederate line. Three of these were directly against Gregg's Brigade. The first two were repulsed, but in the third one the Federals broke through and were driven back only after bloody hand-to-hand fighting by Gregg's men.[36]

Fighting continued around Spotsylvania for nearly two weeks before Grant broke off to continue his sliding movement south. The main Union assault at Cold Harbor on June 3 was slightly to the right of Gregg's Brigade, so casualties among the Texans were relatively light. When Grant crossed the James and moved toward Petersburg, Gregg's Brigade moved with the Army of Northern Virginia into trenches south of the Appomattox River and east of Petersburg. The brigade remained there for five weeks and then moved to a defense line north of the James River and southeast of Richmond.[37]

The hard campaigning took its toll on Gregg's Brigade. Gregg's predecessor, Jerome B. Robertson, had requested that the brigade be allowed to return to Texas for the purpose of recruiting, but no approval had been forthcoming. In early summer of 1864, Gregg brought up the issue again. In a letter to Adj. Gen. Samuel Cooper, Gregg noted that the number of muskets in his command was only about 435, too small for effective brigade operations. He proposed that additional troops be found west of the Mississippi. His division commander, General Field, agreed, observing that Gregg's Brigade had "fought too long and gallantly to be permitted to disappear from pure exhaustion of men." General Lee endorsed the proposal to move men from the Trans Mississippi, but was opposed to releasing men from the brigade for recruiting purposes. "General Gregg cannot be spared from this army at this time, when every man is wanted at his post," wrote Lee.[38] During the next four months, Gregg's Brigade was involved in several engagements with the enemy. Most of these were no more than skirmishes, but in late September heavy fighting occurred when two Union corps launched a major attack on Confederate positions at Fort Harrison and Fort Gilmer. Although the Federals overran Harrison, which was the outer fort, Gregg's and Benning's brigades beat back several assaults on Gilmer, the inner fort.[39]

Lee was determined to retake Fort Harrison. On October 7 Field's Division and Robert Hoke's Division were ordered to attack the Union position between Darbytown and New Market roads while two other Confederate brigades outflanked the Federals and attacked from the rear. In the attack Gregg's Brigade attempted to take a strongly defended enemy position. Although some of the brigade managed to get within a hundred yards of their objective, they were driven back by massive enemy fire.[40]

Casualties in the fighting were high. Gregg was killed instantly by a ball through the neck as he was leading the attack. His body lay in a pool of blood but was recovered by several Texans who crawled through enemy fire. Gregg's body was taken to Richmond, where it lay in state in the hall of the House of Representatives. Members of the brigade were permitted to attend the funeral on October 9. The casket was placed in a private vault in Hollywood Cemetery, where it remained until Gregg's widow, Mary, arrived at Richmond to claim the body. She had the body taken to Aberdeen, Mississippi, for final burial. Gregg County, Texas, created in 1873, was named in his honor.[41]

THOMAS HARRISON

Thomas Harrison, younger brother of Confederate Brig. Gen. James E. Harrison, was born on May 1, 1823, in Jefferson County, Alabama, and raised in Monroe County, Mississippi. He moved to Brazoria County, Texas, in 1843 and studied law in the office of his brother-in-law, William H. Jackson. He returned to Aberdeen, Mississippi, where he practiced law. In 1846 he joined Jefferson Davis' First Mississippi Rifles for service in the Mexican War. After the war he moved to Houston, Texas, where he was elected to the Texas legislature. In 1851 he moved to Marlin, Texas, where he lived for four years prior to making his permanent home in Waco. He married Sarah Ellis McDonald, niece of North Carolina Governor John Ellis, in 1858; the couple had five children.[42]

Thomas Harrison
(photo taken after war)
—Courtesy of Harold B. Simpson Research Center, Hillsboro, Texas

In 1860 Harrison served as a captain in William C. Dalrymple's Ranger company pursuing Indians in the Texas Panhandle.

When the Civil War began, Harrison became captain of a militia company that helped force the surrender of U.S. troops at Camp Cooper. The militia company was later mustered into Confederate service as Company A of Benjamin Terry's cavalry regiment, officially the Eighth Texas Cavalry but better known as Terry's Texas Rangers.[43]

Terry's Rangers traveled from Houston via Beaumont, New

Orleans, and Nashville to Bowling Green, Kentucky, where Albert Sidney Johnston was assembling his army. There the regiment was formally organized and field officers chosen. Terry was elected colonel, Tom Lubbock lieutenant colonel, and Harrison major. Following the deaths of Terry and Lubbock in the winter of 1861-1862, the regiment selected John A. Wharton, commander of Company B, as the new regimental commander. Harrison became lieutenant colonel and second-in-command.[44]

Wharton led the Rangers in the Battle of Shiloh on April 6-7, 1862, and was wounded in the fight. Although he refused to leave the field while the battle raged, Wharton turned over temporary command to Harrison after the battle ended. Under Harrison's leadership, the Rangers helped cover the withdrawal of the Confederates to Corinth. When Union troops drew too close to the retreating Confederates, Harrison joined Nathan Bedford Forrest in driving back the enemy. According to one Texan, the Rangers "went like a cyclone" when the orders for attack were given and rode to within twenty paces of the enemy before unloading both barrels of their shotguns. The effect was devastating; the enemy suffered more than one hundred casualties, compared to only ten for the Texans.[45]

During the summer of 1862, the Rangers, again under Wharton's command, were part of Forrest's Brigade in raids against Buell's supply line in Tennessee. When Forrest turned over command of the brigade to Wharton in late September, Harrison became regimental commander. After the Battle of Perryville in early October, Harrison was promoted to colonel. In the Battle of Murfreesboro, fought in late December and early January, Wharton divided the brigade into three commands and selected Harrison to command one consisting of the Eighth Texas, Third Confederate, and Second Georgia cavalries. Harrison led the three regiments in the fighting on December 31, when the brigade swung around the Union right flank and captured 1,500 prisoners. In the second day of fighting at Murfreesboro, Harrison, who had eluded injury so far and gained the nickname "Old Iron Sides" because he seemed to be shielded against enemy bullets, was wounded in the hip. Nevertheless, he stayed with his command throughout the battle.[46]

In February 1863, Wharton's Brigade accompanied Maj. Gen. Joseph Wheeler in an unsuccessful raid on Fort Donelson. According to Ranger L. B. Giles, the "wild-goose chase" was exceeded only by Napoleon's Russian campaign in terms of "suffering, hardships, and barrenness of results." After preliminary attacks on the fort failed, Wheeler called off the campaign and ordered retreat.[47]

During the spring and early summer the cavalry staged some minor raids in Tennessee, but the search for forage for the animals became a major concern. In August Wharton was given command of a division in Wheeler's Cavalry Corps, with Harrison taking command of the brigade consisting of the Eighth Texas, Eleventh Texas, First Kentucky, and Third Confederate Cavalry. Although the composition of the brigade would change from time to time, Harrison remained in command from August 1863 to the end of the war.

Wharton's cavalry, including Harrison's Brigade, took part in the Battle of Chickamauga in September 1863, but was on the left flank of the army and missed the heavy fighting that occurred in the center. In late November the cavalry was attached to James Longstreet's Corps and participated in the unsuccessful Knoxville campaign. Harrison's Brigade remained in East Tennessee during the winter months, but in April 1864 was transferred to William C. Y. Humes' Division in Wheeler's Cavalry Corps near Dalton, Georgia.[48]

Harrison's Brigade saw considerable action during the late spring and early summer as a part of Joseph E. Johnston's army in its efforts to block Sherman's move toward Atlanta. General Wheeler praised Harrison and his cavalry for their role in the battles at Resaca, Dug Gap, and Varnell's Station. At Big Shanty and New Hope Church, Harrison's troopers fought as dismounted cavalry. The brigade saw only limited action in the major battles around Atlanta in July, but played a significant role in defending vital railroad lines from enemy hands.[49]

Harrison and his brigade were part of Wheeler's massive raid in northern Georgia and middle Tennessee in mid-August 1864. Wheeler was impressed with Harrison's performance in fighting near Nashville. "Harrison's brigade charged the enemy and drove him rapidly for two miles," reported Wheeler, "capturing 3 stands of colors, a number of prisoners, and arms." Even though the raiders destroyed much property, they failed to stop Sherman in his moves around Atlanta.[50]

When Hood moved his army northward toward Nashville in

the autumn of 1864, he left Wheeler's Cavalry Corps to oppose Sherman's march to the sea. Harrison's Brigade, still part of Humes' Division, took part in several of the delaying actions as the Confederates fell back to Savannah. When Sherman headed into the Carolinas the brigade continued to harass the enemy.

Harrison was promoted to brigadier general on February 18, with date of rank January 14, 1865. At the Battle of Monroe's Crossroads on March 10, 1865, Harrison was severely wounded in a clash with Judson Kilpatrick's cavalry. Harrison went to Greensboro to recover from his wound, but the war ended before he could rejoin his command.[51]

Harrison returned to his home in Waco after the surrender of Confederate forces in North Carolina. Described by one of his soldiers as "a small, nervous irascible man," Harrison was never popular with his troops, but like John Gregg he was generally respected. He entered politics after the war, winning election as district judge in 1866. He was a Democratic presidential elector in 1872. He died in Waco on July 14, 1891, and was buried in the First Street Cemetery, where his brother James was buried sixteen years earlier.[52]

ADAM RANKIN JOHNSON

Adam Rankin Johnson, who gained the sobriquet "Stovepipe" in the War for Southern Independence, was born in Henderson, Kentucky, on February 8, 1834, the son of a physician. As a young lad he worked in a local drug store. By the age of sixteen he was a factory foreman supervising eighty people. When he was twenty he moved to Burnet County, Texas. During the next few years he was a surveyor, contractor for the Butterfield Overland Mail, and Indian fighter. On the eve of the Civil War, January 1861, he married Josephine Eastland of Burnet. The couple had nine children, but three of them died early in life.[53]

When the Civil War began, Johnson returned to Kentucky to serve as a scout with Nathan Bedford Forrest. After some brief skirmishes with the enemy, Forrest and his cavalry were assigned to the defense of Fort Donelson in early 1862. When the Confederate commanders there decided to surrender, Forrest assigned Johnson the responsibility of finding a way out of the besieged fort. Having completed this assignment Johnson was then given the task of assisting John B. Floyd and Gideon Pillow to make good their escape from Donelson.[54]

In the summer of 1862 Johnson returned to Kentucky to recruit Confederate sympathizers into a partisan ranger company. In command of the company, Johnson made the first Confederate raid on a northern town. On July 18, 1862, with only thirty-five men, Johnson crossed the Ohio River and rode into Newburgh, Indiana. By placing an old stovepipe and a charred log on two wagons, he convinced Federal troops that he had two pieces of artillery. The

Adam Rankin Johnson
—Courtesy of Center for American History, UT at Austin

Federals, who outnumbered Johnson by six-to-one, surrendered the city, and thereafter Johnson gained the nickname "Stovepipe."[55]

With weapons taken at Newburgh, Johnson returned to Kentucky, where he recruited and equipped new troops into what became the Tenth Kentucky Cavalry. Johnson was commissioned colonel of the regiment which was assigned to John Hunt Morgan's Brigade. In August Johnson led his regiment in the capture of Hopkinsville, Kentucky, and Clarksville, Tennessee, where additional weapons were taken from the Federals. That fall, when Morgan split his command into two separate brigades, Johnson was offered command of one but declined, citing his belief that he would be freer to carry out raids into western Kentucky if he were not burdened with brigade responsibilities.[56]

In late 1862 Johnson returned to Texas on what he later described as a "special mission," probably relating to recruiting. When he rejoined Morgan in February 1863, Johnson agreed to take command of the Second Cavalry Brigade. Johnson commanded one brigade and Basil W. Duke the other when Morgan made his July raid into Ohio and Indiana. Although Morgan and Duke were forced to surrender when they were surrounded, Johnson and several hundred of his brigade managed to escape across the Ohio River into western Virginia.[57]

As the senior officer in Morgan's command not captured in the Ohio raid, Johnson issued a call for all of Morgan's men who had escaped (or were not in the raid) to rendezvous at Morristown in eastern Tennessee. Within two months Johnson had assembled 1,200 men. Some of the reformed brigade took part in the Chickamauga campaign, but Johnson himself was apparently not in the battle. Following Chickamauga, Braxton Bragg, who had been critical of both Morgan and Johnson, divided the command, sending some with Forrest and others with Wheeler in operations around Knoxville and Chattanooga.[58]

When Morgan escaped from his imprisonment in Ohio and returned to his command in the spring of 1864, Johnson received permission to resume recruiting Confederate sympathizers in southwestern Kentucky. Once more he was highly successful, enlisting several hundred volunteers and preparing to cross the Ohio again. Union authorities were alarmed at reports that Johnson was preparing to resume his raiding activities. Union Brig. Gen. Hugh Ewing, writing to another officer, believed authorities "should treat Johnson and his gang as without the protection of the laws of war; Johnson should be assailed without delay; he is doing much harm."[59]

Johnson's role as a raider came to an end suddenly. Before dawn on August 21, Johnson was accidentally hit in the eye by fire from his own men while leading an attack on a Federal camp at Grubbs Crossroads, near Canton, Kentucky. The bullet passed through the right eye and came out the left temple, cutting both eyes and leaving Johnson blind. He was taken to the home of Southern sympathizers where he received medical and nursing care. That night Union troops surrounded the house and Johnson was made prisoner. He was taken to Fort Warren, where he remained as a prisoner until an exchange was arranged in February 1865. While in prison Johnson was promoted to brigadier general on September 6, 1864, with date of rank assigned as June 1.[60]

Johnson returned to Texas after his release from prison. He opened a small store and became a leader in local civic affairs. In the 1880s he founded the town of Marble Falls. He worked to develop the water resources of the Colorado River and founded the Texas Mining Improvement Company. In 1904 his memoir *Partisan Rangers of the Confederate States of America*, an account of his experiences both in military and civilian life, was published. He died from heart failure at Burnet, Texas, on October 20, 1922, at the age of eighty-eight, one of the last surviving Confederate generals. His funeral services were held in the State Capitol and he was buried in the Texas State Cemetery in Austin.[61]

JOHN CREED MOORE

John Creed Moore, born in Hawkins County, Tennessee, on February 18, 1824, had little contact with Texas before the Civil War and yet is usually listed among the state's Civil War generals. This is probably because his first assignment as Confederate officer was in Texas and much of his war service was either as regimental or brigade commander of Texas troops. From statements made during the war, Moore came to consider himself a Texan; when the war ended he returned to Texas to live there.[62]

Moore attended Emory and Henry College in Virginia for four years prior to his enrollment at the U.S. Military Academy. He graduated from West Point seventeenth in a class of forty-three in 1849. He served as an artillery officer in the Seminole War of 1849-1850 and then spent several years in garrison duty on the frontier. Moore resigned from the army in 1855 and became a civil engineer. He married Augusta Clark of Orange County, New York; the couple had four children.[63]

In 1860 Moore accepted a position as a professor at Shelby College in Kentucky. A steadfast supporter of states' rights, he received an appointment as an artillery captain in the Louisiana militia following the secession of the lower South. He resigned this position on April 5, 1861, to take a commission as captain in the regular Confederate army. He was sent to Texas immediately with orders to construct defensive fortifications for Galveston. Soon thereafter he helped raise an infantry regiment from local militia

John Creed Moore

—Courtesy of Alabama Department
of Archives and History, Montgomery

units in Central Texas and along the Texas coast. This regiment, the Second Texas Infantry, was formally organized in September 1861, with Moore as colonel and William P. Rogers, a Mexican War veteran and friend of Sam Houston, as lieutenant colonel. Among those serving in the regiment were Dr. Ashbel Smith, former surgeon-general of the Texas Army, diplomat, and secretary of state of the Texas Republic; Sam Houston, Jr., the oldest son of Sam Houston; and Albert Jones, son of Dr. Anson Jones, the last president of the Republic of Texas.[64]

Moore, regarded as a strict disciplinarian, spent the fall and winter of 1861-1862 training the men. The regiment was originally intended for Texas coastal defense, but in March 1862, Moore received orders to report to Corinth, Mississippi, where Albert Sidney Johnston was concentrating all available forces for an attack on Grant's army at Pittsburg Landing. The regiment proceeded by train, steamboat, and overland march, arriving at Corinth on April 1. Supplies of the regiment were virtually exhausted on the long journey, but the Confederate commissary could provide Moore with rations for only two and one-half days.

After only a day's rest, the regiment marched with Johnston's army on April 3 as it headed toward Pittsburg Landing. The regiment was not only low on rations, but many of the men had worn out their shoes on the march from Texas and were barefoot.[65]

The Second Texas Infantry was in the thick of fighting in the

Battle of Shiloh. As part of Brig. Gen. Jones M. Withers' Division, the Texans were on the right flank of the Confederate army in the attack. They overran the outlying Federal camps and took part in the heavy fighting around the Hornet's Nest. In the early afternoon nearly 1,000 troops of Benjamin Prentiss' Division surrendered to the Second Texas.[66]

On the second day at Shiloh the Second Texas became the center of a controversy between Moore and corps commander William J. Hardee that resulted in much bitterness and clouded Moore's Civil War career. The regiment had performed so well under Moore's leadership on the first day at Shiloh, General Withers appointed Moore as temporary brigade commander. In the confused fighting that took place as Grant's army, joined the previous night by troops under Don Carlos Buell, began pushing the Confederates back, the Second Texas gave ground and fell back. Hardee, who was on the scene, blamed the Texans for breaking and fleeing "disgracefully from the field."[67]

In his report of the battle Hardee criticized both officers and men for the Confederate defeat on the second day. "In one instance," wrote Hardee, "that of the Second Texas Regiment, commanded by Col. Moore, the men seemed appalled, fled from the field without apparent cause, and were so dismayed that my efforts to rally them were unavailing."[68]

Moore responded angrily to Hardee's charges, pointing out that Col. William Rogers was in command of the regiment that day while Moore commanded the brigade. Moore also noted that the proper chain of command was not followed. Several officers, including a member of Hardee's staff, had shouted orders to the Texans, adding to the confusion of the battle. Some men in the regiment had heard orders to fall back, contended Moore. Joseph E. Chance, who wrote the most complete account of Moore and the Second Texas, pointed out that numerous errors were made by Hardee and his staff in the incident, but concluded that "the Second Texas and General Moore . . . made a very powerful enemy in General Hardee," an officer with strong influence in Confederate affairs.[69]

Not everyone agreed with Hardee concerning Moore's role at Shiloh. General Withers, the division commander, cited Moore for "great gallantry" and recommended his promotion to brigadier general. Braxton Bragg, who was commanding the corps at the time, endorsed the promotion which was made on May 26, 1862. Moore was assigned command of a brigade in Dabney H. Maury's Division in the Army of the West commanded by Sterling Price. The brigade included the Second Texas, the Fifteenth and Twenty-third Arkansas, the Thirty-fifth Mississippi, and an artillery battalion. Later the Forty-second Alabama was added to the brigade.[70]

In late summer 1862, Moore's Brigade was camped near Tupelo, Mississippi. Part of the brigade, including the Second Texas, took part in the battle at Iuka, thirty miles east of Corinth, in the third week of September. Moore himself had been ordered to remain in Tupelo to receive and organize a group of exchanged prisoners of war, so he was not involved in the fighting at Iuka. In early October, Moore was in command of the brigade in the battle at Corinth, in which the combined armies of Earl Van Dorn and Sterling Price attempted to recapture the town from Union troops commanded by William S. Rosecrans. Moore's Brigade was in heavy fighting on October 3, capturing three enemy batteries and a redoubt. The next day the brigade, with the Second Texas in the lead, fought its way into the center of town before being driven back by devastating enemy musket and cannon fire. Col. William P. Rogers, commanding the Second Texas, was killed as he planted a Texas flag on the enemy battery. Moore's Brigade suffered heavy casualties that day and the following day as it helped cover the army's retreat over the Hatchie Bridge. In all, the brigade sustained 1,295 casualties, highest loss of any Confederate brigade in the campaign.[71]

Although Moore received praise from Sterling Price for his services at Corinth, the old wounds from Shiloh were reopened when General Hardee used his influence to block Moore's confirmation as brigadier general in the regular Confederate army. In a letter written to Adj. Gen. Samuel Cooper, December 18, 1862, Moore appealed the injustice of the charges. No further action was taken, however. Moore retained his rank as brigadier general in the provisional army, but he remained a captain in the regular army.[72]

In late December 1862, Moore and his brigade were sent to the Vicksburg area, where they took part in the repulse of Sherman's troops at Chickasaw Bluffs. In March the brigade was ordered to Yazoo City to support Maj. Gen. William Loring in stopping

Union movements there. In late April Moore and his troops returned to Vicksburg, where they remained during the siege by Grant's army. The brigade was under heavy enemy fire in both the attacks of May 19 and 22, when Grant assaulted the Confederate lines. In the fighting on the 22nd the enemy made repeated assaults against Moore's Brigade but was driven back with heavy losses.[73]

Moore and other Confederates were paroled when Vicksburg surrendered to the enemy on July 4, 1863. Moore was ordered to Demopolis, Alabama, with his Alabama and Mississippi regiments to await exchange, but his old regiment, the Second Texas, was sent back to the Lone Star State. Moore hoped that upon being exchanged he would be transferred to Mobile for service with his old division commander, Dabney H. Maury, but to his great displeasure he learned that his brigade had been assigned to the corps commanded by his old nemesis, William J. Hardee.[74]

Moore and his brigade, now consisting of the Thirty-seventh, Fortieth, and Forty-second Alabama regiments, was ordered to Chattanooga in early November. The brigade was assigned to Frank Cheatham's Division defending Lookout Mountain, a position of strategic importance to the Army of Tennessee in its siege of Chattanooga. Cheatham was on leave and J. K. Jackson, the senior brigade commander, was in charge of the division. Moore's Brigade was placed on the northern slope of the mountain with the Cravens house serving as headquarters.

On November 24, 1863, Union troops attacked the pickets at the base of Lookout Mountain and then pushed back Edmund W. Walthall's Brigade. Moore launched a counterattack and temporarily drove the enemy back before a shortage of ammunition forced the Confederates to retreat. Assisted by Brig. Gen. Edmund W. Pettus' Brigade, Moore was able to form a defense line and held until 2:00 A.M. on November 25, when ordered to withdraw from the mountain and occupy positions on adjacent Missionary Ridge. When Union troops broke through the center of the Confederate line on the ridge, Jackson's Brigade, to Moore's right, gave way and rushed through the ranks of Moore's Brigade. After some confusion Moore was able to restore some order to Jackson's Brigade and held back the enemy until dark, when Hardee ordered his corps to retreat.[75]

After the defeat at Chattanooga, Moore was delighted when he received orders transferring him to Dabney Maury's command at Mobile. He proceeded at once to Mobile, where Maury assigned Moore to command the eastern division of the Department of the Gulf. This assignment apparently confused the adjutant general's office in Richmond, which believed Moore was being assigned as chief of artillery under Maury, not commander of a departmental division. On December 23 Adjutant General Cooper sent a new order transferring Moore back to Hardee's command.

This latest turn of events was both frustrating and embarrassing to Moore. On January 15, 1864, he submitted his resignation as brigadier general in the provisional army. General Cooper declined to accept the resignation, so Moore traveled to Richmond to discuss the issue with President Davis. Although the Confederate president was polite, he refused to change the order returning Moore to Hardee's command. Moore once again submitted a letter of resignation, this time requesting a return to his position as captain of artillery in the regular army. The resignation was accepted, and Moore was ordered to report to Col. Josiah Gorgas, chief of Confederate ordnance.

Moore was promoted to lieutenant colonel and assigned to the command of the Savannah Arsenal. He continued in this capacity until September 1864, when he was transferred to command the Selma Arsenal in Alabama. He remained in this position until James H. Wilson's cavalry raid in April 1865 forced evacuation. He went to Mobile, but was captured by Federal troops on April 24, 1865.[76]

After the war Moore returned to Texas, where he spent the rest of his career as a teacher and school administrator. He died on December 31, 1910, at Osage, Texas, and was buried in the city cemetery there.[77]

FELIX HUSTON ROBERTSON

Felix Huston Robertson, born at Washington-on-the-Brazos on March 9, 1839, was the only native Texan to serve as a general officer in the Confederacy. He was also the only Lone Star general in gray whose father (Jerome Bonaparte Robertson) was a general and the only Texas general officer who spent most of his military career with the artillery. The last Confederate general to die, Robertson was one of the youngest to hold the rank. Among Texas general officers only Wilburn H. King, born three months after Robertson, was younger. Robertson was also the only Texan whose promotion to general officer was approved by President Davis but rejected by the Confederate Senate.

Felix Huston Robertson
(photo taken after war)
—Courtesy of Harold B. Simpson Research Center, Hillsboro, Texas

Felix Robertson had the poorest reputation of all Lone Star generals in terms of character. Historian William C. Davis described Robertson as a "perjurer, sycophant, [and] quite possibly a murderer," who "was almost without doubt the most reprehensible man in either army to wear the uniform of a general." Perhaps this evaluation is too severe, but admittedly Felix Robertson was a controversial individual, admired by some for his personal bravery and courage but disliked by others for flaws in his character.[78]

Robertson attended Baylor University prior to his appointment to West Point in 1857. A classmate of Tom Rosser, George A. Custer, and Judson Kilpatrick, Robertson resigned from the Academy on January 19, 1861, shortly before graduation, to accept appointment as an artillery officer in the Confederate army. Assigned to Charleston, South Carolina, he took part in the bombardment of Fort Sumter. Soon thereafter he was transferred to Pensacola, Florida, where he established a close relationship with Braxton Bragg. When Bragg was ordered to Corinth to join Albert Sidney Johnston's army, Robertson went, too, as captain of a Florida artillery battery. His battery was assigned to the first brigade of the Second Division of Bragg's Corps commanded by Brig. Gen. Adley H. Gladden. Robertson's battery of four guns was at the southeastern edge of the peach orchard in the fighting at Shiloh on April 6. On the next day Robertson's battery was on the Confederate right flank in the Sarah Bell field, where the Second Texas Infantry had such an unpleasant encounter at midday.[79]

In the battle at Murfreesboro, or Stone's River, fought in late December-early January 1862-1863, Robertson commanded a six-gun battery assigned to Jones M. Withers' Division in Polk's Corps. On January 2 Braxton Bragg, commanding the Confederate army in the battle, ordered Maj. Gen. John C. Breckinridge to attack a strongly defended position on the enemy's left flank. Bragg assigned Robertson's and another battery to support Breckinridge's infantry in the attacks. Breckinridge and Robertson disagreed over the placement of the battery. Breckinridge wanted Robertson to move forward during the attack and give close support; the Texan believed the battery should remain behind in the woods. When the attack was not successful, Bragg and Breckinridge blamed each other for the failure.

Even if Robertson had moved his battery, the attack may have been unsuccessful given the strength of the enemy position. However, Bragg was not willing to let the matter rest. He found a willing ally to help him embarrass Breckinridge. In his first report on the engagement, written on January 12, Robertson had not criticized Breckinridge. Bragg, looking for ways to undercut Breckinridge, requested that Robertson write a second report. Robertson, eager to please Bragg, complied. In his second report, on February 16, the Texan denounced Breckinridge's conduct of the battle and charged the Kentuckian with failing to follow Bragg's orders. In so doing Robertson strengthened his standing with Bragg, but made a mortal enemy of Breckinridge.[80]

Robertson was now firmly established with Braxton Bragg. While many fellow officers criticized Bragg, Robertson praised him. In March 1863 the young Texan was in Richmond defending Bragg to Confederate congressmen investigating military affairs in Tennessee. In July Robertson was promoted to major, the first of three promotions he received within a twelve-month period. He was given command of a four-battery artillery battalion. The battalion formed the artillery reserve for Bragg's army in the September battle at Chickamauga, where for the first time Robertson served in the same army with his father, who commanded the Texas Brigade in Longstreet's Corps. For his role in the defeat of Rosecrans, Robertson was promoted to lieutenant colonel and assigned to command the artillery in Wheeler's Cavalry Corps. He remained with Wheeler throughout the Chattanooga and Atlanta campaigns. On July 26, 1864, Robertson was appointed brigadier general by President Davis and given command of a small cavalry brigade.[81]

In the autumn of 1864 Robertson, whose harsh manners and Indian-like features earned him the nickname "Comanche," was involved in the most controversial act of his military career. Federal Brig. Gen. Stephen Burbridge moved into southwestern Virginia with a large raiding party determined to destroy a saltworks vital to the Confederacy. Robertson and his brigade accompanied Confederate Brig. Gen. John S. Williams in an effort to block Burbridge. At Saltville, Virginia, on October 2, 1864, the Confederates drove off Union raiders. The next morning, however, Confederate troops, apparently encouraged by Robertson, began killing wounded Federals, many of them black troopers. Only the arrival of the departmental commander, John C. Breckinridge, ended the carnage in which over one hundred blacks were killed.[82]

Breckinridge reported the affair to General Lee, who ordered Robertson's arrest. Before Robertson could be apprehended, however, he rejoined Wheeler in Georgia and was outside Breckinridge's jurisdiction. On November 28, 1864, Robertson was severely wounded at Buck Head, Georgia, when an enemy bullet broke his left elbow and carried away two pieces of bone. Although General Wheeler reported to Braxton Bragg in January that Robertson "is fast recovering," the Texan did not recover in time to see additional action.[83]

Meanwhile, Breckinridge, now Confederate secretary of war, was determined to bring Robertson to justice for the Saltville deaths. Orders were issued directing Robertson to return to Virginia, but they either did not reach him or he ignored them. The Confederate Senate, influenced no doubt by Breckinridge, rejected Robertson's nomination as brigadier general. Robertson's immediate superior, Joe Wheeler, still believed in and supported him. On January 5, 1865, Wheeler wrote to Bragg, now President Davis' military advisor, that "General Robertson is to-day as good a division commander as can be found in any of our armies." Two weeks later Wheeler wrote to Bragg again, stating that "Robertson is brave and efficient, and his brigade under him will be the best in service." On February 8, two weeks before the Senate rejected Robertson's promotion to brigadier, Wheeler recommended that Robertson be promoted to major general.[84]

At war's end Robertson, who had married Sarah Davis on September 11, 1864, returned to Texas. He settled in Waco, studied law, and was admitted to the bar. He was an active member of the United Confederate Veterans, serving as commander of the Texas Division in 1911. After the death of his first wife he married Elizabeth Dwyer in 1892. He had four children by his first wife and one by his second. At the time of his death in Waco on April 10, 1928, he was the last surviving Confederate general. He was buried in Oakwood Cemetery, Waco.[85]

JEROME BONAPARTE ROBERTSON

Jerome Bonaparte Robertson, who commanded Hood's Texas Brigade longer than any other officer, was one of the most beloved Confederate general officers from Texas. Referred to affectionately by his men as "Aunt Polly" because of his genuine regard and consideration for the troops under his command, Jerome B. Robertson had personal characteristics and qualities much unlike those of his son, Felix Robertson. While the son was impetuous, harsh, and occasionally even ruthless in his behavior, the older Robertson was "by nature easy going, patient, and understanding." His only failure as a military commander may have been that he cared for his troops too much, placing their welfare above other considerations, including his own military career.[86]

Robertson was born in Woodford County, Kentucky, on March 14, 1815. His father, a Scottish immigrant who admired Napoleon Bonaparte, died when Jerome, the fourth of five children, was only three. His mother was forced to apprentice Jerome to a hatter when the lad was eight years of age. Despite his hardships Robertson was able to study medicine at Transylvania University, where he graduated in 1835.[87]

In 1836 Dr. Robertson joined a local company of Kentucky

volunteers for service in the Texas War for Independence. The company, of which he was a captain, arrived after San Jacinto, but Robertson remained in the Texas Army until early 1837. He returned to Kentucky briefly, married Mary Elizabeth Cummins, and came back to Texas in December 1837 with his wife, father-in-law, and brother. He settled at Washington-on-the-Brazos, where he opened his medical practice. He and his wife had three children, Felix being the oldest.[88]

Jerome Bonaparte Robertson
—Courtesy of Harold B. Simpson Research Center, Hillsboro, Texas

In 1845 Robertson moved to Independence, Texas, where he farmed and practiced medicine. He served in Indian and Mexican campaigns, including the Somervell expedition. He was a substantial property holder, possessing $50,000 in personal and real property in 1860. He was highly respected in the county and served in numerous public offices including postmaster, coroner, mayor, and state legislator. In 1861 he was chosen as one of Washington County's delegates to the Texas secession convention.[89]

Following the secession of Texas from the Union, Robertson raised a company of volunteers from Washington County. The company was assigned to the Fifth Texas Infantry, which was sent to Virginia to become part of Hood's Texas Brigade. Robertson was promoted to lieutenant colonel on October 10, 1861. On June 2, 1862, he became colonel and regimental commander, replacing James J. Archer, who was given command of a Tennessee brigade. Robertson led the regiment in the successful attack at Gaines' Mill later that month but was wounded in the shoulder. At Second Manassas in late August, Robertson was wounded again, this time in the groin. In the battle Robertson's regiment suffered the most severe losses for any regiment in Lee's army—261 casualties.[90]

Robertson led his regiment in Lee's march into Maryland in early September and took part in the fighting at Boonsboro, or South Mountain, on September 14. However, he collapsed from exhaustion and had to be carried from the field. He was confined to the hospital and did not take part in the battle at Sharpsburg, or Antietam. He was with the regiment during the retreat back into Virginia. On November 1 he was promoted to brigadier general and succeeded Hood, who became division commander, in command of the Texas Brigade.[91]

Robertson's first battle as brigade commander came at Fredericksburg in December 1862. The brigade was in the center of the Confederate line, but avoided heavy casualties as the main fighting was to the left and right. Hood's Division, including the Texas Brigade, was detached from Lee's army in the spring and sent on foraging duty in the Suffolk area. As a result Robertson and his brigade did not take part in the Chancellorsville campaign.

Hood's Division and the Texas Brigade rejoined Lee's army in time to take part in the march north in June 1863. In the Battle of Gettysburg, Robertson and his brigade were in the assault against the Union left flank on the afternoon of July 2. In this attack General Hood was severely wounded by a shell that shattered his left arm. Robertson was wounded above the right knee; three of his four regimental commanders were also wounded. Although the brigade saw only limited action the following day, the casualty rates for the Gettysburg campaign were high: 597 casualties, or 54.3 percent of its effective strength.[92]

After the Gettysburg campaign, Robertson's Brigade moved back to Culpepper, Virginia, with other brigades of Hood's Division. In August the division was ordered to the Rappahannock River near Fredericksburg, where most of the men expected to remain during the autumn and winter. In early September, however, the division boarded trains at Richmond for the move to northern Georgia to support Braxton Bragg's army.

In the third week of September the division, including the Texas Brigade, was in the Battle of Chickamauga. For the first time

Robertson and his men fought along with other Texans, including Robertson's son, Felix, who commanded the reserve artillery in Bragg's army. Ironically, Robertson complained of lack of proper artillery support for his brigade in the fighting on September 19. Once again casualties were high. The brigade sustained 570 casualties, or almost 44 percent of its total strength, in the battle. General Hood, the division commander, was again a casualty. While talking with Robertson on September 20, Hood was struck by a bullet that shattered his right leg.[93]

Following the Battle of Chickamauga, Robertson and the Texas Brigade moved to the Knoxville area with Longstreet's Corps and took part in unsuccessful operations there before going into winter quarters at Morristown in the Holston Valley. There the brigade spent the winter chasing Federal cavalry and trying to stay warm in the bitter cold. Robertson, unhappy with Micah Jenkins, the temporary division commander who replaced the wounded Hood, and fearful that the Texas Brigade, now reduced to 784 effectives, might be consolidated with another brigade, proposed a recruiting plan for the brigade. Under his proposal the entire brigade would return to Texas and Arkansas in January 1864, conduct a mass recruiting drive, and then march east to rejoin Longstreet's Corps.

The Robertson recruiting plan was supported by both General Hood and the Texas delegation in the Confederate Congress. The Confederate War Department refused to consider the plan, however, and the proposal was temporarily shelved. As noted earlier, John Gregg, the next commander of the brigade, brought the plan up again in the summer of 1864, but was no more successful than Robertson.[94]

Robertson, meanwhile, found himself out of favor with interim division commander Micah Jenkins and corps commander James Longstreet. In late October 1863, Jenkins complained about Robertson's ability to command the brigade, leading Longstreet to relieve Robertson of command. After an investigation, Bragg restored Robertson to command. In late December Jenkins filed charges that Robertson, who had disagreed with some orders that he considered injurious to his men, had insulted Jenkins' generalship and judgment. In late February 1864 the court appointed by Longstreet to hear the charges acquitted Robertson of "improper motives" but disapproved of "his conduct." Robertson was reprimanded and relieved of command of the Texas Brigade.[95]

The decision to remove Robertson was not well received by the officers and men of the brigade. Although they occasionally complained about his excessive "mothering," they were unhappy to see him go. Several petitions protesting the action were signed by officers of the brigade and forwarded to Richmond, but to no avail. One Texas soldier later wrote "this action [the court-martial] came very near destroying the efficiency of Hood's Texas Brigade." He added, "The boys love Aunt Polly, and would have fought for him to the last extremity."[96]

After a sad farewell to the Texas Brigade, Robertson returned to Texas. He never again held a field command. In May 1864 he was ordered to report to John B. Magruder, commander of the Texas district. On June 24, 1864, he took command of the reserve forces of the state, a position he held until the war ended.

Robertson returned to his home at Independence after the war and resumed the practice of medicine. In 1874 he became state superintendent of the Bureau of Immigration. After the death of his first wife in 1868, he married Mrs. Hattie Hendley Hook. During the next few years he was active in the Masonic Order and was an organizer of Hood's Texas Brigade Association. He was elected president of the association in 1875 and reelected president eleven times. In 1887 his former comrades named him lifetime president of the association.

Robertson died on January 7, 1891, and was buried at Independence next to his first wife and mother. In 1894 his son had all three bodies moved to Oakwood Cemetery in Waco. Thirty-four years later his son, Felix, would be buried beside his father, the beloved "Aunt Polly."[97]

LAWRENCE SULLIVAN ROSS

Texas Ranger, Confederate general, state senator, governor of Texas, and president of Texas A&M, Lawrence Sullivan "Sul" Ross was born at Bentonsport, Iowa, on September 27, 1838. The spring following his birth the Ross family migrated to Texas, eventually settling in Waco. His father, Shapley Prince Ross, was an entrepeneur, landowner, and Texas Ranger highly respected in the Waco community.

The son, Sul Ross, was involved in an Indian fight while still a young lad. He wished to become a Texas Ranger like his father, but recognized the importance of education so enrolled first at Baylor University at Independence and later Wesleyan University at Florence, Alabama, where he graduated with honors in 1859. While home on summer vacation in 1858 he served with Earl Van Dorn's troopers in a campaign against the Comanches in Indian Territory. Although he sustained a serious wound, Ross returned to Wesleyan to finish his education.[98]

Lawrence Sullivan Ross
(photo taken after war)
—Courtesy of Harold B. Simpson
Research Center, Hillsboro, Texas

Ross' military talents were recognized early. Winfield Scott, commanding general of the U.S. Army, offered the young Texan an army commission, but Ross declined in order to finish college. In 1860 Ross served as an officer in Middleton T. Johnson's campaign against hostile Comanches and Kiowas. That fall Governor Sam Houston authorized Ross, only twenty-two years of age, to raise a company of Rangers for Indian service. In the Battle of Pease River in December 1860, Ross and his Rangers won a decisive victory over the Comanches. In this engagement Ross won enduring fame and recognition by rescuing Cynthia Ann Parker, a young white woman who had been held captive since childhood. Governor Houston offered to make Ross his aide-de-camp with the rank of colonel, but the young Ranger declined.[99]

On May 28, 1861, Ross married Elizabeth "Lizzie" Tinsley,

daughter of a wealthy physician-planter of Waco. The honeymoon was cut short, however, when Ross accepted assignment as a state peace commissioner to various Indian tribes. When he returned from this mission he joined a volunteer cavalry company formed by his brother, Pete, for service in the Confederate army. The company was incorporated into the Sixth Texas Cavalry, commanded by Col. B. Warren Stone, a lawyer and judge from Dallas County. Because of his reputation as a soldier and Indian fighter, Ross was elected major of the new regiment.[100]

In early October 1861, the Sixth Cavalry joined Ben McCulloch's army in Arkansas. McCulloch, who knew Ross from service with the Rangers, utilized Ross' talents during the late fall and winter months. In November he sent Ross on a scouting mission into southwestern Missouri. In February 1862, Ross, with over 500 men, made a raid behind enemy lines near Keetsville, Missouri. In this operation Ross destroyed several wagonloads of commissary supplies, captured sixty horses and mules, took eleven Union prisoners, and enhanced his reputation as a bold and daring officer. Colonel Stone, commander of the Sixth Texas, praised the young Texan for his performance, declaring that he could not "too highly estimate the chivalry and gallantry of this intrepid, daring knight."[101]

Ross and the Sixth Cavalry were with McCulloch's forces in the Battle of Pea Ridge, fought on March 6-7, 1862. In the fighting on March 6 Ross led a battalion of cavalry in a fierce charge against the enemy but was driven back by Federal artillery. Still the Confederates seemed to have the upper hand until the deaths of Generals McCulloch and McIntosh in the afternoon. The next morning General Van Dorn, commanding the Confederate army, launched an attack on the Union right near Elkhorn Tavern but pulled away after encountering heavy opposition. Ross was disappointed about the failure of Confederate arms. "The truth of the whole matter," he wrote his wife, "is we had them badly whipped the first evening." And in a letter to his father-in-law, Ross concluded "we whipped ourselves."[102]

After the Battle of Pea Ridge, the Sixth Cavalry was ordered to Corinth, Mississippi, as part of the Confederate concentration by Albert Sidney Johnston. The Sixth Texas and the rest of Van Dorn's army arrived too late for the fighting at Shiloh but remained in Corinth for several weeks as P. G. T. Beauregard planned a strategic withdrawal. In early May, Ross was elected colonel and commanding officer of the Sixth Texas, succeeding B. Warren Stone, who left the regiment to seek a generalship. Under Ross' leadership the regiment helped cover the Confederate withdrawal from Corinth in late May and took part in several skirmishes along the Mobile and Ohio Railroad during the summer. In mid-September the regiment took part in the fighting around Iuka, Mississippi.[103]

Ross and the Sixth Cavalry were in the thick of fighting in the unsuccessful effort by Van Dorn to retake Corinth in early October 1862. As part of Brig. Gen. Charles W. Phifer's Brigade the Texans helped drive back the Federals on October 3 but had to give ground later due to heavy enemy resistance. The following day Van Dorn ordered a frontal assault against strong Federal defenses. In the attack Phifer's Brigade managed to reach the enemy's breastworks before being forced to retire under murderous artillery and musket fire. In the fighting Ross was thrown from his horse, giving rise to the rumor that he had been killed. Ross was not severely hurt, but losses in the regiment were high. When the Confederates retreated on October 5, Ross, temporarily commanding the brigade due to Phifer's illness, and his troopers held the Hatchie Bridge against repeated enemy attacks during the withdrawal.[104]

In November Ross received a furlough which allowed him to return to Texas for a visit with his wife. While Ross was in Texas his regiment, now part of John W. Whitfield's Brigade, took part in Van Dorn's celebrated raid against the Union supply depot at Holly Springs, Mississippi. When Ross returned to his unit in January 1863, the brigade moved into Tennessee, where it participated in a series of raids against enemy communications and supply lines. In a battle at Thompson's Station near Spring Hill, Tennessee, on March 5, the regiment, fighting dismounted, made three charges before carrying the Federal position. In the weeks that followed Ross was often in command of the brigade while Colonel Whitfield was on sick leave or in Richmond seeking promotion. Gen. William H. Jackson, the division commander, and Stephen D. Lee, who became corps commander after Van Dorn's death in May, wanted Ross assigned as permanent brigade commander, but Whitfield fought the move. While the issue was being debated, Lee gave Ross detached service as temporary commander of a small brigade consisting of the Sixth Texas and First Mississippi. In this capacity Ross took part in Joe Wheeler's cavalry raid in middle Tennessee in October 1863.[105]

While Ross was away on the Tennessee raid, Stephen D. Lee, commanding Confederate cavalry in Mississippi, continued his efforts to relieve Whitfield, whose poor health was increasingly a problem. In late October Whitfield was placed on sick leave and returned to Texas. When Ross came back from the cavalry raid into Tennessee he was assigned as commander of the brigade. His promotion to brigadier general was approved on February 5, 1864, with date of rank effective the date of his appointment as brigade commander, December 21, 1863. Ross, aged twenty-five, was one of the youngest generals in the Confederate army.[106]

Ross' health was not good at the time of his appointment to brigade command. Between late September 1863 and April 1864, he had fever and chills almost every three days, apparently from malaria. Even so, he was not off duty for illness at any time.

In late December 1863, Ross and his brigade were assigned duty along the Yazoo River when William T. Sherman raided Meridian, Mississippi. In March Ross' Brigade was engaged in a bitter fight at Yazoo City in which the Texans drove the enemy from their defenses. For the first time Ross' men faced black troops. In negotiating over surrender terms, Ross and the Federal commander engaged in a heated controversy. The Union officer charged that the Texans had murdered several black prisoners, while Ross claimed that two of his men had been killed by the Federals after surrendering.[107]

In late spring 1864, Ross' Brigade was ordered to join Joe Johnston's army in northern Georgia. The brigade, many of its members unhappy to be sent farther away from Texas, arrived in May. During the next three months, the brigade was involved in eighty-six separate clashes with the enemy. Most were small affairs with few casualties, but at Brown's Mill near Newnan, Georgia, in late July the Texans engaged in hand-to-hand combat with Iowa troops. Ross himself was captured, but was rescued when Confederate cavalry successfully counterattacked.[108]

In mid-August 1864, Ross' Brigade was involved in a battle with Judson Kilpatrick's Union cavalry near Lovejoy's Station south of Atlanta. In the fighting Ross' heavily outnumbered Texans were overrun by two Federal brigades and suffered more than fifty casualties, but helped prevent Kilpatrick from cutting the vital Confederate supply line. Even so, Confederate commander John Bell Hood, fearing encirclement by Sherman's troops, was forced to evacuate Atlanta on the first day of September.[109]

The attrition in Ross' Brigade in the four months of campaigning in Georgia was high. With a little more than 1,000 men under his command when he entered Georgia, Ross could count only slightly more than 700 in September. Morale was low as many of the men had not seen home in two years. In late autumn the brigade rode north with Hood's army in the disastrous Tennessee campaign. Although the brigade did not participate in the major battles at Franklin and Nashville, the Texans, now in Nathan Bedford Forrest's command, were in several skirmishes with the enemy. When Hood's defeated army retreated back into Alabama, Ross' Brigade was part of the rear guard brunting attacks of pursuing Union troops.[110]

In January 1865 Ross and his brigade were assigned to picket duty in Mississippi. Several weeks later about half of the brigade received the long sought furloughs to go home. On March 13, Ross, whose health continued to be poor, was given a ninety-day leave of absence and headed for home. A month later Lee surrendered at Appomattox. Other capitulations took place during the following month. Ross was not present when his brigade was surrendered at Jackson, Mississippi, on May 13, 1865.[111]

After the war, Ross purchased a small plantation on the Brazos near Waco. He served as sheriff of McLennan County in 1873, delegate to the state constitutional convention in 1875, and state senator from 1881 to 1885. In 1886 he was elected governor of Texas and was reelected in 1888. When he left the chief executive office in 1891, he was chosen president of Texas A&M College, a position he held until his death at his home in College Station at the age of fifty-nine on January 3, 1898. Ross was buried in Oakwood Cemetery in Waco, the burial site of two other Texas Confederate generals, Jerome and Felix Robertson.[112]

JOHN WILKINS WHITFIELD

Born on March 11, 1818, in Williamson County, Tennessee, John Wilkins Whitfield had a colorful career before moving to Texas to purchase land in 1860. He served as a lieutenant colonel in the Second Tennessee Infantry in the Mexican War followed by two terms in the Tennessee legislature, 1848-1851. He moved to Independence, Missouri, in 1853, and he was appointed agent to the Potawatomi tribe. A strong advocate of making Kanasas a slave state, Whitfield led a group of Missourians into Kansas. He served as Kansas territorial delegate to the U.S. Congress, 1854-1857. From 1857 to 1861 he was registrar at the land office in Doniphan, Kansas. Whitfield married twice; to Catherine Carter in 1838 and to Sarah B. Dribrell in 1853.[113]

John Wilkins Whitfield
—Courtesy of Harold B. Simpson Research Center, Hillsboro, Texas

Disappointed that Kansas was not going to become a slave state, Whitfield followed the example of his brothers by relocating to Texas. In 1860 he purchased 1,500 acres of land on the Navidad River in Lavaca County and moved to Texas the following year. He organized a cavalry company in Lavaca County in August 1861. The company, known as Whitfield's Rifles, was assigned to Ben McCulloch's Army of the West at Fort Smith, Arkansas. There it combined with three other independent companies from East Texas to form the Fourth Texas Cavalry Battalion. Whitfield was assigned as battalion commander with the rank of major. In

February 1862 McCulloch sent Whitfield and his battalion on a raid into Missouri at the same time he dispatched Sul Ross on a similar expedition. As noted previously, Ross was highly successful in his mission. Whitfield, on the other hand, never reached his objective.[114] Whitfield's battalion saw limited action in the Battle of Pea Ridge in March 1862, serving with Louis Hebert's Brigade. After Pea Ridge the battalion was augmented by the addition of eight small companies of recruits from Texas. This unit, commanded by Whitfield as colonel, was officially designated as the Twenty-seventh Texas Cavalry Regiment, but was generally referred to as "Whitfield's Legion."[115]

In mid-April Whitfield was ordered to dismount his command, cross the Mississippi, and join Sterling Price's army at Memphis. Under Price's command Whitfield and his legion participated in the Battle of Iuka on September 19, 1862. In the fighting the Legion captured a Federal battery and according to Sterling Price "won their gallant leader a reputation for dashing boldness and steady courage." Casualties for the Legion were high: 106 officers and men killed and wounded. Whitfield was wounded twice. The wound in his right shoulder produced a fracture of the humerus near its surgical neck, which kept Whitfield from active duty for several weeks.[116]

While Whitfield recuperated from his wounds the Legion, temporarily commanded by Lt. Col. Edwin R. Hawkins, took part in the Battle of Corinth, October 3-4, 1862. Later that month the Legion was remounted and brigaded with the Third, Sixth, and Ninth Texas cavalries. As senior colonel Whitfield became commander of the new brigade, but because of continuing medical problems he frequently allowed other officers to lead the brigade. Under Earl Van Dorn's command the brigade took part in the Holly Springs raid in December 1862. Whitfield was in command of the brigade in the Battle of Thompson's Station, March 5, 1863. In that engagement the brigade, fighting dismounted, drove the enemy forces back in a series of bold charges.[117]

In April 1863, Whitfield, suffering from severe rheumatism, was on sick leave during which time he traveled to Richmond, Virginia. Sul Ross, who was left in command of the brigade, believed Whitfield used the trip to scheme for appointment as brigadier general. Apparently the Richmond visit was fruitful, for on May 9, 1863, Whitfield was promoted to brigadier general.[118]

In late May Whitfield's Brigade was ordered to Mississippi to join Joseph E. Johnston, who was putting together an army in central Mississippi to aid John C. Pemberton in the defense of Vicksburg. Whitfield's Texans formed the second brigade of a new cavalry division commanded by William H. "Red" Jackson. Jackson, a young West Point graduate from Tennessee, believed Whitfield was not healthy enough to command a cavalry brigade. On June 5, 1863, orders were issued by his headquarters relieving Whitfield of command and assigning Maj. Sul Ross to brigade command. Joe Johnston approved the order but was overridden by Confederate Secretary of War James A. Seddon, a Whitfield ally. For the next three months Whitfield remained in command as the brigade took part in a series of skirmishes along the Big Black River. His health continued to be a problem, however, and in October, Stephen D. Lee, who was now in command of all cavalry in Mississippi, repeated the request that Whitfield be replaced as brigade commander. In late October Whitfield was placed on medical leave and returned to Texas. The war ended before Whitfield recovered from his illnesses.[119]

Recovery for Whitfield was slow. Dr. Jack D. Welch, in his book *Medical Histories of Confederate Generals*, noted that "symptoms from his whole muscular and osseous system along with intermittent chronic diarrhea and the residual difficulties from his wounds added to his problems." He recovered sufficiently that he was able to attend the state constitutional conventions of 1866 and 1875 as a delegate from Lavaca County. He resumed farming and was listed in the 1870 Federal census as having $18,000 in property. He died October 27, 1879, near Hallettsville and was buried in the Hallettsville cemetery.[120]

LOUIS TREZEVANT WIGFALL

Louis Trezevant Wigfall, the passionate, aggressive champion of Southern rights, is better known for his long and colorful career as a Southern extremist and political leader than he is for his brief tenure as a Confederate general. The volatile native son of South Carolina, described by the diarist Mary Chesnut as the "stormy petrel," is usually remembered for his activities in the American and

Confederate Senates rather than as the first commander of the Texas Brigade.

Wigfall was born on April 21, 1816, in the Edgefield District of South Carolina. The son of prosperous parents who died when he was young, Wigfall attended the University of Virginia and graduated from South Carolina College. While a student in South Carolina Wigfall gained brief military experience during a summer of service in the Seminole Wars. After graduation from college he established a law practice in Edgefield but demonstrated more interest in dueling than in practicing law. His biographer, Alvy L. King, reported that within a five-month period around 1842 Wigfall "was involved in a fist fight, three near-duels, two duels, and one shooting—all of which left one dead and two, including Wigfall, wounded."[121]

Louis Trezevant Wigfall
—Courtesy of Harold B. Simpson
Research Center, Hillsboro, Texas

Wigfall curbed his interest in dueling after his marriage to a second cousin, Charlotte Marie Cross, in 1841. He developed a keen interest in politics and became a vocal defender of slavery and states' rights. He experienced financial difficulties in the 1840s, in part due to the expenses incurred relating to the illness of his first son and in part due to his own excessive spending habits. After his son's death, Wigfall determined to move to Texas. His cousin James Hamilton, who had migrated to Texas some years earlier, arranged a law partnership for Wigfall with a young Texas attorney, William B. Ochiltree, in Nacogdoches.[122]

Wigfall arrived in Texas in the fall of 1846. He was joined the next year by his wife, Charlotte, young son Halsey, aged two, and infant daughter Louise Sophia, born in April 1847.[123]

Wigfall practiced law briefly in Nacogdoches but soon moved his law office to Marshall. He quickly established himself as a successful trial lawyer, but his main interest was in politics. He became a leader in the state Democratic Party and was elected to the Texas legislature in 1849. In that body he supported reopening the African slave trade, filibustering in Latin America, and lowering the tariff. He became an outspoken critic of the moderate policies of Senator Sam Houston and campaigned against Houston's election as governor in 1857. In that year Wigfall was elected to the Texas Senate, where he continued to attack Houston and other Texas unionists. Following John Brown's raid upon Harpers Ferry in October 1859, Wigfall was chosen by the Texas legislature to the seat in the U.S. Senate vacated by the death of James Pinckney Henderson.[124]

Wigfall took his seat in the 36th Congress on January 4, 1860. Ignoring the Senate tradition that freshmen say little on the floor, he seized the opportunity to express his views on various subjects. In the two months Congress was in session that winter he quickly earned the reputation as an eloquent speaker and a pugnacious debater, ready to challenge those with whom he disagreed. He particularly seemed to enjoy taunting and ridiculing his Northern colleagues with his sharp tongue and sarcastic wit.[125]

During the summer of 1860, Wigfall campaigned in Texas for the election of John C. Breckinridge as president of the United States. After Lincoln's election Wigfall returned to Congress more determined than ever to support secession and to oppose any compromise. In mid-December Wigfall and Senator James L. Pugh of Alabama drafted a "Southern Manifesto," signed by cotton state congressmen expressing support for the organization of a Southern confederacy. When Senator John J. Crittenden of Kentucky attempted to avert secession by a series of compromise proposals, Wigfall led the opposition.[126]

The secession of the seven states of the lower South, including Texas, in the winter of 1860-1861 delighted Wigfall. He was pleased that the Texas secession convention selected him as a delegate to the Montgomery convention creating the Southern confederacy, but decided to stay on in Congress until officially notified by the state that he should leave. He believed he could be of more value to the South through his activities in Washington. He remained during most of the special session of the new Congress, which met March 4 through March 24. During this time he assisted Confederate agents in recruiting and arming troops. He also met with the Confederate commissioners who were working to achieve the evacuation of Forts Pickens and Sumter.[127]

When it was apparent that the Federal government was not prepared to evacuate the two forts, Wigfall left Washington and journeyed to Charleston, South Carolina. There he was greeted with great enthusiasm by the local citizenry. In a series of public appearances he praised the work of the Montgomery convention in drafting the Confederate constitution and selecting Jefferson Davis as president. He accepted an appointment on the staff of volunteer aides to P. G. T. Beauregard, who was now in charge of the Charleston defenses, and urged President Davis by telegraph to order the capture of Fort Sumter. When the firing on Sumter began, Wigfall was on Morris Island, a key Confederate artillery position. When, after a day and a half of bombardment, fires were burning at Fort Sumter, Wigfall, on his own volition and without any orders or authority, commandeered a small boat and two black oarsmen and set out for the fort. Upon landing, Wigfall found a gun casemate to crawl through and asked for a parley with Maj. Robert Anderson, Union commander of the fort. After some discussion over surrender terms, Anderson agreed to evacuate the fort.[128]

The daring action of Wigfall enchanced his reputation as a bold and courageous individual. He was accorded a hero's reception by the Charlestonians for his role at Sumter. According to his biographer, "there seemed to be no end of listeners to hear Wigfall's own account of his deed, nor did Wigfall tire of telling it." His future appeared bright as he and his wife boarded the train for Montgomery, where he would serve in the Confederate Provisional Congress.[129]

Wigfall took his seat in the Confederate Congress on April 19, 1861. Although the session was brief, Wigfall made his presence felt. He introduced and secured passage of a bill increasing the size of the Confederate army. He also established a good relationship with Jefferson Davis. When Congress adjourned on May 21, to convene the next month in the new capital at Richmond, the Wigfalls prepared to return to Texas for a visit; however, Davis insisted that Wigfall accompany him to Richmond as a member of his staff, an offer that Wigfall accepted.[130]

Wigfall arrived in Richmond with the Davis party in late May. For the next several months Wigfall divided his time between making speeches, visiting the first Texas troops to arrive in Virginia, and attending sessions of Congress. His relationship with President Davis had begun to cool, but officially he remained an aide to the chief executive. In early July Wigfall, who had only brief military experience as a college student, was named commander of the Texas troops in Virginia. At the time the Texas companies were only at battalion strength, so Wigfall had the rank of lieutenant colonel. Wigfall's command was ordered to Manassas in mid-July, but due to an accident they arrived too late to take part in the battle. The battalion was increased to regimental size in August by the arrival of additional troops from Texas. On August 28, 1861, Wigfall was promoted to colonel of what was now the First Texas Infantry Regiment.[131]

In the early fall months Wigfall spent more and more time with the Texans camped north of Richmond. The number of Texas troops was steadily increasing. In late September two new regiments, the Fourth and Fifth Texas infantries, were organized under the commands of R. T. P. Allen (soon replaced by John Bell Hood) and James J. Archer. The number of troops was now at brigade level. On November 21, 1861, President Davis appointed Wigfall brigadier general. That same month an additional regiment, the Eighteenth Georgia, was added to what had become known as Wigfall's Brigade.[132]

Several days before Davis appointed Wigfall brigadier general the Texas legislature selected Wigfall and W. S. Oldham to represent the state in the Senate of the first regular, or permanent, Confederate Congress. Wigfall now had to choose between military and political service. Although he enjoyed his role as an army officer, Wigfall believed he could be of greater service in Congress than on active duty in the field. Accordingly, he decided to resign his military commission, but only in February 1862, when the permanent congress convened. In the meantime he continued to perform his duties as brigade commander and member of the provisional congress. Even after he did resign his generalship, he continued on occasion to play a military role. When the Senate was in recess in the summer of 1862 he served on James Longstreet's staff as an aide, helping care for the wounded during the battles of Seven Pines and the Seven Days around Richmond.[133]

As a member of the Confederate Senate, Wigfall's main interest was in military matters. Although philosophically a believer in states' rights, Wigfall supported legislation strengthening the national government's authority in the military realm. He supported conscription, suspension of habeas corpus, and impresssment, and opposed exemptions for frontier service, discharges for age, and substitution for military service. He opposed legislation that would allow arming slaves as soldiers. While favoring the use of blacks for military labor, he was totally against arming or emancipating them.[134]

As the war continued, Wigfall became a bitter critic of the Davis administration. Although he supported the president in the early phases of the war, Wigfall believed that Davis showed poor judgment in his appointment and support of incompetent generals such as John C. Pemberton and Braxton Bragg. He was displeased with the president's treatment of his friend Joseph E. Johnston, whom Wigfall considered the Confederacy's most able field general. The removal of Johnston as commander of the Army of Tennessee in the Atlanta campaign angered Wigfall. In the closing days of the war, Wigfall worked to curb the powers of the president. He took particular delight in the passage of a bill requiring the president to appoint a general-in-chief of the army.[135]

When the war ended, Wigfall made his way back to Texas. Fearful of being captured and punished for treason, he shaved his beard and obtained a private's uniform to disguise himself. In the spring of 1866 he fled to London, where his family joined him. He remained there until 1872. Although he attempted to find some legal work, his debts mounted and he decided to return to the United States. He and his wife lived in Baltimore until 1874, when they returned to Texas. He planned to reopen his law office in Marshall, but died in Galveston on February 18, 1874, from apoplexy. He was buried in the Episcopal Cemetery in Galveston.[136]

WILLIAM HUGH YOUNG

One of the youngest Texans to attain the rank of brigadier general in the Confederate army, William Hugh Young of Grayson County was still a university student when the war began. Once in

William Hugh Young
—Courtesy of Harold B. Simpson
Research Center, Hillsboro, Texas

the army Young showed himself to be a brave, courageous soldier who often exposed himself to enemy fire. Wounded in battle five times, the North Texan was captured by the enemy and spent the last months of the war in Federal hospitals and the prison on Johnson's Island, Ohio.

William Hugh Young was born in Booneville, Missouri, on January 1, 1838. His father, Hugh Franklin Young, was a Virginian who had fought pirates and Indians along the Mississippi frontier before settling in Missouri. The family moved to Red River County, Texas, in 1840 when William was only two years old. There the senior Young was active in militia affairs and served in the Snively expedition and the Mexican War. In 1853 the family moved to Sherman in Grayson County, where Hugh Young served as chief justice. The son, William, attended Washington College, Tennessee, and McKenzie College, Texas, before enrolling at the University of Virginia in 1859. He graduated in early summer of 1861, but stayed on several weeks to participate in studying military tactics at an affiliated military academy. William was cadet captain of one of the academy's two companies; Robert E. Lee, Jr., was captain of the other company.[137]

Young returned to Texas in September to raise a company of volunteers in northeast Texas. The recruits, who became part of Sam Maxey's Ninth Texas Infantry, elected Young as their captain. In December the regiment was ordered to join Albert Sidney Johnston's command in Kentucky. However, when the Texans reached Memphis they were diverted to Iuka, Mississippi, to protect the Memphis and Charleston Railroad. Maxey, who was promoted to brigadier general, was transferred from the regiment in early March. Wright A. Stanley, a major in the regiment, was chosen as Maxey's successor as regimental commander.[138]

In late March 1862, the Ninth Texas was ordered to join Confederate forces at Corinth, Mississippi. In the Battle of Shiloh, fought in early April, the regiment was part of Patton Anderson's Brigade in Bragg's Corps. The Ninth took part in the Confederate assault on the Federal right on the morning of April 6, but was forced to fall back after sustaining heavy casualties.[139]

Following the Battle of Shiloh, the Ninth Texas retreated back to Corinth with Beauregard's army. In the general reorganization in May, Young, at the age of twenty-four, was elected regimental commander with the rank of colonel. When the Confederates evacuated Corinth in June, Young and the Ninth Texas moved with the army, now under the command of Braxton Bragg, to the Chattanooga area. The regiment took part in Bragg's Kentucky campaign during the fall of 1862. Assigned to Preston Smith's Tennessee Brigade, the Texans were involved in the fighting on the Union left in the Battle of Perryville on October 8.[140]

At Murfreesboro in late December, Young and the Ninth Texas were in the center of the Confederate assault against Rosecrans' army. When the attack failed, Col. A. J. Vaughan, now commanding Smith's Brigade, ordered the brigade to fall back. Young and the Ninth Texas did not hear the order to retreat and continued to fight. They worked their way around the Union flank and delivered an enfilading fire against the enemy lines with telling effect. In the course of the battle Young had two horses killed under him and was himself wounded by a minié ball in the right shoulder. Although the battle eventually became a stalemate, Young was recognized by both the division and brigade commanders for his leadership. In his report Colonel Vaughan praised Young for driving the enemy from the woods "in most gallant style." Vaughan observed that "Colonel Young of the Ninth Texas Infantry, seized the colors of his regiment in one of the most gallant charges and led it through."[141]

On January 21, 1863, the Ninth Texas was transferred from Smith's Brigade to Ector's Brigade in J. P. McCown's Division. The transfer was welcomed by both Young and members of the regiment. For the first time they were serving in a brigade commanded by a Texan and made up of other Texas regiments. From this time forward, Young's Civil War service was with Ector's Brigade.[142]

Ector's Brigade spent the summer of 1863 in central Mississippi. The brigade took part in several skirmishes as Joe Johnston attempted to thwart Union efforts to capture Vicksburg and occupy central Mississippi. In an engagement at Jackson on July 13, Young was wounded in the right thigh and disabled from duty for a month. In September the brigade, now part of W. H. T. Walker's Division, was in the fight at Chickamauga. Casualties were high. Young was shot in the left chest and forced to spend several weeks recuperating. He was back with the brigade, now assigned to Maj. Gen. Samuel French's Division, in Meridian, Mississippi, in early 1864.[143]

In May, Ector's Brigade was ordered to join Joe Johnston's army in northern Georgia. In the next two months the brigade, including Young and the Ninth Texas, took part in several battles as the Confederates fought to keep Sherman from Atlanta. At Kennesaw Mountain, Young was wounded in the neck and jaw but continued fighting. On July 27, in the fighting around Atlanta, Ector was seriously injured, requiring amputation of his leg. Young assumed command of the brigade that evening and directed the brigade in the remainder of the Atlanta campaign. He was promoted to brigadier general on August 16.[144]

After the evacuation of Atlanta in early September, John Bell Hood, now commanding the Army of Tennessee, moved northward in a bold attempt to draw Sherman after him. French's Division, which included Young and the old Ector Brigade, was ordered to attack the Federal positions at Allatoona, Georgia. In the assault on October 5 Young's horse was shot from under him but the general continued to lead the brigade on foot until he was severely wounded in the left leg by an enemy artillery projectile. He was taken to the rear in an ambulance, but, when the vehicle made a wrong turn, was captured by the Federals. The wound became infected before Young could receive medical treatment, and he recovered only after a painful operation and four months in Federal hospitals. He was sent to Johnson's Island, where he remained a prisoner until July 24, 1865.[145]

Young moved to San Antonio after the war. He studied law and was admitted to the bar, but practiced only briefly. He was involved in several business ventures including a freight line, the Nueces River Irrigation Company, and the *San Antonio Express*. He returned to Virginia in November 1869, to marry Frances Kemper, whom he had met as a student before the war. The couple had one son, Hugh H. Young, who appropriately, considering his father's various wounds, became a surgeon.

Young had at least one additional medical mishap. Years later, when he was traveling from Denver, the train was stopped by thousands of buffalo. The old general got out of the train to shoot one; when he fired, the rifle burst. Pieces of steel gashed his forehead and knocked him unconscious. The engineer put him back on the train, and gradually Young regained his consciousness and was able to continue his journey.[146]

General Young died in San Antonio on November 28, 1901. Cause of death was given as pulmonary congestion and cardiac degeneration. He was buried in the Confederate Cemetery in San Antonio.[147]

CHAPTER SIX

Final Inspection

AS WE HAVE SEEN in the preceding chapters the thirty-seven Texans who served as Confederate generals in the Civil War had varied experiences as military commanders. Two of them, Albert Sidney Johnston and John Bell Hood, led great armies in major battles and campaigns of the war. Early in the war Ben McCulloch commanded the so-called "Army of the West," which was actually only a large brigade. Later, at Pea Ridge, McCulloch led a division in Earl Van Dorn's army. His brother, Henry, commanded a division of infantry in Arkansas, in 1862, and Sam Bell Maxey commanded an infantry division late in the war. Several others, including John A. Wharton, Tom Rosser, A. P. Bagby, and Tom Green, headed cavalry divisions. John Gregg, Jerome B. Robertson, Matthew D. Ector, and Hiram Granbury directed their infantry brigades in great battles in Virginia, Tennessee, and Georgia. Others spent their careers in the Trans Mississippi, where they received less attention and publicity than their comrades east of the river but nevertheless played important roles in defending the area from the enemy.

In completing this study of Lone Star generals in gray, some judgments should be made as to how well they carried out their assignments in the war. Which of them performed so well as battlefield commanders that they could be labeled as "outstanding"? Which of them carried out their duties better than average but not quite as effectively as those who were outstanding? Which generals handled their tasks in a satisfactory manner but somehow failed to rise above average as leaders in combat? And which Texans, either through lack of ability, illness, injury, opportunity, or simply bad luck, were less successful than their comrades in arms? An attempt will be made below to answer some of these questions.

ARMY COMMANDERS

Neither Albert Sidney Johnston nor John Bell Hood, the only Texans to command major armies in the Civil War, could be judged as successful in the role. Johnston never lived up to the great things that were expected of him by Jefferson Davis and the Southern people. Faced with enormous obstacles and saddled with weak (Gideon Pillow, John B. Floyd, Leonidas Polk, George Crittenden, and Felix Zollicoffer) or temperamental subordinates (Pierre Beauregard, Braxton Bragg, and William J. Hardee), Johnston was overwhelmed in the early days of the war by the complexities of defending the vast western department. Described, perhaps unfairly, by U.S. Grant as "vacillating and undecided in his actions," Johnston initially attempted to hold everything by a cordon defense that scattered his forces and left the Confederates vulnerable to attacks by a determined enemy. His biographer, Charles P. Roland, agreed that Johnston made a critical error in trying to hold Fort Donelson with an inadequate force.[1]

Johnston learned from his mistakes, and made the right decision in concentrating his forces at Corinth. Even then, however, his trusting nature caused him to allow his strong-willed subordinate, Pierre Beauregard, to draw up the plan of attack against Grant's army. The result was what historian Steven Woodworth described as "a disastrous plan" which had the Confederates attacking in a linear formation, with one corps behind another, rather than side by side. In addition, the plan failed to provide a heavier attacking force on the Confederate right side where Johnston intended to cut off the Union army from Pittsburg Landing. By adopting this plan of attack, the Confederates, according to James L. McDonough, "may well have lost the opportunity to break the Union army at Shiloh."[2]

Once the battle began, Johnston did his best to lead his men to victory. He was at the front the entire day, directing and encouraging his green, inexperienced troops as they pushed the enemy back. His death that afternoon has left historians debating "what might have been" had he lived.

Because of his early death, it may be unfair to evaluate Albert Sidney Johnston as a Civil War commander. Roland pointed out in his biography of Johnston that if Robert E. Lee, U. S. Grant, and William T. Sherman were judged at this time in their careers they would not enjoy the high reputations they have as wartime commanders. All three made numerous mistakes early in the war but overcame these to be successful leaders later in the war.

Based upon what he did accomplish in his brief Civil War career, Johnston is not regarded highly by most historians. Of the seven Confederates who were full generals and commanded armies in the field, Johnston would fall somewhere in the middle, behind Robert E. Lee and Pierre Beauregard, and possibly Joseph E. Johnston, but ahead of Edmund Kirby Smith, Braxton Bragg, and John Bell Hood.[3]

John Bell Hood probably should not have been placed in command of the Army of Tennessee in the summer of 1864. Peerless as a combat leader and fighter, Hood was ideally suited for brigade and division command. Under the best of circumstances he would have had difficulty in commanding an army. In poor physical condition as a result of major injuries suffered at Gettysburg and Chickamauga, Hood had only several weeks' experience directing a corps. Taking over command when the army was backed up to the outskirts of Atlanta, Hood received no cooperation from his predecessor, Joseph E. Johnston, and less than full support from his principal subordinate, William J. Hardee, in carrying out a bold plan of attack.

Critics have dismissed Hood's actions as rash and erratic, but Joseph B. Mitchell in his book *Military Leaders of the Civil War* argued that the timing and planning for the attacks was sound, and almost succeeded. David Coffey, *John Bell Hood and the Struggle for Atlanta*, pointed out that Hood's strategy was "conceptually sound"; his failure "came in trying to do too much with too little." Steven Woodworth in his *Jefferson Davis and His Generals* credited Hood with staving off the loss of Atlanta for a month when Joe

Johnston would have lost it within days. After Atlanta fell, Hood's campaign against Sherman's supply lines in northern Georgia was "well conceived, well executed, and probably about the best thing he could have undertaken," wrote Woodworth.[4]

The disaster for Hood came in his ill-fated Tennessee campaign. The plan for the campaign was questionable to begin with; Hood threw away any chance of success in a series of frontal attacks at Franklin before his artillery and part of his infantry were in place. Then, after laying siege to Nashville, he made a serious error in dispatching Forrest and his cavalry to Murfreesboro. W. J. Wood, an historian who has analyzed Civil War generalship, surmised that Hood became submerged in "a sort of dream world" where reality gave way to the idea that when Thomas came out of his fortifications he would be defeated. The result was the destruction of Hood's army and the loss of his reputation.[5]

While recent works by Steven Woodworth, Joseph Mitchell, David Coffey, and Richard McMurry have made Hood's actions more understandable, they have not changed the overall consensus, most fully enunciated by Thomas L. Connelly in his seminal studies of the Army of Tennessee, that Hood was a failure as an army commander.[6]

DIVISION AND BRIGADE COMMANDERS

With the exception of Albert Sidney Johnston, all of the Civil War generals from the Lone Star State served at one time or another as division or brigade commanders. John Bell Hood was the only one of the group to command an infantry division for any length of time. Ben McCulloch, who had earlier commanded the so-called Army of the West, was in command of a division consisting of an infantry brigade and a cavalry brigade in one battle, Pea Ridge. Sam Maxey, who directed cavalry in Indian Territory, was assigned command of an infantry division only in the closing months of the war. John A. Wharton, Tom Green, Adam Johnson, A. P. Bagby, and Hamilton P. Bee all headed cavalry divisions, but usually these were smaller in size than infantry divisions. Thomas N. Waul and John Whitfield each commanded a so-called "legion," but neither was as large as an infantry division.

The majority of Texas general officers commanded brigades consisting of several regiments. These ranged in size from two to three thousand men early in the war to several hundred men late in the conflict. About half of these brigadiers were in the cavalry, a high proportion in an army in which only fifteen percent of its soldiers were in mounted service. More than half of the general officers from Texas served primarily in the Trans Mississippi, where the nature of the war favored cavalry operations.[7]

On the whole, the general officers from Texas who commanded divisions and brigades performed their duties as well as those from other states. A few did so in an outstanding manner, several either failed or had little opportunity to achieve anything significant in the war, and many carried out their assignments satisfactorily but without any spectacular accomplishments or successes.

Outstanding Commanders

Six general officers from Texas performed in an outstanding manner as division and/or brigade commanders. These were, in alphabetical order:

1. Matthew D. Ector
2. Hiram Granbury
3. Tom Green
4. John Gregg
5. John Bell Hood
6. John A. Wharton

Each of these officers was highly successful in leading his division or brigade in combat. Hood and Wharton were promoted to major general; Tom Green was recommended for promotion to this rank but was killed before presidential and congressional action confirming the appointment was taken. All three commanded divisions: Wharton and Green in the cavalry and Hood the infantry. The other three outstanding commanders, Ector, Granbury, and Gregg, commanded infantry brigades. Of the six, only Ector and Hood survived the war.

All six had some form of college education, but Hood was the only professional soldier and graduate of the U.S. Military Academy. Five of the six served at some time with the Army of Tennessee, although Gregg and Hood gained their greatest reputations as brigade commanders with Lee's Army of Northern Virginia. Tom Green was the only one of the six whose Civil War service was exclusively in the Trans Mississippi.

Hood, who was not successful as army commander, was one of the Civil War's outstanding combat officers. Even the most vocal critics of his tenure as army commander agree that as a brigade and division commander he was unexcelled. Lee's only general who enhanced his reputation in the Seven Days fighting around Richmond in early summer of 1862, Hood carried out his orders with precision and efficiency at Second Manassas. At Sharpsburg (Antietam) he won the praise of Stonewall Jackson for his role in stopping the Federals in Miller's corn field. At Gettysburg, after failing to convince Longstreet to alter his attack orders, Hood led his division in the bitter fighting in and around the Devil's Den. At Chickamauga he led the attack that broke through the Union line. Had his career ended in 1863, Hood would have been considered one of the war's most successful soldiers.[8]

The other Texas generals listed on the previous page received less publicity than Hood but were nevertheless men of outstanding ability. John Gregg, who died while commanding Hood's Texas Brigade, served well in three different Confederate armies—the Army of Mississippi, the Army of Tennessee, and the Army of Northern Virginia. Never as popular with the troops in the Texas Brigade as Hood and Jerome B. Robertson, Gregg was nevertheless respected by the men who served under him. He led the Texas Brigade in its most famous hour when it stopped the enemy advance in the Wilderness, as Robert E. Lee looked on approvingly. By the time of his death in October 1864, Gregg was regarded as Lee's most able brigadier and doubtlessly would have been promoted to major general had he lived.

The same might be said of Gregg's one-time deputy, Hiram Granbury. As Gregg's successor as commander of the Seventh Texas Infantry, Granbury displayed many of the same charactertistics as his former chief. At Raymond, Chickamauga, and Missionary Ridge he demonstrated his capacity for higher command. As brigade commander he led his Texas troops in one of the few successful night attacks at Pickett's Mill, Georgia. Like Gregg, he died while leading an attack in the autumn of 1864.[9]

Matthew D. Ector, like Gregg a lawyer with little military experience before the war, was an outstanding regimental commander before his promotion to brigade command in September 1862. In the fighting at Murfreesboro, Chickamauga, New Hope Church, Kennesaw Mountain, and around Atlanta, Ector demonstrated his ability to lead his brigade to achieve its objectives against heavy odds.

Tom Green and John A. Wharton, the two cavalry officers in the group, were successful in most of their Civil War assignments. Green, whose entire war career was west of the Mississippi, took part in several of the area's best known military engagements—Valverde, Galveston, Mansfield, and Pleasant Hill. A rather quiet, unassuming man, Green remained extremely popular with his troops, often under the most difficult of circumstances. John A. Wharton, who succeeded Green following the latter's death at Blair's Landing, won his laurels in Kentucky and Tennessee, where he led his cavalry in the battles of Shiloh, Perryville, Murfreesboro, and Chickamauga. The futile attack he ordered at Yellow Bayou, Louisiana, in May 1864 was the one major mistake he made as a military commander. He was generally well liked by his men, but his brusque manner sometimes offended fellow officers. A quarrel with Joe Wheeler led to Wharton's transfer to Louisiana, and his treatment of George W. Baylor resulted in the tragic altercation in which Wharton was killed.

Above Average Commanders

Several Confederate generals from Texas demonstrated that they were above average as military commanders but for various reasons—oftentimes lack of opportunity—would not be considered outstanding. These are, alphabetically:

1. Richard Gano
2. Thomas Harrison
3. Samuel Bell Maxey
4. Lawrence Sullivan Ross
5. William R. Scurry
6. Thomas N. Waul

Among this group Sam Bell Maxey and Lawrence S. "Sul" Ross are the best known and probably the most able. Indeed, some historians would put them in the higher category of outstanding commanders. Maxey did a good job wherever he commanded troops, but his reputation suffers from missed opportunities; for a variety of reasons he just missed the fighting at Shiloh, Murfreesboro, Port Hudson, and Vicksburg. Transferred to Indian Territory, he did a creditable job as a district administrator but failed to participate in any major battles. On the one occasion where he had an opportunity to command, Poison Spring, he allowed a junior officer (Marmaduke) to direct the attack. Wisely, he interceded to stop the fighting after victory, thus saving the lives of many black troops. Lack of resources and internal politics eventually led to his transfer to command of a division, but by that time the war was nearly over.[10]

Sul Ross was another Texas general who performed well but lack of opportunity to command his brigade in major battles detracts from his wartime record. Ross was involved in many military engagements—135 according to his biographer. But so often these were small affairs in which his troopers skirmished with the enemy. His success at Thompson's Station, Yazoo City, and Newnan demonstrated that Ross was a military leader of some ability, but he was not involved in the larger battles at Murfreesboro, Chickamauga, Franklin, and Nashville.

The other four Texans in this category, Tom Harrison, Richard Gano, William R. Scurry, and Thomas N. Waul, while not as well known as Maxey and Ross, also demonstrated military talents above average. Harrison had the fortune, or misfortune, to follow John A. Wharton, first as commander of Terry's Texas Rangers and then as head of the cavalry brigade. Harrison was never as colorful as Wharton, nor as popular with the troops in his command, but he did perform in a dependable fashion in the Murfreesboro, Chickamauga, and Atlanta campaigns. William R. Scurry led the attack at Valverde, commanded Magruder's ground troops at Galveston, and directed his brigade at Mansfield, Pleasant Hill, and Jenkins' Ferry. He won a tactical victory at Glorieta Pass, but the failure to guard his supply train was a mistake that keeps him from the "outstanding" category. Thomas N. Waul commanded his Legion with distinction in the fighting and siege at Vicksburg and later showed considerable ability leading a brigade in Walker's Division at Mansfield, Pleasant Hill, and Jenkins' Ferry. Richard Gano is probably the least known of the group, but his service with Morgan's Raiders, in Bragg's Kentucky campaign, in the cavalry raid near Fort Gibson, and victory at Cabin Creek mark him as a highly capable officer. Had his health been better he might have risen even higher as a Civil War commander.

Average Commanders

As noted earlier, the majority of Texas generals in gray carried out their duties satisfactorily but not above the performance level expected of general officers. These individuals are listed below (in alphabetical order) with brief comments about each.

1.   Arthur P. Bagby—signs of brilliance shown in the bayou country and a favorite of Kirby Smith, but never quite lived up to prewar expectations.

2.   Xavier Debray—solid performance at Mansfield and Pleasant Hill but did not command in other major battles.

3.   William Hardeman—steady performer at Valverde and Galveston; prevented Union forces from outflanking the Missouri Brigade at Pleasant Hill, but limited oppotunities elsewhere.

4.   James Harrison—dependable commander of Fifteenth Texas Infantry; well liked by officers and men but did not become a brigade commander until late in the war.

5.   Adam Johnson—an independent spirit, excellent at recruiting and organizing troops; avoided brigade command for some time so that he could operate on his own.

6.   Wilburn H. King—another steady performer, and youngest Texan to be appointed general; severe wound at Mansfield limited opportunities for higher command.

7.   Walter P. Lane—courageous, brave, a legend in his own time; something of a maverick who occasionally allowed personal ambition to take precedence over needs of Confederacy.

8.   Ben McCulloch—a bold fighter; enjoyed great reputation when war began, but was killed too early in the war to reach full potential.

9.   John C. Moore—man of considerable ability and intelligence; performed well at Shiloh, Corinth, Vicksburg, and Missionary Ridge, but controversy with William J. Hardee damaged his reputation.

10.   Horace Randal—handled brigade well at Mansfield, Pleasant Hill, and Jenkins' Ferry, but never quite reached prewar expectations.

11.   Jerome B. Robertson—the beloved "Aunt Polly" of the Texas Brigade; truly concerned about welfare of men in his command; led Texas Brigade longer than any other commander; quarrel with superiors ended his Civil War career.

12.　Tom Rosser—prototype of the dashing, bold, headstrong cavalry raider; excessively ambitious officer who distrusted and disliked most of his superiors; capable of outstanding performance such as at Kelly's Ford, Wilderness, and Shenandoah Valley raid, but also of monumental failures such as Tom's Brook.[11]

13.　William Steele—probably the most disappointing of any Texas general; with West Point background and extensive prewar experience as a professional soldier should have risen to higher rank and command; served in New Mexico, Indian Territory, and Louisiana, but never in a major battle; bitter over experiences as commander in Indian Territory.

14.　Richard Waterhouse—one of the better regimental commanders; became a brigadier late in the war; given greater opportunities he may have shown superior talents.

15.　William H. Young—often seriously wounded; without question one of the bravest officers in the Confederate army; became brigade commander in summer of 1864, captured soon thereafter.

"They Also Served"

Several Texans were not successful as brigade or division commanders. It would not be fair to consider all as failures because various factors, including poor health and lack of opportunity, affected their performance. Yet they did not achieve the degree of success as their previously discussed comrades. Charitably, they are listed under the category "They Also Served."

1.　Hamilton P. Bee—given a command beyond his military experiences and capability; would have been better in an administrative rather than a field command; his caution at Monett's Ferry saved lives but thwarted Taylor's plan to attack Banks' army.

2.　Elkanah Greer—carried out Van Dorn's wishes after death of Ben McCulloch; resigned after reaching Corinth; desire for promotion led him to accept an administrative post, which he handled fairly well, but nevertheless he was removed from this position before war's end.

3.　Joseph L. Hogg—secured position because of political connections; died early in the war without opportunity to demonstrate his ability.

4.　Henry McCulloch—a man of integrity; showed some ability as an organizer and administrator, but was a failure as a field commander; removed first as division commander and later as brigade commander; did a good job in charge of northern sub-district of Texas.

5.   Allison Nelson—promising Civil War career cut short by early death; had the experience and characteristics that should have resulted in military success.

6.   Felix Robertson-—capable individual, but serious character flaws became a liability as a brigade commander.

7.   A. W. Terrell—limited opportunities as brigade commander; apparently had some difficulty in maintaining discipline in his command.

8.   John Whitfield—ambitious, independent-minded political general; poor health forced retirement from active duty.

9.   Louis T. Wigfall—the *"enfant terrible"* of the Confederacy; impetuous, volatile, headstrong individual with limited military experience and questionable ability.[12]

Other Texas "Generals" in Gray

In addition to the thirty-seven Confederate general officers described in the text, there were a number of Texans who were generals in the state army or militia or who were listed in one or more contemporary lists as general officers. These thirteen Texans are discussed in a recent work by Bruce Allardice, *More Generals In Gray* (Baton Rouge: Louisiana State University Press, 1995), which includes a total of 137 officers for the Confederacy. Short sketches of each of these with data from Allardice's book supplemented by information from other sources including the *New Handbook of Texas* (Austin: Texas State Historical Association, 1997) are provided below:

Charles D. Anderson—Born in South Carolina in July 1827. Moved to Texas in 1839. Attended, but did not graduate from, the U.S. Military Academy at West Point. An artillery officer, U.S. Army, 1856-1861. In the Civil War served primarily in Alabama, commanded Fort Gaines when surrendered to Federal forces. Imprisoned in New Orleans. Returned to Texas after the war. Two years city engineer in Austin. Builder and keeper of Galveston Lighthouse. Died in Galveston, November 21, 1901.

James W. Barnes—A brigadier general of Texas state troops. Born on October 5, 1815, in Hancock County, Georgia. Educated at Sparta Academy. Served in Seminole War. Moved to Mississippi in 1839, then to Polk County, Texas, in 1841. In 1842 settled in Anderson, Grimes

County, where he established a farm. Active Baptist layman, treasurer of Baptist state convention in 1848 and regular contributor to Texas *Baptist Herald*. Colonel of Fourth Regiment, Texas state troops, commander of Camp Groce prison, appointed brigadier general of Fifth Brigade, Texas state troops, by Governor Pendleton Murrah. After the war, vice-president of International Railroad Company. Died on October 22, 1892, in Anderson.

John R. Baylor—Colorful frontiersman and Indian fighter. Born on July 27, 1822, in Paris, Kentucky. Prominent Virginia family background. Father an army surgeon. Attended Woodward College in Cincinnati, Ohio, 1835-1837. Moved to Texas in 1839, settled near Weatherford, became a rancher. State representative, 1853-1854, Indian subagent, editor of Democratic Party newspapers. Elected lieutenant colonel of Second Texas Mounted Rifles; promoted to colonel in December 1861. Led regiment into New Mexico Territory, captured Union troops under Maj. Isaac Lynde at San Augustine Pass. Proclaimed governor of Confederate Territory of Arizona. Advocated extermination of Apaches. Removed from office by President Davis. As volunteer participated in recapture of Galveston. Elected to Confederate Congress in 1863. Reappointed colonel in Confederate army on March 25, 1865. After the war practiced law and ranched. Active in politics. Involved in several postwar gunfights. Died on February 6, 1894, in Montell, Uvalde County. Several sources list him as a general.

Santos Benavides—Highest-ranking Mexican American to serve in Confederate army. Born in Laredo on November 1, 1863. Distinguished family background; great-grandfather founded Laredo. Uncle, Basilio Benavides, three times *alcalde* under Mexican rule and later mayor and state representative. Santos Benavides became successful merchant and rancher, mayor of Laredo, and county chief justice. Led several campaigns against Lipan Apaches. Supported secession, commissioned captain in Thirty-third Texas Cavalry. Drove Juan Cortina back into Mexico in 1861. Promoted to colonel in December 1863. Defeated Union First Texas Cavalry in Battle of Laredo on March 19, 1864. Mentioned in several places as brigadier general, but no official record that he was a general officer. After war resumed mercantile business. Elected to Texas legislature three times; twice elected Laredo alderman. Died November 9, 1891.

Robert H. Cumby—Legislator and planter. Born on August 24, 1824, in Charlotte County, Virginia. Moved to Mississippi in 1836, and to Texas in 1849, settling in Rusk County. In 1860 possessed $60,000 in property, including thirty slaves. Served in Texas legislature, 1859-1861. Raised

Company B of Third Texas Cavalry Regiment. Fought in battles of Wilson's Creek and Pea Ridge. In May 1862 elected colonel of Third Texas Cavalry, but because of poor health resigned command in June 1862. In 1864 Governor Murrah appointed Cumby as brigadier general commanding Fourth Brigade, Texas state troops. After war moved to Sulphur Springs, where he ran grocery store. Died in Sulphur Springs on November 19, 1881.

John S. Ford—A true Renaissance man who was lawyer, doctor, elected official, editor, soldier, Ranger, trailblazer, and politician. Born in Greenville District, South Carolina, on May 26, 1815. Moved to Texas in June 1836, served in Texas army for two years. Settled in San Augustine, where he practiced medicine and law. Elected to Texas Congress in 1844. In 1845 moved to Austin; became editor of *Texas Democrat*. During Mexican War served as adjutant in Jack Hays' Regiment, where he acquired nickname "Rip" because when sending out death notices he included message "Rest in Peace," later shortened to "R.I.P." After Mexican War he and Robert S. Neighbors explored country between San Antonio and El Paso. In 1849 made captain in Texas Rangers. Elected to state senate in 1852 and founded newspaper, the *State Times*. In 1858 accepted commission in state troops; defeated Indians in two engagements. In 1859 sent to Rio Grande, where he conducted operations against Juan Cortina. Member of secession convention in 1861. Elected colonel of Second Texas Cavalry with a command along the Rio Grande. In 1862 appointed chief of conscription for the state. In December 1863 General Magruder ordered him to lead state and Confederate troops to retake South Texas from Federals. Appointed brigadier general of District No. 1, Texas state troops, in 1864. In May 1865 commanded Confederate troops in last battle of the war, a victory at Palmito Ranch. Active political career after the war. Mayor of Brownsville in 1874, Texas Senate, 1875-1879, Texas Constitutional Convention of 1875, superintendent of Texas Deaf and Dumb School. Active role in promoting Texas history; a charter member of Texas State Historical Association. Died in San Antonio on November 3, 1897.

John S. Griffith—Born on June 17, 1829, in Montgomery County, Maryland. Moved to San Augustine, Texas, in 1839. Clerk in mercantile store in 1850, then established own store. Moved to Kaufman County in 1859, raised cotton and livestock. Joined volunteer cavalry company; elected lieutenant colonel of Sixth Texas Cavalry. Led charge against Federal Indians at Chustenahlah in 1861. Responsible for planning and execution of Holly Springs raid of 1862, but poor health forced him to resign commission. Returned to Texas, elected to state legislature. In March 1864 appointed by Governor Murrah as brigadier general of state troops, District No. 2. After the war moved to Terrell, Texas. Elected to state legislature in 1876. Died in Terrell on August 6, 1901.

Philip N. Luckett—Physician and soldier. Born in Augusta County, Virginia, in either 1823 or 1824. Family moved to Ohio before 1830. Received appointment to West Point, but apparently did not enroll. Studied medicine, moved to Texas, settled in Corpus Christi, where Luckett established medical practice. Served as surgeon to Texas Ranger companies in South Texas. In 1860 listed with $5,000 in real and $6,000 in personal property. One of the three commissioners appointed to negotiate surrender of Federal property in Texas. Served briefly as quartermaster and commissary general of Texas. In fall 1861 became colonel of Third Texas Infantry. Assigned to western sub-district of Texas, 1861-1862. In July 1863 made acting brigadier general of eastern sub-district of Texas. In April 1864, Third Texas assigned to Walker's Texas Division; took part in Red River campaign. When William R. Scurry was killed at Jenkins' Ferry, Luckett commanded brigade. In December 1864 assigned to detached duty on military court of inquiry into Price's Missouri raid. Fled to Mexico after end of war, and returned to Texas in November 1865. Arrested by Federal authorities and imprisoned at Fort Jackson, Louisiana, for several months. Died of bronchial disease on May 21, 1869, and is buried in Cincinnati, Ohio.

Hinche P. Mabry—According to various sources was promoted to brigadier general by Edmund Kirby Smith in 1864, but no record of appointment has been found. Born at Laurel Hill, Georgia, on October 27, 1829. Attended University of Tennessee but forced to leave school due to lack of funds. In 1851 moved to Jefferson, Texas, where he became a merchant. Practiced law; state representative, 1856-1861. Opposed secession but raised Company B, Third Texas Cavalry. Captain of company; later adjutant of Third Texas. Fought at Wilson's Creek and Pea Ridge. In May 1862 elected lieutenant colonel of Third Texas. Severely wounded and captured at Iuka. After being exchanged was promoted to colonel. During 1864 and 1865 led a Mississippi cavalry brigade in operations in that state. Regarded as an outstanding leader and repeatedly recommended for promotion by superiors. In April 1864 his brigade captured Union gunboat *Petrel* near Yazoo City. Resumed legal practice after the war. Member of 1866 constitutional convention. Judge of district court but removed by Sheridan as "impediment to Reconstruction." Active in local Ku Klux Klan affiliate. Died in Sherman, Texas, on March 24, 1884 from accidental pistol wound.

John F. Marshall—Newspaper editor and staunch secessionist. Born in Virginia, probably in 1823 (Allardice said "Marshall's origins were shrouded in mystery"). Moved to Mississippi, became assistant editor of Jackson *Southern Reformer*. Later bought interest in and edited Jackson *Mississippian*. Moved to Austin, Texas, in 1852. Became editor of *Texas State Gazette*, which he made the leading Texas forum for Southern extremist views. Became chairman of Texas Democratic Party in 1856, helped secure election of Hardin Runnels over Sam Houston in 1857. In October 1861, President Jefferson Davis, an old friend, appointed Marshall lieutenant colonel of the Fourth Texas Infantry. When John B. Hood, commander of Fourth Texas, was promoted to brigade commander, Marshall was promoted to colonel and commander of the regiment. Led the regiment in battles of Eltham's Landing and Seven Pines. Killed while leading charge at Gaines' Mill on June 27, 1862. Listed in several sources as a general officer; no evidence that such appointment was made.

William H. Parsons—Born on April 23, 1826, in New Jersey. Family moved to Montgomery, Alabama, when Parsons was quite young. Attended Emory College but left to serve in Mexican War. After the war, settled near Tyler, Texas. Became editor of *Tyler Telegraph*. Moved several times in Central Texas. In 1860 founded a newspaper, the *South West*, in Waco. When war broke out, raised and commanded volunteer cavalry regiment which became the Twelfth Texas Cavalry. Under his leadership the regiment helped defend Little Rock, Arkansas, from Federal forces in summer of 1862. By October commanded a brigade of Texas cavalry which operated along the west bank of the Mississippi River. Led his cavalry brigade in Red River campaign of 1864. Recommended for brigadier general several times but not promoted due to controversy with Col. George W. Carter of the Twenty-first Texas over seniority. After the war Parsons went to British Honduras briefly but soon returned to Houston, where he was active in railroad promotion, newspapers, and politics. Elected to the Texas Senate as a Republican in 1870. Received several Federal appointments in later life. Died in Chicago, Illinois, on October 2, 1907. Although he had commanded a brigade and later claimed the rank of brigadier, he was never promoted to that rank.

Elijah S. C. Robertson—Son of Texas empresario Sterling C. Robertson, Elijah S. C. Robertson was born on August 2, 1820, in Nashville, Tennessee. The family moved to Texas in 1832. In 1835-1836 young Robertson was a member of a company of Texas Rangers that repelled Indian attacks. Attended Jackson College in Tennessee, 1837-1839. Returned to Texas; served in several governmental offices. Admitted to the bar in 1845. Moved to Bell County in 1852; purchased plantation and raised livestock. In 1860 owned $150,000 in real and $30,000 in personal property including thirty slaves. Elected to Texas secession convention in 1861. Commissioned brigadier general in state militia. Served briefly on staff of Henry McCulloch in 1862. After the war continued farming and ranching. Member of Texas Constitutional Convention of 1875. Died on October 8, 1879.

James W. Throckmorton—Legislator, brigadier general of state troops, governor of Texas. Born on February 1, 1825, in Sparta, Tennessee. Moved with his father, a physician, to Collin County, Texas, in 1841. Studied medicine with an uncle in Princeton, Kentucky. Returned to Texas at outbreak of Mexican War. Served as surgeon in Ranger company in Mexican War. Received medical discharge on June 8, 1847, because of kidney disease. Studied law, commenced practice in McKinney, Texas. A leader of Whig Party in Texas, served in Texas House of Representatives, 1851-1857, and Senate, 1857-1861. Owned $9,500 in property (including one slave) in 1860. Elected to Texas secession convention; one of the eight delegates who opposed secession. Although a leader of Texas unionists, he served as lieutenant colonel in William Young's regiment that occupied abandoned army posts in Indian Territory. A captain in Sixth Texas Cavalry, fought at Chustenahlah and Pea Ridge. In May 1862 discharged from Confederate army because of poor health. Rejoined Sixth Cavalry with rank of major in February 1863; served in Louisiana until poor health again forced him to resign in September 1863. Elected to Texas Senate in fall 1863. Appointed brigadier general of Third District, Texas state troops, by Governor Murrah in March 1864. In December 1864 assigned command of First Frontier District in northwest Texas. President of Texas Constitutional Convention of 1866. Elected governor, but removed in 1867 on orders of General Sheridan. Returned to law practice in Collin County. Elected to Congress, served 1875-1879 and 1883-1887. Unsuccessful candidate for U.S. Senate, 1888. Died in McKinney on April 21, 1894.

* * * * * *

In *More Generals In Gray*, Bruce Allardice pointed out that in addition to the 137 officers listed as generals in one or more standard sources there are a large number of other Confederates who were called general officers. Although Allardice noted that "in no credible sense were these officers Confederate generals," he provided brief sketches of each in an appendix (pp. 243-258).

Allardice's appendix contains sketches for twenty Texans. Their names are listed below. For additional information see *More Generals In Gray* and the *New Handbook of Texas*.

Frederick S. Bass

August Buchel

Thomas Jefferson Chambers

Edward Clark

George M. Flournoy

William N. Hamman

Thomas B. Howard

William Hudson

Hugh McLeod

David B. Martin

Ebenezer B. Nichols

Alexis T. Rainey

William P. Rogers

Nathan G. Shelley

Sidney Sherman

Darwin M. Stapp

Nathaniel Terry

William G. Webb

James Willie

Hugh F. Young

Endnotes

CHAPTER ONE

1. Several Texans, including Thomas Lubbock, Benjamin F. Terry, and Thomas Goree, were at First Manassas. They had come to Richmond in early summer, 1861, to inquire as to Confederate military needs. All three served as volunteer aides on the staff of James Longstreet at First Manassas. Goree remained on Longstreet's staff throughout the war; Terry and Lubbock returned to Texas to form the Eighth Texas Cavalry, or Terry's Texas Rangers. See Ralph A. Wooster, ed., *Lone Star Blue and Gray* (Austin: Texas State Historical Association, 1995), ix-x.

2. Texan Felix Robertson, later a brigadier general in the Confederate army, served on the staff of Gen. Adley H. Gladden at Pensacola, Florida, in the autumn of 1861. William C. Davis, "Felix Huston Robertson," in *The Confederate General* (Harrisburg, PA: National Historical Society, 1991), 5:100-101.

3. Davis appointed Robertson brigadier general on July 26, 1864. Robertson had ingratiated himself with his commanding officer, Braxton Bragg, who probably urged Davis to make the appointment. However, Robertson's command was subsequently involved in the killing of black prisoners. This, and a running controversy with Secretary of War John C. Breckinridge, led the Senate on February 22, 1865, to reject the appointment. *Ibid.*, 5:100-101.

4. Not surprising perhaps, there is disagreement over who were the general officers from Texas in the Confederate army. In the main I have used the list given in Marcus J. Wright, comp., *Texas in the War, 1861-1865*, ed. Harold B. Simpson (Hillsboro: Hill Jr. College Press, 1965), 3-18. This varies slightly from Ezra J. Warner, *Generals in Gray: Lives of Confederate Commanders* (Baton Rouge: Louisiana State University Press, 1959), and William C. Davis, ed., *The Confederate General*, 6 vols. I have not, however, included Hinche P. Mabry of Jefferson described by Wright and Simpson, p. 86, as "promoted to brigadier general E. Kirby Smith sometime in 1864 but . . . never confirmed by Jefferson Davis or the Confederate Senate." Bruce S. Allardice, *More Generals in Gray* (Baton Rouge: Louisi-

ana State University Press, 1995), 146, points out that Mabry was not in the Trans Mississippi at the time of the supposed promotion and still signed himself as colonel as late as January 6, 1865. Since I have not found any written evidence that Smith appointed Mabry I have not included him in this study. Nor have I included James P. Major, a native of Missouri who commanded a Texas cavalry brigade in Louisiana. Major is listed as a general officer from Texas by Richard M. McMurry, *Two Great Rebel Armies: An Essay in Confederate Military History* (Chapel Hill: University of North Carolina Press, 1989), 163-164. He is not listed as a Texas general by Wright and Simpson.

5. Neither Albert S. Johnston, John Bell Hood, nor John C. Moore are included in these calculations for places of residence. Johnston, whose last Texas residence was Travis County, was stationed in California when the war began. Hood, a native of Kentucky, was in West Texas with the U.S. Second Cavalry when the war began. When Kentucky delayed taking action on secession, Hood entered Confederate service from Texas. See his explanation in *Advance and Retreat: Personal Experiences in the United States and Confederate Armies* (New Orleans: Published for the Hood Orphan Memorial Fund, 1880), 16. John C. Moore, a native of Tennessee, had not lived in Texas prior to the war. He was sent to Texas by the Confederate army immediately after receiving his commision in April 1861. He is listed as a Texas general in both Wright and Simpson, *Texas in the War* and McMurry, *Two Great Rebel Armies*.

6. Robertson resigned on January 19, 1861, and was commissioned in the Confederate artillery on March 9, 1861, in time to participate in the reduction of Fort Sumter. Rosser resigned on April 22, 1861, two weeks before graduation. He was commissioned as first lieutenant of artillery dated March 16, 1861, and assigned to the famed Washington Artillery of New Orleans. *The Confederate General*, 5:113, and Warner, *Generals in Gray*, 260, 264-265.

7. Both Anne J. Bailey, "Xavier Blanchard Debray," in Ron Tyler, et. al., eds., *The New Handbook of Texas*, 6 vols. (Austin: Texas State Historical Association, 1996), 2:554, and Ella Lonn, *Foreigners in the Confederacy* (Chapel Hill: University of North Carolina Press, 1940), 136-137, state Debray attended St. Cyr Academy. Alwyn Barr, "Xavier Blanchard Debray," in *The Confederate General*, 5:180, states Debray "achieved his schooling in the military academy of his native country." Allardice, *More Generals in Gray*, 74-75, points out that in response to his queries both St. Cyr and L'Ecole Polytechnique stated they had no record of Debray attending.

8. Ralph A. Wooster, "Notes on Texas' Largest Slaveholders, 1860," *Southwestern Historical Quarterly* 65 (July 1961): 72-79; Wooster, "Wealthy Texans, 1860," ibid. 71 (October 1967): 163-179; Randolph B. Campbell, *An Empire for Slavery: The Peculiar Institution in Texas* (Baton Rouge: Louisiana State University Press, 1989), 274-276.

9. Data gathered from Warner, *Generals in Gray*; Davis, ed., *The Confederate General*, 6 vols.; Allardice, *More Generals in Gray*; Tyler, ed., *New Handbook of Texas*, 6 vols.; and Wright and Simpson, *Texas in the War*.

10. *New Handbook of Texas*, 3:450-451, 5:617; Joseph Milton Nance, *Dare-Devils All: The Texian Mier Expedition*, ed. Archie P. McDonald (Austin: Eakin Press, 1998), 26, 30-31.

11. Cynthia Ann Parker was the most celebrated Texas captive of the Indians.

She was taken by the Comanches on a raid in Limestone County in 1836 and held for twenty-five years. She married an Indian chief, Pete Nocona, and had two sons and a daughter. She was never reconciled to living in white society after her recapture by Ross. For more on Parker see *New Handbook of Texas*, 5:57-58, and Margaret S. Hacker, *Cynthia Ann Parker: The Life and Legend* (El Paso: Texan Western Press, 1990). For Ross see Judith Ann Benner, "The Making of a Soldier: The Indian Fighting Career of Lawrence Sullivan Ross, 1858-1861," *Military History of Texas and the Southwest* 16 (No. 4, 1982): 205-222, and Benner, *Sul Ross: Soldier, Statesman and Educator* (College Station: Texas A & M University Press).

    12. *New Handbook of Texas*, 5:976, 6:945; *The Confederate General*, 4:195, 5:130-131.

    13. The standard biography of Johnston is Charles P. Roland, *Albert Sidney Johnston: Soldier of Three Republics* (Austin: University of Texas Press, 1964).

    14. Thomas W. Cutrer, *Ben McCulloch and the Frontier Military Tradition* (Chapel Hill: University of North Carolina Press, 1993), 176.

    15. Harold B. Simpson, *Hood's Texas Brigade: Lee's Grenadier Guard* (Waco: Texian Press, 1970), 48, 66, 72-74, 88.

    16. *The Confederate General*, 3:113; *New Handbook of Texas*, 3:653-654; W. Buck Yearns, ed., *The Confederate Governors* (Athens: University of Georgia Press, 1985), 196-197.

    17. *The Confederate General*, 6:122-123; Ralph A. Wooster, *Texas and Texans in the Civil War* (Austin: Eakin Press, 1995), 51, 59, 84-87.

    18. Wooster, *Texas and Texans in the Civil War*, 177; Harold B. Simpson, "West Pointers in the Texas Confederate Army," *Texas Military History* 6 (Spring 1962): 82-83.

    19. *New Handbook of Texas*, 3:486-487; and Jack D. Welsh, *Medical Histories of Confederate Generals* (Kent, OH: Kent State University Press, 1995), 95.

    20. Terrell was one of a group of southern officers and govenment officials who went to Mexico rather than surrender in early summer, 1865.

    21. Cutrer, *Ben McCulloch*, 224-244, 291-309; *The Confederate General*, 5:195; *New Handbook of Texas*, 4:976.

    22. *The Confederate General*, 4:120-121.

    23. Bagby and Hardeman spent the Civil War west of the Mississippi. Lane, who was in the Trans Mississippi most of the war, was in the fighting at Corinth, Mississippi.

    24. Apparently, Harrison was on leave in Texas when his horse ran away. See Alwyn Barr, *Polignac's Texas Brigade* (1964; new ed., College Station: Texas A&M University Press, 1998), 39.

    25. *The War of the Rebellion: A Compilation of the Official Records of the Union and Confederate Armies*, 128 vols. (Washington: Government Printing Office, 1880-1901), Series I, 34:563-564 [hereinafter cited as *Official Records;* unless indicated all citations are to Series I]; *Supplement to the Official Records of the Union and Confederate Armies*, 10 vols. (Wilmington, NC: Broadfoot Publishing Co., 1996), 6:348-350; Anne J. Bailey, *Between the Enemy and Texas: Parsons's Texas Cavalry in the Civil War* (Fort Worth: Texas Christian University Press, 1989), 181-182; Richard Taylor, *Destruction and Reconstruction* (New York: Longmans, Green, and Co., 1955), 220, 221, 225; J. P. Blessington, *The Campaigns of Walker's Texas Division* (Reprint; Austin: State House Press, 1994), 182-200.

26. Thomas L. Connelly, *Army of the Heartland: The Army of Tennessee, 1861-1862* (Baton Rouge: Louisiana State University Press, 1967), 3-5; *The Confederate General*, 6:130-131.

27. Ibid., 2:154-155, 3:34-35, 4:171-172; Louise Horton, *Samuel Bell Maxey: A Biography* (Austin: University of Texas Press, 1974); W. C. Nunn, ed., *Ten More Texans in Gray* (Hillsboro: Hill Jr. College Press, 1980), 59-70.

28. *The Confederate General*, 6:113-115, 122-123.

29. Ibid., 2:94-95, 5:110-111.

30. Ibid., 3:24-25, 70-71, 4:180-181; Wooster, *Texas and Texans in the Civil War*, 158-159, 162-168.

31. *The Confederate General*, 3:169-171. See Johnson's own account: *The Partisan Rangers of the Confederate States Army*, ed. William J. Davis (Reprint; Austin: State House Press, 1995).

32. *The Confederate General*, 6:172-173; *New Handbook of Texas*, 6:1130.

33. *The Confederate General*, 5:100.

34. Robertson's removal from command is covered fully in Simpson, *Hood's Texas Brigade*, 383-387.

35. Douglas Southall Freeman, *Lee's Lieutenants: A Study in Command*, 3 vols. (New York: Charles Scribner's Sons, 1942-1944), 3:737, 764-765.

36. See Welsh, *Medical Histories of Confederate Generals*.

37. Many sources say that Johnson's eyes were completely destroyed, but William C. Davis, *The Confederate General*, 3:170, points out that an extant photograph of him wearing crude goggles with what appear to be lenses indicates he retained some limited eyesight.

38. Welsh, *Medical Histories*, 243; *The Confederate General*, 6:172-173.

39. Johnson, *Partisan Rangers*, 197-198; Allardice, *More Confederate Generals*, 146-147; Welsh, *Medical Histories*, 115-116; Douglas S. Hale, *The Third Texas Cavalry in the Civil War* (Norman, OK: University of Oklahoma Press, 1993), 127.

40. See Wooster, *Texas and Texans in the Civil War*, 187-194.

41. Based on information in *New Handbook of Texas*, *Generals in Gray*, Clement A. Evans, ed., *Confederate Military History* (Atlanta: Confederate Publishing Co., 1889), 11; *More Generals in Gray*, *The Confederate General*, Wright and Simpson, *Texas in the War*, and Jon Wakelyn, *Biographical Directory of the Confederacy* (Westport, CT: Greenwood Press, 1977).

42. See Eric H. Walter, *The Fire-Eaters* (Baton Rouge: Louisiana State University Press, 1992), and Alvy L. King, *Louis T. Wigfall: Southern Fire-eater* (Baton Rouge: Louisiana State University Press, 1970), for more on Wigfall.

CHAPTER TWO

1. Charles P. Roland, *Albert Sidney Johnston: Soldier of Three Republics* (Austin: University of Texas Press, 1964), 353. Neither John P. Dyer, *The Gallant Hood* (Indianapolis: Bobbs-Merrill Co., 1950) nor Richard McMurry, *John Bell Hood and the War for Southern Independence* (Lexington: The University Press of Kentucky, 1982) mentions Hood's role in Johnston's reburial.

2. Roland, *Albert Sidney Johnston*, 11-14; William Preston Johnston, *The Life*

of Gen. Albert Sidney Johnston (New York: D. Appleton and Co., 1879), 7-12; Edward C. Boynton, *History of West Point . . .* (Freeport, NY: Books for Libraries Press, 1863), 217-222; Stephen Ambrose, *Duty, Honor, Country: A History of West Point* (Baltimore: Johns Hopkins University Press, 1966), 62-105; Joseph J. Ellis and Robert Moore, *School for Soldiers: West Point and the Profession of Arms* (New York: Oxford University Press, 1974), 32-37.

3. Roland, *Albert Sidney Johnston*, 16-19; Johnston, *Life of Gen. Albert Sidney Johnston*, 10-13. Steven E. Woodworth, *Jefferson Davis and His Generals: The Failure of Confederate Command in the West* (Lawrence: The University Press of Kansas, 1990), 46, notes that Johnston was second in his class most of his academy career but dropped in standing as a result of a senior mathematics final.

4. Johnston's son, William Preston Johnston, covers the Black Hawk War and death of family members thoroughly in his *Life of Gen. Albert Sidney Johnston*, 19-55.

5. Roland, *Albert Sidney Johnston*, 54.

6. Ibid., 81-103.

7. Johnston, *Life of Gen. Albert Sidney Johnston*, 133-145.

8. Johnston's biographer, Charles P. Roland, finds his failure to receive a military command "puzzling." Johnston's son, William Preston Johnston, believes partisan politics were involved, writing "it was almost an avowed policy to confer military command as the reward for political acitivity." Ibid., 145.

9. Roland, *Albert Sidney Johnston*, 140-153. William Preston Johnston later purchased China Grove plantation from his father's creditors in order to free his father of the debt he still owed.

10. William C. Davis, *Jefferson Davis: The Man and His Hour* (New York: Harper, Collins, 1991), 29. Davis notes that Johnston and Jefferson Davis had both attended Transylvania University although Johnston left a year before Davis arrived. When the two West Point cadets learned they had this in common they began a friendship that lasted through the years. See also Charles P. Roland and Richard C. Robbins, eds., "The Diary of Eliza (Mrs. Albert Sidney) Johnston," *Southwestern Historical Quarterly* 60 (April 1957): 464-465.

11. In addition, two officers who joined the regiment in 1856, Fitzhugh Lee (Virginia) and James P. Major (Missouri), became generals in the Civil War. A complete roster of officers in the Second Cavalry may be found in Harold B. Simpson, *Cry Comanche: The 2nd U.S. Cavalry in Texas, 1855-1861* (Hillsboro: Hill Junior College Press, 1979), 172-176. Half of the eight men who became full generals in the Confederate States Army (Johnston, Lee, Smith, and Hood) were in the Second Cavalry.

12. Roland, *Albert Sidney Johnston*, 173-184; Simpson, *Cry Comanche*, 65-82.

13. Roland, *Albert Sidney Johnston*, 191-204; Johnston, *Life of Gen. Albert Sidney Johnston*, 207-220.

14. Future Civil War general Ben McCulloch of Texas and Senator-elect Lazarus W. Powell of Kentucky were the two peace commissioners. For McCulloch's role see Thomas W. Cutrer, *Ben McCulloch and the Frontier Military Tradition* (Chapel Hill: University of North Carolina Press, 1993), 151-159.

15. Johnston, *Life of Gen. Albert Sidney Johnston*, 221-246.

16. Roland, *Albert Sidney Johnston*, 236-242.

17. Johnston had been a small slaveholder. When he was assigned to duty in California, he disposed of his two slaves; one was sold, the other emancipated but accompanied the family to California as a servant. Ibid., 246-248; Johnston, *Life of Gen. Albert Sidney Johnston*, 269-272.

18. Roland, *Albert Sidney Johnston*, 251-252.

19. For Johnston's New Mexico experience see Martin Hardwick Hall, "Albert Sidney Johnston's First Confederate Command," *McNeese Review* 13 (1962): 3-12, and Jerry Don Thompson, *Colonel John Robert Baylor: Texas Indian Fighter and Confederate Soldier* (Hillsboro: Hill Junior College Press, 1971), 44-46.

20. Johnston, *Life of Gen. Albert Sidney Johnston*, 241.

21. Davis, *Jefferson Davis*, 356-357, 360; *Official Records*, 2: 687-688, 4: 405.

22. Roland, *Albert Sidney Johnston*, 263-265.

23. Shelby Foote, *The Civil War: A Narrative*, 3 vols. (New York: Random House, 1958-1974), 1: 170-176; W. C. Nunn, ed., *Ten More Texans in Gray* (Hillsboro: Hill Junior College Press, 1980), 44-45; *Official Records*, 4: 412, 417, 419-420.

24. *Official Records*, 7: 103. The battle of Mill Springs is described in some detail by Johnston, *Life of Gen. Albert Sidney Johnston*, 394-406, and Woodworth, *Jefferson Davis and His Generals*, 60-70.

25. T. Harry Williams, *P. G. T. Beauregard: Napoleon in Gray* (Baton Rouge: Louisiana State University Press, 1954), 113-114.

26. Ibid., 114; Roland, *Albert Sidney Johnston*, 282-283. When Beauregard learned the disparity in numbers he declared that his presence in Kentucky was useless. Only with difficulty did Johnston persuade him to stay.

27. Benjamin Franklin Cooling, *Forts Henry and Donelson: The Key to the Confederate Heartland* (Knoxville: University of Tennessee Press, 1987), 123-128; Roland, *Albert Sidney Johnston*, 289-291.

28. Roland, 290.

29. Ibid. See also Roland's article "Albert Sidney Johnston and the Loss of Forts Henry and Donelson," *Journal of Southern History* 23 (February 1957): 45-69.

30. Woodworth, *Jefferson Davis and His Generals*, 80.

31. For a full account see Cooling, *Forts Henry and Donelson*, 122-223.

32. *Official Records*, 7: 255-256. Johnston noted in his report that Floyd had evacuated his Virginia brigade of about 1,000 men. Confederate cavalry commanded by Col. Nathan Bedford Forrest also escaped from Donelson.

33. Davis, *Jefferson Davis*, 398-399. For criticisms of Johnston see Larry J. Daniel, "'The Assaults of the Demogogues in Congress': General Albert Sidney Johnston and the Politics of Command," *Civil War History* 37 (December 1991): 328-335.

34. *Official Records*, 7: 257-258.

35. Ibid., 7: 258-261.

36. Johnston, *Life of Gen. Albert Sidney Johnston*, 514.

37. Roland, *Albert Sidney Johnston*, 302-310. Roland notes that after the war there was argument between Johnston's friends and Beauregard's supporters over who selected Corinth as the concentration point.

38. Bruce Catton, *Grant Moves South* (Boston: Little, Brown, 1960, 198-221); Larry Daniel, *Shiloh: The Battle That Changed the Civil War* (New York: Simon & Schuster, 1997), 100-111.

39. Charles P. Roland, "Albert Sidney Johnston and the Shiloh Campaign," *Civil War History* 4 (December 1958): 364-366; Grady McWhiney, *Braxton Bragg and Confederate Defeat* (New York: Columbia University Press, 1969), 211-218.

40. Johnston, *Life of Gen. Albert Sidney Johnston*, 566-569; Daniel, *Shiloh*, 127-128; Roland, "Albert Sidney Johnston and the Shiloh Campaign," 370-372. Thomas L. Connelly, *Army of the Heartland*, who is most critical of Johnston's role as a military commander, found Johnston's decisiveness here "surprising." Ibid., 157.

41. For accounts of this phase of the battle see Daniel, *Shiloh*, 143-225; James Lee McDonough, *Shiloh—in Hell before Night* (Knoxville: University of Tennessee Press, 1977), 86-150; Wiley Sword, *Shiloh: Bloody April* (New York: William Morrow & Co., 1974), 141-270.

42. Johnston's personal physician, Dr. D. W. Yarnell, had earlier been sent by Johnston to care for some wounded prisoners. Daniel, *Shiloh*, 226-227; Sword, *Shiloh: Bloody April*, 270-271. Roland, *Albert Sidney Johnston*, 338, notes that it is puzzling that Johnston's officers failed to care for the wound. There was a tourniquet on his person that could have been used to stop the flow of blood. Roland speculates that Harris and others were blinded by panic or ignorant of the danger from bleeding. Sword, *Shiloh: Bloody April*, 444, believes that the bullet that killed Johnston may have been fired by his own men during the confused fighting. Welsh, *Medical Histories of Confederate Generals*, 118-119, points out in addition to the fatal wound Johnston was struck three times in the lower limbs.

43. Roland, *Albert Sidney Johnston*, 352-353.

44. Jefferson Davis, *The Rise and Fall of the Confederate Government*, 2 vols. (New York, 1881), 2: 68; Grady McWhiney, "General Beauregard's 'Complete Victory' at Shiloh: An Interpretation," *Journal of Southern History* 49 (August 1983): 430-431; McWhiney, *Braxton Bragg*, 250-251; Nathaniel C. Hughes, *General William J. Hardee: Old Reliable* (Baton Rouge: Louisiana State University Press, 1965), 109; William Preston Johnston, "Albert Sidney Johnston at Shiloh," Robert U. Johnston and Clarence C. Buel, eds., *Battles & Leaders of the Civil War*, 4 vols. (Reprint, New York: Thomas Yoseloff, 1956), 1: 568.

45. P. G. T. Beauregard, "The Campaign of Shiloh," *Battles & Leaders*, 1: 569-593. This position is defended by Stanley Horn, *The Army of Tennessee* (Indianapolis: Bobbs-Merrill Co., 1951), 135, who writes "Beauregard appears to have done just about everything humanly possible during the few hours of daylight that were left."

46. Among the Johnston critics are Connelly, *Army of the Heartland*, McDonough, *Shiloh—Hell before Night*, and Daniel, *Shiloh*. Sam Houston was another critic of Johnston, writing in February 1863 that "Johnston was a good man and a gentleman—but [had] not one particle of military capacity, and as for statesmanship he did not comprehend it." See "Civil War Letters of Sam Houston," ed. David P. Smith, *Southwestern Historical Quarterly* 81 (April 1978): 421-422. Defenders of Johnston include Sword, *Shiloh: Bloody April*, McWhiney, *Braxton Bragg*, and Woodworth, *Jefferson Davis and His Generals*.

47. Roland, *Albert Sidney Johnston*, 347.

48. Woodworth, *Jefferson Davis and His Generals*, 101.

49. Donald E. Everett, ed., *Chaplain Davis and Hood's Texas Brigade* (San Antonio: Principia Press of Trinity University, 1962), 54-55; McMurry, *John Bell Hood*, 36-37.

50. John Bell Hood, *Advance and Retreat: Personal Experiences in the United States and Confederate Armies* (New Orleans: Hood Orphan Memorial Fund, 1880), 16; McMurry, *John Bell Hood*, 23-35. The definitive account of the brigade is Harold B. Simpson, *Hood's Texas Brigade*, 4 vols. (Waco: Texian Press, 1968-1977).

51. Dyer, *Gallant Hood*, 26, notes that Hood, with a flourish of curves and curlicues, dated the signed acceptance notice March 9, *1848*, instead of *1849*. This, Dyer believes, was characteristic of Hood: "a master of dramatic flourish but . . . often careless about details."

52. McMurry, *John Bell Hood*, 9. In his memoirs *Advance and Retreat*, Hood devotes only two sentences to his West Point years.

53. Years later, when the two commanded opposing armies, Schofield said he "came very near thinking once or twice that perhaps I had made a mistake." John M. Schofield, *Forty-Six Years in the Army* (New York: Century, 1897), 138. Apparently neither Lee nor Hood retained any ill-feeling over the reprimand. McMurry, *John Bell Hood*, 10. In his own *Advance and Retreat*, 7, Hood wrote that while a cadet he "had become very much attached to Lee."

54. Dyer, *Gallant Hood*, 30-33.

55. Hood, *Advance and Retreat*, 6. Hood later received a draft for one thousand dollars in gold as his share of profits in the wheat crop. Ibid., 7.

56. Hood, *Advance and Retreat*, 7. Richard McMurry, *John Bell Hood*, 15, speculates as to Hood's appointment to the elite Second Cavalry. His West Point record was undistinguished and he had done little as a junior officer to impress authorities. Hood had applied for transfer to the new regiment and had requested boyhood friend John C. Breckinridge, who had been in Congress, to use his influence to secure the transfer.

57. For accounts of the march see Roland and Robbins, eds., "The Diary of Eliza (Mrs. Albert Sidney) Johnston," 463-500; Richard W. Johnson, *A Soldier's Reminiscences in Peace and War* (Philadelphia: J. B. Lippincott Co., 1886), 98-107; and George F. Price, *Across the Continent with the Fifth Cavalry* (New York: D. Van Nostrand Co., 1883), 31-35.

58. Hood, *Advance and Retreat*, 8-15; Simpson, *Cry Comanche*, 83-101.

59. Hood, *Advance and Retreat*, 7-8.

60. Ibid., 16.

61. Ibid., 18; Dyer, *Gallant Hood*, 51-53; Paul D. Casdorph, *Prince John Magruder: His Life and Campaigns* (New York: John Wiley & Sons, 1996), 133-134; *Official Records*, 2: 296-298. McMurry, *John Bell Hood*, 209, states there is no indication that Hood was ever a lieutenant colonel although there are official records that refer to him as such.

62. Everett, ed., *Chaplain Davis and Hood's Texas Brigade*, 44. Chaplain Davis notes that at Camp Clark, Texas, the men had "with remarkable unanimity, come to the conclusion that he [Allen] did not suit their views of a commander."

63. Ibid., 149.

64. Simpson, *Hood's Texas Brigade: Lee's Grenadier Guard* (Waco: Texian Press, 1970), hereinafter cited as *Hood's Texas Brigade*, 71-74; McMurry, *John Bell Hood*, 29-30.

65. Simpson, *Hood's Texas Brigade*, 82-84; Simpson, *Hood's Texas Brigade: A Compendium* (Waco: Texian Press, 1977), viii-ix; Everett, ed., *Chaplain Davis and Hood's Texas Brigade*, 4.

66. McMurry, *John Bell Hood*, 35, states "Hood's promotion to brigadier is the major mystery of his career," but points out that neither Archer nor William T. Wofford of the Eighteenth Georgia, the two senior colonels in the brigade, were West Point graduates.

67. Hood, *Advance and Retreat*, 21-23; *Official Records*, 11, Part 1: 626-632; Stephen W. Sears, *To the Gates of Richmond: The Peninsula Campaign* (New York: Ticknor & Fields, 1992), 85-86; J. B. Polley, *Hood's Texas Brigade: Its Marches, Its Battles, Its Achievements* (New York: Neale Publishing Co., 1910), 23-28.

68. Simpson, *Hood's Texas Brigade*, 103.

69. Polley, *Hood's Texas Brigade*, 31-33; Douglas Southall Freeman, *R. E. Lee: A Biography*, 4 vols. (New York: Scribner's, 1935), 2:73-74.

70. Hood, *Advance and Retreat*, 25-29; Sears, *To the Gates of Richmond*, 210-242.

71. Simpson, *Hood's Texas Brigade*, 122-124; Everett, ed., *Chaplain Davis and Hood's Texas Brigade*, 74-92; McMurry, *John Bell Hood*, 45-50.

72. Ibid., 52. For changes in Lee's army see Douglas Southall Freeman, *Lee's Lieutenants*, 3 vols. (New York: Scribner's 1945), 1: 605-619.

73. Technically, Col. William T. Wofford of the Eighteenth Georgia, as senior officer, now commanded the brigade. In his memoirs, *Advance and Retreat*, 37, Hood wrote that his adjutant, Maj. W. H. Sellers, led the Texas Brigade in the Second Manassas campaign.

74. *Official Records*, 12, Pt. 2: 609-618; Hood, *Advance and Retreat*, 31-37; John J. Hennessy, *Return to Bull Run: The Campaign and Battle of Second Manassas* (New York: Simon & Schuster, 1991), 365-406; Mamie Yeary, comp., *Reminiscences of the Boys in Gray, 1861-65* (Dallas: Smith & Lamar, 1912), 816-817.

75. Freeman, *Lee's Lieutenants*, 2: 138. Freeman describes Hood's performance at Second Manassas as "magnificent."

76. Hood, *Advance and Retreat*, 38-39; Everett, ed., *Chaplain Davis and Hood's Texas Brigade*, 124-125; McMurry, *John Bell Hood*, 56. "Shanks" Evans, who had served with Hood in the Second Cavalry, was promoted brigadier general six months before Hood. He was a controversial officer who was twice charged with intoxication and disobedience of orders. Although acquitted by the courts martial he lost command of his brigade.

77. For details of these operations and the controversy over the "lost order," see Stephen W. Sears, *Landscape Turned Red: The Battle of Antietam* (New Haven: Ticknor & Fields, 1983), 82-114, 349-352; Freeman, *Lee's Lieutenants*, 2: 144-165; James V. Murfin, *The Gleam of Bayonets: The Battle of Antietam and the Maryland Campaign of 1862* (South Brunswick, NJ: Thomas Yoseloff, 1965), 328-338.

78. Hood, *Advance and Retreat*, 39-40; Polley, *Hood's Texas Brigade*, 114; Simpson, *Hood's Texas Brigade*, 165-166; McMurry, *John Bell Hood*, 57.

79. In his account of the battle Chaplain Davis was critical of McLaws for tar-

diness in relieving Hood's Division. This incensed McLaws, who blamed Hood. McMurry, *John Bell Hood*, 72-73; *Official Records*, 1, Pt. 1: 922-925, 927-937; Hood, *Advance and Retreat*, 42-46; William R. Hamby, "Hood's Texas Brigade at Sharpsburg," *Confederate Veteran* 16 (January 1908): 19-22; D. H. Hamilton, *History of Company M, First Volunteer Infantry: Hood's Brigade* (Waco: W. M. Morrison, 1962), 22-24; John M. Priest, *Antietam: The Soldier's Battle* (New York: Oxford University Press, 1989), 55, 60-67, 73, 82-94.

80. Simpson, *Hood's Texas Brigade*, 176-177, 187-188; Sears, *Landscape Turned Red*, 295-296; Everett, ed., *Chaplain Davis and Hood's Texas Brigade*, 187-191. These figures differ slightly from Priest, *Antietam*, 323.

81. This account is based upon Polley, *Hood's Texas Brigade*, 134. Polley is giving Stephen D. Lee's version of a meeting between Lee and his senior officers. Both Dyer, *Gallant Hood*, 143, and McMurry, *John Bell Hood*, 59, repeat the story. Douglas S. Freeman, *Lee's Lieutenants*, 2: 221 fn, believes that Stephen D. Lee was confused about the meeting. Hood himself does not mention this in his account of the battle and its aftermath in *Advance and Retreat*, 42-44. Herman Hattaway, the biographer of Stephen D. Lee, making no reference to Hood's comments, believes that Stephen D. Lee may have embellished the story after the meeting. Hattaway, *General Stephen D. Lee* (Jackson: University Press of Mississippi, 1976), 59-60.

82. Hood, *Advance and Retreat*, 45-46; McMurry, *John Bell Hood*, 60-61.

83. The Eighteenth Georgia Infantry and Hampton's South Carolina Legion were transferred from the Texas Brigade. They were replaced by the Third Arkansas, which remained with the Texas Brigade the rest of the war. The two Mississippi regiments of Law's Brigade were reassigned; their place filled by Alabama and North Carolina units. For more on army reorganization see Freeman, *Lee's Lieutenants*, 2: 250-268.

84. Polley, *Hood's Texas Brigade*, 138-139; Dyer, *Gallant Hood*, 155-157. Although Hood's Division sustained comparatively few casualties at Fredericksburg, it was rumored at the time that Hood himself had been wounded. See J. B. Jones, *A Rebel War Clerk's Diary*, 2 vols. (New York: Old Hickory Bookshop, 1935), 1: 212.

85. Hood, *Advance and Retreat*, 51.

86. Ibid., 51-52; Simpson, *Hood's Texas Brigade*, 224-234.

87. Hood, *Advance and Retreat*, 51-53.

88. Arthur J. L. Fremantle, *The Fremantle Diary, Being the Journal of Lieutenant Colonel Arthur James Lyon Fremantle, Coldstream Guards, and his Three Months in the Southern States*, ed. Walter Lord (New York: Capricorn Books, 1954), 191.

89. McMurry, *John Bell Hood*, 74-75; Dyer, *Gallant Hood*, 190-198. Much controversy surrounds Longstreet's role at Gettysburg. See Robert K. Krick, "'If Longstreet . . . Says So, It Is Most Likely Not True': James Longstreet and the Second Day at Gettysburg," *The Second Day at Gettysburg: Essays on Confederate and Union Leadership*, ed. Gary W. Gallagher (Kent, OH: Kent State University Press, 1993), 56-86; William Garrett Pison, "Longstreet, Lee, and Confederate Attack Plans for July 3 at Gettysburg," *The Third Day at Gettysburg & Beyond*, ed. Gary W. Gallagher (Chapel Hill: University of North Carolina Press, 1994), 31-

55; and Kent Gramm, "The Charm of War: Lee, Longstreet, Sickles, and the First Minnesota Volunteers," *The Gettysburg Nobody Knows*, ed. Gabor S. Boritt (New York: Oxford University Press, 1997), 86-91.

90. *Official Records*, 27, Pt. 2: 404-412; Hood, *Advance and Retreat*, 55-60; Edward B. Coddington, *The Gettysburg Campaign: A Study in Command* (New York: Charles Scribner's Sons, 1968), 385-410; Simpson, *Hood's Texas Brigade*, 268-282.

91. McMurry, *John Bell Hood*, 68, 76; C. Vann Woodward, *Mary Chesnut's Civil War* (New Haven: Yale University Press, 1981), 441-443, 509-510. Mrs. Chesnut described Hood in September 1863 as having a "sad Quixote face, the face of an old crusader who believed in his cause, his cross, his crown . . ." Dyer, *Gallant Hood*, 202, notes that Sally Preston seemed to cast a deadly curse on her lovers. Three previous suitors had met death. Johnny Chesnut, Mary Boykin Chesnut's nephew, warned that it was safer to face a Federal battery than fall in love with her.

92. Hood, *Advance and Retreat*, 61-62; Peter Cozzens, *This Terrible Sound: The Battle of Chickamauga* (Urbana: University of Illinois Press, 1992), 110-111, 119; Simpson, *Hood's Texas Brigade*, 308-310.

93. *Official Records*, 30, Pt. 2: 21-27, 287-292; Simpson, *Hood's Texas Brigade*, 314-325; Cozzens, *This Terrible Sound*, 406-412; Steven Woodworth, *Six Armies in Tennessee: The Chickamauga and Chattanooga Campaign* (Lincoln: University of Nebraska Press, 1998), 119-124.

94. Hood, *Advance and Retreat*, 64-65; Dyer, *Gallant Hood*, 210-212; McMurry, *John Bell Hood*, 77-79. Initial reports indicated that Hood had been killed in battle. See Jones, *A Rebel War Clerk's Diary*, 2: 49, 51.

95. Quotation found in Dyer, *Gallant Hood*, 221; see also Thomas B. Buell, *The Warrior Generals: Combat Leadership in the Civil War* (New York: Crown Publishers, 1997), 349. For more on the Hood-Preston romance see Woodward, ed., *Mary Chesnut's Diary*, 442-443, 509-510, 551-554, 555-559, 567-568, 647.

96. Ibid., 552. Thomas Connelly, *Autumn of Glory: The Army of Tennessee, 1862-1865*, 433, states that Hood "apparently never learned to walk with his artificial leg, and only hobbled without it on crutches."

97. McMurry, *John Bell Hood*, 86. McMurry points out that some historians have argued that Hood was sent by President Davis and his military advisor, Braxton Bragg (both of whom depised Johnston), to undermine Johnston to justify his removal. McMurry believes that there is little evidence to support such charges.

98. It is difficult to know Hood's motives in writing these letters. He may have been scheming to win promotion or he may have sincerely believed Johnston was wrong. There is no question that the writing of letters to his superiors criticizing Johnston in this manner was unprofessional. Johnston's most recent biographer, Craig L. Symonds, *Joseph E. Johnston: A Civil War Biography* (New York: W. W. Norton and Co., 1992), 264, concedes that "Hood did not set out to denigrate Johnston: there is evidence that at first he genuinely admired his commander, but he was trapped by his compulsion for promotion."

99. Late on the night of May 11-12, Hood was baptized by his fellow lieutenant general Episcopal Bishop Leonidas Polk at Hood's quarters near Dalton. Buell, *Warrior Generals*, 362; McMurry, *John Bell Hood*, 103.

100. Woodworth, *Jefferson Davis and His Generals*, 282-283.

101. Ibid., 283-284; *Official Records*, 39, Pt. 2: 713-714.

102. Ibid., 38, Pt. 5: 885; Albert Castel, *Decision in the West: The Atlanta Campaign of 1864* (Lawrence: University Press of Kansas, 1992), 357-361.

103. Norman Brown, ed., *One of Cleburne's Command: The Civil War Reminiscences and Diary of Captain Samuel T. Foster, Granbury's Texas Brigade, C.S.A.* (Austin: University of Texas Press, 1980), 106, 159; Lucia Rutherford Douglas, ed., *Douglas's Texas Battery* (San Antonio: Principia Press of Trinity Univesity, 1962), 114; Schofield, *Forty-Six Years in the Army*, 232. For more on the removal of Johnston and the appointment of Hood see Connelly, *Autumn of Glory*, 421-424; Woodworth, *Jefferson Davis and His Generals*, 282-285; Castel, *Decision in the West*, 352-365; Richard M. McMurry, "Confederate Morale in the Atlanta Campaign of 1864," *Georgia Historical Quarterly* 54 (Summer 1970): 221-243; Thomas R. Hay, "The Davis-Hood-Johnston Controversy of 1864," *Mississippi Valley Historical Review* 11 (1924): 54-87.

104. *Official Records*, 38, Pt. 5: 894-897; Hood, *Advance and Retreat*, 162-172; Castel, *Decision in the West*, 365-383.

105. McMurry, *John Bell Hood*, 129-130; Connelly, *Autumn of Glory*, 441-444; Craig L. Symonds, *Stonewall of the West: Patrick Cleburne & The Civil War* (Lawrence: University Press of Kansas, 1997), 223-224. Even Hardee's biographer, Nathaniel C. Hughes, Jr., *General William J. Hardee*, 225, concedes that "Peachtree Creek does stand as one of Hardee's poorest performances."

106. McMurry, *John Bell Hood*, 132, blames Hood for the failure to coordinate Cheatham's attack with Hardee's. Albert Castel, *Decision in the West*, 413, believes that Hood "tried to do too much with too little in too short a time." Castel does point out that many historians have mistakenly accepted Sherman's estimate that 8,000 Confederates were casualties.

107. Ibid., 414-436; Connelly, *Autumn of Glory*, 453-455; Hattaway, *General Stephen D. Lee*, 128-130. In his *Shades of Blue and Gray* (Columbia: University of Missouri Press, 1997), 223, Professor Hattaway writes that "his subordinates . . . were more to blame for the disaster [Ezra Church] than Hood himself."

108. Hood, *Advance and Retreat*, 193-210; Connelly, *Autumn of Glory*, 455-469. Hood blamed Hardee for the failure at Jonesboro. Hughes, *General William J. Hardee*, 241, notes that Hood was correct in criticizing Hardee for lack of vigor in attacking the enemy.

109. McMurry, *John Bell Hood*, 158, and Dyer, *Gallant Hood*, 275, state that Hood presented the plan to President Davis. William C. Davis, *Jefferson Davis*, 565, writes that Davis advised raiding the railroad line.

110. Hood, *Advance and Retreat*, 242-270; Davis, *Jefferson Davis*, 565-566; McMurry, *John Bell Hood*, 135-162.

111. Alfred Roman, *The Military Operations of General Beauregard in the War Between the States, 1861-1865*, 2 vols. (New York: Harper & Brothers, 1984), 2: 281-300.

112. Wiley Sword, *The Confederacy's Last Hurrah: Spring Hill, Franklin, and Nashville* (Lawrence: University Press of Kansas, 1992), 152, states that "the failure of the Confederate high command at Spring Hill has endured even to this day as one of the greatest missed opportunities of the entire war." Stanley Horn, "The

Spring Hill Legend—A Reappraisal," *Civil War Times Illustrated* 8 (April 1969), 20-32, and Richard McMurry, *John Bell Hood*, 173, question the emphasis placed upon the Spring Hill affair.

113. *Official Records*, 45, Pt. 1: 684-685, 707-708; James Lee McDonough and Thomas L. Connelly, *Five Tragic Hours: The Battle of Franklin* (Knoxville: University of Tennessee Press, 1983), 92-168; Sword, *The Confederacy's Last Hurrah*, 197-248; Symonds, *Stonewall of the West*, 255-260.

114. Hood, *Advance and Retreat*, 292-300.

115. Connelly, *Autumn of Glory*, 508; McMurry, *John Bell Hood*, 177.

116. *Official Records*, 45, Pt. 1: 709-710; Stanley Horn, *The Decisive Battle of Nashville* (Baton Rouge: Louisiana State University Press, 1956), 73-153; Thomas R. Hay, *Hood's Tennessee Campaign* (New York: Walter Neale, 1929), 148-170; W. J. Wood, *Civil War Generalship: The Art of Command* (Westport, CT: Praeger, 1997), 219-222, 229-230.

117. *Official Records*, 45, Pt. 1: 664-669; Wood, *Civil War Generalship*, 224-225; Hood, *Advance and Retreat*, 304-307.

118. Preston later told Mrs. Chesnut that she would have married Hood if he had been persistent and not given in to her family. But the affair was ended. "Buck" was soon being seen by Capt. Rawlins Lowdnes. The couple married in March 1868. Woodward, *Mary Chesnut's Civil War*, 769; Sword, *The Confederacy's Last Hurrah*, 436-437; Winston Groom, *Shrouds of Glory: From Atlanta to Nashville, The Last Great Campaign of the Civil War* (New York: Atlantic Monthly Press, 1995), 286-289.

119. For Hood's later years see McMurry, *John Bell Hood*, 192-203, and Dyer, *Gallant Hood*, 304-321.

CHAPTER THREE

1. Warner, *Generals In Gray*, 143, 265, 322.

2. Maxey's biographer, Louise Horton, *Samuel Bell Maxey: A Biography* (Austin: University of Texas Press, 1974), 39, states that after the war Maxey learned from "Texas Confederate Senator H. C. Burnet that the assignments made by General Kirby Smith had been nominated and confirmed by the Senate." This is repeated in her article on Maxey in the *New Handbook of Texas*, 4: 580, except the senator's name is spelled "Burnett." There was no Texas Confederate senator named Burnet or Burnett. There was a Henry C. Burnett, who served as Confederate senator from Kentucky. See Thomas B. Alexander and Richard E. Beringer, *The Anatomy of the Confederate Congress* (Nashville: Vanderbilt University Press, 1972), 358.

3. Warner, *Generals In Gray*, 117, 351; *New Handbook of Texas*, 1: 332, 2: 316-317; *The Confederate General*, 1: 32-22, 6: 178-179. David J. Eicher, *The Civil War in Books: An Analytical Bibliography* (Urbana: University of Illinois Press, 1997), 305-306, is quite critical of Warner and others for including individuals not confirmed by President Davis and the Senate. He would doubtlessly disagree with their inclusion here.

4. *The Confederate General*, 6: 122; *New Handbook of Texas*, 6: 907. For more on the family background see Laura Hale, "The Groces and Whartons in the

Early History of Texas" (M.A. thesis, University of Texas, 1942); *New Handbook of Texas*, 2: 750, 3: 348, 6: 908-909; and James A. Creighton, *A Narrative History of Brazoria County* (Waco: Brazoria County Historical Commission, 1975), 483.

5. *New Handbook of Texas*, 3: 348, 6: 907-909; William Wharton Groce, "Major General John A. Wharton," *Southwestern Historical Quarterly* 19 (January 1916): 271-273.

6. Randolph B. Campbell, *An Empire for Slavery: The Peculiar Institution in Texas* (Baton Rouge: Louisiana State University Press, 1989), 274; Ralph A. Wooster, "Notes on Texas' Largest Slaveholders, 1860," *Southwestern Historical Quarterly* 65 (July 1961): 72-79; Ralph A. Wooster, "Wealthy Texans, 1860," *Southwestern Historical Quarterly* 71 (October 1967): 163-179.

7. *Journal of the Secession Convention of Texas, 1861*, ed. E. W. Winkler (Austin, 1912), 25-26; Ralph A. Wooster, *The Secession Conventions of the South* (Princeton: Princeton University Press, 1962), 129-131; Walter L. Buenger, *Secession and the Union in Texas* (Austin: University of Texas Press, 1984), 145-148.

8. Anne J. Bailey, *Texans in the Confederate Cavalry* (Fort Worth: Ryan Place Publishers, 1995), 29, 38; *The Confederate General*, 6: 122; Simpson, *Hood's Texas Brigade*, 41; *New Handbook of Texas*, 4: 320.

9. Wharton himself missed the fighting at Woodsonville. According to Welsh, *Medical Histories of Confederate Generals*, 231, Wharton was in Nashville from November 7, 1861, through January 7, 1862, on sick leave due to measles.

10. Giles, who believed Wharton had future political aspirations, wrote that Wharton "never forgot during a wakeful moment that the soldier who survived the war would be a voter." L. B. Giles, "Terry's Texas Rangers," *Terry Texas Ranger Trilogy* (Austin: State House Press, 1996), 18. See also J. K. P. Blackburn, "Reminiscences of the Terry Rangers," 106, and Thomas W. Cutrer, "Introduction," xiii-xiv, in the same volume.

11. Giles, "Terry's Texas Rangers," 21-22; Blackburn, "Reminiscences of the Terry Rangers," 107-111.

12. Giles, "Terry's Texas Rangers," 23-24. George W. Baylor, who was later involved in the altercation leading to Wharton's death, was on Johnston's staff at the time. In an account written years later, Baylor declared that Wharton was placed under arrest but appealed to Johnston that he would rather be shot than not allowed to take part in the battle. See "With Gen. A. S. Johnston at Shiloh," *Confederate Veteran* 5 (1897): 609.

13. For Wharton and the Rangers at Shiloh see *Official Records*, 10, Pt. 1: 569, 626-627; Blackburn, "Reminiscences of the Terry Rangers," 113-122; Giles, "Terry's Texas Rangers," 24-26, Daniel, *Shiloh*, 190-191, 241, 280; Sword, *Shiloh*, 333.

14. Daniel, *Shiloh*, 296-297; Sword, *Shiloh*, 425-426.

15. *Official Records*, 10, Pt. 2: 509-510, 16, Pt. 1: 810-811; Giles, "Terry's Texas Rangers," 27-30; Blackburn, "Reminiscences of the Terry Rangers," 123-127; Brian Steele Wills, *A Battle from the Start: The Life of Nathan Bedford Forrest* (New York: Harper Collins, 1992), 72; Welsh, *Medical Histories of Confederate Generals*, 231.

16. Quotation from *Official Records*, 16, Pt. 1: 1094, 1109-1100; see also Robert W. Williams and Ralph A. Wooster, eds., "With Terry's Texas Rangers: The

Letters of Dunbar Affleck," *Civil War History* (Spring 1963): 311; James Lee McDonough, *War in Kentucky: From Shiloh to Perryville* (Knoxville: University of Tennessee Press, 1994), 233, 241.

17. *Official Records*, 20, Pt. 1: 661, 665, 670, 774, 966-970; Edwin C. Bearss, "Cavalry Operations in the Battle of Stones," *Tennessee Historical Quarterly* 19 (June 1960), Pt. 2: 118-120, 136-137. James McDonough, *Stone's River—Bloody Winter in Tennessee* (Knoxville: University of Tennessee Press, 1980), 146, argues that the Confederates missed an opportunity to alter the outcome of the battle by failing to provide more support for Wharton.

18. *Official Records*, 23, Pt. 1: 33-35, 39, 40-41; Giles, "Terry's Texas Rangers," 41-42; Wills, *A Battle from the Start*, 98-102; Jack Hurst, *Nathan Bedford Forrest: A Biography* (New York: Alfred A. Knopf, 1993), 113-114; John P. Dyer, *"Fightin' Joe" Wheeler* (Baton Rouge: Louisiana State University Press, 1941), 91-96.

19. *Official Records*, 23, Pt. 1: 152, 219-221; 30, Pt. 4: 500.

20. "Diary of Ephraim Shelby Dodd," in *Terry Texas Rangers Trilogy* (Austin: State House Press, 1996), 196, 208; Giles "Terry's Texas Rangers," 43; H. J. H. Rugeley, ed., *Batchelor-Turner Letters, 1861-1864, Written by Two Terry's Texas Rangers* (Austin: Steck Co., 1961), 20; Williams and Wooster, eds., "With Terry's Texas Rangers," 318; Welsh, *Medical Histories of Confederate Generals*, 232.

21. *Official Records*, 30, Pt. 2: 519-523.

22. Ibid., 30, Pt. 2: 725; Dyer, *"Fightin' Joe" Wheeler*, 125-137.

23. *Official Records*, 32, Pt. 3: 643-644; Connally, *Autumn of Glory*, 27, 57, 316. Dyer, *"Fightin' Joe" Wheeler*, does not mention this affair.

24. *Official Records*, 32, Pt. 2: 670; Symonds, *Joseph E. Johnston*, 251-253; *The Confederate General*, 6: 123.

25. *Official Records*, 34, Pt. 3: 782.

26. B. P. Gallaway, *The Ragged Rebel: A Common Soldier in W. H. Parsons' Texas Cavalry, 1861-1865* (Austin: University of Texas Press, 1988), 102-121; Ludwell Johnson, *The Red River Campaign: Politics and Cotton in the Civil War* (Baltimore: Johns Hopkins Press, 1958), 231-276.

27. Quotations taken from Anne J. Bailey, *Between the Enemy and Texas: Parsons's Texas Cavalry in the Civil War* (Fort Worth: Texas Christian University Press, 1989), 187-188; and Bailey, *Texans in the Confederate Cavalry*, 73.

28. *Official Records*, 34, Pt. 1: 615-616. In his report of the Louisiana campaign Richard Taylor praised Wharton for his "skill, energy, and idefatigable industry." *Official Records, Supplement*, 6, Pt. 1: 350.

29. Contrasting views of Wharton may be seen in the memoirs of former Texas Governor Francis R. Lubbock, an officer on Wharton' staff, and the letters of Pvt. Dunbar Affleck, a relative of Wharton's and member of his escort company. Lubbock described Wharton as in "buoyant humor, full of fun and sentiment," whereas Affleck, who had served with Wharton in Tennessee and Kentucky, believed Wharton was no longer as friendly as he once had been and was "as crabid [sic.] as an old bear besides." Francis R. Lubbock, *Six Decades in Texas: The Memoirs of Franics R. Lubbock*, ed. C. W. Raines (Austin: Pemberton Press, 1968), 546; Ralph A. Wooster, "With the Confederate Cavalry in the West: The Civil War Experiences of Isaac Dunbar Affleck," *Southwestern Historical Quarterly* 83 (July 1979): 17-18.

30. *Official Records*, 41, Pt. 4: 1061-1062, 48, Pt. 1, 1351-1352, 1392-1393, 1396-1397; Kevin R. Young, *To the Tyrants Never Yield* (Plano: Wordware Publishing Co., 1992), 182. Jerry D. Thompson, who has edited Baylor's memoirs, *Into the Far, Wild Country: True Tales of the Old Southwest* (El Paso: Texas Western Press, 1996), 18, points out that the trouble between Wharton and Baylor began on Marksville Prairie in May 1864, when Wharton, who had only recently taken command of Confederate cavalry in Louisiana, criticized Baylor's handling of his regiment.

31. Young, *To the Tyrants Never Yield*, 184. For Baylor's version of the affair see his "My Troubles with General John A. Wharton," *Into the Far, Wild Country*, 232-246.

32. Thompson, ed., *Into the Far, Wild Country*, 19-20.

33. Paul D. Casdorph, *Prince John Magruder: His Life and Campaigns* (New York: John Wiley & Sons, 1996), 293; *New Handbook of Texas*, 6: 907.

34. McMurry, *Two Great Rebel Armies*, 164-165, lists Rosser as a Virginia general. Marcus J. Wright, *Texas in the War, 1861-1865*, 3-18, includes Rosser among the general officers from Texas, as does Harold B. Simpson, "West Pointers in the Texas Confederate Army," *Texas Military History* 6 (Spring 1962) 82-83. For Custer's view, see his article "Battling With the Sioux on the Yellowstone," *Galaxy Magazine* (July 1876), reprinted in *The Custer Reader*, ed. Paul A. Hutton (Lincoln: University of Nebraska Press, 1992), 203.

35. *The Confederate General*, 5: 113; Millard Kessler Bushong and Dean McKoin Bushong, *Fightin' Tom Rosser* (Shippenburg, PA: Beidel Printing House, 1983), 1-2.

36. Bushong, *Fightin' Tom Rosser*, 1-2; *New Handbook of Texas*, 5: 691. The population schedule of the manuscript census returns for Panola County, 1850, does not list any real property for John Rosser, but eleven slaves are enumerated for Rosser in the slave schedule. In 1860 John Rosser owned fourteen slaves.

37. Custer, "Battling with the Sioux on the Yellowstone," 203, notes that he and Rosser occupied adjoining rooms at West Point, were in the same company, and often marched side by side in performance of their duties. See also Mary Elizabeth Sergent, "Classmates Divided," *American Heritage* 9 (February 1958): 35; Bushong, *Fightin' Tom Rosser*, 6-10; Charles G. Milham, *Gallant Pelham: American Extraordinary* (Washington: Public Affairs Press, 1959), 21-22; Jay Monaghan, *Custer: The Life of General George Armstrong Custer* (Boston: Little, Brown and Co., 1959), 25-29; Jeffrey D. Wert, *Custer: The Controversial Life of George Armstrong Custer* (New York: Simon & Schuster, 1996), 29.

38. Rosser's letters are quoted in Bushong, *Fightin' Tom Rosser*, 11. A summary of the letters to Davis is found in Lynda L. Crist, ed., *The Papers of Jefferson Davis* (Baton Rouge: Louisiana State University Press, 1989, 1992), 6: 672, 7: 63. Houston's response to Rosser is in Amelia W. Williams and Eugene C. Barker, eds. *The Writings of Sam Houston, 1813-1863* (Austin: Pemberton Press, 1971), 8: 199-200.

39. Bushong, *Fightin' Tom Rosser*, 13. Stephen E. Ambrose, "The War Comes to West Point," *Civil War Times Illustrated* 4 (August 1965): 36, points out that most of the southern cadets were gone by May 1861. Out of a total corps of 278 there were 86 southerners, of whom 65 resigned.

40. Milham, *Gallant Pelham*, 34-35; William C. Davis, *Battle at Bull Run* (Garden City, NY: Doubleday & Co., 1977), 24, 124-125; Freeman, *Lee's Lieutenants*, 1: 648-649; William M. Owen, *In Camp and Battle with the Washington Artillery of New Orleans* (2nd ed.; Boston: Ticknor and Company, 1885), 24-25, 43-44.

41. Thomas L. Rosser, *Riding With Rosser*, ed. S. Roger Keller (Shippensburg, PA: Burd Street Press, 1997), 2; Freeman, *Lee's Lieutenants*, 1: 648; *Official Records*, 5: 183-184; Welsh, *Medical Histories of Confederate Generals*, 189; Emory M. Thomas, *Bold Dragoon: The Life of Jeb Stuart* (New York: Harper & Row, 1986), 91, 139; Owen, *In Camp and Battle with the Washington Artillery*, 85-86.

42. *Official Records*, 9, Pt. 2: 521; Freeman, *Lee's Lieutenants*, 1: 648-649; Sears, *To the Gates of Richmond*, 291.

43. Hennessy, *Return to Bull Run*, 61-62, 64, 77, 227, 233, 365, 462; Thomas, *Bold Dragoon*, 154-157, 191, 193; *Official Records*, 31: 738-739.

44. Thomas, *Bold Dragoon*, 186, 202, 261-262. Thomas points out that Rosser had a drinking problem. Rosser's biographers, Millard and Dean Bushong, *Fightin' Tom Rosser*, 58, state that Rosser tried to drown the promotion disappointment by drinking.

45. *Official Records*, 35, Pt. 1: 58-59, 62. Pelham's death was a shock to all Confederates, especially Stuart and Rosser, both of whom later named sons for the Alabamian. Rosser had asked Pelham to be his best man at his forthcoming marriage to Betty Barbara Winston of Hanover County.

46. Thomas, *Bold Dragoon*, 234-235; Edward C. Longacre, *The Cavalry at Gettysburg* (Lincoln: University of Nebraska Press, 1993), 104-109; Emory Thomas, "Eggs, Aldie, Shepherdstown, and J. E. B. Stuart," *The Gettysburg Nobody Knows* (New York: Oxford University Press, 1991), 101-107.

47. Thomas, *Bold Dragoon*, 234-235; Longacre, *Cavalry at Gettysburg*, 220-244; Mark Nesbitt, *Saber and Scapegoat: J. E. B. Stuart and the Gettysburg Campaign* (Mechanicsburg, PA: 1994), xv-xvii, 88-92. Gregory J. W. Urwin, *Custer Victorious: The Civil War Battles of General George Armstrong Custer* (Lincoln: University of Nebraska Press, 1990), 73-82, presents a somewhat different view of the cavalry engagement at Gettysburg. Rosser himself was highly critical of Robert E. Lee's conduct of the Battle of Gettysburg and years later became involved in controversy with a number of former Confederate officers concerning the battle. Bushong, *Fightin' Tom Rosser*, 55-56.

48. Ibid., 60, 75; William N. McDonald, *A History of the Laurel Brigade* (Baltimore: priv. printed, 1907), 17-18. Rosser's promotion to brigadier general was confirmed by the Confederate Senate on February 17, 1864.

49. *Official Records*, 29, Pt. 1: 905; Freeman, *Lee's Lieutenants*, 3: 274-275, 278-279.

50. McDonald, *Laurel Brigade*, 215-220; Freeman, *Lee's Lieutenants*, 3: 328-329. The relationship between Early and Rosser improved, but that between Stuart and Rosser did not. Rosser continued to be highly critical of the cavalry commander.

51. Quotations from *Official Records*, 33: 1081-1082; see also Keller, ed., *Riding With Rosser*, 19-20; Charles C. Osborne, *Jubal: The Life and Times of General Jubal A. Early, CSA, Defender of the Lost Cause* (Chapel Hill: Algonquin Books, 1992), 224.

52. McDonald, *Laurel Brigade*, 225-233; Gordon C. Rhea, *The Battle of the Wilderness, May 5-6, 1864* (Baton Rouge: Louisiana State University Press, 1994), 113-117, 256-257, 344-349, 378-379; Gordon C. Rhea, "Union Cavalry in the Wilderness," *The Wilderness Campaign*, ed. Gary W. Gallagher (Chapel Hill: University of North Carolina Press, 1997), 106-135; Urwin, *Custer Victorious*, 133-134.

53. Keller, ed., *Riding With Rosser*, 24-38; William D. Matter, *If It Takes All Summer: The Battle of Spotsylvania* (Chapel Hill: University of North Carolina Press, 1988), 287-288; Gordon C. Rhea, *The Battles for Spotsylvania Court House and the Road to Yellow Tavern* (Baton Rouge: Louisiana State University Press, 1997), 30; McDonald, *Laurel Brigade*, 249-254.

54. Keller, ed., *Riding With Rosser*, 38-41; Bushong, *Fightin' Tom Rosser*, 102. For more on the cattle raid see Edward Boykin, *Beefsteak Raid* (New York: Funk & Wagnalls Co., 1960), 200, 208, 226-230, 258-259, 262-267.

55. Elizabeth B. Custer, *Boots and Saddles, Or Life in Dakota with General Custer* (New York: Harper & Brothers, 1885), 91-92; Osborne, *Jubal*, 350-357; Urwin, *Custer Victorious*, 195-202; Monaghan, *Custer*, 212. Jeffrey Wert, *Custer*, 190, states that during the early phases of the battle Rosser pointed to the Union lines and told his men "that's General Custer, the Yanks are so proud of, and I intend to give him the best whipping to-day that he ever got. See if I don't." Rosser does not mention that in his memoirs, *Riding With Rosser*, 47, but states that while using his glasses before the battle he recognized Custer, who apparently recognized him at the same time "for he wheeled his horse around facing me and galantly [sic.] raised his hat and made me a profound bow."

56. First quote, Robert K. Krick, "Thomas Lafayette Rosser," in *The Confederate General*, 5: 115; second quote, Osborne, *Jubal*, 357. Rosser blamed Early for not properly supporting him at Tom's Brook. *Riding With Rosser*, 49.

57. Jubal A. Early, *Lieutenant General Jubal Anderson Early, C.S.A., Autobiographical Sketch and Narrative of the War Between the States* (Philadelphia: J. B. Lippincott Co., 1912), 440-452; Stephen Z. Starr, *The Union Cavalry in the Civil War*, 3 vols. (Baton Rouge: Louisiana State University Press, 1981), 2: 302-322; Gary Gallagher, *Stephen Dotson Ramseur: Lee's Gallant General* (Chapel Hill: University of North Carolina Press, 1985), 162.

58. *Official Records*, 43, Pt. 1: 586, 669, 46, Pt. 1: 451; Keller, ed., *Riding With Rosser*, 55-60; Edward B. Williams, ed. *Rebel Brothers: The Civil War Letters of the Trueharts* (College Station: Texas A&M University Press, 1995), 206-207, 263-264.

59. Keller, ed., *Riding With Rosser*, 61-62; Osborne, *Jubal*, 386-397; Early, *Autobiographical Sketch*, 461-466.

60. Freeman, *Lee's Lieutenants*, 3: 666; Bushong, *Fightin' Tom Rosser*, 172-178; Keller, ed., *Riding With Rosser*, 64-65.

61. Freeman, *Lee's Lieutenants*, 3: 708-709; Owen, *Washington Artillery*, 376-377.

62. Custer, "Battling with the Sioux on the Yellowstone," 203-204; Bushong, *Fightin' Tom Rosser*, 185-189.

63. Quoted in Bushong, 192. For more on the Rosser-Custer relationship see Monaghan, *Custer*, 343-344; Louise Barnett, *Touched by Fire: The Life, Death and Mystic Afterlife of George Armstrong Custer* (New York: Henry Holt & Co., 1996),

243; Lawrence Frost, *General Custer's Libbie* (Seattle: Superior Publishing Co., 1976), 117, 204, 313; Elizabeth B. Custer, *Boots and Saddles*, 90-92, 275; Shirley A. Leckie, *Elizabeth Bacon Custer and the Making of a Myth* (Norman: University of Oklahoma Press, 1993), 156, 261.

64. Bushong, *Fightin' Tom Rosser*, 192-193; Robert M. Utley, *Custer and the Great Controversy: The Origin and Development of a Legend* (Pasadena, CA: Westernlore Press, 1980), 47.

65. *The Confederate General*, 5: 115.

66. Bushong, *Fightin' Tom Rosser*, 202-206.

67. Louise Horton, *Samuel Bell Maxey: A Biography* (Austin: University of Texas Press, 1974), 5-8. For more on the family background see Kathleen Neils Conzen, "A Saga of Families," in *Oxford History of the West*, ed. Clyde A. Milner II, et. al. (New York: Oxford University Press, 1994), 332-339.

68. This class has been the subject of John C. Waugh, *The Class of 1846: From West Point to Appomattox: Stonewall Jackson, George McClellan and Their Brothers* (New York: Warner Books, 1994). Waugh mentions Maxey only twice in the book; once for a physical assault on a fellow student and the other as a U.S. senator after the Civil War. Horton, *Maxey*, 11, says that Maxey was a roommate of Stonewall Jackson during one of his West Point years. Neither Waugh, *Class of 1846*, nor James I. Robertson, Jr., *Stonewall Jackson: The Man, The Soldier, The Legend* (New York: Macmillan Co., 1997) mentions this.

69. Horton, *Maxey*, 12.

70. K. Jack Bauer, *The Mexican War* (New York: Macmillan Publishing Co., 1974), 19, 49-50, 97; Justin H. Smith, *The War With Mexico*, 2 vols. (Gloucester, MA: Peter Smith, 1913), 1: 143, 163, 209, 245, 247.

71. David B. Gracy, II, ed. and introd., *Maxey's Texas* (Austin: Pemberton Press, 1965), 8-9; Horton, *Maxey*, 12-13.

72. Gracy, ed., *Maxey's Texas*, 9; Horton, *Maxey*, 13-14.

73. Sam's father, Rice Maxey, replaced him in the Texas Senate. J. Elden Spencer, "Samuel Bell Maxey," in *Ten More Texans in Gray*, ed. W. C. Nunn (Hillsboro: Hill Junior College Press), 61.

74. Horton, *Maxey*, 18-22.

75. Ibid., 23-28; *Official Records*, 10, Pt. 2: 358, 367, 371-372; Joseph H. Parks, *Edmund Kirby Smith, C.S.A.* (Baton Rouge: Louisiana State University Press, 1954), 163, 164-165.

76. *Official Records*, 16, Pt. 1: 889-891.

77. *Official Records*, 16, Pt. 2: 761, 835, 854, 905, 951, 998, 1001.

78. *Official Records*, 15: 934; 17, Pt. 2: 796; 20, Pt. 2: 447-449; Lawrence Lee Hewitt, *Port Hudson, Confederate Bastion on the Mississippi* (Baton Rouge: Louisiana State University Press, 1987), 45; Edward Cunningham, *The Port Hudson Campaign* (Baton Rouge: Louisiana State University Press, 1963), 21, 36.

79. Hewitt, *Port Hudson*, 59-95.

80. *Official Records*, 15: 1071, 1076; 24, Pt. 3: 828.

81. Ibid., 24, pt. 1: 221-222, 242, 259; pt. 3: 222, 871, 881.

82. Ibid., 14, Pt. 3: 1048; Horton, *Maxey*, 33-34.

83. *Official Records*, 22, Pt. 2: 1112-1113, 1127; John C. Waugh, *Sam Bell Maxey and the Confederate Indians* (Fort Worth: Ryan Place Publishers, 1995), 16-

19; Robert L. Kerby, *Kirby Smith's Confederacy: The Trans-Mississippi South, 1863-1865* (New York: Columbia University Press, 1972), 237-238.

84. Waugh, *Maxey and Confederate Indians*, 44-51; Annie Heloise Abel, *The American Indian as Participant in the Civil War* (Cleveland: Arthur H. Clark Company, 1919), 315, 320-321, 329-330; L. W. Horton, "General Sam Bell Maxey: His Defense of North Texas and the Indian Territory," *Southwestern Historical Quarterly*, 74 (April 1971): 509-512. Ms. Abel, one of the first historians to study the role of Native Americans in the Civil War, concluded that "without Maxey the war for the Indians would have ended the preceding winter [1863-64]."

85. Waugh, *Maxey and Confederate Indians*, 52-56; Gracy, ed., *Maxey's Texas*, 16-17.

86. It is difficult to determine the number of troops involved at Poison Spring. Maxey reported that the Confederates with less than 1,800 men defeated the enemy with 2,500 troops. *Official Records*, 34, Pt. 1: 842, 844. Don Richards, "The Battle of Poison Spring," *Arkansas Historical Quarterly* 18 (Winter 1959): 342-344, estimated 1,170 Federals and 3,335 Confederates. Kirby Smith believed the Federals had 2,700 men and the Confederates 2,000. Horton, "General Sam Bell Maxey," 514 fn.

87. Gregory J. W. Urwin, " 'We Cannot Treat Negroes . . . As Prisoners of War': Racial Atrocities and Reprisals in Civil War Arkansas," *Civil War History*, 42 (September 1996): 197; Anne J. Bailey, "Was There a Massacre at Poison Spring?" *Military History of the Southwest* 20 (Fall 1990): 162. Albert Castel, *General Sterling Price and the Civil War in the West* (Baton Rouge: Louisiana State University Press, 1968), 177, believes the Federal losses would have been greater had Maxey not stopped the pursuit. For Maxey's report see *Official Records*, 34, Pt. 1: 841-844; for Marmaduke's report see ibid., 34, pt. 1: 818-820, 821-827.

88. Waugh, *Maxey and Confederate Indians*, 62-63, describes the confusion surrounding Maxey's promotion. Apparently Maxey had been recommended before the other brigadiers but through an oversight at Smith's headquarters Maxey had not been informed.

89. James L. Nichols, *The Confederate Quartermaster in the Trans-Mississippi* (Austin: University of Texas Press, 1964), 40-41.

90. Waugh, *Maxey and Confederate Indians*, 67-80; *Official Records*, 41, Pt. 1: 29; Marvin J. Hancock, "The Second Battle of Cabin Creek," *Chronicles of Oklahoma* 39 (Winter 1961-62): 409-419; Lary C. Rampp, "Confederate Sinking of the *J. R. Williams*," *Journal of the West* 11 (January 1972): 43-50; Lary C. Rampp and Donald L. Rampp, "The Civil War in the Indian Territory: Confederate Guerrilla Operations End," *Military History of Texas and the Southwest* 11 (No. 4, 1973): 257-263.

91. *Maxey and Confederate Indians*, 41-43, 81-82. Lary C. Rampp and Donald L. Rampp, "The Civil War in the Indian Territory: The Phillips' Expedition and Stalemate," *Military History of Texas and the Southwest* 11 (No. 2, 1973): 83, describe Cooper as "a man of possessing more ambition that ability."

92. Waugh, *Maxey and Confederate Indians*, 43; Kerby, *Kirby Smith's Confederacy*, 405. Waugh says Cooper "had inordinate influence with Jefferson Davis," and describes him as Davis' friend, but Davis' biographer, William C. Davis, says "Cooper and Davis definitely were not friends." *Jefferson Davis*, 135.

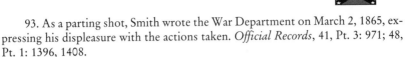

93. As a parting shot, Smith wrote the War Department on March 2, 1865, expressing his displeasure with the actions taken. *Official Records*, 41, Pt. 3: 971; 48, Pt. 1: 1396, 1408.

94. Waugh, *Maxey and Confederate Indians*, 84-85; Gracy, ed., *Maxey's Texas*, 20.

95. For Maxey's postwar years see Horton, *Maxey*, 46 ff; and Alwyn Barr, *Reconstruction to Reform: Texas Politics, 1876-1906* (Austin: University of Texas Press, 1971), 30, 40, 50, 60-61, 100-103.

96. Published accounts give different birthdates for Green. Odie Faulk, *General Tom Green: Fightin' Texan* (Waco: Texian Press, 1963), 2, and Alwyn Barr, "Thomas Green," *New Handbook of Texas*, 3: 316, give the day as July 8. Warner, *Generals in Gray*, 117, and Anne Bailey, *The Confederate General*, 3: 32, give January 8. Kathleen Williams, "Thomas Green," in *Ten More Texans in Gray*, ed. W. C. Nunn (Hillsboro: Hill Junior College Press, 1980), 19, and Jon L. Wakelyn, *Biographical Directory of the Confederacy*, 210, give June 8.

97. Faulk, *General Tom Green*, 2-3; Sam Houston Dixon and Louis Wiltz Kemp, *The Heroes of San Jacinto* (Houston: Anson Jones Press, 1932), 78-79; Alwyn Barr, "Tom Green: The Forrest of the Trans-Mississippi," *Lincoln Herald* 88 (Summer 1986): 39; *New Handbook of Texas*, 3: 316.

98. Dixon and Kemp, *Heroes of San Jacinto*, 78-79. For more on the "Twin Sisters," see Jeffrey William Hunt, "Twin Sisters," *New Handbook of Texas*, 6: 604-605; Stephen L. Hardin, *Texian Iliad* (Austin: University of Texas Press, 1994), 189, 202-203, 210; E. W. Winkler, "The 'Twin Sisters' Cannon, 1836-1865," *Southwestern Historical Quarterly* 21 (July 1917): 36-60; Mike Kaury, "Cannon for Texas: Artillery in the Revolution and the Republic," *Military History of Texas and the Southwest* 10 (1972): 128-131.

99. Faulk, *General Tom Green*, 9-12; Williams, "Thomas Green," 20.

100. Faulk, *General Tom Green*, 13-17; Dixon and Kemp, *Heroes of San Jacinto*, 79.

101. Faulk, *General Tom Green*, 17-19; Thomas W. Cutrer *Ben McCulloch and the Frontier Military Tradition* (Chapel Hill: University of North Carolina Press, 1993), 60-62. For more on this subject see Joseph Milton Nance, *Attack and Counterattack: The Texas-Mexican Frontier, 1842* (Austin: University of Texas Pres, 1964); Nance, *Dare-Devils All—The Texan-Mier Expedition*, ed. Archie P. McDonald (Austin: Eakin Press, 1998); and Sam W. Haynes, *Soldiers of Misfortune: The Somervell and Mier Expeditions* (Austin: University of Texas Press, 1990).

102. Williams, "Thomas Green," 21-23; Stephen B. Oates, "The Texas Rangers in the Mexican War," *Texas Military History* 3 (Summer 1963): 68-69; Charles Spurlin, "Mobilization of the Texas Militia for the Mexican War," *Military History of Texas and the Southwest* 15 (No. 3, 1975): 25-44.

103. Williams, "Thomas Green," 23; *New Handbook of Texas*, 2: 27.

104. Fredericka Ann Meiners, "The Texas Governorship, 1861-1865: Biography of an Office" (Ph. D. dissertation, Rice University, 1975), 34; Martin H. Hall, *The Confederate Army of New Mexico* (Austin: Presidial Press, 1978), 133-134.

105. Donald S. Frazier, *Blood & Treasure: Confederate Empire in the Southwest*

(College Station: Texas A&M University Press, 1995), 75-136; Martin H. Hall, *Sibley's New Mexico Campaign* (Austin: University of Texas Press, 1961), 29-58; Jerry Thompson, *Confederate General of the West: Henry Hopkins Sibley* (College Station: Texas A&M University Press, 1996), 215-243.

106. The most complete account of the battle is John M. Taylor, *Bloody Valverde: A Civil War Battle on the Rio Grande, February 21, 1862* (Albuquerque: University of New Mexico Press, 1995).

107. *Official Records*, 9: 505-506; Hall, *Sibley's New Mexico Campaign*, 101-103, Thompson, *Confederate General of the West*, 267-269. The total casualty figures given are those in Taylor, *Bloody Valverde*, 102. They differ slightly from those reported by Green, *Official Records*, 9: 521. Taylor lists Green as one of those wounded; other accounts do not mention this.

108. Frazier, *Blood & Treasure*, 178-196; Don E. Alberts, ed., *Rebels on the Rio Grande: The Civil War Journal of A. B. Peticolas* (Albuquerque: Merit Press, 1993), 55-75; Thompson, *Confederate General of the West*, 270-274.

109. Frazier, *Blood & Treasure*, 199-207; Hall, *Sibley's New Mexico Campaign*, 121-123.

110. Don E. Alberts, *The Battle of Glorieta: Union Victory in the West* (College Station: Texas A&M University Press, 1998), 94-138; Thomas S. Edrington and John Taylor, *The Battle of Glorieta Pass: A Gettysburg in the West, March 16-28, 1862* (Albuquerque: University of New Mexico Press, 1998), 77-100.

111. Frazier, *Blood & Treasure*, 228-229; Hall, *Sibley's New Mexico Campaign*, 165-168.

112. Frazier, *Blood & Treasure*, 239-240; Thompson, *Confederate General of the West*, 294-295.

113. Hall, *Sibley's New Mexico Campaign*, 168-169; Alberts, ed., *Rebels on the Rio Grande*, 102n.

114. See Don E. Alberts, "The Battle of Peralta," *New Mexico Historical Review* 58 (October 1983): 369-379.

115. Theophilus Noel, *A Campaign From Santa Fe to the Mississippi: Being a History of the Old Sibley Brigade* (Shreveport: News Printing, 1865), 26-39; Hall, *Sibley's New Mexico Campaign*, 189-214. Frazier, *Blood & Treasure*, 249-250, notes that Green intitally favored the detour through the mountains but as the discussion among Sibley's council wore on, Green "became sullen and detached, realizing, according to one observer, that one plan meant 'death in a northern prison, the other death in the mountains.'"

116. Curtis M. Milburn, "Brigadier General Tom Green of Texas," *East Texas Historical Journal* 32 (Spring 1994): 5, 10; Donald S. Frazier, *Cottonclads! The Battle for Galveston and the Defense of the Texas Coast* (Fort Worth: Ryan Place Publishers, 1996), 56.

117. Donald S. Frazier, "Sibley's Texans and the Battle of Galveston," *Southwestern Historical Quarterly* XCIX (October 1995): 176-178; Frazier, *Cottonclads!*, 56-57; Faulk, *General Tom Green*, 49; Edward T. Cotham, Jr., *Battle on the Bay: The Civil War Struggle for Galveston* (Austin: University of Texas Press, 1998), 111.

118. Frazier, *Cottonclads!*, 39-60; Faulk, *General Tom Green*, 48-50; Robert M. Franklin, *Battle of Galveston, January 1, 1863* (Reprint, Galveston: San Luis Press, 1975), 4-5.

119. *Official Records of the Union and Confederate Navies in the War of Rebellion,* 30 vols. (Washington: Government Printing Office, 1894-1922), hereinafter cited as *Official Records, Navies,* 19: 473-474; Alwyn Barr, "Texas Coastal Defense," *Southwestern Historical Quarterly* 65 (July 1961): 14-16; Edward B. Williams, ed., "A 'Sprited' Account of the Battle of Galveston, January 1, 1863," ibid. 99 (October 1995): 212-215.

120. *Official Records, Navies,* 19: 474-475; *Official Records,* 15: 210-217; Alwyn Barr, "The 'Queen City of the Gulf' Held Hostage: The Impact of the War on Confederate Galveston," *Military History of the West* 27 (Fall 1997): 123-124.

121. *Official Records,* 15: 217; Frazier, "Sibley's Texans and the Battle of Galveston," 197; Cotham, *Battle on the Bay,* 132-133.

122. Donald S. Frazier, "Texans on the Teche: The Texas Brigade at the Battles of Bisland and Irish Bend, April 12-14, 1863," *Louisiana History* 32 (Fall 1991): 417-435; Thompson, *Confederate General of the West,* 320-329; Stephen S. Michot, "In Relief of Port Hudson: Richard Taylor's 1863 Lafourche Offensive," *Military History of the West* 23 (Fall 1993): 103-117; Faulk, *General Tom Green,* 52-56.

123. Taylor, *Destruction and Reconstruction,* 166-174; T. Michael Parrish, *Richard Taylor: Soldier Prince of Dixie* (Chapel Hill: University of North Carolina Press, 1992), 297-302; L. Boyd Finch, "Surprise at Brashear City: Sherod Hunter's Sugar Cooler Cavalry," *Louisiana History* 26 (Fall 1984): 403-434; James T. Matthews, "A Time for Desperate Valor: The Confederate Attack on Fort Butler, Louisiana, 1863," *Military History of the West* 26 (Spring 1996): 23-34.

124. Taylor, *Destruction and Reconstruction,* 173-176; Parrish, *Richard Taylor,* 302-304; Milbourn, "Brigadier General Thomas Green of Texas," 7; Michot, "In Relief of Port Hudson," 130-133.

125. *Official Records,* 26, Pt. 1: 695-698; Parrish, *Richard Taylor,* 304-309. Banks' plans are described fully by Richard Lowe, *The Texas Overland Expedition of 1863* (Abilene: McWhiney Foundation Press, 1998), 25-35.

126. Alwyn Barr, ed., "The Battle of Bayou Bourbeau, November 3, 1863: Col. Oran M. Roberts' Report," *Louisiana History* 6 (Winter 1965): 83-91; David C. Edmonds, "Surrender on the Bourdeaux: Honorable Defeat or Incompetency Under Fire," ibid. 18 (Winter 1977): 63-86; Lowe, *Texas Overland Expedition,* 63-100. Taylor praised Green and his troops for their action at Bayou Bourbeau. See Parrish, *Richard Taylor,* 312.

127. *Official Records,* 25, Pt. 1: 385; Milbourn, "Brigadier General Thomas Green of Texas," 8.

128. Taylor, *Destruction and Reconstruction,* 193-198; Parrish, *Richard Taylor,* 322-352; Faulk, *General Tom Green,* 59-60.

129. Parrish, *Richard Taylor,* 356-361. Taylor defended Green's decision, writing in his memoirs that "the charge was premature and cost valuable lives, but was of use in moral effect." *Destruction and Reconstruction,* 204.

130. Ibid., 202-205; Noel, *Campaign From Santa Fe to the Mississippi,* 79-81; Johnson, *The Red River Campaign,* 160-162.

131. Faulk, *General Tom Green,* 62-63; Bailey, *Between the Enemy and Texas,* 170-176; Alwyn Barr, "The Battle at Blair's Landing," *Louisiana History* 2 (Winter 1963): 204-212.

132. Taylor, *Destruction and Reconstruction*, 216; Milbourn, "Brigadier General Tom Green," 9-10; Noel, *A Campaign from Santa Fe to the Mississippi*, 110-116.

133. *New Handbook of Texas*, 1: 332; *The Confederate General*, 6: 178; Martin Hardwick Hall, "The Court-Martial of Arthur Pendleton Bagby, C.S.A.," *East Texas Historical Journal* 19 (Fall 1981): 61; Lowe, *Texas Overland Expedition*, 77. Bagby graduated 36th in a West Point class of 43. George Crook, who later became famous as an Indian fighter, graduated 38th in the class. According to Craig H. Roell, *New Handbook of Texas*, 1: 332, Bagby became the youngest graduate of West Point to be commissioned a second lieutenant of infantry.

134. Frazier, *Blood & Treasure*, 99, 120.

135. Hall, "The Court-Martial of Arthur Pendleton Bagby," 60-67, covers the proceedings fully. Hall believes that Bagby had over-imbided at Dona Ana, but "if an officer possessed Bagby's innate warrior characteristics, drinking on duty, or even getting drunk, was no deterrent in gaining promotion and recognition in the Confederate army," Ibid., 65.

136. *Official Records*, 15: 210, 212, 217; Frazier, "Sibley's Texans and the Battle of Galveston," 179, 197; Frazier, *Cottonclads!*, 57, 59; Cotham, *Battle on the Bay*, 111-112.

137. *Official Records*, 15: 395, 397-398; William Arceneaux, *Acadian General: Alfred Mouton and the Civil War* (Lafayette: Center for Louisiana Studies, University of Southwestern Louisiana, 1981), 75-76, 78, 82; John D. Winters, *The Civil War in Louisiana* (Baton Rouge: Louisiana State University Press, 1963), 224-225.

138. Quotation from *The Confederate General*, 6: 179; see also *Official Records*, 26, Pt. 1: 339, 394; Noel, *A Campaign from Santa Fe to the Mississippi*, 62-66, 69; Lowe, *Texas Overland Expedition*, 78, 88.

139. *Official Records*, 34, Pt. 1: 524, 563, 570-571; Winters, *Civil War in Louisiana*, 339-349; Parrish, *Richard Taylor*, 374-375; Johnson, *Red River Campaign*, 211.

140. Fredericka Meiners, "Hamilton P. Bee in the Red River Campaign," *Southwestern Historical Quarterly* 78 (July 1974): 33-38; Alwyn Barr, ed., "William T. Mechling Journal of the Red River Campaign, April 7-May 10, 1864," *Texana* 1 (Fall 1963): 373-374; Winters, *Civil War in Louisiana*, 362-365.

141. Parrish, *Richard Taylor*, 377-379; Taylor, *Destruction and Reconstruction*, 220-221; Winters, *Civil War in Louisiana*, 374-377; Bailey, *Texans in the Confederate Cavalry*, 63-74.

142. Kerby, *Kirby Smith's Confederacy*, 332-333; *Official Records*, 41, Pt. 2,: 854, 1049-1050, 1060, Pt. 4, 1141-1146; 48, Pt. 1: 728, 1198, Pt. 2: 87, 1278.

143. *Official Records*, 48, Pt. 2: 1307.

144. *The Confederate General*, 6: 179; *New Handbook of Texas*, 1: 332; Allardice, *More Generals In Gray*, 24-25.

CHAPTER FOUR

1. There were thirty-seven general officers from Texas; however, one, Albert Sidney Johnston, never served as brigadier general.

2. As noted in Chapter Two there is some question concerning the rank of Sam Maxey. His biographer, Louise Horton, believed he was confirmed late in the war.

3. Thomas N. Waul, who was in the Vicksburg campaign east of the Mississippi, could easily be considered an eastern brigadier. He is included among the western brigadiers, because his only service as a general officer was in the Trans Mississippi.

4. The most complete account of the Monett's Ferry affair is Fredericka Meiners, "Hamilton P. Bee in the Red River Campaign of 1864," *Southwestern Historical Quarterly* 78 (July 1974): 21-44.

5. *The Confederate General*, 1: 96; *New Handbook of Texas*, 1: 458. Hamilton P. Bee's younger brother, Barnard Elliott Bee, Jr., was appointed to West Point, became an army officer, and later a brigadier general in the Confederate army. Killed at First Manassas, he is best remembered for his statement "yonder stands Jackson like a stone wall," leading to the nickname "Stonewall" for Thomas J. Jackson. *The Confederate General*, 1: 94-95.

6. *New Handbook of Texas*, 1: 458; *The Confederate General*, 1: 96-97; Fredericka Ann Meiners, "Hamilton Prioleau Bee" (M.A. thesis, Rice University, 1972), 2-6; Ralph A. Wooster, "Wealthy Texans, 1860" *Southwestern Historical Quarterly* 71 (October 1967): 163-179.

7. Meiners, "The Texas Governorship," 49-51; Meiners, "Hamilton P. Bee in the Red River Campaign," 23.

8. Meiners, "Hamilton P. Bee," 23. Only five Texans were appointed general officer prior to Bee. Sam Maxey received his appointment the same day as Bee. For more on Bee's efforts to regulate the cotton trade see Fredericka Ann Meiners, "The Texas Border Cotton Trade, 1862-1863," *Civil War History* 23 (December 1977): 293-306.

9. *Official Records*, 26, Pt. 1: 434-435; Kerby, *Kirby Smith's Confederacy*, 287. In his official report Bee noted that the local militia disappeared on the morning of November 3 and that not more than a dozen citizens of Brownsville assisted him in the effort to save the supplies. James A. Irby, *Backdoor to Bagdad: The Civil War on the Rio Grande* (El Paso: Texas Western Press, 1977), 29, states that "Bee's pent-up nervous tension caused him to panic." Jerry Thompson, *A Wild and Vivid Land* (Austin: Texas State Historical Association, 1998), 110, points out that Richard Fitzpatrick, Confederate commercial agent in Matamoros, believed the fire was an attempt by Bee to cover up massive corruption in the Confederate cotton trade.

10. *Official Records*, 34, Pt. 1: 273-274, 421-422, 563-565, 606-607; X. A. Debray, *A Sketch of Debray's (26th) Regiment of Texas Cavalry* (Austin: Von Boeckmann, 1884), 18-19; Winters, *Civil War in Louisiana*, 340-347; Meiners, "Hamilton P. Bee in the Red River Campaign," 24-28.

11. Winters, *Civil War in Louisiana*, 349-355; Johnson, *Red River Campaign*, 155-162; *Official Records*, 34, Pt. 1: 608-609; Stanley S. McGowen, "Augustus Buchel: A Forgotten Texas Patriot," *Military History of the West* 25 (Spring 1995): 18-20.

12. H. P. Bee, "Battle of Pleasant Hill—An Error Corrected," *Southern Historical Society Papers* 8 (April 1880): 184-186; J. E. Sliger, "How General Taylor

Fought the Battle of Mansfield, La.," *Confederate Veteran* 31 (December 1923): 456-458; Parrish, *Richard Taylor*, 368.

13. Meiners, "Hamilton P. Bee in the Red River Campaign," 31; *Official Records*, 36, Pt. 1: 606-610; Taylor, *Destruction and Reconstruction*, 204. In August 1864 Walker wrote a blistering letter to Kirby Smith's chief of staff in which he charged that Bee had failed to carry out his assignment at Mansfield and Pleasant Hill. Walker concluded that he "would regard it as a public calamity to know of his [Bee's] being assigned to an important command." *Official Records*, 41, Pt. 2: 1066-1067.

14. Meiners, "Hamilton P. Bee in the Red River Campaign," 33-38; Johnson, *Red River Campaign*, 225-232. Frank Price, a soldier in Walter P. Lane's regiment, writing to his sister, was highly critical of Bee's action. "I regret to say that we have no General," he wrote. "Genl Bee gave up the Ferry without any resistance and came very near sacrificing half of our cavalry." Jimmy L. Bryan, Jr., ed., "'Whip Them Like The Mischief': The Civil War Letters of Frank and Mintie Price," *East Texas Historical Journal* 36 (Fall 1998): 77.

15. *Official Records*, 34, Pt. 1: 580-581; Parrish, *Richard Taylor*, 376-377.

16. *Official Records*, 34, Pt. 1: 610-615; Meiners, "Hamilton P. Bee in the Red River Campaign," 39-44. Although most historians agree that Bee made mistakes in the campaign, they also believe that Bee could not prevent Banks' army from crossing the Cane. "It seems clear," writes Ludwell W. Johnson, *Red River Campaign*, 234, "that even if Bee had conducted a letter-perfect defense, the Federals would have been able to force a crossing . . ." Fredericka Meiners, "Hamilton P. Bee in the Red River Campaign," 42, says "Taylor's plan of encirclement and destruction of the Union army was audacious, but almost too much so. He just did not have enough men to pull it off." See also Parrish, *Richard Taylor*, 379; Curt Anders, *Disaster in Deep Sand: The Red River Expedition* (Carmel, IN: Guild Press of Indiana, 1997), 106-107; William R. Brooksher, *War Along the Bayous: The 1864 Red River Campaign in Louisiana* (Washington: Brassey's, 1998), 176-182.

17. *Official Records*, 41, Pt. 2: 1071-1072, 48, Pt. 1: 1372, 1457-1458, Pt. 2: 1086, 1300, 1303.

18. *New Handbook of Texas*, 1: 458; Welsh, *Medical Histories of Confederate Generals*, 20.

19. Allardice, *More Generals In Gray*, 74; Ella Lonn, *Foreigners in the Confederacy* (Chapel Hill: University of North Carolina Press, 1940), 136-137. Both the *New Handbook of Texas* and *The Confederate General* entries give 1819 as the year of birth, but Allardice, *More Generals In Gray*, states that 1818 is the date taken from the grave marker in the State Cemetery.

20. Allardice, *More Generals In Gray*, 74; *New Handbook of Texas*, 2: 554.

21. Allardice, *More Generals In Gray*, 74; Debray, *History of Debray's Regiment*, 3-4; Stewart Sifakis, *Compendium of the Confederate Armies: Texas* (New York: Facts on File, 1995), 83, 108.

22. Debray, *History of Debray's Regiment*, 6.

23. Ibid., 7-10; Casdorph, *Prince John Magruder*, 225-226, 228, 235; *Official Records*, 15: 210-217.

24. Debray, *History of Debray's Regiment*, 10-11; *The Confederate General*, 2: 180-181. In August 1863 Debray had to disarm the men of two regiments in

Galveston who mutinied over poor food and lack of pay. *Official Records*, 26, Pt. 1, 242-243; Cotham, *Battle on the Bay*, 156.

25. Debray, *History of Debray's Regiment*, 12-18.

26. Ibid., 24.

27. Allardice, *More Generals In Gray*, 75; *The Confederate General*, 6: 181.

28. *The Confederate General*, 2: 154; *New Handbook of Texas*, 3: 79; *Generals in Gray*, 96.

29. *Official Records*, 16, Pt. 1: 767-774; Basil W. Duke, *A History of Morgan's Cavalry* (Bloomington: Indiana University Press, 1960), 190-191, 197, 201; Dee Brown, *The Bold Cavaliers: Morgan's 2nd Kentucky Cavalry Raiders* (Philadelphia: J. B. Lippincott, 1959), 78, 91.

30. *Official Records*, 16, Pt. 1: 881.

31. Edison H. Thomas, *John Hunt Morgan and His Raiders* (Lexington: University Press of Kentucky, 1975), 55-58; Brown, *Bold Cavaliers*, 130-133.

32. Welsh, *Medical Histories of Confederate Generals*, 75; Duke, *History of Morgan's Cavalry*, 386.

33. Meiners, "Texas Governorship," 226-227, 237-240; *Official Records*, 26, Pt. 2: 121, 127.

34. *Official Records*, 22, Pt. 2: 1048, 1062, 1076, 1083, 1127.

35. Ibid., 34, Pt. 1: 779-784, 841-848.

36. Kerby, *Kirby Smith's Confederacy*, 352-355; Marvin J. Hancock, "The Second Battle of Cabin Creek, 1864," *Chronicles of Oklahoma* 39 (Winter 1963): 414-426; Laurence M. Hauptman, *Between Two Fires: American Indians in the Civil War* (New York: Free Press, 1995), 54-57; Waugh, *Sam Maxey and the Confederate Indians*, 73-78; Welsh, *Medical Histories of Confederate Generals*, 75.

37. *Official Records*, 41, Pt. 4: 1036, 48, Pt. 1: 1334-1336, 1347-1348.

38. Welsh, *Medical Histories of Confederate Generals*, 75; *New Handbook of Texas*, 3: 79; *The Confederate General*, 2: 155.

39. *The Confederate General*, 3: 34-35; *New Handbook of Texas*, 3: 325; Roy Sylvan Dunn, "The KGC in Texas," *Southwestern Historical Quarterly* 70 (April 1967): 543-573.

40. Cutrer, *Ben McCulloch*, 197; Douglas Hale, *The Third Texas Cavalry in the Civil War* (Norman: University of Oklahoma Press, 1993), 29; S. B. Barron, *The Lone Star Defenders: A Chronicle of the Third Texas Cavalry, Ross' Brigade* (New York: Neale Publishing Co., 1908), 23-27; A. W. Sparks, *The War Between the States, As I Saw It* (Tyler: Lee & Burnett, 1901), 130-131.

41. *Official Records*, 3: 104-107; Cutrer, *Ben McCulloch*, 226-237; Sparks, *War Between the States*, 138-148; Barron, *Lone Star Defenders*, 44-46; Hale, *Third Texas Cavalry*, 50-69.

42. Sparks, *War Between the States*, 158-162; Hale, *Third Texas Cavalry*, 77-83; Douglas John Cater, *As It Was: Reminiscences of a Boy Soldier of the Third Texas Cavalry and the Nineteenth Louisiana Infantry* (Reprint; Austin: State House Press, 1990), 100-105. While on leave Greer apparently paid a visit to the Confederate capital to discuss affairs in Arkansas and Missouri with President Davis. See letter from the Confederate governor of Missouri, Claiborne R. Jackson, to Jefferson Davis, October 12, 1861, in which the governor states "the bearer of this note Col. Greer of Texas is probably better known to you than myself . . ." *Official Records*, 3: 717-718.

43. William L. Shea & Earl J. Hess, *Pea Ridge: Civil War Campaign in the West* (Chapel Hill: University of North Carolina Press, 1992), 146; Hale, *Third Texas Cavalry*, 85-97.

44. Shea and Hess, *Pea Ridge*, 143-185; William L. Shea, *War in the West: Pea Ridge and Prairie Grove* (Abilene: McWhiney Foundation Press, 1998), 63. Greer himself apparently received a slight wound at Elkhorn Tavern, but does not mention it in his report. Welsh, *Medical Histories of Confederate Generals*, 87-88.

45. Hale, *Third Texas Cavalry*, 111.

46. Ibid., 114; *The Confederate General*, 3: 35. In his report of the Battle of Pea Ridge, Van Dorn fails to mention Greer's role. *Official Records*, 8: 183-186.

47. Ibid., 26, Pt. 2: 493-495, 34, Pt. 2: 1093-1095, Pt. 3: 739-741, 41, Pt. 3: 986-987; Kerby, *Kirby Smith's Confederacy*, 277; Meiners, "Texas Governorship, 1861-1865," 238-239, 313-316; Yearns, ed., *Confederate Governors*, 210-211.

48. James L. Nichols, *The Confederate Quartermaster in the Trans-Mississippi* (Austin: University of Texas Press, 1964), 50; Anne J. Bailey, "Elkanah Brackin Greer," in *The Confederate General*, 3: 35; *Official Records*, 41, Pt. 4: 110l.

49. *Official Records*, 22, Pt. 2: 1129, 41, Pt. 4, 1094.

50. Ibid., 48, Pt. 1: 1146-1147.

51. *New Handbook of Texas*, 3: 325. Welsh, *Medical Histories of Confederate Generals*, 88, lists phthisis pulmonary as the cause of death.

52. *New Handbook of Texas*, 3: 450; Hall, *The Confederate Army of New Mexico*, 61. Gotch's father, Thomas J. Hardeman, was later a member of the Texas Congress and the state legislature. Gotch's uncle, Bailey, was a signer of the Texas Declaration of Independence. For more on this distinguished family see Nicholas P. Hardeman, *Wilderness Calling: The Hardeman Family in the Western Movement, 1750-1900* (Knoxville: University of Tennessee Press, 1977).

53. *New Handbook of Texas*, 3: 450; Hall, *Confederate Army of New Mexico*, 61-62.

54. Hall, 62.

55. *Official Records*, 9: 513-516; Wooster, "Membership of Texas Secession Convention," 331; Hall, *Sibley's New Mexico Campaign*, 98-99, 172-173; Frazier, *Blood & Treasure*, 198, 274-275.

56. *Official Records*, 26, Pt. 1: 227-228, 393-395, Pt. 2: 512; Casdorph, *Prince John Magruder*, 227-228.

57. Taylor, *Destruction and Reconstruction*, 193-198, 201-202; *Official Records*, 34, Pt. 1: 603.

58. Ibid., 34, Pt. 1: 587, 589-590.

59. Ibid., 41, Pt. 4: 1017-1019.

60. Ibid., 41, Pt. 3: 989-990, Pt. 4: 1122; *The Confederate General*, 3: 63.

61. *Official Records*, 48, Pt. 1: 1392-1393; *New Handbook of Texas*, 3: 451.

62. *New Handbook*, 3: 485; *The Confederate General*, 3: 69.

63. Barr, *Polignac's Texas Brigade*, 11-12.

64. Ibid., 14-16.

65. Ibid., 23-27; *Official Records*, Pt. 1: 331.

66. Barr, *Polignac's Texas Brigade*, 28-29.

67. Ibid., 30-36; *Official Records*, 26, Pt. 1: 393-395.

68. Alwyn Barr, *Polignac's Texas Brigade*, 39, notes that Harrison, on leave in

Texas, was delayed in returning to his regiment because his horse had run away and he was on foot when the Battle of Mansfield occurred.

69. Ibid., direct quotation, 42, other material, 42-29; *Official Records*, 41, Pt. 3: 996, 989-990.

70. Quote, Barr, *Polignac's Texas Brigade*, 50; *Official Records*, 41, Pt. 4: 1017, 1124. Ironically, the promotion of King, who was recommended by Smith with Harrison and others, was not approved by President Davis.

71. *Official Records*, 48, Pt. 1: 1371, 1390, 1427; Baylor, "My Troubles with General John A. Wharton," 237-239.

72. The author wishes to thank Ron Ellison, a religious historian in Beaumont, Texas, for information pertaining to Harrison's role in Baptist affairs. J. M. Carroll, *A History of Texas Baptists* (Dallas: Baptist Standard Publishing Co., 1923), 423-424; B. F. Riley, *History of the Baptists of Texas* (Dallas: priv. publ., 1907), 233-234; Welsh, *Medical Histories of Confederate Generals*, 94.

73. *New Handbook of Texas*, 3: 653; *The Confederate General*, 3: 113.

74. Wooster, "Membership of the Texas Secession Convention," 329; Ralph A. Wooster, *Texas and Texans in the Civil War* (Austin: Eakin Press, 1995), 13.

75. Barron, *Lone Star Defenders*, 18-19.

76. *New Handbook of Texas*, 3: 653-654.

77. *Official Records*, 10, Pt. 2: 434, 436, 475; Barron, *Lone Star Defenders*, 85-89; Welsh, *Medical Histories of Confederate Generals*, 103.

78. W. H. King, "Early Experiences in Missouri," *Confederate Veteran*, 17 (August 1908): 502-508; *New Handbook of Texas*, 6: 186; L. David Norris, ed., *With the 18th Texas Infantry: The Autobiography of Wilburn Hill King* (Hillsboro: Hill Junior College Press, 1996), 11-34; *The Confederate General*, 6: 186.

79. Ibid., 6: 186; Norris, ed., *Autobiography of Wilburn Hill King*, 61-63; J. P. Blessington, *The Campaigns of Walker's Texas Division* (Reprint; Austin: State House Press, 1994), 46-47, 110-111.

80. Blessington, *The Campaigns of Walker's Texas Division*, 138-145; Norris, ed., *Autobiography of Wilburn Hill King*, 63-64; *Official Records*, 26, Pt. 1: 393-395.

81. Norris, ed., *Autobiography of Wilburn Hill King*, 69-71; Blessington, *Walker's Texas Division*, 185-191; *New Handbook of Texas*, 3: 1109.

82. Barr, *Polignac's Texas Brigade*, 41-42; Blessington, *Walker's Texas Division*, 270-271; *Official Records*, 41, Pt. 4: 1017-1018, 1371.

83. Barr, *Polignac's Texas Brigade*, 50-51; Blessington, *Walker's Texas Division*, 275-280; L. T. Wheeler, "Gen. Wilbur[n] Hill King," *Confederate Veteran*, 19 (April 1911): 172-173.

84. Barr, *Polignac's Texas Brigade*, 51-52.

85. Ibid., 53-54; Blessington, *Walker's Texas Division*, 291-309; *The Confederate General*, 6: 187; *Official Records*, 48, Pt. 1: 1371, 1390, 1392, 1405.

86. Norris, ed., *Autobiography of Wilburn Hill King*, 91-113. The *New Handbook of Texas*, 3: 1109, and *The Confederate General*, 6: 187, give October 12 as the date of death. Allardice, *More Generals In Gray*, 142, gives December 12 as the date.

87. *New Handbook of Texas*, 4: 62; *The Confederate General*, 4: 20; Welsh, *Medical Histories of Confederate Generals*, 128; Dixon and Kemp, *Heroes of San Jacinto*, 313-314. Lane describes his early military experiences in his memoirs, *The*

Adventures and Recollections of General Walter P. Lane . . . (Marshall, Texas, 1887; reprint, Austin: Pemberton Press, 1970), 12-13, 19-21, 33.

88. *The Adventures and Recollections of General Walter P. Lane*, 42-71; *New Handbook of Texas*, 4: 62-63.

89. *New Handbook of Texas*, 6: 63; Lane, *Adventures and Recollections*, 74-81; Randolph B. Campbell, *A Southern Community in Crisis: Harrison County, Texas, 1850-1880* (Austin: Texas State Historical Association, 1983), 200-202; Hale, *Third Texas Cavalry*, 47.

90. *Official Records*, 3: 120, 297-301, 8: 22-23, 28-29; Shea and Hess, *Pea Ridge*, 97-99; Hale, *Third Texas Cavalry*, 62-63, 68, 79-81, 91-92, 95-97.

91. *Official Records*, 10, Pt. 2: 583-584; *New Handbook of Texas*, 4: 63; Lane, *Adventures and Recollections*, 98.

92. *Official Records*, 22, Pt. 2: 827, 830, 834, 26, Pt. 1: 218-219. Lane does not mention this in his memoirs.

93. Ibid., 34, Pt. 1: 616-618; Welsh, *Medical Histories of Confederate Generals*, 129. For an account of the regiment's participation in the Louisiana campaigns see Bryan, ed., "Civil War Leters of Frank and Mintie Price," 68-84.

94. *Official Records*, 41, Pt. 4: 1017-1019, 1122.

95. *New Handbook of Texas*, 4: 63. Welsh, *Medical Histories of Confederate Generals*, 129, gives January 27, 1892 as the date of death.

96. Cutrer, *Ben McCulloch*, 3-7.

97. Ibid., 6-12; Victor Rose, *The Life and Services of Gen. Ben McCulloch* (Philadelphia, 1888; reprint, Austin: Steck Co., 1958), 26-30.

98. Ibid., 31-38; Cutrer, *Ben McCulloch*, 15-16; Jack W. Gunn, "Ben McCulloch: A Big Captain," *Southwestern Historical Quarterly* 58 (July 1954): 1-2.

99. *New Handbook of Texas*, 4: 384.

100. Ibid., 4: 385; *The Confederate General*, 4: 117-118; Nance, *Dare-Devils All*, 26, 30-31; Samuel C. Reid, *The Scouting Expeditions of McCulloch's Texas Rangers* (Philadelphia, 1847; reprint, Freeport, NY: Books for Libraries, 1970); Walter P. Webb, *The Texas Rangers: A Century of Frontier Defense* (New York, 1935; reprint, Austin: University of Texas Press, 1965), 94-113; Stephen B. Oates, "The Texas Rangers in the Mexican War," *Texas Military History* 3 (Summer 1963): 65-84; Charles Spurlin, "With Taylor and McCulloch Through the Battle of Monterrey," ibid., 6 (Fall 1967): 203-221.

101. Gunn, "Ben McCulloch," 9-14; Cutrer, *Ben McCulloch*, 104-138.

102. Cutrer, 151-176.

103. For McCulloch's roles in the surrender of Federal property see Jeanne T. Heidler, "'Embarrassing Situation': David E. Twiggs and the Surrender of U.S. Forces in Texas in 1861," *Military History of the Southwest* 21 (Fall 1991): 157-172; Russell K. Brown, "An Old Woman with a Broomstick: General David E. Twiggs and the U.S. Surrender in Texas, 1861," *Military Affairs* 48 (April 1984): 57-61; J. J. Bowden, *The Exodus of Federal Forces from Texas, 1861* (Austin: Eakin Press, 1986), 44-63.

104. Cutrer, *Ben McCulloch*, 195.

105. Ibid., 194-244; *Official Records*, 3: 104-107, 118-120; Kel N. Pickens, "The Battle of Wilson's Creek, Missouri, August 10, 1861, *Journal of the West* 19 (October 1980): 10-25. A more complete account of the battle is William R.

Brooksher, *Bloody Hill: The Civil War Battle of Wilson's Creek* (Dulles, VA: Brassey's, 1995).

106. Cutrer, *Ben McCulloch*, 246-277. For more on the differences between McCulloch and Price see William L. Shea, "The Road to Pea Ridge," *Arkansas Historical Quarterly* 52 (Autumn 1993): 209-210; Shea and Hess, *Pea Ridge*, 16-19; and Shea, *War In the West*, 14-18.

107. Shea and Hess, *Pea Ridge*, 62-112; Cutrer, *Ben McCulloch*, 273-309; Edwin C. Bearss, "The Battle of Pea Ridge," *Arkansas Historical Quarterly* 20 (Spring 1961): 74-94; Walter L. Brown, "Pea Ridge: Gettysburg of the West," ibid., 15 (Spring 1956): 3-16; Maynard J. Hanson, "The Battle of Pea Ridge, Arkansas, March 6-8, 1862," *Journal of the West* 19 (October 1980): 39-50.

108. Lane, *Adventures and Recollections*, 94.

109. Cutrer, *Ben McCulloch*, 310-316. McCulloch was the fourth Confederate general to be killed in combat. Robert S. Garnett, killed July 13, 1861, Barnard E. Bee, killed July 22, 1861, and Felix Zollicoffer, killed January 22, 1862, were southern generals killed earlier. Russell Brown, *Fallen in Battle: American General Officer Combat Fatalities From 1775* (Westport, CT: Greenwood Press, 1988), 177.

110. *The Confederate General*, 3: 120; *New Handbook of Texas*, 4: 385-386. For more on McCulloch's early life see David Paul Smith, "In Defense of Texas: The Life of Henry E. McCulloch" (M.A. thesis, Stephen F. Austin State University, 1975).

111. Bowden, *Exodus of Federal Forces*, 65-79; Stanley S. McGowen, *Horse Sweat and Powder Smoke: The First Texas Cavalry in the Civil War* (College Station, Texas A&M University Press, 1999), 3-9; *Official Records*, 1: 558-559, 575-576, 617-618, 4: 101.

112. Ibid., 9: 151-152, 700, 718, 884.

113. Bailey, *Between the Enemy and Texas*, 73-74, 84-86, 95-97; Anne J. Bailey, "Henry McCulloch's Texans and the Defense of Arkansas in 1862," *Arkansas Historical Quarterly* 46 (Spring 1987): 46-49; Blessington, *Walker's Texas Division*, 40-65; *Official Records*, 17, Pt. 2: 787, 810.

114. Ibid., 24, Pt. 2: 459, 462-465, 467-470; Blessington, *Walker's Texas Division*, 95-109; Joseph T. Glatthar, *Forged in Battle: The Civil War Alliance of Black Soldiers and White Officers* (New York: Free Press, 1990), 132-135; Terrence J. Winchel, "To Rescue Gibraltar: John Walker's Texas Division and Its Expedition to Relieve Fort Vicksburg," *Civil War Regiments* 3 (No. 3 1994): 33-58.

115. *Official Records*, 26, Pt. 2: 120, 188.

116. First quote, Smith, *Frontier Defense in the Civil War*, 75; second quote, *Official Records*, 34, Pt. 2: 942; *New Handbook of Texas*, 5: 380; Albert Castel, *William Clark Quantrill: His Life and Times* (New York: Frederick Fell, Inc., 1962), 157-168; Albert Castel, "Quantrill in Texas," *Civil War Times Illustrated* 11 (June 1972): 20-27; Lary C. Rampp, "William Quantrill's Civil War Activities in Texas" *Texas Military History* 8 (No. 2 1970): 224-226; Edward E. Leslie, *The Devil Knows How to Ride* (New York: Random House, 1996), 285-287, 292-293, 297-298.

117. Smith, *Frontier Defense in the Civil War*, 64-65, 112-128; Richard B. McCaslin, *Tainted Breeze: The Great Hanging at Gainesville, Texas, 1862* (Baton Rouge: Louisiana State University Press, 1994), 139-148; Richard B. McCaslin,

"Dark Corner of the Confederacy: James G. Bourland and the Border Regiment," *Military History of the West* 24 (Spring 1994): 57-70.

118. Smith, *Frontier Defense in the Civil War*, 131-134; David Paul Smith, "The Elm Creek Raid, 1864: State and Confederate Defense and Response," *Military History of the Southwest* 19 (Fall 1989): 121-136; Kenneth Neighbors, "Elm Creek Raid in Young County, 1864," *West Texas Historical Association Year Book* 40 (October 1964): 83-89.

119. *The Confederate General*, 4: 121; *New Handbook of Texas*, 4: 386.

120. *New Handbook of Texas*, 4: 976; *The Confederate General*, 4: 195; Stephen B. Oates, ed., *Rip Ford's Texas* (Austin: University of Texas Press, 1963), 224, 227, 233-235; William C. Pool, *Bosque County, Texas* (San Marcos: San Marcos Record Press, 1954), 19-30. Nelson was listed in the manuscript returns of the Federal census for 1860 as owning $1,500 in real and $400 in personal property. No slaves were enumerated for him in the census slave schedule for Bosque County.

121. *Official Records*, 13: 36.

122. Ibid., 13: 884; Evans, ed., *Confederate Military History*, 11: 250; *New Handbook of Texas*, 4: 976; *The Confederate General*, 4: 195.

123.Quotation from *Official Records*, 13: 887; see also Welsh, *Medical Histories of Confederate Generals*, 160. Nelson was the sixth of nineteen Confederate generals to die from disease or accident. Brown, *Fallen In Battle*, 185-186.

124. *The New Handbook of Texas*, 5: 436, and *The Confederate General*, 6: 192, give January 1, 1863, as the date of birth, but Bruce Allardice, *More Generals In Gray*, 193n, observes that an 1849 letter from Randal's father to the secretary of war cites the January 4 date.

125. From Gilbert E. Govan and James W. Livingood, eds., *The Haskell Memoirs: The Personal Narrative of a Confederate Officer* (New York, 1960), 10, quoted by both Allardice, *More Generals In Gray*, 193, and Norman Brown, "Horace Randal," *The Confederate General*, 6: 192.

126. Blessington, *Walker's Texas Division*, 95-128; *Official Records*, 13: 884; M. Jane Johansson, *A Peculiar Honor: A History of the 28th Texas Cavalry* (Fayetteville: University of Arkansas Press, 1998), 8-9, 26-29, 38-58. Ms. Johansson notes in the fall of 1862 Col. O. M. Roberts of the Eleventh Infantry challenged Randal's seniority. The issue was eventually referred to the secretary of war, who decided in Randal's favor. Ibid., 45.

127. Parrish, *Richard Taylor*, 335-361; Jane Harris Johansson and David H. Johansson, "Two 'Lost' Battle Reports: Horace Randal's and Joseph L. Brent's Reports of the Battles of Mansfield and Pleasant Hill, 8 and 9 April, 1864," *Military History of the West* 23 (Fall 1993): 169-190; Johansson, *A Peculiar Honor*, 91-111.

128. *New Handbook of Texas*, 5: 436; Johansson, *A Peculiar Honor*, 113-122; Allardice, *More Generals In Gray*, 193.

129. Frazier, *Blood & Treasure*, 78-79; Hall, *Confederate Army of New Mexico*, 53; Oates, ed., *Rip Ford's Texas*, 21. Cotham, *Battle on the Bay*, 101, says another explanation for the "Dirty Shirt" nickname is that Scurry used his shirt to signal at the Battle of Glorieta Pass.

130. *New Handbook of Texas*, 6: 946; Hall, *Confederate Army of New Mexico*, 53.

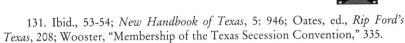

131. Ibid., 53-54; *New Handbook of Texas*, 5: 946; Oates, ed., *Rip Ford's Texas*, 208; Wooster, "Membership of the Texas Secession Convention," 335.

132. Frazier, *Blood & Treasure*, 78-86.

133. Martin Hall, *Sibley's New Mexico Campaign*, 101, points out that Scurry's voice cheering his men on could be heard throughout the battle. See also *Official Records*, 9: 513-516; Frazier, *Blood & Treasure*, 157-185; Alberts, ed., *Rebels on the Rio Grande*, 43n, 48-49; Taylor, *Bloody Valverde*, 79-82, 97-98, 101-102.

134. *Official Records*, 9: 540-545; Hall, *Sibley's New Mexico Campaign*, 141-167; Frazier, *Blood & Treasure*, 208-240; Don E. Alberts, *The Battle of Glorieta: Union Victory in the West* (College Station: Texas A&M University Press, 1998), 100-127, 173. Thomas S. Edrington and John Taylor, *The Battle of Glorieta Pass: A Gettysburg in the West, March 26-28, 1862* (Albuquerque: University of New Mexico Press, 1998), 57-105, provide the most complete coverage of Scurry's role in the fighting at Pigeon's Ranch.

135. First quote, Alberts, ed., *Rebels on the Rio Grande*, 18; second quote, Jerry Thompson, *Confederate General of the West*, 283. See also Edrington and Taylor, *The Battle of Glorieta Pass*, 108-111, and Alberts, *The Battle of Glorieta*, 79-80, 142-148.

136. Cotham, *Battle on the Bay*, 101, 120-123; Ralph A. Wooster, "The Battle of Galveston," *Texas Gulf Historical and Biographical Record* 28 (November 1992): 28-38; Casdorph, *Prince John Magruder*, 227, 232. Casdorph incorrectly states that the attacking force was "under the overall command of General Tom Green." Green, only a colonel at the time, was clearly outranked by Scurry.

137. *The Confederate General*, 5: 133-135; Casdorph, *Prince John Magruder*, 238-239, 243. Lt. Col. Arthur Fremantle of the British Coldstream Guards visited Scurry in May 1863. Fremantle was quite impressed by Scurry, who at the time was suffering from a severe inflammation of the eye. Fremantle described Scurry as a congenial host who was "very amusing, and . . . an admirable mimic." Fremantle, *Diary*, 52.

138. First quote, Blessington, *Walker's Texas Division*, 136; second quote, Norman D. Brown, ed., *Journey to Pleasant Hill: The Civil War Letters of Captain Elijah P. Petty* (San Antonio: University of Texas Institute of Texan Cultures, 1982), 271. Captain Petty, 286, tells an interesting story of how Scurry dealt with men caught stealing a hog. He forced them to wear the skin of a hog while parading back and forth before the brigade.

139. Taylor, *Destruction and Reconstruction*, 196-205; Parrish, *Richard Taylor*, 363-367; Blessington, *Walker's Texas Division*, 182-198; Brooksher, *War Along the Bayou*, 98-134.

140. Blessington, *Walker's Texas Division*, 256-258; *New Handbook of Texas*, 5: 946.

141. Hall, *The Confederate Army of New Mexico*, 217-218; *The Confederate General*, 6: 280.

142. Given his experience in the old army it is surprising that Steele was not made a general in 1861. Among fellow graduates of 1840 who were appointed general that year were William T. Sherman, George H. Thomas, Richard Ewell, and Paul O. Hebert. *Official Records*, 4: 143, 9: 522; Frazier, *Blood & Treasure*, 97, 120, 188, 196-197, 273-283; Hall, *Sibley's New Mexico Campaign*, 209, 217-218, 223-224.

143. *Official Records*, 22, Pt. 1: 28-33; Allan C. Ashcraft, ed., "A Civil War Letter of General Steele, CSA," *Arkansas Historical Quarterly* 22 (Autumn 1963): 278-281.

144. Steele made an exception of Stand Waite in his criticism, noting the Cherokee was "a gallant and daring officer." *Official Records*, 22, Pt. 1: 32-35, Pt. 2: 948-949, 981, 986; Lary C. Rampp and Donald L. Rampp, "The Civil War in Indian Territory: Blunt's Pursuit," *Military History of Texas and Southwest* 10 (No. 4, 1972): 249-272; Edwin C. Bearss, "General Wiliam Steele Fights to Hold Unto Northwest Arkansas," *Arkansas Historical Quarterly* 25 (Spring 1966): 36-93; Edwin C. Bearss, "The Federals Capture Fort Smith, 1863," ibid., 28 (Summer 1969): 156-190.

145. *Official Records*, 22, Pt. 2: 1108-1109.

146. Bailey, *Texans in the Confederate Cavalry*, 63-75; Bailey, *Between the Enemy and Texas*, 181-192.

147. *Official Records*, 41, Pt. 33: 966-971; 48, Pt. 1, 1458.

148. Webb, *Texas Rangers*, 288; Clarence P. Denman, "The Office of Adjutant General in Texas, 1835-1881," *Southwestern Historical Quarterly* 28 (April 1925): 318-320; Welsh, *Medical Histories of Confederate Generals*, 204.

149. Charles K. Chamberlain, "Alexander Watkins Terrell: Citizen, Statesman" (Ph. D. dissertation, University of Texas, 1957), 3-6; John W. Spencer, *Terrell's Texas Cavalry* (Burnet: Eakin Press, 1982), 92-93; *New Handbook of Texas*, 6: 258-259.

150. Chamberlain, "Alexander Watkins Terrell," 6-60; Spencer, *Terrell's Texas Cavalry*, 93-94. Spencer, v-vi, discusses the confusion over the regiment's name. He notes that Terrell's men used both names.

151. *Official Records*, 26, Pt. 2: 237-239, 469-471, 536; Spencer, *Terrell's Texas Cavalry*, 3-7.

152. Spencer, 14-40; *Official Records*, 26, Pt. 2: 563, 34, Pt. 2: 932, 1096; *The Confederate General*, 6: 195.

153. Spencer, *Terrell's Texas Cavalry*, 50-55; McGowen, *Horse Sweat and Powder Smoke*, 162-163. The November 21, 1864, report of the Trans Mississippi inspector general was critical of Terrell's Brigade for depredations against local citizens and cited the "want of discipline and restraint." *Official Records*, 41, Pt. 4: 1071.

154. Spencer, *Terrell's Texas Cavalry*, 55-63; McGowen, *Horse Sweat and Powder Smoke*, 165-166.

155. Ibid., 66-71, 95-96. Terrell's experiences in Mexico are recounted in his *From Texas to Mexico and the Courts of Maximilian in 1865* (Dallas: Dallas Book Club, 1933).

156. *New Handbook of Texas*, 6: 258-259; Spencer, *Terrell's Texas Cavalry*, 96-99; Allardice, *More Generals In Gray*, 218.

157. *The Confederate General*, 6: 108; *New Handbook of Texas*, 6: 840.

158. *Official Records*, 22, Pt. 1: 903-905, 24, Pt. 2: 967-970.

159. *Official Records*, 24, Pt. 2, 967, quoted by Anne J. Bailey, "Richard Waterhouse," *The Confederate General*, 6: 108.

160. O. M. Roberts, in Evans, *Confederate Military History*, 11: 259; Blessington, *Walker's Texas Division*, 193-197.

161. *Official Records*, 34, Pt. 3: 823, 967, Pt. 4: 1017-1018; 48, Pt. 1: 1430.

162. Jack D. Welsh, *Medical Histories of Confederate Generals*, 229, says that a business rival tried to get Waterhouse drunk so he could not attend to his duties. Waterhouse was either drugged or intoxicated when he fell down the stairs. An inquest was supposedly held but records of the inquest are no longer available.

163. *New Handbook of Texas*, 6: 852; *The Confederate General*, 5: 113; Alexander and Beringer, *The Anatomy of the Confederate Congress*, 388-389; Buenger, *Secession and the Union in Texas*, 38.

164. The legislature selected Williamson S. Oldham for the Senate position. William C. Davis, *"A Government of Our Own:" The Making of the Confederacy* (New York: Free Press, 1994), 13, 182, 259, 358; *New Handbook of Texas*, 6: 852; James B. Warner, "A Legislative History of Texas During the Civil War" (M.A. thesis, Lamar State College of Technology, 1971), 40.

165. Quotation from *Official Records*, 24, Pt. 1: 416. See also Pt. 3: 640-641, 705; *New Handbook of Texas*, 6: 852; Robert A. Hasskarl and Leif R. Hasskarl, *Waul's Texas Legion, 1862-1865* (priv. publ., 1985) 16-21; Samuel E. Carter, III, *The Final Fortress: The Campaign for Vicksburg, 1862-1863* (New York: St. Martin's Press, 1980), 137-141.

166. Quotation from *Official Records*, 24, Pt. 2: 351. See also James R. Arnold, *Grant Wins the War: Decision at Vicksburg* (New York: John Wiley & Sons, 1997), 254-255; Laura Simmons, "Waul's Legion From Texas to Mississippi," *Texana* 7 (Spring 1969): 1-16; Wayne Flynt, "The Texas Legion at Vicksburg," *East Texas Historical Journal* 17 (Spring 1979): 60-67; Herman Hattaway, *General Stephen D. Lee* (Jackson: University Press of Mississippi, 1976), 94.

167. Ibid., 26, Pt. 2: 249-250, 427; Arnold, *Grant Wins the War*, 272-273.

168. *Official Records*, 26, Pt. 2: 425, 427, 460, 519, 34: Pt. 2: 946, 961; Blessington, *Walker's Texas Division*, 165.

169. Taylor, *Destruction and Reconstruction*, 196-197, 202-205; Blessington, *Walker's Texas Division*, 185-190, 195-196. Stewart Sifakis, *Compendium of the Confederate Armies: Texas*, 124, points out that the Twelfth Infantry was also known as the Eighth Infantry.

170. *Official Records*, 34, Pt. 1: 816-818; Edwin C. Bearss, *Steele's Retreat From Camden and the Battle of Jenkins' Ferry* (Little Rock: Arkansas Civil War Centennial Commission, 1967), 114-169.

171. Blessington, *Walker's Texas Division*, 271, 176, 198-306; Welsh, *Medical Histories of Confederate Generals*, 230.

172. Welsh, 230; *New Handbook of Texas*, 6: 852. Waul's cause of death was tuberculosis.

CHAPTER FIVE

1. Lawrence Hewitt, "Matthew Duncan Ector," *The Confederate General* 2: 94, states that Ector served in a Georgia regiment during the Mexican War. Neither the *New Handbook of Texas*, 2: 780; Evans, ed., *Confederate Military History*, 11: 228; Warner, *Generals in Gray*, 81; nor Wright and Simpson, *Texas in the War*, 77, mention any Mexican War service.

2. Quotation from *Official Records*, 16: 934; Hale, *Third Texas Cavalry*, 29,

48, 63-64, 116; James Lee McDonough, *War in Kentucky: From Shiloh to Perryville* (Knoxville: University of Tennessee Press, 1994), 134-135. Hale, *Third Texas Cavalry*, 44, notes that Ector's thirteen-year-old son, Walton, also served in the regiment.

3. *Official Records*, 16, Pt. 2: 984; 20, Pt. 1: 660; 20, Pt. 2: 413; 23, Pt. 2: 655; 30, Pt. 2: 14; 32, Pt. 3: 659, 863; *The Confederate General*, 2: 95. The Fifteenth Texas Cavalry was later referred to as the Thirty-second Texas Cavalry. See Sifakis, *Compendium of the Confederate Armies: Texas*, 72, 88.

4. *Official Records*, 20, Pt. 1: 915, 923, 926-930; James L. McDonough, *Stones River—Bloody Winter in Tennessee* (Knoxville: University of Tennessee Press, 1980), 86-91.

5. First quote, Peter Cozzens, *This Terrible Sound: The Battle of Chickamauga* (Urbana: University of Illinois Press, 1992), 135; second quote, *Official Records*, 30, Pt. 2: 524. See also *Official Records*, 24, Pt. 1: 222, Pt. 3, 889, 920, 925, 1041; 30, Pt. 2: 243; Judy Watson McClure, *Confederate From East Texas: The Civil War Letters of James Monroe Watson* (Austin: Eakin Press, 1970), 11, 23, 26-27; Welsh, *Medical Histories of Confederate Generals*, 61. The *New Handbook of Texas*, 2: 780, states that Ector received "three slight wounds" at Chickamauga.

6. *Official Records*, 31, Pt. 3: 228, 573, 726; 32, Pt. 2: 584, 701, 719, 721, 724, 730. The inspector general's report on May 2 indicated Ector's Brigade "was poorly armed and not well clothed, but still presented a most soldierly appearance." Ibid., 34, Pt. 2: 569.

7. Ibid., 38, Pt. 3: 903-904, 909; Evans, ed., *Confederate Military History*, 11: 185-186; Castel, *Decision in the West*, 204-205; 426-428; Welsh, *Medical Histories of Confederate Generals*, 60.

8. *Official Records*, 38, Pt. 3: 909.

9. David Stroud of Kilgore College, who has studied Ector's career carefully, states in the *New Handbook of Texas*, 2: 780, "the war ended before he had recovered [from his wounds] enough to resume his duties." The journal of Confederate Senator Williamson S. Oldham indicates that Ector was in La Grange, Georgia, in late April 1865. According to Oldham, Ector and his wife traveled with him to Montevallo, Alabama, and then proceeded on to Marion, Alabama, where he was to receive his parole under terms arranged by departmental commander Richard Taylor. See Buck Yearns, ed., *From Richmond to Texas: The 1865 Journey Home of Confederate Senator Williamson S. Oldham* (Dayton, OH: Morningside House, 1998), 28, 33, 36, 30-40.

10. *New Handbook of Texas*, 2: 780; *The Confederate General*, 2:95; Randolph B. Campbell, *Grass-Roots Reconstruction in Texas, 1865-1880* (Baton Rouge: Louisiana State University Press, 1997), 110-112, 115, 127.

11. *New Handbook of Texas*, 3: 275; *The Confederate General*, 2: 24. The 1860 manuscript census returns for McLennan County list Granbury as the owner of one slave and $4,000 in property.

12. *Official Records*, 7: 374, 376; James Lynn Newsom, "Intrepid Gray Warriors: The 7th Texas Infantry, 1861-1865" (Ph. D. dissertation, Texas Christian University, 1995), 16-38. Benjamin F. Cooling, *Forts Henry and Donelson: The Key to the Confederate Heartland* (Knoxville: University of Tennessee Press, 1987), 57, 137.

13. Newsom, "Intrepid Gray Warriors," 47-48, notes that Grant allowed Granbury to visit his wife in Hopkinsville before he reported to prison. Cooling, *Forts Henry and Donelson*, 220, 259-260; *Official Records*, Series II, 2: 307. For a description of Fort Warren see Lonnie R. Speer, *Portals to Hell: Military Prisons of the Civil War* (Mechanicsburg, PA: Stackpole Books, 1992), 41-44.

14. *Official Records*, Series I, 24, Pt. 3: 800-801; Series II, 4: 445; Lawrence L. Hewitt, *Port Hudson: Confederate Bastion on the Mississippi* (Baton Rouge: Louisiana University Press, 1987), 62; Newsom, "Interpid Gray Warriors," 59-65, 75-78.

15. *Official Records*, 24, Pt. 1: 737-739, 747-748; Newsom, "Intrepid Gray Warriors," 80-89; Samuel Carter III, *The Final Fortress: The Campaign for Vicksburg, 1862-1863* (New York: St. Martin's Press, 1980), 189-191.

16. Newsom, "Intrepid Gray Warriors," 91-100; Craig L. Symonds, *Joseph E. Johnston: A Civil War Biography* (New York: W. W. Norton & Co., 1992), 205-216.

17. *Official Records*, 30, Pt. 2: 456-458; Newsom, "Intrepid Gray Warriors," 108-117; Cozzens, *This Terrible Sound*, 199-201, 233, 259-262.

18. Newsom, "Intrepid Gray Warriors," 118-119; James M. McCaffrey, *This Band of Heroes: Granbury's Texas Brigade, C.S.A.* (Austin: Eakin Press, 1985), 85-88.

19. *Official Records*, 31, Pt. 2: 748-753, 773-775; McCaffrey, *This Band of Heroes*, 88-96; Wiley Sword, *Mountains Touched with Fire: Chattanooga Besieged, 1863* (New York: St. Martin's Press, 1995), 243-247, 335-338; James Lee McDonough, *Chattanooga—A Death Grip on the Confederacy* (Knoxville: University of Tennessee Press, 1984), 126, 144, 149, 233; Craig L. Symonds, *Stonewall of the West: Patrick Cleburne & the Civil War* (Lawrence: University Press of Kansas, 1997), 167, 172-173, 176; Norman D. Brown, ed., *One of Cleburne's Command: The Civil War Reminiscences and Diary of Capt. Samuel T. Foster, Granbury's Texas Brigade, CSA* (Austin: University of Texas Press, 1980), 58-65.

20. Symonds, *Stonewall of the West*, 185-195. Some believe that the proposal kept Cleburne, one of the most highly respected division commanders in the Confederate army, from being promoted to lieutenant general. Hewitt, *The Confederate General*, 3: 25, believes Granbury's failure to endorse Cleburne's proposal influenced his confirmation as permanent brigade commander.

21. *Official Records*, 38, Pt. 3: 720-726; McCaffrey, *This Band of Heroes*, 101-111; Castel, *Decision in the West*, 233-241; Newsom, "Intrepid Gray Warriors," 130-142; Brown, ed., *One of Cleburne's Command*, 82-88.

22. *Official Records*, 38, Pt. 3: 515-546, 564-565, 731-732, 747-754; McCaffrey, *This Band of Heroes*, 120-121; Brown, ed., *One of Cleburne's Command*, 108-112. In the fighting on the 22nd Union general James McPherson, commander of one of Sherman's armies, was killed, probably by a member of Granbury's Brigade. See Castel, *Decision in the West*, 399.

23. Quotations from Symonds, *Stonewall of the West*, 237. See also *Official Records*, 38, Pt. 3: 727, 747, 756; Castel, *Decision in the West*, 499-503;

24. Quotations from Douglas, ed., *Douglas's Texas Battery*, 150. See also Symonds, *Stonewall of the West*, 259; McCaffrey, *This Band of Heroes*, 134-139; Brown, ed., *One of Cleburne's Command*, 150-151; James Lee McDonough and Thomas L. Connelly, *Five Tragic Hours: the Battle of Franklin* (Knoxville: University of

Tennessee Press, 1983), 92-168; Wiley Sword, *The Confederacy's Last Hurrah: Spring Hill, Franklin & Nashville* (Lawrence: University of Kansas Press, 1992), 221-224.

25. McDonough and Connelly, *Five Tragic Hours*, 161, point out that tradition maintains that the bodies of two other Confederate generals, John C. Carter and States Rights Gist, rested on the same gallery but that research by historians Howell and Elizabeth Perdue has shown this to be incorrect. Palmer Bradley, writing in the *New Handbook of Texas*, 3: 275, notes the correct spelling of the last name has been debated; some relatives claim that it is Granberry, as written on the original tombstone, but most historians accept the spelling Granbury.

26. William C. Davis, "John Gregg," *The Confederate General*, 3: 38; Douglas Southall Freeman, *R. E. Lee: A Biography*, 4 vols. (New York: Charles Scribner's Sons, 1936), 3: 509n.

27. *New Handbook of Texas*, 3: 328.

28. Walter L. Buenger, *Secession and the Union in Texas* (Austin: University of Texas Press, 1984), 147, 153; William C. Davis, *"A Government of Our Own:" The Making of the Confederacy* (New York: Free Press, 1994), 138, 162.

29. Newsom, "Intrepid Gray Warriors," 4-12; Cooling, *Forts Henry and Donelson*, 259-260; *Official Records*, 7: 374, 376.

30. *Official Records*, 17, Pt. 1: 666, 669, 673-674; 24, Pt. 1: 737-739, 747-748; Hewitt, *Port Hudson*, 45, 62, 122; Newsom, "Intrepid Gray Warriors," 78-91; Stephen E. Ambrose, "Struggle for Vicksburg," in *Americans at War* (Jackson: University Press of Mississsippi, 1997), 18-24.

31. Simpson, *Hood's Texas Brigade*, 321. See also Cozzens, *This Terrible Sound*, 260.

32. *Official Records*, 32, Pt. 2: 536, 546; Simpson, *Hood's Texas Brigade*, 383-388.

33. J. B. Polley, *Hood's Texas Brigade: Its Marches, Its Battles, Its Accomplishments* (New York: Neale Publishing Co., 1910), 226-227, later wrote that Gregg "held himself aloof from his inferiors in rank," and never won their hearts.

34. Quotation, Freeman, *R. E. Lee*, 3: 287. There are many versions of this dramatic incident. Dayton Kelley, *General Lee and Hood's Texas Brigade at the Battle of the Wilderness* (Hillsboro: Hill Junior College Press, 1969), discusses fully the incident and accounts by members of the brigade; see especially the appendix, 57-70. A more recent account is given by Robert E. Krick, "'Lee to the Rear' the Texans Cried," in Gary W. Gallagher, ed., *The Wilderness Campaign* (Chapel Hill: University of North Carolina Press, 1997), 160-200.

35. Simpson, *Hood's Texas Brigade*, 398-403; Gary E. Gallagher, ed., *Fighting for the Confederacy: The Personal Recollections of General Edward Porter Alexander* (Chapel Hill: University of North Carolina Press, 1989), 358; E. P. Alexander, *Military Memoirs of A Confederate* (Reprint; Bloomington: Indiana University Press, 1962), 504-507; Rhea, *Battle of the Wilderness*, 302-306; Evander M. Law, "From the Wilderness to Cold Harbor," *Battles and Leaders*, 4: 125.

36. Simpson, *Hood's Texas Brigade*, 410-412. See also William D. Matter, *If It Takes All Summer: The Battle of Spotsylvania* (Chapel Hill: University of North Carolina Press, 1988), 154-155; and Gordon C. Rhea, *The Battles for Spotsylvania Court House and the Road to Yellow Tavern, May 7-12, 1864* (Baton Rouge: Louisiana State University Press, 1997), 146-147.

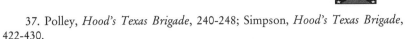

37. Polley, *Hood's Texas Brigade*, 240-248; Simpson, *Hood's Texas Brigade*, 422-430.

38. *Official Records*, 36, Pt. 3: 894-895.

39. Ibid., 42, Pt. 2: 1301, 1304; Simpson, *Hood's Texas Brigade*, 249-255; Richard Sommers, *Richmond Redeemed: The Siege at Petersburg* (Garden City, NY: Doubleday & Co., 1981), 17-18, 28-34, 45-47, 434.

40. Simpson, *Hood's Texas Brigade*, 438-440.

41. Ibid., 441-442; Freeman, *Lee's Lieutenants*, 3: 594; *New Handbook of Texas*, 3: 329.

42. *New Handbook of Texas*, 3: 486; *The Confederate General*, 3: 70.

43. *The Confederate General*, 3: 70; *New Handbook of Texas*, 3: 486; Bowden, *The Exodus of Federal Forces from Texas, 1861*, 71-73.

44. L. B. Giles, "Terry's Texas Rangers," 11-19; J. K. P. Blackburn, "Reminiscences of the Terry Rangers," 96-106.

45. *Official Records*, 10, Pt. 1: 627, 923-924; Blackburn, "Reminiscences of the Terry Rangers," 117-120. Blackburn claims that the Rangers attacked so quickly that Forrest's men did not get in the battle. The version in Wyeth, *That Devil Forrest*, 64-67, is somewhat different.

46. *Official Records*, 20, Pt. 1: 774, 966-967; Giles, "Terry's Texas Rangers," 34-39; Blackburn, "Reminiscences of the Terry Rangers," 134-138; McDonough, *Stone's River*, 90-91.

47. Giles, "Terry's Texas Rangers," 41-43; *Official Records*, 23, Pt. 2: 821, 827, 834, 848, 960.

48. Ibid., 30, Pt. 1: 232; 30, Pt. 2: 522; 31, Pt. 1: 453, 545, 549.

49. Ibid., 38, Pt. 3: 642, 657, 945, 950; Giles, "Terry's Texas Rangers," 63-66; *The Confederate General*, 3: 71.

50. *Official Records*, 38, Pt. 3: 964.

51. Tom Harrison's brother, James, had been promoted to brigadier general three weeks earlier. Ibid., 44: 407, 409; 47, Pt. 1: 1045, 1132; Blackburn, "Reminiscences of the Terry Rangers," 174.

52. Giles, "Terry's Texas Rangers," 13; *The Confederate General*, 3: 71; *New Handbook of Texas*, 3: 486-487; Campbell, *Grass-Roots Reconstruction in Texas*, 169-172, 174, 184. Frank Batchelor, a young lieutenant who served as acting adjutant under Harrison stated that he found no fault with Harrison "except that he is addicted to getting drunk & does it when a battle is pending & has thus lost the confidence of his men." Rugeley, *Batchelor-Turner Letters*, 44-45.

53. William J. Davis, ed., *The Partisan Rangers of the Confederate States Army: Memoirs of General Adam R. Johnson* (Austin: State House Press, 1995), 1-37; *New Handbook of Texas*, 3: 951; *The Confederate General*, 3: 169.

54. Johnson, *Partisan Rangers*, 52-70; Cooling, *Forts Henry and Donelson*, 138, 147, 151, 158, 201.

55. Johnson, *Partisan Rangers*, 104-109; Lorine Letcher Butler, *John Morgan and His Men* (Philadelphia: Dorrance & Co., 1960), 190-191.

56. Johnson, *Partisan Rangers*, 112-133.

57. Ibid., 134-150; Cecil F. Holland, *Morgan and His Raiders: A Biography of the Confederate General* (New York: Macmillan Co., 1943), 227-228, 233-234, 243-244.

58. Johnson, *Partisan Rangers*, 150-161; Holland, *Morgan and His Raiders*, 268-269, 299-300; Basil Duke, *A History of Morgan's Cavalry* (Reprint; Bloomington: Indiana University Press, 1960), 507-508.

59. Quotation from General Ewing, *Official Records*, 39, Pt. 2: 245; Holland, *Morgan and His Raiders*, 312; Johnson, *Partisan Rangers*, 158-172.

60. Johnson, *Partisan Rangers*, 173-174, 178-179, 196-200. William C. Davis, "Adam Rankin Johnson," *The Confederate General*, 3: 170, notes that while many sources say that Johnson's sight was completely destroyed an extant photograph (shown on p. 168, Vol. 3, *The Confederate General*) shows him wearing crude goggles with what appear to be lenses, indicating he must have retained some sight.

61. *New Handbook of Texas*, 3: 951; *Medical Histories of Confederate Generals*, 116; Johnson, *Partisan Rangers*, 203-204.

62. Both Gen. Marcus J. Wright, *Texas in the Civil War*, 13-14, and Richard McMurry, *Two Great Rebel Armies*, 164, list Moore as a Texas Civil War general.

63. *New Handbook of Texas*, 4: 821; *The Confederate General*, 4: 180.

64. Joseph E. Chance, *The Second Texas Infantry: From Shiloh to Vicksburg* (Austin: Eakin Press, 1981), 1-14.

65. *Official Records*, 4: 155, 166, 169; 10, Pt. 1: 560-561; Chance, *Second Texas Infantry*, 15-25.

66. Chance, *Second Texas Infantry*, 26-33.

67. *Official Records*, 10, Pt. 1: 572.

68. Ibid., 570 (quotation); Daniel, *Shiloh*, 273; Sword, *Shiloh: Bloody April*, 391.

69. *Official Records*, 10, Pt. 1: 563-564; Chance, *Second Texas Infantry*, 37. I agree with Kevin R. Young, *To The Tyrants Never Yield: A Texas Civil War Sampler* (Plano: Wordware Publishing, Inc., 1992), 116, who writes "it is highly possible that Hardee was using Moore and his regiment as a scapegoat for his own military blundering."

70. *Official Records*, 10, Pt. 1: 533, 789, Pt. 2: 549; Chance, *Second Texas Infantry*, 47; *The Confederate General*, 4: 180.

71. *Official Records*, 17, Pt. 1: 378, 383, 393-400, 443; Chance, *Second Texas Infantry*, 43-81; Young, *To The Tyrants Never Yield*, 111-122; Peter Cozzens, *The Darkest Days of the War: The Battles of Iuka and Corinth* (Chapel Hill: University of North Carolina Press, 1997), 181-182, 259-270.

72. Chance, *Second Texas Infantry*, 86-89. Nathaniel C. Hughes, Jr., *General William T. Hardee: Old Reliable* (Baton Rouge: Louisiana State University Press, 1965), makes no mention of the controversy.

73. *Official Records*, 24, Pt. 1: 380-383; Chance, *Second Texas Infantry*, 89-108; Walter H. Mays, ed., "The Vicksburg Diary of M. K. Simons, 1863," *Texas Military History* 5 (Spring 1965): 28-29; Arnold, *Grant Wins the War*, 247-248, 252-255.

74. Chance, *Second Texas Infantry*, 146-149.

75. *Official Records*, 31, Pt. 2: 704-706; Sword, *Mountains Touched With Fire*, 208-209, 215-219, 313-314; McDonough, *Chattanooga*, 134-140, 207-208. After the battle Moore, Walthall, and Pettus were all highly critical of J. K. Jackson's role in the battle.

76. Ibid., 31, Pt. 3: 741, 849, 852-853; Chance, *Second Texas Infantry*, 154-158.

77. *New Handbook of Texas*, 4: 821.

78. William C. Davis, "Felix Hutson Robertson," in *The Confederate General*, 5: 100. Robertson, a harsh disciplinarian, was not well liked by his men. Larry J. Daniel, *Cannoneers in Gray: The Field Artillery of The Army of Tennessee* (University of Alabama Press, 1984), 88, states that Robertson "was the most unpopular officer in the artillery."

79. Ibid., 100; "The Life Story of Brig. Gen. Felix Robertson," *Texana*, 8 (No. 2, 1970): 161-168; Daniel, *Shiloh*, 154, 195, 229, 273; McDonough, *Shiloh—Hell Before Night*, 201, 243-244; Sword, *Shiloh: Bloody April*, 166, 236, 239-241, 392-393; Nathaniel C. Hughes, Jr., *The Pride of the Confederate Artillery: The Washington Artillery in the Army of Tennessee* (Baton Rouge: Louisiana State University Press, 1997), 42.

80. *Official Records*, 20, Pt. 1: 665-666, 758-759; William C. Davis, *Breckinridge: Statesman, Soldier, Symbol* (Baton Rouge: Louisiana State University Press, 1974), 340-346, 351-353; Thomas L. Connelly, *Autumn of Glory: The Army of Tennessee, 1862-1865* (Baton Rouge: Louisiana State University Press, 1971), 63-65, 83; Daniel, *Cannoneers in Gray*, 66-68.

81. *Official Records*, 10, Pt. 2: 288, 32, Pt. 3: 872, 38, Pt. 3: 643, 659, 961; "Life Story of Brig. Gen. Felix Robertson," 171-174; Connelly, *Autumn of Glory*, 91; Cozzens, *This Terrible Sound*, 203, 300, 496.

82. Davis, *Breckinridge*, 457-461; William C. Davis, "Massacre at Saltville," *Civil War Times Illustrated* 9 (February 1971): 4-11, 43-48; Thomas D. Mays, *The Saltville Massacre* (Abilene: McWhiney Foundation Press, 1998), esp. 54-56, 66-67. In an interview many years later with Helen Pool Baldwin recounting his Civil War experiences, Robertson did not mention this affair. "Life Story of Brig. Gen. Felix Robertson," 154-182.

83. Welsh, *Medical Histories of Confederate Generals*, 186.

84. *The Confederate General*, 5: 101; *Official Records*, 47, Pt. 2: 986-987, 1028, 1127.

85. *New Handbook of Texas*, 5: 616; "Life Story of Brig. Gen. Felix Robertson," 181.

86. Quotation, Harold B. Simpson, ed., Jerome B. Robertson, *Touched with Valor: Civil War Papers and Casualty Reports of Hood's Texas Brigade* (Hillsboro: Hill Junior College Press, 1964), 1.

87. Most sources, including *New Handbook of Texas*, 5: 617, and *The Confederate General*, 5: 102, give Woodford as the county of birth, but Simpson, ed., *Touched with Valor*, 2 fn, notes that his son stated that Christian County was the place of birth.

88. Simpson, ed., *Touched with Valor*, 3-7.

89. Ibid., 7-9; Wooster, "Membership of the Texas Secession Convention," 163-179.

90. *Official Records*, 11, Pt. 2: 444-446, 12, Pt. 2: 609-618; *Official Records, Supplement*, 2, Pt. 1: 430-434; Mamie Yeary, comp., *Reminiscences of the Boys in Gray, 1861-65* (Dallas: Smith & Lamar, 1912), 816-817; Polley, *Hood's Texas Brigade*, 66-70, 103-108; Simpson, *Hood's Texas Brigade*, 124-125, 150-157.

91. Simpson, ed., *Touched with Valor*, 12; Simpson, *Hood's Texas Brigade*, 167, 194-198.

92. *Official Records*, 27, Pt. 2: 339-340, 404-412; Simpson, *Hood's Texas Brigade*, 268-289; Hood, *Advance and Retreat*, 54-59.

93. *Official Records*, 30, Pt. 2: 510-519; Simpson, *Hood's Texas Brigade*, 297-328; Steven E. Woodworth, *A Deep Steady Thunder: The Battle of Chickamauga* (Abilene: McWhiney Foundation, 1998), 49-51, 86-87.

94. Robertson, *Touched with Valor*, 52-57. Harold Simpson, 416 who wrote the definitive history of Hood's Brigade, doubts that the recruitment plan would have worked. There were few potential volunteers left in Texas by 1864 and the Brigade would not accept conscripts. Simpson notes that Robertson did not give up on the plan. In October 1864 he wrote to Texas Governor Pendleton Murrah urging the chief executive to write President Davis requesting that the Brigade be allowed to come home to recruit during the winter of 1864-65. Simpson, *Hood's Texas Brigade*, 379 fn.

95. Ibid., 384-385; *Official Records*, 31, Pt. 1: 467; Robertson, *Touched with Valor*, 13-15; Mrs. A. V. Winkler, *The Confederate Capital and Hood's Texas Brigade* (Austin: Von Boeckmann, 1894), 151.

96. Miles V. Smith, "Reminiscences of the Civil War," 48, quoted in Simpson, *Hood's Texas Brigade*, 386. See also Polley, *Hood's Texas Brigade*, 225-226. For a more critical view of Robertson by a fellow Texan, see Langston James Goree, ed., *The Thomas Jewett Goree Letters* (Bryan: Family History Foundation, 1981), 200.

97. Simpson, ed., *Touched with Valor*, 15-21; *New Handbook of Texas*, 5: 618.

98. Judith Ann Benner, *Sul Ross: Soldier, Statesman, Educator* (College Station: Texas A&M University Press, 1983), 3-34; T. Michael Parrish, introduction, *Personal Civil War Letters of General Lawrence Sullivan Ross*, ed. Shelly Morrison (Austin: prev. pub., 1994), ix.

99. Benner, *Sul Ross*, 35-61; Parrish, *Personal Civil War Letters of Ross*, ix.

100. May 28, 1861, is the date of marriage given by Judith Ann Benner in her essay on Ross, *New Handbook of Texas*, 5: 668, but in her biography *Sul Ross*, 63-65, she states that the wedding had to be postponed until a date in June.

101. Quotation from *Official Records*, 8: 302; see also *Official Records, Supplement*, 1, Pt. 1: 542-544; Morrison, ed., *Personal Civil War Letters of Ross*, 18-20; William C. Billingsley, ed., "'Such Is War': The Confederate Memoirs of Newton Asbury Keen," *Texas Military History* 6 (Winter 1967): 248; Cutrer, *Ben McCulloch*, 287.

102. Morrison, ed., *Personal Civil War Letters of Ross*, 21-26; Shea and Hess, *Pea Ridge*, 102, 105, 187-188, 267, 313.

103. Benner, *Sul Ross*, 78-81; Homer L. Kerr, ed., *Fighting With Ross' Texas Cavalry Brigade: The Diary of George L. Griscom, Adjutant, 9th Texas Cavalry Regiment* (Hillsboro: Hill Junior College Press, 1976), 38-43; Victor M. Rose, *Ross' Texas Brigade: Being a Narrative of Events Connected with Its Service in the Late War Between the States* (1881; reprint, Kennesaw, GA: Continental Book Co., 1960), 163-164.

104. *Official Records*, 17, Pt. 1: 393-394; A. W. Sparks, *The War Between the States As I Saw It* (Tyler: Lee & Burnett, 1901), 275-276; Cozzens, *The Darkest Days of the War*, 266-267, 286.

105. *Official Records*, 33, Pt. 1: 123; Pt. 3, 947, 959, 1027, 1041; Benner, *Sul Ross*, 88-93. In letters to his wife, Ross complained "Col Whitfield has been frol-

icing around seeing his friends & Enjoying himself and scheming to get the appointment of Brigd Genl, leaving me all the work to do." Morison, ed., *Personal Civil War Letters of Ross*, 49.

106. Parrish, introduction, *Personal Civil War Letters of Ross*, xi.

107. *Official Records*, 32, Pt. 1: 326-328, 365-369, 385-386; Welsh, *Medical Histories of Confederate Generals*, 189.

108. *Official Records*, 38, Pt. 3: 955, 963-965; Billingsley, ed., "Such Is War," Pt. 2: 56, Pt. 3: 111; Barron, *The Lone Star Defenders*, 200-204.

109. *Official Records*, 38, Pt. 2: 826; Barron, *Lone Star Defenders*, 205-215.

110. Kerr, ed., *Fighting with Ross' Texas Cavalry*, 186-198; Wyeth, *That Devil Forrest*, 496-507.

111. Benner, *Sul Ross*, 112-113.

112. Ibid., 115-132. Welsh, *Medical Histories of Confederate Generals*, 189, states that death was from "acute congestion of the stomach and bowels."

113. *The Confederate General*, 6: 130; *New Handbook of Texas*, 6: 945; *Biographical Directory of the American Congress, 1774-1949* (Washington: Government Printing Office, 1950), 2006.

114. *New Handbook of Texas*, 6: 945; Sifakis, *Compendium of the Confederate Armies: Texas*, 50; Cutrer, *Ben McCulloch*, 287; Sparks, *War Between the States*, 171.

115. Tom Cutrer in an article on Whitfield's Legion, *New Handbook of Texas*, 6: 945, points out the unit was not properly a legion, which contains artillery, cavalry, and infantry. Whitfield's command consisted entirely of cavalry, although the unit was dismounted from April to October 1862.

116. *Official Records*, 17, Pt. 1: 123, 128-129; Cozzens, *Darkest Days of the War*, 86-92, 96-99, 101-106. Welsh, *Medical Histories of Confederate Generals*, 233; Sparks, *War Between the States*, 220-221.

117. *Official Records*, 13, Pt. 1: 123, Kerr, ed., *Fighting With Ross' Texas Cavalry Brigade*, 59-60; Barron, *Lone Star Defenders*, 127-142; Cozzens, *Darkest Days of the War*, 182-284.

118. Morrison, ed., *Personal Civil War Letters of Ross*, 49, 53; *The Confederate General*, 6:130.

119. *Official Records*, 24, Pt. 3: 941, 959; 30, Pt. 2: 815; 52, Pt. 2: 490, 497, 577; Welsh, *Medical Histories of Confederate Generals*, 233; Sparks, *War Between the States*, 237-240. Sparks, a member of Whitfield's Brigade, remembered Whitfield as "straight as an arrow—he looked every inch the soldier." Ibid., 351.

120. Welsh, *Medical Histories of Confederate Generals*, 233; Charles Hale, "Political Leadership in Texas During Reconstruction" (M.A. thesis, Lamar State College of Technology, 1965), 23.

121. Alvy L. King, *Louis T. Wigfall: Southern Fire-eater* (Baton Rouge: Louisiana State University Press, 1970), 29.

122. Ibid., 36-46; Eric H. Walther, *The Fire-eaters* (Baton Rouge: Louisiana State University Press, 1992), 162-164, 168-169.

123. Another daughter, Fanny, was born six years later.

124. Walther, *The Fire-eaters*, 171-172; King, *Louis T. Wigfall*, 48-78; Patsy McDaniel Spaw, ed., *The Texas Senate: Republic to Civil War, 1836-1861* (College Station: Texas A&M University Press, 1990), 279-280, 312-313; Billy D. Led-

better, "The Election of Louis T. Wigfall," *Southwestern Historical Quarterly* 77 (October 1973): 241-154. Most writers have attributed Wigfall's victory to the impact of John Brown's raid, but Ledbetter argues that Wigfall's election was *not* a reaction to the affair but "was a party victory more than anything else, and the October raid in Virginia had no determinable impact on the Texas senate race." Ibid., 254.

125. King, *Louis T. Wigfall*, 19-90, 97-99; Walther, *The Fire-eaters*, 172, 179-182.

126. King, *Louis T. Wigfall*, 103-105.

127. Ibid., 108-115; Walther, *The Fire-eaters*, 188-189.

128. King, *Louis T. Wigfall*, 118-121; W. A. Swanberg, *First Blood: The Story of Fort Sumter* (New York: Charles Scribner's Sons, 1959), 177-278, 318-320.

129. King, *Louis T. Wigfall*, 122. William H. Russell, the well-known British journalist, was among those to whom Wigfall related his exploit. According to Russell, Wigfall was under the influence of alcohol at the time, a characteristic not uncommon to the South Carolina-Texas fire-eater. See William H. Russell, *My Diary North and South* (Reprint; New York: Harper & Row, 1954), 62-63.

130. King, *Louis T. Wigfall*, 126-128; Davis, *A Government of Our Own*, 327, 394-395.

131. King, *Louis T. Wigfall*, 129-134; Simpson, *Hood's Texas Brigade*, 47-48. Simpson, 74, points out that for a short period of time the regiment was referred to as the Second Texas Infantry, but Wigfall protested the "second ranking" and Col. John C. Moore's Texas regiment, also raised at the time, became the Second Texas Infantry Regiment.

132. Ibid., 60-64, 71-74.

133. King, *Louis T. Wigfall*, 135-141; James B. Warner, "A Legislative History of Texas During the Civil War" (M.A. thesis, Lamar State College of Technology, 1971), 40; Simpson, *Hood's Texas Brigade*, 88. In his work on the brigade, Colonel Simpson, 88-89 fn, quotes a young Texan who wrote "during the winter General Wigfall was elected a Confederate State's [sic.] Senator from Texas, for which Texas has our thanks, thereby ridding us of a braggadocio—and causing to be placed at our head, the great and gallant Hood."

134. Wilfred Buck Yearns, *The Confederate Congress* (Athens: University of Georgia Press, 1960), 65, 70, 150, 158, 200; King, *Louis T. Wigfall*, 137-138, 142-151, 205-208.

135. Ibid., 186-193, 209-213; Symonds, *Joseph E. Johnston*, 177-180, 329, 341-343, Walther, *The Fire-eaters*, 190.

136. Both King, *Louis T. Wigfall*, 231, and Walther, *The Fire-eaters*, 191, state that his death was from an undisclosed cause. Welsh, *Medical Histories of Confederate Generals*, 235, using the Internment Record, Galveston Health Department, gives apoplexy as cause of death.

137. Hugh H. Young, "Two Texas Patriots," *Southwestern Historical Quarterly* 44 (July 1940), 18-23; *New Handbook of Texas*, 6: 1130.

138. Horton, *Maxey*, 22-27; *The Confederate General*, 6: 172.

139. Sword, *Shiloh: Bloody April*, 206.

140. *Official Records*, 17, Pt. 2: 764; McDonough, *War in Kentucky*, 264, 272, 280; *The Confederate General*, 6: 172.

141. Quotation from *Official Records*, 20, Pt. 1: 745; see also McDonough, *Stone's River*, 97-100; Welsh, *Medical Histories of Confederate Generals*, 242.

142. *Official Records*, 23, Pt. 2: 613, 735.

143. Welsh, *Medical Histories of Confederate Generals*, 242; *The Confederate General*, 6: 173.

144. Welsh, *Medical Histories of Confederate Generals*, 60, 142-143; *Official Records*, 38, Pt. 3: 903-904, 909.

145. Ibid., 39, Pt. 1: 760, 766, 816-819, 822-823; Welsh, *Medical Histories of Confederate Generals*, 243; Young, "Two Texas Patriots," 24-25.

146. Ibid., 28-32; *New Handbook of Texas*, 6: 1130; Welsh, *Medical Histories of Confederate Generals*, 243.

147. Ibid., 243.

CHAPTER SIX

1. E. B. Long, ed., *Personal Memoirs of U.S. Grant* (Cleveland: World Publishing Co., 1950), 187; Roland, *Albert Sidney Johnston*, 290; Thomas L. Connelly and Archer Jones, *The Politics of Command: Factions and Ideas in Confederate Strategy* (Baton Rouge: Louisiana State University Press, 1972), 95-99.

2. Woodworth, *Davis and His Generals*, 98; McDonough, *Shiloh*, 73. See also Steven E. Woodworth, "When Merit Was Not Enough: Albert Sidney Johnston and Confederate Defeat in the West, 1862," in Woodworth, ed., *Civil War Generals in Defeat* (Lawrence: University of Kansas Press, 1999), 9-27.

3. This is based upon reading of contemporary Civil War literature. Such evaluations are obviously quite subjective. Although R. E. Lee has had his critics, notably Tom Connelly and Alan T. Nolan, in recent years, most historians would probably agree with Gary W. Gallagher that "the greatest single obstacle to Northern victory after June 1862 was R. E. Lee and his army of Northern Virginia." *Lee the Soldier* (Lincoln: University of Nebraska Press, 1996), 286. Beauregard, for all his idiosyncrasies, was a competent strategist. Joseph E. Johnston is perhaps the most difficult to evaluate. Frank Vandiver and others have written favorably of Johnston, but recent works by Albert Castel, William C. Davis, Joseph T. Glatthaar, Richard McMurry, and Steven Woodworth have raised serious questions about his ability to command a large army.

For an interesting and informative comparative study of Confederate commanding generals see Richard M. McMurry, *Two Great Rebel Armies: An Essay in Confederate Military History* (Chapel Hill: University of North Carolina Press, 1989), 118-139. See also Joseph B. Mitchell, *Military Leaders in the Civil War* (New York: Putman, 1972) and W. J. Wood, *Civil War Generalship: The Art of Command* (Westport, CT: Praeger, 1997). Neither Mitchell nor Wood include evaluations of Albert Sidney Johnston.

4. Mitchell, *Military Leaders in the Civil War*, 204-209; Woodworth, *Jefferson Davis and His Generals*, 303; David Coffey, *John Bell Hood and the Struggle for Atlanta* (Abilene: McWhiney Foundation Press, 1998), 114. Albert Castel, who believes Hood, with the possible exception of Ambrose Burnside, was the least intelligent of all Civil War commanders, concedes that Hood inherited "a virtually impossible situation which it is doubtful [Robert E.] Lee himself could have salvaged." Castel, *Decision in the West*, 562, and Castel, *Winning and Losing in the*

Civil War (Columbia: University of South Carolina Press, 1996), 122. In a satire on "The Wizard of Oz," William C. Davis, *The Lost Cause: Myths and Realities of the Confederacy*, 30, joins Castel in questioning Hood's intelligence. He likens Joe Johnston to the Lion of Oz, who lacked courage, Pierre Beauregard to the Tin Man, who did not have a heart, and Hood to the Scarecrow, who had no brain.

5. Wood, *Civil War Generalship*, 228.

6. Woodworth, *Jefferson Davis and His Generals*; Mitchell, *Military Leaders in the Civil War*; McMurry, *John Bell Hood*; Connelly, *Autumn of Glory*, esp. 321-323, 430-431, 502-504, 506-509. In an essay on Civil War generals in Gabor S. Borritt, ed., *Why the Confederacy Lost* (New York: Oxford University Press, 1992), 89, Gary W. Gallagher links Hood with John Pope and Benjamin Butler "on a lower rung of proficiency" than John C. Pemberton, Nathaniel P. Banks, William S. Rosecrans, and Don Carlos Buell.

7. Some examples of brigade strength: Hood's Brigade—1,922 effectives (April 1862), 1,110 effectives (Gettysburg campaign), 431 effectives (July 1864); Wharton's Brigade—2,305 effectives (January 1863); Tom Harrison's Brigade—1,618 effectives (July 1864); Maxey's Brigade—2,622 effectives (May 1863). Often the effective strength, i. e., present for duty, was much smaller than the overall strength which included those ill, on leave, and absent without leave. Simpson, *Hood's Texas Brigade*, 94, 285, 453; *Official Records*, 17, Pt. 2, 835; 24, Pt. 3: 734, 936; 38, Pt. 2: 761.

8. See Douglas Southall Freeman, *Lee's Lieutenants*, 1: 198, 534, 853; 2: 695; McMurry, *John Bell Hood*, 58-59, 88-89.

9. Granbury's only mistake as a commander came at Jonesboro, when he led his brigade after Kilpatrick's cavalry rather than hitting the flank of the Union infantry.

10. In studying his Civil War career, one admires Maxey for his patient forbearance. Time and time again he was transferred just before a major battle in which he would have an opportunity to show his military skills.

11. Robert E. Krick, one of the most knowledgable authorities of the Army of Northern Virginia, says that "Rosser's subordinates invariably attested to the general's bravery, but with almost as much unanimity they complained of his incompetence, particularly when he assumed division command in 1864." *Encyclopedia of the Confederacy*, 3: 1347.

12. Krick, writing in *The Second Day at Gettysburg: Essays on Confederate and Union Leadership*, ed. Gary W. Gallagher (Kent, OH: Kent State University Press, 1993), 63, describes Wigfall as "a military failure as pronounced as any in the army, excepting, always [Robert] Toombs."

Bibliography

Sources for a study of Texas Confederate generals are abundant. Most important are the 128 volumes of *The War of the Rebellion: A Compilation of the Official Records of the Union and Confederate Armies* (Washington: Government Printing Office, 1880-1901). These volumes, particularly those in Series I, are indispensable as they contain the correspondence and reports for all Civil War military operations that were available at the time of publication. In recent years a number of additional materials have been located. These are being published as *Supplement to the Official Records of the Union and Confederate Armies*, 10 volumes (Wilmington, NC: Broadfoot Publishing Company, 1996); additional volumes to be forthcoming. Additional accounts by participants, first published in *Century Magazine* two decades after the war and then published in book form, are found in Robert U. Johnson and Clarence C. Buel, eds., *Battles & Leaders of the Civil War*, 4 vols. (New York, 1888; reprint, New York: Thomas Yoseloff, 1956).

A number of general works provide biographical information on Confederate generals from Texas. Particularly valuable are the six volumes edited by William C. Davis, *The Confederate General* (National Historical Society, 1991). These volumes provide a photograph and brief (usually two pages) biographical sketch of every Confederate general officer including those individuals appointed by Edmund Kirby Smith but not confirmed by the president and Senate. The entries, written by leading scholars including Anne J. Bailey, Alwyn Barr, Norman Brown, Thomas Cutrer, and Lawrence L. Hewitt, are most helpful in putting together data on Texas Confederates. The same may be said for the six-volume *New*

Handbook of Texas, ed. Ron Tyler (Austin: Texas State Historical Association, 1996), which also includes entries for Texas general officers.

Biographical information, including photographs, is also found in Marcus J. Wright, comp., *Texas in the War, 1861-1865*, ed. Harold B. Simpson (Hillsboro: Hill Junior College Press, 1965). As noted in the endnotes, I have used this work heavily in determining the names of general officers from Texas. The list provided in this work differs slightly from Ezra J. Warner, *Generals in Gray: Lives of Confederate Commanders* (Baton Rouge: Louisiana State University Press, 1959), a valuable work containing photographs and short sketches of Confederate general officers.

Jon Wakelyn, *Biographical Directory of the Confederacy* (Westport, CT: Greenwood Press, 1977); Richard Current, ed., *Encyclopedia of the Confederacy,* 4 vols. (New York: Simon and Schuster, 1993); and Stewart Sifakis, *Who's Who in the Civil War* (New York: Facts on File, 1988), also contain brief biographical sketches on some Texas Confederate generals. O. M. Roberts, chair of the Texas secession convention, Confederate colonel, and later governor of Texas, provides biographical information on most Lone Star generals in Volume 11 of Clement A. Evans, ed., *Confederate Military History*, 12 vols. (Atlanta: Confederate Publishing Company, 1899). Stewart Sifakis, *Compendium of Confederate Armies: Texas* (New York: Facts on File, 1995) is helpful in determining information on Texas regiments and their commanders.

Medical Histories of Confederate Generals (Kent, OH: Kent State University Press, 1995) by Jack D. Welsh, M.D., is a particularly valuable work in tracing injuries and illnesses of Confederate general officers in the war. This work also provides information on the death and burial of general officers, often based upon death certifcates and burial records. Helpful also is Bruce S. Allardice, *More Generals In Gray* (Baton Rouge: Louisiana State University Press, 1995), a companion volume to Warner's *Generals in Gray* cited above. Allardice's work is especially useful in finding information for Texans appointed brigadier general by Kirby Smith but not approved by the president and the Senate.

Biographies have been written for a number of the Lone Star generals in gray. Albert Sidney Johnston's son, William Preston Johnston, wrote the first work biography of his father, *The Life of General Albert Sidney Johnston* (New York: D. Appleton & Co., Inc., 1878) based upon interviews with contemporaries and reports and papers available at the time. Not surprising, this study is highly favorable of Johnston. More objective and better balanced is the modern account by Charles P. Roland of Tulane University, *Albert Sidney Johnston: Soldier of Three Republics* (Austin: University of Texas Press, 1964). Based upon a careful examination of manuscript and published materials, *Soldier of Three Republics* weighs both the strengths and weaknesses of the Confederacy's highest ranking field commander. Roland concedes that Johnston made mistakes but points out that Grant, Sherman, and Lee made similar errors early in the war and went on to become outstanding army commanders. Roland believes Johnston learned from his failures and had he lived would have been "an incalcuable asset to the Confederacy" (p. 351).

John Bell Hood, the other Texan to command a major army, defended his actions in his memoirs, *Advance and Retreat: Personal Experiences in the United States and Confederate States Armies* (New Orleans: Published for the Hood Orphan Memorial Fund, 1880). Hood was the subject of two biographies written in the late 1940s: Richard O'Connor, *Hood: Cavalier General* (New York: Prentice Hall, Inc., 1949) and John P. Dyer, *The Gallant Hood* (Indianapolis: Bobbs-Merrill Co., Inc., 1950). The Dyer volume is the stronger of the two. More recently Richard M. McMurry's *John Bell Hood and the War for Southern Independence* (Lexington: University Press of Kentucky, 1982) has provided the most in-depth picture of Hood available. McMurry depicts the Texan as a tragic figure who while possessing courage, audacity, and a strategic sense lacked "important attributes necessary to any army commander" (p. 167). Mary Boykin Chesnut, the famous Confederate diarist, provides additional insights into Hood's character in *Mary Chesnut's Civil War*, ed. C. Vann Woodward (New Haven: Yale University Press, 1981).

Three of the five Texans who commanded divisions as major generals (Sam Maxey, Tom Rosser, and Tom Green) have been the subject of biographies. *Samuel Bell Maxey: A Biography* by Louise Horton (Austin: University of Texas Press, 1974) is a scholarly, well-researched volume but devotes only one chapter to Maxey's Civil War years. The majority of the book covers Maxey's long postwar career in the United States Senate. For additional information on Maxey one should read Mrs. Horton's "General Sam Bell Maxey: His Defense of North Texas and Indian Territory," *Southwestern Historical Quarterly* 74 (April 1971): 507-524, and her "Samuel Bell Maxey on the Coke-Davis Controversy," ibid. 72 (April 1969): 519-525; "The Star Route Conspiracies" *Texana* 7 (No. 3, 1969): 220-233; and "Samuel Bell Maxey," *New Handbook of Texas*, 4: 580-581. In addition see John C. Waugh, *Sam Bell Maxey and the Confederate Indians* (Fort Worth: Ryan Place Publishers, 1995); David B. Gracy, II, ed. and introd., *Maxey's Texas* (Austin: Pemberton Press, 1965); and J. Elden Spencer, "Samuel Bell Maxey," in *Ten More Texans in Gray*, ed. W. C. Nunn (Hillsboro: Hill Junior College Press, 1980).

Millard Kessler Bushong and Dean McKoin Bushong, *Fightin' Tom Rosser* (Shippenburg, PA: Beidel Printing House, 1983) provides a good outline for Rosser's Civil War years but contains little information on his youth in Texas. A more recent publication, *Riding With Rosser*, ed. by S.

Roger Keller (Shippenburg, PA: Burd Street Press, 1997), is Rosser's personal account of his war experiences written for a Virginia newspaper, preserved by family members, and edited by Keller. Since George A. Custer was a close friend of Rosser, Custer's biographies contain references to Rosser. See also Custer's own "Battling with the Sioux on the Yellowstone," *Galaxy Magazine* (July 1876) reprinted in Paul A. Hutton, ed., *The Custer Reader* (Lincoln: University of Nebraska Press, 1992), 201-219; and Elizabeth B. Custer, *Boots and Saddles, Or Life in Dakota with General Custer* (New York: Harper & Brothers, 1885).

Odie B. Faulk, *General Tom Green: Fightin' Texan* (Waco: Texian Press, 1963) is a brief biography of the popular Texan. See also Alwyn Barr, "Tom Green: The Forrest of the Trans-Mississippi," *Lincoln Herald* 88 (Summer 1986): 39-42; Sam Houston Dixon and Louis Wiltz Kemp, *The Heroes of San Jacinto* (Houston: Anson Jones Press, 1932), 78-79; Kathleen Williams, "Thomas Green," *Ten More Texans in Gray*, 19-39; Curtis M. Milburn, "Brigadier General Tom Green of Texas," *East Texas Historical Journal* 32 (Spring 1994): 3-11; and Anne Bailey, "Thomas Green," in *The Confederate General*, 3: 32-33.

Surprisingly, there is no major biography for John A. Wharton, the wealthy Texas planter who became a highly successful cavalry officer. Most accounts of Terry's Texas Rangers (described below) give considerable information on Wharton. Anne Bailey's "John Austin Wharton," in *The Confederate General*, 6: 122-123, is especially strong and probably the best single source of information on Wharton. For the tragic events leading to Wharton's death see George W. Baylor, "My Troubles with General John A. Wharton," in *Into the Far, Wild Country: True Tales of the Old Southwest*, ed. Jerry D. Thompson (El Paso: Texas Western Press, 1996), 232-246.

Arthur Pendleton Bagby, promoted to major general by Kirby Smith but not approved by either President Davis or the Confederate Senate, has not been the subject of a biography. The best accounts of Bagby are Alwyn Barr, "Arthur Pendleton Bagby," *The Confederate General*, 6: 178-179, and Craig H. Roell, "Arthur Pendleton Bagby," *New Handbook of Texas*, 1: 332. See also Martin Hardwick Hall, "The Court-Martial of Arthur Pendleton Bagby, C. S. A.," *East Texas Historical Journal* 19 (Fall 1981): 60-67.

Biographies for several Texas brigadiers have been written. Outstanding in this respect is Thomas W. Cutrer's *Ben McCulloch and the Frontier Military Tradition* (Chapel Hill: University of North Carolina Press, 1993). Well-researched and skillfully written, this biography depicts McCulloch as a capable officer who never received the rank or responsibility he deserved because of his lack of a West Point education. Cutrer's work should be supplemented by the earlier account by Victor Rose, *The*

Life and Services of Ben McCulloch (Philadelphia, 1888; reprint, Austin: Steck Company, 1958), and master's theses "Life of Ben McCulloch" (University of Texas, 1947) by Jack W. Gunn and "The Confederate Services of General Ben McCulloch" (University of Arkansas, 1957) by Neal Terry Bulloch.

Judith Ann Benner, *Sul Ross: Soldier, Statesman, Educator* (College Station: Texas A&M University, 1983) is a solid biography of the Texas general, Indian fighter, and governor. For the Civil War years readers should see also *Personal Civil War Letters of General Lawrence Sullivan Ross*, transcribed and compiled by Perry Wayne Shelton and edited by Shelly Morrison (Austin, Texas, 1994). The introduction by Civil War scholar T. Michael Parrish provides an excellent brief account of Ross' life. The book also contains a bibliography of essential works relating to Ross and his brigade.

Louis T. Wigfall, who served briefly as commander of the Texas Brigade in Virginia, is the subject of a biography by Alvy L. King, *Louis T. Wigfall: Southern Fire-eater* (Baton Rouge: Louisiana State University Press, 1970). Eric H. Walter, *The Fire-eaters* (Baton Rouge: Louisiana State University Press, 1992), 160-194, has an excellent chapter on Wigfall but deals primarily with his political career.

Full-length biographies for other Texas generals have not been published, but several theses and dissertations have been written about them. See especially Fredericka Ann Meiners, "Hamilton Prioleau Bee" (M. A. thesis, Rice University, 1972); David Paul Smith, "In Defense of Texas: The Life of Henry McCulloch" (M.A. thesis, Stephen F. Austin State University, 1975); and Charles K. Chamberlain, "Alexander Watkins Terrell: Citizen, Statesman" (Ph. D. dissertation, University of Texas, 1957).

Several Texas Confederate brigadiers wrote memoirs or regimental histories. The most complete of these is Adam Rankin Johnson, *Partisan Rangers of the Confederate States Army*, ed. William J. Davis (Louisville, Kentucky, 1904; reprint, Austin: State House Press, 1995). Johnson's account covers not only his own career but also includes articles by several comrades in the Rangers. Walter P. Lane, *The Adventures and Recollections of General Walter P. Lane . . .* (Marshall, TX, 1887; reprint, Austin: Pemberton Press, 1970) provides a colorful and sometimes embellished account of Lane's role in the Civil War. Containing less self-praise is L. David Norris, ed., *With the 18th Infantry: The Autobiography of Wilburn Hill King* (Hillsboro: Hill Junior College Press, 1996). Xavier Debray, *A Sketch of the History of Debray's (26th) Regiment of Texas Cavalry* (Austin: Von Boeckmann, 1884) is a brief account of that regiment.

Unit histories provide much material relating to their Texas commanders. Histories of Hood's Texas Brigade contain much information about the four general officers—Wigfall, Hood, Jerome Robertson, and John Gregg—who commanded the brigade. Indispensable are the four volumes by Col. Harold B. Simpson which are the definitive works on the Texas Brigade: *Hood's Texas Brigade in Poetry and Song*; *Hood's Texas Brigade: Lee's Grenadier Guard*; *Hood's Texas Brigade in Reunion and Memory*; and *Hood's Texas Brigade: A Compendium* (Waco: Texian Press, 1968-1977). Simpson's work is supplemented by earlier primary accounts, including Hood's *Advance and Retreat* (cited earlier); J. B. Polley, *Hood's Texas Brigade* (New York: Neale Publishing Co., 1910); Nicholas A. Davis, *Chaplain Davis and Hood's Texas Brigade*, ed. Donald E. Everett (San Antonio: Principia Press of Trinity University, 1962); Mrs. A. V. Winkler, *The Confederate Capital and Hood's Texas Brigade* (Austin: Von Boeckmann, 1894). Personal accounts by soldiers in the brigade provide insights on their commanders. Especially important are William A. Fletcher, *Rebel Private, Front and Rear*, ed. Bell I. Wiley (Austin: University of Texas Press, 1954); Ann Lee (Clark) Dempster and Homer L. Kerr, eds., "Civil War Letters of William C. Edwards, A Soldier in Hood's Texas Brigade," *Texas Military History* 7 (Spring 1968): 5-26; Robert W. Glover, ed., *Tyler to Sharpsburg: The War Letters of Robert H. and William H. Gaston* (Waco: W. M. Morrison, 1960); Mary Laswell, ed., *Rags and Hope: The Memoirs of Val C. Giles, Four Years with Hood's Texas Brigade, Fourth Texas Infantry, 1861-1865* (New York: Coward-McCann, Inc., 1961); and John C. West, *A Texan in Search of a Fight* (Waco: J. C. West, 1901). See also Jerome B. Robertson, comp., *Touched with Valor: The Civil War Papers and Casualty Reports of Hood's Texas Brigade*, ed. Harold B. Simpson (Hillsboro: Hill Junior College Press, 1964). Many of the brigade's soldiers wrote accounts for the *Confederate Veteran*. These are listed in Simpson, *Hood's Texas Brigade: Lee's Grenadier Guard*, 481-486.

Next to Hood's Brigade, the Eighth Texas Cavalry, better known as Terry's Texas Rangers, was probably the most famous Texas unit in the Civil War. Two of its commanders, John A. Wharton and Thomas Harrison, later became Confederate general officers. Much information pertaining to them may be found in the numerous accounts of the Rangers, including L. B. Giles, "Terry's Texas Rangers," J. K. P. Blackburn, "Reminiscences of the Terry Rangers," and E. S. Dodd, "The Diary of Ephraim Shelby Dodd," all together in *Terry Texas Ranger Triology*, introduction by Thomas W. Cutrer (Austin: State House Press, 1996); H. J. H. Rugeley, ed., *Batchelor-Turner Letters, 1861-1864, Written by Two of Terry's Texas Rangers* (Austin: Steck Company, 1961); Thomas W. Cutrer, ed., "'We Are Stern and Resolved': The Civil War Letters of John Wesley Rabb, Terry's Texas Rangers," *Southwestern Historical Quarterly* 91 (October 1987): 185-226; Robert W. Williams and Ralph A. Wooster, eds., "With Terry's Texas Rangers: Letters of Dunbar Affleck," *Civil War History* 9 (September 1963): 199-310; Williams and Wooster, eds., "With Wharton's Cavalry in Arkansas: Civil War Letters of Isaac Dunbar Affleck," *Arkansas Historical Quarterly* 21 (Autumn 1962): 247-268; Ralph A. Wooster, "With the Confederate Cavalry in the West: The Civil War Experiences of Isaac Dunbar Affleck," *Southwestern Historical Quarterly* 83 (July 1979): 1-28; C. C. Jeffries, "The Character of Terry's Rangers," ibid. 64 (April 1961): 454-462; C. C. Jeffries, *Terry's Rangers* (New York: Vantage Press, 1961).

Various accounts of Ross' Texas Cavalry Brigade and its regiments provide information on Generals Elkanah Greer, Walter P. Lane, John Whitfield, and Sul Ross. These include Sam Barron, *The Lone Star Defenders: A Chronicle of the Third Texas Cavalry, Ross' Texas Brigade* (New York: Neale Publishing Co., 1908); William Clyde Billingsly, ed., "Such is War: The Confederate Memoirs of Newton Asbury Kean," *Texas Military History* 6 (Winter 1967): 238-253, 7 (Spring 1968): 44-70, 7 (Summer 1968): 103-119, 7 (Fall 1968): 176-194; Douglas John Cater, *As It Was: Reminiscences of a Soldier of the Third Texas Cavalry and the Nineteenth Louisiana Infantry* (Reprint, Austin: State House Press, 1990); Douglas Hale, *The Third Texas Cavalry in the Civil War* (Norman: University of Oklahoma Press, 1993); William W. Heartsill, *Fourteen Hundred and 91 Days in the Confederate Army: A Journal Kept by W. W. Heartsill . . . of the W. P. Lane Rangers, from April 19th, 1861, to May 20th, 1865* (Reprint, ed. Bell Wiley, Jackson, TN: McCowat-Mercer Press, 1954); Homer L. Kerr, ed., *Fighting with Ross' Texas Cavalry Brigade, C.S.A.: The Diary of George L. Griscom, Adjutant, 9th Texas Cavalry Regiment* (Hillsboro: Hill Junior College Press, 1976); Max S. Lale, ed., "The Boy Bugler of the Third Texas Cavalry: The A. B. Blocker Narrative," *Military History of Texas and the Southwest* 14 (Nos. 2-4, 1978), 71-92, 147-167, 215-225, 15 (No. 1, 1979), 21-34; Max S. Lale and Hobard Key, eds., *The Civil War Letters of David R. Garrett, Detailing the Adventures of the 6th Texas Cavalry, 1861-1865* (Marshall, TX: Port Caddo Press, 1964); Richard Lowe, ed., *A Texas Cavalry Officer's Civil War: The Diary and Letters of James C. Bates* (Baton Rouge: Louisiana State University Press, 1999); Judy Watson McClure, *Confederate from East Texas: The Civil War Letters of James Monroe Watson* (Quanah, TX: Nortex Press, 1976); Victor M. Rose, *Ross' Texas Brigade, Being a Narrative of Events Connected with Its Service in the Late War Between the States* (Louisville, 1881; reprint, Kennesaw, GA: Continental Book Company, 1960); and A. W. Sparks, *The War Between the States as I Saw It: Reminiscent, Historical and Personal* (Tyler, 1901; reprint, Longview: D & D Publishing, 1987).

Five Texans—A. P. Bagby, Tom Green, William P. Hardeman, William R. Scurry, and William Steele—who served with Sibley's Brigade in New Mexico later became Confederate generals. Numerous works relating to that campaign provide significant insights into their evolution as military commanders. Especially important are the pioneering studies by Robert Lee Kerby, *The Confederate Invasion of New Mexico and Arizona, 1861-1862* (Los Angeles: Westernlore Press, 1958), and Martin Hardwick Hall, *Sibley's New Mexico Campaign* (Austin: University of Texas Press, 1960) and *The Confederate Army of New Mexico* (Austin: Presidial Press, 1978). More recent significant studies include Donald S. Frazier, *Blood and Treasure: Confederate Empire in the Southwest* (College Station: Texas A&M University Press, 1995); John Taylor, *Bloody Valverde: A Civil War Battle on the Rio Grande, February 21, 1862* (Albuquerque: University of New Mexico Press, 1995); Thomas E. Edrington and John Taylor, *The Battle of Glorieta Pass: A Gettysburg in the West, March 26-28, 1862* (Albuquerque: University of New Mexico Press, 1998); Don E. Alberts, *The Battle of Glorieta: Union Victory in the West* (College Station: Texas A&M University Press, 1998); Jerry Thompson, *Confederate General of the West: Henry Hopkins Sibley* (Natchitoches, 1987; new ed., College Station: Texas A&M University Press, 1996). These should be supplemented by a number of accounts by participants including Don E. Alberts, ed., *Rebels on the Rio Grande: The Civil War Journals of A. B. Peticolas* (Albuquerque: Merit Press, 1993); Walter A. Faulkner, ed., "With Sibley in New Mexico: The Journal of William Henry Smith," *West Texas Historical Association Year Book* 27 (October 1951): 111-142; David B. Gracy, II, ed., "New Mexico Campaign Letters of Frank Starr, 1861-1862," *Texas Military History* 4 (Fall 1964): 169-188; Oscar Haas, trans., "The Diary of Julius Giesecke," ibid. 3 (Winter 1962): 228-242; Theophilus Noel, *A Campaign from Santa Fe to the Mississippi: Being a History of the Old Sibley Brigade . . .* (Shreveport: News Printing Establishment, 1865); Jerry D. Thompson, ed., *Westward the Texans: The Civil War Journal of Private William Randolph Howell* (El Paso: Texas Western Press, 1990); Michael L. Tate, ed., "A Johnny Reb in Sibley's New Mexico Campaign: Reminiscences of Private Henry C. Wright, 1861-1862," *East Texas Historical Journal* 25 (Spring 1987): 20-33, 26 (Spring-Fall 1988): 23-35, 48-60.

Several of the future Confederate generals who were in Sibley's Brigade were also in the campaign to liberate Galveston from Union occupying forces on January 1, 1863. For their activities in this respect see Edward T. Cotham, Jr., *Battle on the Bay: The Civil War Struggle for Galveston* (Austin: University of Texas Press, 1998); Robert M. Franklin, *Battle of Galveston, January 1, 1863* (Reprint, Galveston: San Luis Press, 1975); Donald S. Frazier, *Cottonclads! The Battle of Galveston and the Defense of the Texas Coast* (Fort Worth: Ryan Place Publishers, 1996); Charles C. Cumberland, "The Confederate Loss and Recapture of Galveston, 1862-1863," *Southwestern Historical Quarterly* 51 (October 1947): 109-130; Alwyn Barr, "Texas Coastal Defense, 1861-1865," ibid. 65 (July 1961): 1-31; Donald S. Frazier, "Sibley's Texans and the Battle of Galveston," ibid. 99 (October 1995): 174-198; Edward B. Williams, ed., "A 'Spirited Account' of the Battle of Galveston, January 1, 1863," ibid. 99 (October 1995): 200-215; Alwyn Barr, "The 'Queen City of the Gulf' Held Hostage: The Impact of the War on Confederate Galveston," *Military History of the West* 27 (Fall 1997): 119-138; and Paul D. Casdorph, *Prince John Magruder: His Life and Campaigns* (New York: John Wiley & Sons, 1996).

Future Confederate generals Elkanah Greer, Matthew D. Ector, and W. P. Lane served under Ben McCulloch at the Battle of Wilson's Creek. These three, plus Sul Ross and John Whitfield, were with McCulloch at Pea Ridge. Works on these two battles contain information on these Texans. In addition to Tom Cutrer's biography of McCulloch previously mentioned, see William R. Brooksher, *Bloody Hill: The Civil War Battle of Wilson's Creek* (Washington: Brassey's, 1995); Kel N. Pickens, "The Battle of Wilson's Creek, Missouri, August 10, 1861," *Journal of the West* 19 (October 1980): 10-25; William L. Shea and Earl J. Hess, *Pea Ridge: Civil War Campaign in the West* (Chapel Hill: University of North Carolina Press, 1992); William L. Shea, *War in the West: Pea Ridge and Prairie Grove* (Abilene: McWhiney Foundation Press, 1998); William L. Shea, "The Road to Pea Ridge," *Arkansas Historical Quarterly* 52 (Autumn 1993): 205-222; Edwin C. Bearss, "The Battle of Pea Ridge," ibid. 20 (Spring 1961): 74-94; Walter L. Brown, "Pea Ridge: Gettysburg of the West," ibid. 15 (Spring 1956): 3-16; Maynard J. Hanson, "The Battle of Pea Ridge, Arkansas, March 6-8, 1862," *Journal of the West* 19 (October 1980): 39-50; Mark K. Christ, ed., *Rugged and Sublime: The Civil War in Arkansas* (Fayetteville: University of Arkansas Press, 1994).

Works relating to campaigns in the Indian Territory and Northwest Arkansas provide information on three Lone Star generals, William Steele, Sam Maxey, and Richard Gano, who served in that divided and bitterly contested region. In addition to the works on Maxey cited above see Edwin C. Bearss, "General William Steele Fights to Hold Onto Northwest Arkansas," *Arkansas Historical Quarterly* 25 (Spring 1966): 36-93; Bearss, "The Federals Capture Fort Smith, 1863," ibid. 28 (Summer 1969): 156-190; Lary C. and Donald L. Rampp, *The Civil War in Indian Territory* (Austin: Presidial Press, 1975); Lary C. Rampp, "Confederate Sinking of the *J. R. Williams*," *Journal of the West* 11 (January 1972): 43-50; Lawrence M. Hauptman, *Between Two Fires: American Indians in the Civil War* (New York: Free Press, 1995); Marvin J. Hancock, "The Second Battle of Cabin Creek, 1864," *Chronicles of Oklahoma* 41 (Winter 1963-

64): 414-426; Annie Heloise Abel, *The American Indian as Participant in the Civil War* (Cleveland: Arthur H. Clark Co., 1919).

Several Texas generals fought in the defense of central and eastern Arkansas during 1862. For their activities see the excellent studies by Anne J. Bailey, *Between the Enemy and Texas: Parsons's Texas Cavalry in the Civil War* (Fort Worth: Texas Christian University Press, 1989) and "Henry McCulloch's Texans and the Defense of Arkansas in 1862," *Arkansas Historical Quarterly* 46 (Spring 1987): 46-59. Joseph B. Blessington, *The Campaigns of Walker's Texas Division* (Reprint; Austin: State House Press, 1994); B. P. Gallaway, *The Rugged Rebel: A Common Soldier in W. H. Parsons' Texas Cavalry, 1861-1865* (Austin: University of Texas Press, 1988); M. Jane Johansson, *Peculiar Honor: A History of the 28th Texas Cavalry, 1862-1865* (Fayetteville: University of Arkansas Press, 1998); and Robert Weddle, *Plow-Horse Cavalry: The Caney Creek Boys of the Thirty-fourth Texas* (Austin: Madrona Press, 1974) provide additional information on Texas generals, particularly Henry McCulloch, Allison Nelson, and Horace Randal, involved in fighting in Arkansas and northern Louisiana.

Various accounts describe the efforts of Henry McCulloch to administer the northern sub-district of Texas. Especially helpful are David Paul Smith, *Frontier Defense in the Civil War: Texas' Rangers and Rebels* (College Station: Texas A&M University Press, 1992); Richard B. McCaslin, *Tainted Breeze: The Great Hanging at Gainesville, Texas 1862* (Baton Rouge: Louisiana State University Press, 1994); Richard B. McCaslin, "Dark Corner of the Confederacy: James G. Bourland and the Border Regiment," *Military History of the West* 24 (Spring 1994): 57-70; Albert Castel, *William Clarke Quantrill: His Life and Times* (New York: Frederick Fell, Inc., 1962); Lary C. Rampp, "William C. Quantrill's Civil War Activities in Texas," *Texas Military History* 8 (No. 2, 1970): 221-231; Edward Leslie, *The Devil Knows How to Ride* (New York: Random House, 1996); David Paul Smith, "The Elm Creek Raid, 1864: State and Confederate Defense and Response," *Military History of the Southwest* 19 (Fall 1989): 121-136; Kenneth Neighbours, "Elm Creek Raid in Young County, 1864," *West Texas Historical Association Year Book* 40 (October 1964): 83-89.

Fourteen Texas Confederates who were generals before the end of the Civil War took part in the fighting in the bayou country and/or the Red River campaign in Louisiana, 1863-1864. For works pertaining to the 1863 campaigns in the bayou country see (in addition to works previously mentioned): Donald S. Frazier, "Texans on the Teche: The Texas Brigade at the Battles of Bisland and Irish Bend, April 12-14, 1863," *Louisiana History* 32 (Fall 1991): 417-435; Stephen S. Michot, "In Relief of Port Hudson: Richard Taylor's 1863 Lafourche Offensive," *Military*

History of the West 23 (Fall 1993): 103-117; James T. Matthews, "A Time for Desperate Valor: The Confederate Attack on Fort Butler, Louisiana, 1863," ibid. 26 (Spring 1996): 23-34; L. Boyd Finch, "Surprise at Brashear City: Sherod Hunter's Sugar Cooler Cavalry," *Louisiana History* 26 (Fall 1984): 403-434; Alwyn Barr, ed., "The Battle of Bayou Bourbeau, November 3, 1863: Colonel Oran M. Roberts' Report," ibid. 6 (Winter 1965): 83-91; David C. Edmonds, "Surrender on the Bourdeaux: Honorable Defeat or Incompetency Under Fire," ibid. 18 (Winter 1977): 63-86; David C. Edmonds, *Yankee Autumn in Acadiana: A Narrative of the Great Texas Overland Expedition through Southwestern Louisiana, October-December, 1863* (Lafayette: Acadiana Press, 1979); and Richard Lowe, *The Texas Overland Expedition of 1863* (Abilene: McWhiney Foundation Press, 1998).

T. Michael Parrish's biography of the Confederate commander in Louisiana, *Richard Taylor: Soldier Prince of Dixie* (Chapel Hill: University of North Carolina Press, 1992), provides much material on Texas generals as do Taylor's memoirs, entitled *Destruction and Reconstruction: Personal Experiences of the Late War*, ed. Richard Harwell (New York: Longmans, Green, and Co., 1955). For the Red River campaign see also Ludwell H. Johnson, *Red River Campaign: Politics and Cotton in the Civil War* (Baltimore: Johns Hopkins Press, 1958); Curt Anders, *Disaster in Deep Sand: The Red River Expedition* (Carmel, IN: Guild Press of Indiana, 1997); William R. Brooksher, *War Along the Bayous: The 1864 Red River Campaign in Louisiana* (Washington: Brassey's, 1998); Anne J. Bailey, *Texans in the Confederate Cavalry* (Fort Worth: Ryan Place Publishers, 1995); Alwyn Barr, *Polignac's Texas Brigade* (new ed., College Station: Texas A&M University Press, 1998); Norman E. Brown, ed., *Journey to Pleasant Hill: The Civil War Letters of Captain Elijah P. Petty, Walker's Texas Division, C. S. A.* (San Antonio: Institute of Texan Cultures, 1982); Joseph H. Parks, *General Edmund Kirby Smith, C. S. A.* (Baton Rouge: Louisiana State University Press, 1954); Robert L. Kerby, *Kirby Smtih's Confederacy: The Trans-Mississippi South, 1863-1865* (New York: Columbia University Press, 1972); John Spencer, *Terrell's Texas Cavalry* (Burnet, TX: Eakin Press, 1982); Fredericka Ann Meiners, "Hamilton P. Bee in the Red River Campaign," *Southwestern Historical Quarterly* 78 (July 1974): 21-44; Stanley S. McGowen, "Augustus Buchel: A Forgotten Texas Patriot," *Military History of the West* 25 (Spring 1995): 1-21; H. P. Bee, "Battle of Pleasant Hill—An Error Corrected," *Southern Historical Society Papers* 8 (April 1880): 184-186; Jimmy L. Bryan, Jr., ed., "'Whip Them Like the Mischief': The Civil War Letters of Frank and Mintie Price," *East Texas Historical Journal* 36 (Fall 1998): 68-84.

For those Texas generals who fought beyond the Mississippi River there is an abundance of battle and campaign monographs and articles.

Benjamin F. Cooling, *Forts Henry and Donelson: The Key to the Confederate Heartland* (Knoxville: University of Tennessee Press, 1987), and Charles P. Roland, "Albert Sidney Johnston and the Loss of Forts Henry and Donelson," *Journal of Southern History* 23 (February 1957): 45-69, provide information to supplement the Johnston biographies mentioned above. Lonnie R. Speer's *Portals to Hell: Military Prisons of the Civil War* (Mechanicsburg, PA: Stackpole Books, 1997), contains descriptions of Fort Warren, the Federal prison in Boston harbor, where John Gregg and Hiram Granbury were confined following the surrender at Donelson.

The Shiloh campaign, in which Albert Sidney Johnston and future Texas generals John A. Wharton, John C. Moore, William H. Young, and Tom Harrison participated, is described in various accounts. See James Lee McDonough, *Shiloh—in Hell Before Night* (Knoxville: University of Tennessee Press, 1977); Wiley Sword, *Shiloh: Bloody April* (New York: William Morrow & Co., 1974); Larry J. Daniel, *Shiloh: The Battle That Changed the Civil War* (New York: Simon & Schuster, 1997). These should be supplemented by the works of Thomas L. Connelly, *Army of the Heartland: The Army of Tennessee, 1861-1862* (Baton Rouge: Louisiana State University Press, 1967) and Steven E. Woodworth, *Jefferson Davis and His Generals: The Failure of Confederate Command in the West* (Lawrence: University Press of Kansas, 1990) and biographies of several leading personalities who were in the battle: Grady McWhiney, *Braxton Bragg and Confederate Defeat* (New York: Columbia University Press, 1969); T. Harry Williams, *P. G. T. Beauregard: Napoleon in Gray* (Baton Rouge: Louisiana State University Press, 1954); Nathaniel C. Hughes, Jr., *General William J. Hardee: Old Reliable* (Baton Rouge: Louisiana State University Press, 1965); William C. Davis, *Breckinridge: Soldier, Statesman, Symbol* (Baton Rouge: Louisiana State University Press, 1974); Joseph H. Parks, *General Leonidas Polk: C. S. A.: The Fighting Bishop* (Baton Rouge: Louisiana State University Press, 1962). For the role of John C. Moore and the Second Texas Infantry at Shiloh see Joseph E. Chance, *The Second Texas Infantry: From Shiloh to Vicksburg* (Austin: Eakin Press, 1984).

John C. Moore and Sul Ross both played significant roles in the fighting at Corinth in the autumn of 1862. For their part see (in addition to works on Ross' Brigade and the Second Texas cited above) Peter Cozzens, *The Darkest Days of the War: The Battle of Iuka & Corinth* (Chapel Hill: University of North Carolina Press, 1997); Kevin R. Young, *To the Tyrant Never Yield: A Texas Civil War Sampler* (Plano: Wordware Publishing Inc., 1992): Eleanor Damon Pace, ed., "The Diary and Letters of William P. Rogers," *Southwestern Historical Quarterly* 32 (April 1929): 259-299. Moore and Thomas N. Waul were among the defenders of the Vicksburg garrison in 1863. In addition to Chance's *Second Texas Infantry* cited above, see Laura Simmons, "Waul's Legion, From Texas to Mississippi," *Texana* 7 (Spring 1969): 1-16; Wayne Flynt, "The Texas Legion at Vicksburg," *East Texas Historical Journal* 17 (Spring 1979): 60-67.

Several Texas generals were involved in Joe Johnston's efforts to prevent the Vicksburg garrison from being encircled. See especially James L. Newsom, "Intreprid Gray Warriors: The 7th Texas Infantry, 1861-1865" (Ph.D. dissertation, Texas Christian University, 1995); James M. McCaffrey, *This Band of Heroes: Granbury's Texas Brigade, C.S.A.* (Austin: Eakin Press, 1985); Stephen E. Ambrose, "Struggle for Vicksburg," in *Americans at War* (Jackson: University Press of Mississippi, 1997); and Craig L. Symonds, *Joseph E. Johnston: A Civil War Biography* (New York: W. W. Norton & Co., 1992).

Matthew D. Ector, John A. Wharton, and Thomas Harrison were in the Battle of Murfreesboro, or Stone's River, fought on December 31, 1862, and January 2, 1863. For their role in this engagement see Peter Cozzens, *No Better Place to Die: The Battle of Stone's River* (Urbana, IL: University of Illinois Press, 1990) and James Lee McDonough, *Stones River—Bloody Winter in Tennessee* (Knoxville: University of Tennessee Press, 1980).

Eight Texans who were generals or later became generals fought in the Battle of Chickamauga in September 1863. See Peter Cozzens, *This Terrible Sound: The Battle of Chickamauga* (Urbana, IL: University of Illinois Press, 1992); Steven E. Woodworth, *Six Armies in Tennessee: The Chickamauga and Chattanooga Campaigns* (Lincoln: University of Nebraska Press, 1998); Steven E. Woodworth, *A Deep Steady Thunder: The Battle of Chickamauga* (Abilene: McWhiney Foundation Press, 1998); and Glenn Tucker, *Chickamauga: Bloody Battle in the West* (Indianapolis: Bobbs-Merrill, 1961). Several of these same officers took part in the subsequent siege and battle for Chattanooga. See Peter Cozzens, *The Shipwreck of Their Hopes: The Battles for Chattanooga* (Urbana, IL: University of Illinois Press, 1994); James Lee McDonough, *Chattanooga—A Death Grip on the Confederacy* (Knoxville: University of Tennessee Press, 1984); Wiley Sword, *Mountains Touched With Fire: Chattanooga Besieged, 1863* (New York: St. Martin's Press, 1995).

John Bell Hood, Matthew Ector, Hiram Granbury, Tom Harrison, Sul Ross, and William H. Young were in the Atlanta campaign of 1864. In addition to works previously cited, see Thomas L. Connelly, *Autumn of Glory: The Army of Tennessee, 1862-1865* (Baton Rouge: Louisiana State University Press, 1971); Albert Castel, *Decision in the West: The Atlanta Campaign of 1864* (Lawrence: University Press of Kansas, 1992); David Coffey, *John Bell Hood and the Struggle for Atlanta* (Abilene: McWhiney Foundation Press, 1998); Lucia Rutherford Douglas, ed., *Douglas' Texas Battery* (San Antonio: Principia Press of Trinity University, 1962); Norman D. Brown, ed., *One of Cleburne's Command: The Civil War Reminiscences and Diary of Captain Samuel T. Foster, Granbury's Texas Brigade, C.S.A.* (Austin: University of Texas Press, 1980); Charles D. Spurlin, ed., *The Civil War Diary of Charles A. Leuschner* (Austin: Eakin Press, 1992).

For Hood's Tennessee campaign of 1864, which culminated in the defeats at Franklin and Nashville, see James M. McCaffrey, *This Band of Heroes* (mentioned above); Craig L. Symonds, *Stonewall of the West: Patrick Cleburne & the Civil War* (Lawrence: University Press of Kansas, 1997); Herman Hattaway, *General Stephen D. Lee* (Jackson: University Press of Mississippi, 1976); Wiley Sword, *The Confederacy's Last Hurrah: Spring Hill, Franklin, and Nashville* (Lawrence: University Press of Kansas, 1992); James Lee McDonough and Thomas L. Connelly, *Five Tragic Hours: The Battle of Franklin* (Knoxville: University of Tennessee Press, 1983); Stanley Horn, *The Decisive Battle of Nashville* (Baton Rouge: Louisiana State University Press, 1956); Thomas R. Hay, *Hood's Tennessee Campaign* (New York: Walter Neale, 1929); Winston Groom, *Shrouds of Glory: From Atlanta to Nashville: The Last Great Campaign of the Civil War* (New York: Atlantic Monthly Press, 1995); and W. J. Wood, *Civil War Generalship: The Art of Command* (Westport, CT: Praeger, 1997).

As noted earlier, Harold B. Simpson's four-volume study of Hood's Brigade is basic for information pertaining to the four Texas generals who commanded the brigade. These volumes should be supplemented by Stephen W. Sears, *To the Gates of Richmond: The Peninsular Campaign* (New York: Ticknor and Fields, 1992); John H. Hennessy, *Return to Bull Run: The Campaign and Battle of Second Manassas* (New York: Simon & Schuster, 1993); Joseph H. Harsh, *Confederate Tide Rising: Robert E. Lee and the Making of Southern Strategy, 1861-1862* (Kent, OH: Kent State University Press, 1998); Stephen W. Sears, *Landscape Turned Red: The Battle of Antietam* (New Haven: Ticknor and Fields, 1983); John Michael Priest, *Antietam: The Soldier's Battle* (New York: Oxford University Press, 1989); James V. Murfin, *The Gleam of Bayonets: The Battle of Antietam and the Maryland Campaign of 1862* (New Brunswick, NJ: Thomas Yoseloff, 1965); Gary W. Gallagher, ed., *The Second Day at Gettysburg: Essays on Confederate and Union Leadership* (Kent, OH: Kent State University Press, 1993); Gary W. Gallagher, ed., *The Third Day at Gettysburg & Beyond* (Chapel Hill: University of North Carolina Press, 1994); Gabor S. Boritt, ed., *The Gettysburg Nobody Knows* (New York: Oxford University Press, 1997); Edward Coddington, *The Gettysburg Campaign: A Study in Command* (New York: Charles Scribner's Sons, 1968); Steven E. Woodworth, *Davis and Lee At War* (Lawrence: University Press of Kansas, 1995); Gary Gallagher, ed. *The Wilderness Campaign* (Chapel Hill: University of North Carolina Press, 1997); Gordon C.

Rhea, *The Battle of the Wilderness, May 5-6, 1864* (Baton Rouge: Louisiana State University Press, 1994); Gordon C. Rhea, *The Battles for Spotsylvania Court House and the Road to Yellow Tavern, May 7-12, 1864* (Baton Rouge: Louisiana State University Press, 1997); William D. Matter, *If It Takes All Summer: The Battle of Spotsylvania* (Chapel Hill: University of North Carolina Press, 1988); Richard Sommers, *Richmond Redeemed: The Siege at Petersburg* (Garden City, NY: Doubleday & Co., 1981); Douglas S. Freeman, *Lee's Lieutenants: A Study in Command*, 3 vols. (New York: Charles Scribner's Sons, 1942-1944); Douglas S. Freeman, *R. E. Lee: A Biography*, 4 vols. (New York: Charles Scribner's Sons, 1936).

Felix Robertson, son of Hood Brigade commander Jerome B. Robertson and himself appointed brigadier general by Jefferson Davis, is a central figure in several studies concerning an unfortunate episode at Saltville, Virginia, in which black prisoners were killed. See Thomas Mays, *The Saltville Massacre* (Abilene: McWhiney Foundation Press, 1998); William C. Davis, "Massacre at Saltville," *Civil War Times Illustrated* 9 (February 1971): 4-11, 43-48; and the biography of John C. Breckinridge by William C. Davis cited earlier. The incident is not mentioned in James H. Colqin, ed., "The Life Story of Brig. Gen. Felix Robertson," *Texana* 8 (Spring 1970): 154-182.

Several works were most helpful in analyzing Confederate military leadership. Particularly important are the works by Steven Woodworth described above; Thomas B. Buell, *The Warrior Generals: Combat Leadership in the Civil War* (New York: Crown Publishers, 1997); Gabor S. Boritt, ed., *Jefferson Davis' Generals* (New York: Oxford University Press, 1999); Albert Castel, *Winning and Losing in the Civil War* (Columbia: University of South Carolina Press, 1996); William C. Davis, *The Cause Lost: Myths and Realities of the Confederacy* (Lawrence: University Press of Kansas, 1996); Gary W. Gallagher, *The Confederate War* (Cambridge: Harvard University Press, 1997); Gary W. Gallagher, *Lee and His Generals in War and Memory* (Baton Rouge: Louisiana State University Press, 1998); Richard M. McMurry, *Two Great Rebel Armies: An Essay in Confederate Military History* (Chapel Hill: University of North Carolina Press); Steven H. Newton, *Joseph E. Johnston and The Defense of Richmond* (Lawrence, KS: University Press of Kansas, 1998); and W. J. Wood, *Civil War Generalship: The Art of Command*, cited earlier.

Index

Guess, George, 135
Gulf Prairie, 168
Gutierrez-Magee expedition, 25

H
Hale, Douglas, 130, 143
Halleck, Henry W., 32
Hallettsville City Cemetery, 113
Hallettsville, Texas, 219
Hamilton, A. J., 172
  James, 220
  Sarah Ann, 132
Hamman, William N., 247
Hampton, Wade, 53, 79, 81
Hancock County, Georgia, 241
Hancock, Winfield Scott, 86, 190
Hardee, William J., 27, 31, 33, 35, 38,
  55-56, 58, 59, 62, 69, 70, 185, 200,
  201, 202, 230, 231, 237
Hardee's Corps, 36, 59
Hardeman, Bailey, 131, 132
  Mary Ophelia Polk, 131
  Rebecca, 132
  Sarah, 132
  Thomas Jones, 131
  William P., 3, 4, 6, 7, 11, 13, 17, 19,
  20, 106, 131-134, 172, 237
Hardeman's Brigade, 133, 134
Harpers Ferry, 48, 221
Harpeth River, 61
Harriet Lane, 103-104, 111
Harris, Isham G., 32, 36
Harrison brothers, 3
Harrison County, Texas, 143, 187
Harrison, James, 4, 5, 11, 13, 20, 21,
  74, 134-137, 141, 192, 195, 237
  Mary, 134
  Sarah, 192
  Thomas, 4, 6, 7, 11, 15, 17, 19, 20,
  70, 71, 134, 176, 192-195, 235, 236
Harrison's Brigade, 194-195
Harrison's Landing, 47
Haskell, John Cheves, 157
Hatchie Bridge, 201, 214
Hawkins County, Tennessee, 198
Hawkins, Edwin R., 218
Hays, Jack, 97, 116, 142, 147, 243
Hebert, Louis, 128, 150, 218

Paul O., 152
Hempstead, Texas, 73, 74, 134, 142,
  168
Henderson, James Pinckney, 221
Henderson, Kentucky, 195
Henderson, Texas, 177, 180
Hennen, Anna Marie, 63
High Bridge, 83
Hill, A. P., 189
Hindman, Thomas C., 155
Hobby's Infantry Regiment, 174
Hogg, James Stephen, 9, 137
  Joseph L., 3, 4, 5, 6, 8-9, 10, 13, 16,
  20, 114, 137-139, 177, 238
  Lucanda, 138
Hoke's Division, 191
Holcombe, Anna, 127
Holly Springs, Mississippi, Battle of,
  214, 218, 243
Hollywood Cemetery, 191
Holmes, Theophilus H., 47, 77, 152,
  156
Holmes' Second Division, 156
Holston Valley, 210
Honey Springs, 164
Hood, Anna, 63
  John Bell, 2, 3, 5, 9, 10, 11, 15, 16,
  17, 19, 20, 21, 22, 27, 38, 39-63,
  64, 65, 86, 157, 176, 184, 189,
  194, 210, 216, 223, 227, 229, 230,
  231-232, 233-234, 245
Hood Orphan Memorial Fund, 63
Hood's Corps, 55, 58, 59
Hood's Division, 48-56, 209
Hood's Texas Brigade, 15, 22, 39, 44-
  47, 50, 54, 186, 188, 207, 208,
  209-211, 234
Hood's Texas Brigade Association, 63,
  211
Hook, Hattie Hendley, 211
Hooker, Joe, 49, 51
Hopkinsville, Kentucky, 196
Hornet's Nest, 36, 200
Horton, Louise, 86, 88
Houston, Sam, 25, 66, 76, 96, 97, 116,
  127, 138, 147, 148, 167, 199, 212,
  221, 245
  Sam, Jr., 199